A Multidisciplinary, Multicultural Perspective

Nicole Jafari, Ed.D. | Cynthia Donham, Ph.D. | Erylene Piper-Mandy, Ph.D.

Kona Publishing and Media Group
Higher Education Division
Charlotte, North Carolina
www.konapublishing.com

Designer: Execustaff Composition Services

ISBN: 978-1-935987-68-0

Contents

Acknowledgments

The authors would like to take this opportunity to extend sincere appreciation and to acknowledge the following people:

Each and every one of our family members for supporting us throughput this endeavor even though at times it seemed that there was no end to it! We particularly would like to thank our families for maintaining faith and showering us with their abundant encouragement. This would not have been possible without your sacrifices and continuous support.

In addition, we would like to thank Chana Warnock and Richard Van for their generous time spent reading the book and editing for flow and ease of reading from a reader's perspective. Chana and Richard, your valuable feedback helped keep the flow and the content easy and approachable from a student's point of view. Thank you for your time and effort.

Special thanks and acknowledgment goes to our dear friend, Margaret Goetz, whose editing insight and skills were instrumental in getting the book off the ground. Furthermore, her creative footprints can also be seen all over the pages of this book via her astonishing photographs and beautiful poems. We decided to pay homage to her art by starting some of the chapters with her meaningful poems. Thank you, Margaret, known to us as Peggy, for your beautiful contributions.

Furthermore, we are thankful to our students for encouraging us and actually demanding that we do write a book that befits the field of human development. For years, these students had to compromise by studying from psychology textbooks that were not a good match because of the differences in views and directions in their areas of research. You asked for it and you got it. Thank you.

Last, but not least, we would like to thank our publisher extraordinaire Kyler Ferguson, who actually never gave up on us and kept the light on even if at times, we could not see the light at the end of the tunnel. Kyler, you kept us on task, alert, and focused, and never gave up, so we had to keep moving.

Thank you all and God bless you all.

Preface

Often, textbooks written on human development or child and adolescent studies focus primarily on Western culture and the topics normally examined by Westernized scientists. Although this approach is valid and scientific, it does not view development using a cultural and multidisciplinary approach even though today's globalization phenomenon demands that scientists give attention to the process of development in a global and international fashion. We are living in an amazing time of universal change, and students studying in the fields of social sciences and humanities must be aware of these changes. In addition, the fact that the authors of this textbook come from diverse cultural backgrounds themselves made it necessary to address different developmental processes from both Western and non-Western viewpoints. It also seemed vital and extremely important to address today's global issues concerning change and human development using these multicultural interpretations.

Today, more than ever, we see how globalization is dictating and spearheading development and human growth. A teenager living in Japan, who at one time had more in common with his or her ancestors and thus conformed to traditional customs and ways of life, today is more attuned with an American adolescent than with past generational traditions. Japan, having one of the most traditional acculturation and ethnocentric views on life, has now realized the need for change and for global assimilation. However, this point of view and change in heart regarding flexibility in traditions and becoming globalized did not come easily. It is evident now more than ever that the world is moving toward a unique social dynamic and assemblage of cultures and traditions. Furthermore, the ideas on how and why humans change, the reasons for this plasticity, the acknowledgment of stability and how some things do not change have made it necessary for this book to look at both Western and non-Western views of development. The result of all these considerations brought the authors of this textbook to make a commitment to present purely an unbiased view on human growth to our readers for maximum benefit from such a body of work.

Additionally, the authors made a commitment to make this book user friendly yet to stay true to its vision. In order to maintain such an undertaking without compromising the goals and objectives of this book, the chapters are formatted and constructed in as follows:

THE IMPORTANCE OF HISTORY: The authors decided to start with a brief overview of how the science of human development began; therefore, the first chapter presents a history on how the field of human development got its start and the need for such science, and what makes it unique yet related to psychology and other humanities sciences. We felt it was important for the readers of this book to realize that although most scientists in this field had a psychology degree or background, they were also well versed in the human psyche and its development. This book also pays homage to the human development field and the progress of scientific research practices, which evolved from a one-dimensional view of development to a multidimensional view.

THE STRUCTURE IN WHICH SOCIAL SCIENTISTS WORK: We felt it pertinent to enlighten readers on how and on what premise scientific studies in qualitative methods are done; therefore, Chapter Two not only explains in great detail how a scientific measurement leads to a theory, but also includes the latest ethical standards that a scientist faces while conducting such research studies. This emphasizes how important it is to continuously do research in this field to answer such pertinent questions as why the United States experiences the highest rate of teenage pregnancies compared to other Western and non-Western countries. Or why is there such high rate of crime in America in comparison to other developed industrial countries.

THE IMPORTANCE OF CONTINUOUS RESEARCH: Today, more than ever, universities—whether state funded or private—are acknowledging the importance of students' learning scientific methods and theory- establishment processes. Most universities offer undergraduate research opportunities, which indicate how accepting these academic institutions have become to the need for students to learn about the methodology and statistical side of research findings. This book addresses this need by explaining and expanding on this concept. In addition, the reader must develop an understanding of how to bring theory from the pages of a study to real life and must learn about the applicability of these studies. Therefore, the role of theory is emphasized, explained, and covered in all of the chapters, as well as a discussion that contrasts and debates the role of each of these traditional points of views on development.

OVERVIEW OF THE NATURE OF DEVELOPMENT FROM CONCEPTION: The authors felt that it was necessary for readers to understand the timing and complexity of development from a scientific view and a biological perspective. The in-depth discussion of prenatal development highlights the importance of prenatal care and how the environmental factors may be influential in early stages of conception and later developmental milestones.

THE DIFFERENT ASPECTS OF DEVELOPMENT: The entire body of this book is set up and organized around the different stages and milestones of growth; therefore, these stages of human development are structured in a way that presents both change and stability.

INCLUSION OF MULTIDISCIPLINARY AND MULTICULTURAL VIEWS ON HUMAN GROWTH: This concept is expanded to give an in-depth understanding of non-Western views of human development and why it is important not to dismiss other cultural ideas. Emphasis was given particularly to diverse arrays of theories, age differentiation of each sequence of development, the continuous process that underlines growth, the importance of culture in shaping and molding behavior, the interaction of nature versus nurture, the impact of context on change and stability, the role of biology and environment on growth, and the integration of theory, research, and applicability of research in real life.

TEXT ORGANIZATION: The authors chose a chronological approach in organizing this book, beginning with a brief history of how the field of human development took shape and formed into a discrete area of study. At the same time, this field is contrasted with other disciplines such as psychology, biology, and the social sciences. Beyond the first couple of chapters, which give an overview of development, research methods, theories, and history of human development, the remaining chapters cover prenatal development (in Chapter 2) and end with adolescent problematic behavior (in Chapter 14). In total, 14 chapters present an in-depth study of human development with multicultural and multidisciplinary views of each and every aspect of development in great detail.

The authors of this textbook hope that readers will not only benefit from this diverse and comprehensive academic, scientific, and up-to-date presentation of information, but also find it a practical body of knowledge that can be used in everyday life and beyond the college years.

About the Authors

Dr. Jafari teaches at the California State University, Long Beach in the Human Development Department. She is also a faculty at the California State University, Fullerton, where she teaches in the Child and Adolescent Studies Department. Her research interests are in the areas of cross-cultural and multidisciplinary subjects from prenatal through late adulthood, the application of scientific theories, and the association between social studies and spiritual growth. She has also authored and coauthored several publications on child and adolescent studies, human plasticity and stability, and other related topics; however, in the past few years she has been focusing on research studies related to social issues in Iran. In addition to advocacy, she is a public speaker on matters related to children and youth in today's multicultural and multicontextual environment.

Cynthia A. S. Donham, PhD, currently teaches full time at California State University at Long Beach in the Human Development and Sociology Departments. She received her doctorate and master's from University of California at Irvine in Social Relations and received her bachelor's from University of California at Davis majoring in a combination of Cultural Anthropology and Studio Art. She has particular interests in adolescent and early adulthood problems from a multicultural perspective, as well as expertise in Social Gerontology and the Elderly Deaf subculture. Cynthia also facilitates workshops on social and cultural issues for businesses and community organizations.

Erylene Piper-Mandy, PhD, is currently teaching full time at California State University, Long Beach, in the departments of Human Development and Comparative World Literature. A psychological anthropologist who specializes in cross-cultural competence and American ethnicity, she received a B.A. in African American Studies and a B.S. in Psychology from Vassar College in Poughkeepsie, New York. She continued her studies at Boston University's African American Studies Program, where she received a master's. She completed her education at the University of California, Irvine, where she has received a master's and a PhD in psychocultural anthropology. She has been the recipient of numerous awards and fellowships, including the prestigious Fulbright Fellowship, through which she worked and studied in Senegal, West Africa. A dynamic, engaging and powerful speaker, she has given presentations and taught seminars in over 100 institutions and agencies.

Chapter 1

INTRODUCTION TO CHILDHOOD AND ADOLESCENCE

Children the world over love balloons.
(Photo courtesy of Margaret Goetz)

Magic Remains

By Margaret Goetz

Magic is what we do not understand
Just as a dog cannot read a novel
There will always be magic.

The Century of the Child: A Brief History

Human development is a relatively new field of study in modern science. Freud's inquiry into the childhood roots of psychological disorders marks the initial concern for the importance of understanding childhood influences. The earliest investigations occurred in the field of developmental psychology, but current investigation involves several different disciplines, such as biology, sociology, anthropology, history, and cultural studies. Developmental concerns are commonplace in modern settings. A father in London is concerned about whether his fifteen-year-old daughter should be "single-dating." A teacher in Sydney worries whether the four-year-old in her preschool is developmentally delayed. A mother in San Francisco is interested in whether her fifteen-month-old son should be saying small words. Everyone—everywhere—is interested in how we change as we grow. The sheer complexity of factors and number of perspectives in the field of human development, however, has made it challenging to

Learning to embroider at an evening Boston Massachusetts school, 1909.

(Photo courtesy of Everett Historical/ Shutterstock.com)

establish a definitive statement that captures the character of the discipline. The definition has to encompass the components of interest in the field, as well as the central questions that developmentalists from different disciplines agree form the source of study. Developmental science must also take into account the social environment in which people develop.

Understanding the scope of the discipline of human development requires that we explore its beginnings. Modern inquiry into human developmental processes during childhood blossomed in the late 1800s and the 1900s in three distinct historical phases: the Pre-Industrial, Industrial, and Post-Industrial eras.

The Beginning of Modern Age Human Development

Scientific attention to the developmental processes of childhood in the late nineteenth century was spearheaded by the women of the era. In 1895, Alice McLellan Birney presented the idea of a Congress of Mothers at a Mothers Meeting in Chautauqua, New York (Woyshner, 2004). Her concern was that parents—especially mothers—become educated in those issues that seemed most vital to strong moral, physical, and mental well-being in the nation's children. The idea caught on, not only among prominent mothers, such as Mrs. Adlai Stevenson, wife of then Vice President of the United States, and Mrs. Phoebe Hearst, wife of United States Senator George Hearst and mother of William Randolph Hearst, the famous newspaper publisher, but also among scientists and educators. Each year, the annual congress grew in attendance, and by mid-February 1899, the Third Annual Convention of the National Congress of Mothers held in Washington, D.C., hosted a gathering of over two hundred prominent people, and was met with great anticipation by *The New York Times* (Schoff, 1916). Two of the distinguished speakers at the congress were Dr. Luther Holt, America's first pediatrician, and Dr. G. Stanley Hall, America's premier child psychologist. These pioneers in the field of child development science set out to prove that study of children enhances parenthood, which in turn would ensure physically healthy, socially productive, and morally sound citizens. They were also instrumental in transforming the meaning of childhood from that of an apprenticeship in a naturally recurring labor force to a specific period of human experience that deserved and demanded scientific attention. This paramount shift to viewing childhood as a distinctly different stage from adulthood has encouraged scientists to start collecting data and constructing theories about developmental stages, thus inaugurating "The Century of the Child" (Hulbert, 1999).

Holt and Hall actually offered contrasting models of scientific child rearing. Both developmentalists believed that parenting should be based on scientific information, thereby downsizing advice from grandparents and friends as definitive principles of childrearing. This argument represented a critical shift in Western thinking, the notion that Western scientific inquiry is the superior way of knowing. Hall championed a more child-centered approach while Dr. Holt outlined a parent-centered plan. Holt's manual on "The Care and Feeding of Children", which he wrote in 1894 set the precedence for later experts such as "Dr. Spock." Hall's work greatly influenced Lev Vygotsky and Jean Piaget. The National Congress of Mothers later became the National Parent–Teachers Association (PTA).

By 1925, experts in the field of child development were multiplying almost as fast as the number of children! The need for the education of mothers became obvious as scientific theory about children and childhood became even more complicated. The advisors were predominately male, although the advisees were female. The advice was initially based on little evidence; therefore, the relationship between the professionals and the parents was one of friendly sympathizers. John B. Watson, however, was neither friendly nor sympathetic to parents, declaring that "parents today are incompetent and most of them should be indicted for psychological murder!" (Watson, 1928). At one point, he suggested "infant farms." In 1925 he declared, "Give me a dozen healthy infants, well formed, and my own specified world to bring them up in, and I'll guarantee to take any one at random and train them to become any type of specialist I might select" (Watson, 1930, p. 82). Watson believed that all affection was "physical, self-centered, and indulgent" (Watson, 1930). Most parents found Watson's position hard to take seriously including his own wife, who admitted that she could not contain her affection for her children.

◀ ***A family in the 1950s.***

(Photo courtesy of Elzbieta Sekowska/ Shutterstock.com)

Holt believed that children responded best to controlled environments and strict regimens. He instructed parents to develop carefully thought out and executed schedules and to respond to the children's needs based on the schedule. His motto might be stated as "watch the clock." Responding to Holt's prescription for regularity and timed feedings, Arnold Gesell (1925) developed a different motto: "Don't watch the clock; watch the child." He was also the first human science researcher to use a camera to investigate children's behaviors. His book *Infant and Child Care in the Culture Today* (1943), moved away from parent-centered "regularity" to child-centered "regulation."

Comparison of Family Systems in the Pre-Industrial, Industrial, and Post-Industrial Eras

FAMILY ATTRIBUTE	PRE-INDUSTRIAL ERA	INDUSTRIAL ERA	POST-INDUSTRIAL ERA
Family Motto	"Family rules."	"One for all and all for one."	"Everyone for himself/herself!"
Family Size	Large	Smaller size	Much smaller size
	Extended	Nuclear	New form of families sprouting (single, diverse, multicultural, blended, same sex)
	High infant/child mortality	Better infant/child mortality	Lowest infant/child mortality (depending on ethnicity)
	Average life span 40s	Average life span 60s	Life span of adults and children increases even more (70s and 80s)
Family Economy	Most families live on farms	Families move into cities for better jobs	Families work in the cities but live in the suburbs
	Complete family integration and interaction	Families become more isolated	Individuals within families become more isolated
	Satisfied simply to survive	Attempt to keep up with the "Joneses"	Everyone is the "Joneses"
	Family members depend on each other to survive	Family starting to rely on "available services" more than family members to survive	Children are often left in charge of the conditions of their development
	Stay-at-home moms	A small portion of mothers work	Both parents work

(continues)

Comparison of Family Systems in the Pre-Industrial, Industrial, and Post-Industrial Eras *(continued)*

FAMILY ATTRIBUTE	PRE-INDUSTRIAL ERA	INDUSTRIAL ERA	POST-INDUSTRIAL ERA
Family Society	Patriarchal—Father in charge	Father still in charge but mother taking a more active role in raising and disciplining the child	Both share more equally in responsibilities of raising children and disciplining
	High expectations of children	Still high expectation of children	Lower expectations of children at home and in school
	Family comes first	Tyrannical family style	Child-centered tyranny!
	Family entertains itself	Family gets its entertainment from both inside and outside sources	Family completely relies on outside sources for entertainment
	Divorce means outcast!	Some divorce is surfacing	Divorce nearly inevitable
	Cultural practices stable within regions	Subcultural practices appear within the same region	The subcultures outnumber the subgroups
	Sociopathic behavior handled by individuals	Emerging sociopathic behavior handled by the state	Sociopathic behavior is prevalent and predominantly handled by the state
Family Values	Traditional	Following old traditions blindly creates new problems	Social standards ambivalent or nonexistent; mass media dictates values
	Marriage is sacred	Alternative lifestyles/ behaviors only "in the closet"	No lifestyle is "in the closet"
	Local community involvement	Family conflict starting to surface more	Family conflict is normal (not having conflict is considered abnormal)

The explosion of theory continued. Sigmund Freud (1856–1939) and others credited children with libidinal (sexual) desires. Walter Mischel (1930–) and Albert Bandura (1925–) analyzed personality in the tradition of learning theory but focused particularly on cognitive variables because the human capacity to think is central to personality. In other words, children learn and develop cognitive skills through modeling, that is, they learn through watching others and imitating the behaviors they see. Alfred Adler (1870–1937) believed that parents have an important influence on children. He also believed that better parenting techniques could be taught, so he provided extensive guidelines for childrearing in many different settings. Adler also demonstrated that the relationships between siblings were important to all child development and that birth order powerfully affected personality development. Horney (1885–1952) argued that, based on their parents' attention (or indifferences), children either move toward people, against people, or away from people in a complex pattern of compliance, aggression, and detachment. In her opinion, children needed lots of unconditional love and support. These theorists created the infrastructure of modern developmental studies. Their shifts in focus and their differences in emphasis, have created the multicontextual depth that informs the discipline.

In 1950, the White House held a "Conference on Children and Youth." The atmosphere of this conference became one of a therapy session, where all parties felt free to examine their identities and confess their insecurities. Attendees admitted that child development was more complex than originally thought. Margaret Mead and Erik Erikson each emphasized the role of parents and parenting techniques in child development. On the other hand, Dr. Spock (1903–1998), a prominent and well-known pediatrician, sidestepped this issue with his confident style that declared to parents, "Trust yourself. You know more than you think you do" (Spock, 1946).

Scientific Framework for the Study of Human Development

The Definition of Human Development as a Discipline

As a discipline **human development** is the science that seeks to understand how and why people everywhere change or remain the same over time. Like every other scientific inquiry, human developmentalists create theories to explain their research findings. **Developmental theory** is the systematic statement of principles and generalizations that provide a coherent framework for studying and understanding human development. Theories serve important functions in scientific inquiry. They provide a model for connecting facts and observations, and also offer researchers insight and guidance, by forming the basis for hypotheses that can be tested by new research studies. In turn, theory is constantly modified by new research.

The study of human development differs from other human sciences in its focus. Human development is drawn from a **life-span perspective**, a view that observes changes in people across their entire life's duration from conception to death. For many years scientists were concerned solely with development that was accompanied by obvious, rapid, physical changes—the period of childhood. But modern developmentalists are also concerned with the less obvious, but no less important changes that accompany adulthood, such as the changes that occur when people become parents, or when they enter their careers.

Human development science also differs from other sciences in its perspective. Focusing on different areas that impact the way people change (or don't change) helps developmental scientists to embrace four "multi-" viewpoints:

1. multidisciplinary,
2. multicontextual,
3. multicultural, and
4. multidirectional.

Each of the above viewpoints plays an important role in explaining how, over time, human beings change and at the same time stay the same. Overall, the understanding of how and why we change (plasticity), or how and why we stay the same (stability) is the focal point of human development scientific endeavor (Berger, 2004).

Developmentalists look for changes in multiple contexts because human beings also develop in a number of different settings. The multicontexual aspect of human development science takes into consideration the impacts and influences of all these different settings, which comprise the context(s) with which a person comes in contact. Context is the totality of all environments, which could entail life-changing factors in the development of a child. The **multi-contextual** focus led to a **multi-disciplinary** approach, which draws theory, data, and methodology from many different academic disciplines, such as psychology, cultural studies, biology, and other similar human sciences. Developmentalists make use of whatever they need from other scientific viewpoints that can be effectively applied to developmental and life-span issues in a variety of contexts. Developmentalists may depend on social psychology to understand how a young mother changes her social world to include the mothers of her children's friends. They may then rely on biological explanations of a toddler's first steps. It is important that developmental scientists are not confined to any particular academic lens; they must be able to shift theory and method to account for the changes they observe across the life span.

One of the most important contexts in which change takes place is culture; therefore, developmental science is **multicultural**. A multicultural approach

The Four Multifactorial Aspects of Human Development

Multicontextual	Human development looks for changes in multiple contexts and settings.
Multidisciplinary	Draws theory, data, and methodology from many different academic disciplines, such as psychology, sociology, cultural anthropology, biology, and history.
Multicultural	Draws information from different cultures.
Mulidirectional	Recognizes that development is nonlinear. People can return to earlier stages and skip stages of development in their lives.

helps us to explain why children in Central Africa learn to walk sooner than Western children, or why American children sort information in specific ways. Finally, human development is **multidirectional**—changes can occur in more than one direction at a time, such as when physical, social, and cognitive developments occur simultaneously during infancy. A multidirectional viewpoint also demonstrates that development is nonlinear, that is, it does not occur in a straight line. People can return to former stages of development, while some people actually skip stages that others experience.

The Four Central Questions of Human Development

The study of human development is concerned with growth, that is, how people change as they age. This interest in the processes of change has generated several different questions about the nature of change, as well as becoming pivotal in explaining life span development. The change (plasticity) in development can be viewed as four sets of opposing tensions. The first interest of human development involves continuity. Is human development *continuous*—the result of smooth, imperceptible shifts—or is development *discontinuous*—the product of sudden, dramatic changes in experience, in growth, or in ability? Second and perhaps the best-known concern of developmental studies questions the source of development. Is it heredity or environment that shapes us? Is human development the result of *nature* (genetic inheritance) or *nurture* (the environmental experience), and what is the relationship between the two? Third, human development is also concerned with plasticity—is development fixed or flexible? Is the process of human development stable and consistent no matter what the environmental circumstances are, or is it vulnerable to change based on its context? Finally, developmentalists focus on individual differences. Are differences among children normal or are they indications of deficits? How does a person come to have stable individual characteristics that make him or her different from all other people? Let us look at each of these critical questions individually.

Continuity

Does human growth occur in increments or in stages? Over time, developmentalists agreed that this was not an either–or category and refined the question: *To what extent* is human growth continuous, consisting of gradual accumulation of small changes, as well as discontinuous, involving a series of significant, larger transformations as people age?

The study of **human ontogeny** focuses on the development of an individual from conception to death. The specific study of humanoids' uniqueness among other species, **phylogeny**, however, concentrates on the evolutionary history of human development. Therefore, we can ask the question "How much continuity/discontinuity is there?" not only of each individual across his or her lifetime, but also of the entire human species across human history. A third variation of this question is "How much continuity is there between humans and other species"?

There is certainly evidence that human development is incremental: How many times have we been amazed at how much children we haven't seen for a while have grown, while those who are with them every day don't notice? But it is also clear that individual changes reflect periods of change known as **developmental stages**. In order to qualify as a stage, a period must meet four essential criteria. First, the new stage must be characterized by qualitative changes—there are differences in the quality of the experience or ability. For example, when children begin to walk, they are at some level simply continuing the human capacity to move. But walking qualifies a stage because moving upright on one's feet is qualitatively different from the preceding means of moving through space.

Second, the movement from one stage to the next is marked by simultaneous changes in many aspects of the child's behavior. This means that each stage reflects changes in the child on many levels at once. If we use our previous example, walking reflects not only *physiological* changes, but *psychological* changes as well—the child experiences more autonomy because she can move on her own—and social changes—the relationship between the parents and the child shifts as the now more-restrictive parents must prevent her from moving in ways that will harm her.

The third criterion for a period to qualify as a developmental stage concerns the speed of the transformation, or the rapid rate of change from one stage

◄ ***A toddler learning to walk.***

(Photo courtessy of Dmytro Zinkevych/Shutterstock.com)

to another. Anyone who has ever spent time with a toddler knows that, once the child pulls up on objects to stand, it is a relatively short period—usually days—before the child will take his first step.

Finally, the behavioral and physical changes of a stage form a coherent pattern. Walking is accompanied by behavioral changes, such as learning to respond to the simple command, such as "Come here."

Sources of Development

After several decades, debates about the relative roles of nature and nurture still figure in development studies. Modern developmentalists generally resolve the traditional question of nature versus nurture by arguing that no behavior can be adequately addressed without examining the relationship between nature and nurture. For example, human beings speak using a language because they have the neurological and structural capacity to do so, but which language we speak depends on our social environment.

Explaining human behavior is complicated by a powerful phenomenon associated with human uniqueness. Human beings all operate in a special environment of artifacts, beliefs, and knowledge known as "culture." Every human experience is filtered through our cultural understandings, consequently intercepting and interpreting both our awareness and meaning. Furthermore, we pass our culture from our generation to successive generations. Language acquisition is a function of culture. We learn language from those around us. Language development illustrates both nature and nurture models of explanation. To what extent and in what ways do nature and nurture interact in determining human behavior? This is still a relevant question today.

Plasticity

Although human beings tend to develop in fairly predictable processes, there is considerable variability worldwide between groups and among individuals. Plasticity refers to the degree to which and the circumstances under which developmental processes are vulnerable to change. Are there specific points in the developmental process that can change the entire course of the process? Some of our interest in plasticity comes from research on other species, identifying the existence of critical periods in their development. Ducklings, for example, have a specific period in which they imprint to the mother duck. Imprinting as defined by Konrad Lorenz (1903–1989) is the process through which a young duckling attaches to a moving object, usually the duckling's mother. However, if the duckling does not imprint during that period it becomes incapable of imprinting and undoubtedly dies. The power of imprinting lies in its ability to change the course of the duck's development. It is therefore a *critical period*. The question is, does such a period exist for humans?

Although there is no evidence that certain experiences can induce a specific development in human beings, it is fairly clear that certain experiences can facilitate development at certain stages. For example, children usually learn to speak in the first two years of life; if they do not learn to speak until later, language development is challenged and harder, though not impossible. For this reason, developmentalists argue that human development has *sensitive* periods, rather than *critical* periods. Sensitive periods are times in the development of an organism in which exposure to certain experiences (or the lack of such exposure) will have a more pronounced effect than at other times.

Individual Differences

Although human beings are remarkably alike as a species, each one of us is identifiably different. What makes one individual different from another? How does a person come to have stable individual characteristics that make him or her

Twins, Mary-Kate and Ashley Olsen.

(Photo courtesy of Everett Collection/Shutterstock.com)

different from all other people? Even identical twins are different in some way, which is why their parents and kindergarten teachers can tell them apart. We have watched famous twins, Mary-Kate and Ashley Olsen, grow up on television. Fans can certainly tell Mary-Kate from Ashley. Can you?

Not only is each individual different from every other individual, we are also always changing. Another question about individual differences might be: To what extent are individual differences stable across our lifetimes? The famous Olsen twins grew up from childhood into adulthood on television, each of them changing as she grew. But the individual differences remained stable enough over time so that we can still identify Mary-Kate and can still tell her from Ashley. We are always changing, but we can still recognize ourselves after one decade, two decades, and eight decades of development. The fact that individual differences remain stable to a large extent over time has powerful implications for our ability to predict adult dispositions from infant/childhood behavior. Does a very active baby lead to a very active adult? Does a really inquisitive child become an inquisitive adult? To what extent does our environment shape our individual differences and their stability over time? These important questions can help to shape such issues as should orphaned and abandoned children who cannot be placed with families be raised in group homes.

Four Central Questions/Theories of Human Development

NAMES	CENTRAL QUESTION (A)	CENTRAL QUESTION (B)
Continuity	Is development a smooth continuous event?	Is development not continuous and moves in jumps, or sudden changes?
Plasticity	Is development a fixed pattern?	Can development be influenced by environmental factors?
Sources of Development (Nature versus Nurture)	Is development the source of biological factors?	Is development the source of environmental factors?
Individual Differences	How does a person come to have individual differences from other people?	How does a person come to be similar in many ways to other people?

The following themes appear in various forms over and over again in the following chapters. Sometimes the questions will be obvious; at other times, they may be more challenging to identify. Look carefully at each stage of development and ask:

- What is changing and what is remaining constant?
- What are the relative contributions of nature and nurture in this stage?
- How are the processes of this stage subject to change under different conditions?
- How are individual differences preserved?

Central Concepts in Contemporary Social Sciences

The Power of "Difference" Terms

When attempting to catalog others we tend to use "popular"[1] definitions for classifying different groups. For example, in popular language we use the terms *Black, African American,* and *of African ancestry* interchangeably; we treat the

[1] A popular definition is one that is used by ordinary people; it may or may not be the same as a scientific definition. A scientific definition is one that describes the phenomenon in terms that are necessary, sufficient, and measurable.

terms *handicapped, disabled, impaired,* or the terms *women, girls, females,* as the same.[2] We assume that everyone knows and agrees on what these terms mean, and we often use them in our work in the same way that we do in everyday language. We admit that there is some confusion—certainly some overlap—in popular usage, but generally we treat such terms as *color, disabled, race, gender, ethnicity,* and *culture* as if they were inherent features of human categorization. In other words, we believe that we ***know*** what we mean when we use these terms of "difference."

Even scholars do not all automatically understand these terms in the same way, let alone agree on their complexity. Every time we read or perform scholarly research we must be careful and examine these terms scientifically. We use them as variables in our work and we must openly examine the issue of the validity of our ideas. These terms have power and they give power. Without explicitly examining these ideas, we would not only reproduce social, political, and economic inequalities with all of their meanings and values, we would justify them.

In the next section we look at five of the most basic terms of difference as social scientists have used them in the study of human development: race, ethnicity, culture, gender, and class.

Categories of Group Difference

Like all other social scientists, developmentalists use categories of group difference when they do research. But how do we determine who fits into which category? Three main classification systems used in social science research are: *culture, race,* and *ethnicity*. We often tend to confuse the three terms in popular language.

Race as a Cultural Category

Race as a category has been in use long before our modern understanding of biology. Traditionally race has been based on culturally perceived biological differences. In reality these differences have little biological fact. This becomes clear when we look at the recent progress in the study of the human genome, where it is apparent that, from the standpoint of genetic science, race is not a clear biological category (Gould, 1977). As a result, many researchers have shifted from the use of racial terms to ethnicity terms. The American Anthropological

[2] We also use the terms *White* and *American* interchangeably, but there is less comment on this confusion, for reasons we discuss later.

Association (AAA), for example, reflects the position of the majority of the social science community:

> In the United States both scholars and the general public have been conditioned to viewing human races as natural and separate divisions within the human species based on visible physical differences . . . however, it has become clear that human populations are not unambiguous, clearly demarcated, biologically distinct groups. Evidence from the analysis of genetics (e.g., DNA) indicates that most physical variation, about 94%, lies within so-called racial groups. Conventional geographic "racial" groupings differ from one another only in about 6% of their genes. This means that there is greater variation within "racial" groups than between them. In neighboring populations there is much overlapping of genes and their phenotypic (physical) expressions. Throughout history whenever different groups have come into contact, they have interbred. The continued sharing of genetic materials has maintained all of humankind as a single species. (AAA,1998)

So race is really a culturally determined category. Racial categories still exist today as powerful determinants of human behavior and sociopolitical organization. Race is real because people believe that it is and these beliefs are real in their consequences for different racial groups. The most commonly used racial categories used in the United States are African American, Native American, Caucasian, Pacific Islander, and Asian.

The fact that racial distinctions are actually culturally determined, as opposed to physical, can be challenging to grasp. The markers on which we base our decisions about race—such as *skin color, eye color, hair texture*—do exist, but other differences (e.g., *ear swirl; space between front teeth*) also exist. Skin color, eye color, and hair texture are not the only significant, physically visible differences that could be used to distinguish racial groups, but we are taught to pay attention to those differences, as opposed to other differences. What we are taught is cultural and is based on our systems of defining meaning.

Ethnicity as a Cultural Category

Ethnicity serves as one way to look at distinctions between others and ourselves. Definitions of ethnicity usually involve a collective sense of identity, implying a unique cultural heritage, or cultural background of the group's ancestors. This shared identity includes mutual beliefs and values, collective history, and some commonality of experience. Critical developmentalists emphasize the inclusion of culture as central to the classification of ethnic groups. More specifically, "Ethnicity . . . refers to a group classification in which members share a unique social and cultural heritage passed from one generation to the next" (Rose, as cited in Morten et al., 1989, p. 4).

Racial categories are determined by perceived physical differences that are culturally determined. Ethnicity is culturally determined and learned. These four children are all first cousins and from the same ethnicity.

(Photo courtesy of Cindy Donham)

The definition of ethnicity has three components—a method of distinguishing others and ourselves; a place in a political power system; and a way of explaining differences. Through these components, the ethnic group shares a common tie, a feeling of interdependency, and a sense of identity (Au, 1993; Fisher, Jackson, & Villarruel, 1998). As a method of distinguishing ourselves and others, ethnicity includes a collective sense of identity, based on a unique cultural heritage, which is usually linked to the national background of ancestors, and which incorporates socially recognizable sets of behavior that are taught and maintained through such social institutions as social roles, child rearing, and language. Some examples of commonly known ethnicities are: Hispanics, Germans, Italians, Jews, Islamists, Puerto Ricans, Navahos, among many others.

Ethnicity is both a relationship of power and a cultural identity formed when a cultural group is brought into a single stratified political economy on the basis of its cultural difference. Ethnicity includes a collective sense of identity, based on a unique cultural heritage. It is created by power connections with other ethnic groups to the sources of power within a single society. Ethnicity is used to account for numerous experiences and expressions of scientifically measured disparities, which are actually the result of structured inequality.

Culture

Culture is a dynamic, self-generating, self-determining, and self-regulating process that gives its people a general design for living and patterns for interpreting their reality. Culture is the beliefs and practices of a group of people over generations, which provide them with designs for living and patterns for defining and interpreting reality. This results in traits whose specific combinations renders this group of people unique compared to other groups of people. Culture expresses itself as normative cultural behavior and the visible products of a culture. This includes the organizing principles of a culture, its worldview, its imperatives, and its ethos (Kottak, 2002; Triandis, 1994).

Even though every culture is different, they all share certain essential characteristics. First, culture is preeminently social. It is the product of individuals' interaction with themselves, with their history, and with each other. Culture is therefore shared; no one individual has a culture of his or her own. Culture is practiced and transmitted by groups of people in a specific geographic and historical relationship. The older generations teach their culture to the younger generations. Culture is transmitted from one generation to the next. This also indicates that culture is learned; it is not genetically inherent. It is a set of beliefs and attitudes, perspectives, and behaviors that each member of a cultural unit learns. Culture is all-encompassing. Because culture comprises a blueprint for reality, it defines every aspect of what the people in that culture can know and do. It is continuous, in that it maintains its integrity over time, but culture is also dynamic—each member is constantly modifying and expanding cultural norms.

Prejudice and Discrimination

Prejudice is an ideology or belief that one group of people is superior to another. **Discrimination** is taking this prejudicial belief and acting on it. For example, a person may believe that Hispanics are lazy (this is a prejudicial belief) and as a result will not hire any Hispanics that apply for a job at their company (this is discrimination).

CHAPTER 1 SUMMARY

Human development as a science is relatively new, and it was not until the late nineteenth century that scientists from different disciplines became interested in developing this field, which had been started by mothers who were interested in a more sophisticated and scientific aspect of child rearing. As a discipline, *human development* is the science that seeks to understand how and why people everywhere change and remain the same over time. Human development also differs from other human sciences in its focus. Human development is drawn from a *life-span perspective*, a view that observes changes in people across their entire life's duration from conception to death. Human development also differs from other human sciences in its perspective. Focusing on the way that people change helps developmental scientists to embrace four "multi-" viewpoints: multidisciplinary, multicontextual, multicultural, and multidirectional.

Early developmentalists agreed on the fact that parents need scientific information, thereby downsizing advice from grandparents and friends as definitive principles of childrearing. This shift in point of view later became popular and was vastly accepted by the common population, and soon individuals started to believe that Western scientific inquiry is the superior way of knowing. This way of thinking therefore led to an explosion of scientific theories explaining human development. The explosion of theory development continued for the better half of the nineteenth century. Scientists such as Watson, Freud, and Piaget began to generate notoriety for their theories, which later became the way of life for most parents. These scientists continued to develop theories and present new ideas on child rearing and parenting techniques. Scientists such as Freud introduced the concept of libidinal (sexual) feelings as the foundation for child and adolescent growth and development. Other theorists such as Adler believed parents have an important influence on children, and that better parenting techniques could be taught, therefore providing extensive guidelines for childrearing in many different settings.

Further studies in human development also revealed that human growth might be influenced by different categories such as sequence, source, characteristic, and process in which evolution takes place. Scientists were also able to show continuity, plasticity, and stability, all the while considering individual differences in the process of growth. Early theories were too generalized concerning the process of development; however, as human development progressed as a scientific field, more research hinted at the role played by ethnicity, culture, socioeconomic status, and other distinct factors in this progression.

CHAPTER 1 VOCABULARY

Culture
Developmental stages
Developmental theory
Discrimination
Ethnicity
Human development
Human ontogeny
Life span perspective
Multicontextual
Multicultural
Multidirectional
Multidisciplinary
Phylogeny
Prejudice
Race

Chapter 2

RESEARCH METHODS

Research Design and Methodology

Chinese children dressed for a festival.
(Photo courtesy of Margaret Goetz)

On the Edge

By Margaret Goetz

A good place to be
On the outskirts
Watching
Listening
Smiling
Nodding
Hearing
Seeing
More than they know
A good place to be.
On the edge.

Introduction

Dineen Sykes is a developmental researcher and the mother of three children: Michal, a boy age 7; Nicola, a girl age 5; and Amir, a boy age 3. Nicola has watched her older brother play games on the computer and now she wants to play, too. She asks her mother to let her play a "'puter game," so Dineen reaches to turn on the computer and find a game for her, but Nicola protests. "I can do it, Mommy." Dineen decides to see just how computer literate her daughter may have become, and much to her surprise, Nicola can not only boot up the household desktop and wait appropriately until the machine has initialized, but she can also find her favorite game icon, press it, and start to play.

This is precisely the kind of experience that would intrigue a developmentalist. How did Nicola learn to use a computer? How did she learn exactly which icon represents her game? How did she learn that the computer takes time to boot and offers a number of cues about its status that she must observe but not interrupt? Does Amir know how to use the computer, too? (As it turns out, he did!) Questions form in Dineen's mind: How do young children learn to use the computer? What do the children understand about the computer's functioning? Does this early literacy translate, not only into the actual use of a specific computer, but also an understanding about what to expect on any electronic devise, such as menus, pull-downs, help functions, and so on?

The questions are:

- How should Dineen Sykes design her research?
- What method of research would best suit what she would like to know?

Research Design: The Structure in Which Social Scientists Work

The research process can be divided into five phases: groundwork, design, measurement, analytic interpretation, and ethical standards.

RESEARCH CRITERIA	WHAT TO CONSIDER	ELEMENTS INVOLVED
Groundwork	Choose a topic, formulate a research question, do background literature review	▪ The topic or subject the researcher is interested in studying ▪ Development of a question that can be answered by doing the research ▪ Review of the existing literature and past research done on the topic ▪ Framing a research proposal (especially formulating the hypothesis)
Design	Should this research be done in an experimental or nonexperimental design?	▪ Decide on either qualitative or quantitative design ▪ Careful consideration of whether the research will yield a correlational or causal conclusion ▪ Develop a design that best serves the study and yields authentic results ▪ Control sampling issues
Measurement	Research methods	▪ The method in which data will be collected ▪ How should the information/data/measures be aggregated?
Analysis Interpretation	Data interpretation	▪ Now that the researcher has the data, what do they all mean? ▪ Make sense of the data, and explain why the trends we have identified exist ▪ What next? Where do we go from here?
Ethical Standards	Researcher's ethical conduct	▪ What ethical standards and code of behavior must we consider before, during, and after the research study is done? ▪ What are the implications of these ethical standards?

Groundwork Phase

Before any form of research study can be initiated, the scientist has to first choose a topic and generate a researchable question. This is the beginning of the **groundwork phase**. The scientist suspects that there is a relationship between two or more variables that could be stated. For example, Sykes is interested in the process of informal learning. She knows that her youngest children were not formally taught to use a computer and yet their computer literacy was extensive. She wondered: How is computer literacy achieved in early childhood? Sykes had a topic and a researchable question.

Once the research has a topic and a research question, the researcher must review the current literature on the topic. The **literature review** serves to better formulate the hypothesis, as the researcher begins to note the gaps in the current research. Sykes began reading everything she could find about informal learning and cognitive development in early childhood. The more she read, the more Sykes was convinced that the children were actually tiny "apprentices"—that they watched others in their environment use electronic devises and then mimicked what they saw. Over time Sykes could propose a hypothesis about the relationship she wanted to investigate. She argued that the learning was highly effective (1) because the "mentors" (the slightly older children) were developmentally close enough to the task to be able to teach it in terms easily accessible to the apprentices; (2) because the developmental proximity between the apprentices and the mentors allowed the apprentices to quickly achieve the competency levels of the mentors; (3) because the learning was pragmatic and task specific; and (4) because the rewards of learning were immediate and highly gratifying.

Finally, the scientist drafts a research proposal that includes everything that comprises the experiment, from the hypothesis to the research methods to the anticipated outcome to the costs. Sykes's proposal included a:

1. statement of the problem;
2. literature review;
3. statement of the hypothesis;
4. research design plan; and
5. projection of the anticipated results, which requires the development of the hypothesis.

A **hypothesis** is the scientist's guess about the outcome of an experiment, an educated guess about the relationship between two or more variables. The hypothesis allows the scientist to test a phenomenon, which means that the hypothesis is actually a testable version of the research question. The researcher makes a prediction at the conclusion of the study about whether the data at hand ideally can prove or disprove the research question. Sykes will still have several steps left to carry out the research after the proposal is made.

Design Phase

Once all of the groundwork for the research has been set, the scientist must decide whether the research is best served by an experimental or nonexperimental design. This is called the **design phase**. The five most important considerations of this phase are:

1. whether the design should be experimental or nonexperimental;
2. whether the research will be qualitative or quantitative;
3. whether the design will produce causal or correlational results;
4. sampling considerations; and
5. the choice of an appropriate research method.

Experimental Designs

In **experimental designs**, the researcher actively intervenes in the natural world. The experiment usually takes place in a controlled setting, such as a laboratory, because the scientist is determining as precisely as possible which variables are present and how they are introduced. The researcher often works with two identical groups, a control group and an experimental group. The intervention is then given to the experimental group but not the control group. Then the test is given to both groups and the results are compared. If the intervention has been effective, there will be a difference in the overall scores between the two groups. If the intervention has not been effective, the scores of the two groups will remain relatively the same. Sometimes research study requires direct collection of data, without any manipulation of the environment. This is called a **nonexperimental design**, which relies on conditions and settings that take place naturally.

Qualitative Versus Quantitative Designs

Experimental research methods are often used in social sciences to develop a better understanding of human development. **Quantitative** research is empirical in nature; in other words, it produce data that can be converted to numbers so that some form of statistic can be used to analysis the data. Often questionnaires or surveys are used to collect quantitative data. This approach can have the advantage of large numbers of respondents so it is applicable to a larger population. Because quantitative research is based in numbers and statistics, this type of research lends itself easily to charts, graphs, and other visual representations.

Its disadvantages include its capacity for statistical errors and sampling errors, which can undermine the validity of the study.

Qualitative research is also an inquiry into an identified problem or subject of interest, but it may or may not test a theory that is identified before the research is conducted. **Qualitative** research is frequently designed to develop or discover theory, often through inductive reasoning, which means that the scientists reach a conclusion based on observation. Qualitative research focuses on understanding an individual's thoughts, feelings, experiences, and unique way of interpreting the world. This flexible and focused form of research can produce a large quantity of rich, complex data that can be used in a variety of contexts. The disadvantage of qualitative research is often precisely the fact that it is a difficult, expensive, and time-consuming method of study. Because of its focus on intuitive individual response, qualitative research is not easily projected to a larger sample. Seven common forms of qualitative research are: descriptive; causal-comparative; single-subject; ethnographic; phenomenological; social constructivist; and self-report studies.

Correlational Versus Causal Designs

Correlational research is based on the notion that a connection between two variables does not mean that one variable causes the other. For example, domestic abuse and substance abuse are connected but substance abuse does not necessarily always result in, or cause, domestic abuse. **Causal research** depends on the assumption that one variable causes another (A causes B). For example, research shows that an increase in hormones around the age of nine or ten causes the onset of puberty; this is a cause-and-effect conclusion. Causal experimental research in social sciences studies are particularly challenging due to the fact that social systems, cultures, and people are very complicated and many different variables can affect outcomes. As a result causation is difficult to establish and most research studies in the field of social sciences are based on correlational outcomes.

Independent and Dependent Variables

In experimental designs the general research question is: What is the effect of Variable A (independent variable) on Variable B (dependent variable)? The **independent variable** is the one that the researcher manipulates, that is, deliberately and systematically changes, so that its effect on another variable can be observed.

The **dependent variable** is the one that the researcher observes to see if it changes when the independent variable changes. We can observe the use of independent and dependent variables everywhere. When a bright two-year-old pushes a chair up to the light switch and flicks it on and off, on and off, she is the researcher in an experiment in which the light switch is the independent variable and the lights are the dependent variable. One of the reasons that little children love this experiment involves its reliability—the position of the switch will over and over again allow the young scientist to predict whether the lights will turn on or off. Let us now look at a more sophisticated example of dependent and independent variables from a study that looks at how children lie.

Developmental scientists Lee and Kang were concerned with the relationship between children's capacity to formulate lies and their executive functioning skills, such as memory, impulse control, and planning. They placed a number of eight to sixteen year olds in a room with the answers to a test they were about to take. Each child was given instruction not to look at the answers, but the majority of the children did look. They were then asked a series of questions to determine if they would lie about what they did, and the sophistication of the lie. They were also given a number of questions that tested their brain's executive functioning skills, which are series of mental processes connecting past experiences to present actions. Executive brain functioning is how a person uses complex thoughts to arrive at multifaceted decisions about his or her daily life tasks.

The research question is: What is the relationship between executive brain functioning and the sophistication of lying? The independent variable is executive brain functioning (as a function of one's score on a test) and the dependent variable is whether and how the child lies.

Sampling of Subjects

Sampling is the process of obtaining the appropriate participants for a research study. There are three steps involved. First, developmentalists must specify the **population**, the set of all possible participants who share the characteristic(s) of interest. In the preceding example, the population is eight- to sixteen-year-old children in the United States. Of course, twenty-year-old men, elderly women, and female babies would be excluded from this sample population. Second, we will need a **sample** or a group of participants, who can represent the population being studied. Because we cannot test all children aged eight to sixteen in the United States, we must decide who can represent this group. The most important aspect that the scientists must ensure is that there are no biases in the sample. Next, a **sample size** must be determined. This step usually depends in part on the estimated number of the population. It is convention to test thirty or more participants for any given study; however, given our population size and the degree to which we hope to generalize to the larger population, we may need a fairly large sample size, perhaps somewhere around 6,000 children.

The optimal experimental sampling design would be to have a random sample. In **randomized sampling** all subjects of a population have an equal chance of participating in the study. It is generally impossible to test all of the members of a population; therefore, researchers try to have a population sample that is as representative and random as possible. If scientists want to study the effects of the representation of women in music videos on adolescent female self-esteem in the United States, they certainly cannot test every adolescent girl in the country. We might begin with a single state such as California. One alternative is to randomly select one hundred high schools in California, and then randomly select one hundred girls from each school.

Many studies use **convenience sampling**, a nonrandomized sample of easily accessible subjects. Many researchers, especially those on limited research budgets, use subjects that are readily available. For example, many studies involve college students as subjects because many professors doing research have easy access to this population.

In order to assign subjects to an experimental design, researchers need a **representative sampling** of the population of interest. For example, suppose a researcher is interested in how children typically learn mathematical concepts. The population for this experiment would be a broad group of children from every income bracket and every ability range. The researcher would then choose a certain number of children from each category of interest in the population; for example, six lower-class children, six middle-class children, six upper-class children.

There are other types of sampling that depend on a behavior instead of or in addition to the subjects. One of the most commonly used is **sampling behavior with tasks**. This type of sampling is used when experimenters cannot observe a behavior directly, so they create sample tasks that duplicate the behavior of interest. For example, if a developmental scientist wants to understand how children judge emotion, waiting in real life for examples of the emotions under investigation might take a long time. Instead the researchers might ask children to judge emotion from photographs.

If the investigators are interested in how children group objects in real life, they might place a number of different types of objects on a table and ask the children to group them. Sampling behavior with tasks might not totally sample the behavior of interest as it occurs in real life; for example, children might count toy cars differently than they would count real cars. But the strength of sampling behavior with tasks is that it makes certain behaviors convenient and accessible.

Longitudinal Versus Cross-Sectional Research

The study of human development is the science that seeks to understand how and why all kinds of people change and remain the same over time. Because of this focus, developmentalists also prefer research designs that concentrate on change over time.

Longitudinal research studies a group of individuals or subjects who are the same age over a period of many years, watching for changes as the subjects mature and age. Researchers can trace the course of development as a process that occurs over a long time. For example, studies of developmental changes in rote learning might test one group of subjects who are all four years old, then again when they are eight, twelve, and sixteen.

One of the disadvantages of longitudinal studies is that it can take a long period of time to complete the study. Subjects can also be lost because of death, moving, losing contact, or other reasons. As a result sample sizes in longitudinal studies must start out very large. They are also usually very expensive because of the size of study, the tracking of participants, and the long-term analysis of data.

Cross-sectional research studies individuals who differ in age but share other critical characteristics, such as socioeconomic status (SES), ethnicity, and/or gender. In this way researchers observe the processes of change over short periods of time. Continuing with our previous example of researching rote learning for a cross-sectional study, we would take a sample of four year olds and a different sample of eight, twelve, and sixteen year olds to be used as sample groups. In cross-sectional research, all four sample age groups would be tested at the same time, instead of waiting for the original four year olds to age and retest them at different ages as we would in longitudinal research.

Finally, **microgenetic research** studies individuals at a specific period in time that may cover a few hours or days. The researcher does not begin studying the subject until he or she is on the border of a developmental shift. For example, a researcher interested in the social implications of learning to walk will wait until a baby has pulled up on the furniture before the researcher comes in to study the behavior. This short but comprehensive type of study allows the researcher to collect important information in a short period of time, which could lead to breakthroughs and scientific conclusions.

Each of these methods has inherent challenges and strengths. In longitudinal studies, the subjects may drop out of research that could last decades. The scientists may also have difficulty keeping contact with subjects who move, marry, and miss their mail. Because the subjects are given research questions over a period of time, they grow accustomed to the procedures and the questions; this familiarity can distort the results. Also, given the length of the research, there could be any number of variables that actually account for the findings. There is no way to weed out many of the variables.

Cross-sectional designs were formulated to respond to some of the limitations of longitudinal research designs, in that they can be carried out in a relatively shorter time period. One of the issues associated with cross-sectional designs, however, is the **cohort effect**, that is, when a group of people of the same generation is affected by an historical event or time period. For example, consider the question: Do people become more religious as they age and near death? Cross-sectional studies may find that people do get more religious as they age. However, a longitudinal study may find that people do not get more religious but rather that older generations started out more religious than younger generations. So people do not change in their religious beliefs significantly as they age. This is a good example of the cohort effect. Another example is the effect of September 11, 2001 on the American population and the fear of being vulnerable to terrorists. Future generations that did not live through this event may feel differently about America's vulnerability.

Measurement Phase

There are a variety of different methods used to collect data for research, all of which have advantages and disadvantages. Researchers must be able to identify and understand the strengths and shortcomings of the data collection methods that they have chosen. This way researchers can account for biases that are built into research. Four of the most popular data collection methods in the social sciences are:

1. interviews;
2. questionnaires and surveys;
3. observation; and
4. content analysis.

Interviews

Interviews can elicit detailed information that is impossible or very difficult to get from any other data collection technique. It is also a time-consuming method. A researcher can distribute a questionnaire or survey that can be completed in a very short time to a whole room full of subjects, but interviews must be done one-on-one or in fairly small groups. Because interviewing is labor and time intensive, sample sizes are often relatively small in size.

There are several biases inherent in the interviewing process. One of these is that the data are **self-reported** information, which are only as accurate as the interviewee's memory and reliability. The subject's memory may be faulty or inaccurate, or the interviewee may purposely provide incorrect information. The amount and kind of information gathered may also be influenced by the skill of the interviewer. Another issue is how to analyze the information gathered from the interview. This process is by definition subjective and can lead to validity problems. However, these issues can be systematically overcome by methods of triangulation, the use of two or more methods used as a means of "cross-check" by comparing the results of one method within the study to another.

Questionnaires or Surveys

Questionnaires or surveys are the most commonly used method to gather social science research data. They have the advantage of being relatively fast, cost-effective, and easy to analyze. They are usually quantitative in nature and therefore a variety of statistical analyses are available. Since questionnaires are relatively easy to distribute, it is easier to get large sample sizes.

Questionnaires also have some basic biases. First of all they are only as valid as the questions asked. In other words, if the questions are not well written, or lead a person to respond in a specific manner, or elicit different meanings for different populations, problems with validity can occur. During an interviewing process additional questions may be asked if the need arises, but one cannot do this with a written questionnaire. Questionnaires are, of course, self-reported information and therefore they can have the validity issues that are associated with interviews. Another challenge of this method is that they are usually written; therefore, only people who can read and write can be subjects. As a result they are inappropriate for certain populations, such as young children or people who do not have a written language or populations with high illiteracy rates. Furthermore, the vocabulary used must be appropriate for the educational level of the participants in the study.

Observation

Observation, watching and recording what is seen, is another method used in social science research. Observational research is highly structured. Researchers explicitly define what variables are being observed, as well as the precise methods for observing those variables, such as systematically counting and tabulating the observed variables or recording the exact timing of the behavior. This kind of data also has the advantage of being easily statistically analyzed. Qualitative observation techniques are plentiful and varied, and the range of these methods is constantly changing based on the creativity of the researchers and the advances of observation technology.

Observation research techniques have the advantage of observing actual behavior and are useful in many kinds of research. For example, it is useful in observing play-pattern differences for boys and girls that are toddlers. Obviously this method is not very useful for research that seeks opinions, beliefs, reasons behind behavior, or behavior that cannot be observed.

Observation Techniques in Quantitative Research and Their Descriptions

OBSERVATION TECHNIQUES	DESCRIPTION
Narrative recording	Writes a story-like account of the behavior
Environmental measures	Focuses on the sociopsychological environment in which the behavior transpires
Event recording	Counts every occurrence of the behavior within a specific observation period
Duration recording	Times the occurrence of a single instance of the behavior
Interval recording	Divides the observation period into equal intervals and records the occurrence of the behavior in each
Time sampling	Records observations made at specific points in time
Sequential act coding	Records events in the precise order that they occur
Global rating scales	Makes an overall assessment, often of the quality of the behavior

Content Analysis

Content analysis is a research method designed to analyze the content of data that were not produced for research purposes. For example, if one wants to study women's roles in the 1800s in the United States, there was no formal research done on this topic in that era and there are no women still living that can be interviewed. As a result a researcher looks to diaries, letters, novels, laws, and other historical records to interpolate the roles of women in the 1800s. Social historians often use content analysis.

Content analysis is also used in present-day research to study the stereotypes, social conventions, and norms portrayed in visual media. For example, if one wants to study how women's images were portrayed in advertising over the last fifty years, the researcher would use content analysis of advertising campaigns.

Data Analysis Phase

The final stage of the research process involves making sense of the data. **Data analysis** falls into two measures. Quantitative analysis can be exploratory or confirmatory, depending on the research questions, while qualitative analysis develops a set of themes or a conceptual framework that expresses the main ideas in the data. By using statistics appropriate to each measure, the researchers can analyze, interpret, and explain the data they have collected.

Since the invention of the computer, complex statistical analysis has become easier to carry out and, as a result, much more common than in the past. There is a wide variety and many levels of complexity involved in statistical analysis available today.

Reliability and Validity

All experiments depend on two basic criteria for establishing whether the results of the research are sound. These two measures are **reliability** and **validity**. Good research depends on being able to get the same or similar results every time the research is performed using the same measurement. A measure is considered reliable when the results remain consistent every time the experiment is conducted. For example, Asher (1979) was interested in the reliability of a sociometric technique for predicting preschoolers' friendships, so he employed a test–retest strategy. The same test is given twice at a specific interval. If Asher's sociometric test is given to a subject a second time, and the two scores are the same or nearly the same, then the test is considered reliable. On the other hand, Saylor et al. (1984), using the test–retest strategy, observed that the Childhood Depression Inventory (CDI) will produce variable responses in any given subject, depending on the distance between the first and second tests. The CDI is therefore not reliable.

The second criterion of good research asks the question: Does the measure we are using really test for the reality we are trying to measure? This is called validity. Suppose that, in order to test pre-teen girls' social skills with boys, a researcher uses the number of social interactions girls have with boys as the measure of skill. But as the researcher collects the data, the researcher may notice that some girls who have a high number of interactions with boys may not seem socially skilled because the interactions are mostly negative. This observation will cause the researcher to question the validity of the measure. A measure may be reliable but not valid; a ruler may be a very reliable measure of length, but it will not measure time.

Ethical Standards

Modern research today has to be evaluated not only for its scientific merit but also for its ethical soundness. Most universities and government agencies worldwide have Institutional Review Boards, which are charged with the responsibility of evaluating and ensuring the ethical soundness of their researchers. Worldwide interest in the development of uniform ethical standards was galvanized by the horrific experiments done on human subjects, who were forced to participate in experiments that resulted in extreme pain, permanent disability, or death. An international council held in Nuremberg, Germany, after World War II convicted sixteen German physicians of war crimes as a result of their experimentation. After the trial the council developed the Nuremberg Codes.

The **Nuremberg Codes** share fundamental concerns with the guidelines of international, national, state, and institutional agencies. The three most important of these standards include:

- **Freedom from Harm**—Subjects cannot suffer a detrimentally unique experience or long-term consequences.
- **Informed Consent**—Subjects cannot be forced, coerced, or offered inappropriate incentives. Scientists are required to describe the research to potential participants so they can determine if they wish to participate. Researchers must also avoid deception; if the participants must be deceived, researchers must provide a thorough explanation of the true nature of the research as soon as possible.
- **Confidentiality**—Information gathered must not be made public in a manner that would embarrass or harm the subjects.

In addition to the requirement to keep the identifiable information about the subjects safe and confidential, scientists are also mandated to report research findings honestly and carefully. Specific guidelines are also set up to deal with specific population groups or situations. For example, in addition to the overall ethical standards already discussed, the Society for Research in Child Development has devised a set of ethical standards especially for children, who themselves are not in a position to consent, and who are especially vulnerable to harm. Religious constraints can restrain research questioning as well as subjects' responses. These and other factors have to be addressed in an effort to maintain our overall concern for ethics.

CHAPTER 2 SUMMARY

Social scientists do their research in a structured process that includes groundwork, design, measurement, and analytic interpretation. The initial phase—groundwork—establishes the topic and the specific question under investigation by reviewing existing literature on the topic and framing a research proposal. In the design phase the researcher develops the research method that will yield the best results. The decisions of whether to use a qualitative or quantitative method, and whether the research should attempt a causal or correlational result will determine the course of the rest of the research process. In this phase the research will also identify the independent and dependent variables and decide on the best method of choosing subjects.

Because developmentalists study change over the life span, they prefer those designs that measure change. Longitudinal studies are ideally suited to developmental research because they take place over years, often decades; unfortunately they are also costly, unwieldy, and difficult to generalize. Cross-sectional designs improve somewhat on the longitudinal design. They take less time by sampling subjects at different developmental stages, rather than waiting for subjects to pass through the stages. It is difficult to compare data in cross-sectional designs, however, because different subjects introduce different variables into the design. Microgenetic designs are designed to address the challenges of both longitudinal and cross-sectional designs by studying subjects at the precise point of a developmental change. These designs are relatively short, sometimes lasting only a few days.

The next task is to design the data collection method and the various statistical and analytic methods best suited to interpreting the data. Experimental designs usually involve comparing test groups with control groups and outlining the difference between the two sets of results. Nonexperimental research methods that are particularly useful to developmentalists include interviews, surveys, and a variety of observation methods.

In the analysis phase the researcher must make sense of the data, confirming or refining existing theory and/or generating new theory. The two most important research concerns are reliability, the degree to which the test can be repeated and yield similar results, and validity, how well the test represents the reality it is designed to record.

Finally, all researchers around the world are concerned with the central issues of ethics: freedom from harm, confidentiality, and informed consent.

CHAPTER 2 VOCABULARY

Causal Designs
Cohort Effect
Confidentiality
Content Analysis
Convince Sample
Correlation
Cross-Sectional
Data Analysis
Dependent Variable
Design Phase
Experimental Designs
Freedom from Harm
Groundwork
Hypothesis
Independent Variable
Informed Consent
Literature Review
Longitudinal
Microgenetic Research
Nonexperimental Designs
Nuremberg Codes
Observation
Population
Qualitative
Quantitative
Questionnaires or Surveys
Random Sample
Reliability
Representative Sample
Research Proposal
Sample
Sample Size
Sampling Behavior with Tasks
Self-Reported
Validity

Chapter 3

GRAND THEORIES AND THEORETICAL APPROACHES

Racially mixed families are becoming common place in America today.
(Photo courtesy of DNF Style/Shutterstock.com)

Theoretical Approaches

If we want to understand how people change over time, we cannot simply collect facts. Facts do not speak for themselves. Although human beings are remarkably alike as a species, each one of us is identifiably different. Einstein is reputed to have said, "Theory decides what we observe." We actually create and act on theories all the time. For example, a well-dressed, well-mannered, attractive woman bumps into you as you walk down a crowded street on the way to a coffeehouse. A quick brush, and she says, "Excuse me—I'm so sorry" before she continues on down the street. You smile back, murmuring "Oh, no problem" and you continue on to the coffee house. A set of facts has taken place: the bump, the brush, the polite apology, and the equally polite response. Our belief about these "facts" is a theory of sorts; it tells us how to interpret the facts in this case because it is your belief system that dictates you to expect a certain behavior in such a social setting. You know exactly how to behave and what to expect in return. You would probably interpret it as a simple accidental brush with a harmless stranger. That is also why you probably would not notice that your wallet is missing until you go to pay for your double mocha latte. Thieves and con artists count on our "theories" about human experience to thwart our recognition of their true intents.

Approaches and Contexts in Human Development

There is no broad theory that unifies the discipline of human development. As we have already indicated, the study of human development is multidisciplinary. We use the input of several disciplines because humans are complex beings living in complex interactions in a number of contexts. The study of human development originally focused its central questions on two specific domains of human experience, biological and psychological. But now we focus on both knowledge and systems of inquiry from anthropology, history, sociology, cultural studies, gender studies, and ethnic studies as well as others.

Biosocial Approaches

From conception through adolescence individuals undergo an extensive series of changes that bring them from a single fertilized cell to a complex, multidimensional mature person. For this reason developmentalists draw heavily on biological sciences in order to understand physical development. **Biological approaches** in human development focus on growth and change in the body, with a special concentration on brain development and the processes of sensory input.

Psychological Approaches

No less spectacular than the physical changes that underlie childhood are the equally expansive growth in our ability to think; to analyze and interpret emotional states; to strengthen and extend our awareness; and to discern, reason, and make complex judgments based on a variety of inputs. We rely on the work of the psychological sciences to capture psychological–cognitive development. **Psychological approaches** actually dominated our investigation of human development during the first half of the twentieth century, focusing on changes in thought processes, perceptual abilities, and language, as well as the growth of emotions, personality, and individual responses to interpersonal relationships.

These two domains allowed **developmentalists** to focus on individuals as their basic unit for analysis and interpretation of behavior without considering other factors involved in human development. However, individuals grow and change within social contexts. The first of these contexts is historical. People of roughly the same age comprise a **cohort** and they pass through history together. Major historical events will have an effect on all of the members of a cohort. For example, the Second World War created a significant impact on everyone who went through it. Historical events also impact social institutions and constructions such as the National Association for the Advancement of Colored People, the Jewish Defense League, the American Indian Movement, and the League of United Latin American Citizens, which were all created in response to particular historical incidents.

Furthermore, we live in a social world, in a variety of types of families, schools, work places, religious institutions, and neighborhoods, which all have a significant effect on our development. Sociology's contribution to the study of human development centers in its focus on cohorts and social institutions. *Sociological approaches* are also concerned with socioeconomic status (SES), with special attention paid to poverty because of its effects on human developmental processes. This discipline also sheds light on the developmental contexts represented by families, neighborhood, community institutions, and ethnic groupings.

Finally, developmentalists grew interested in cultural contexts. These contexts included community practices, religious traditions, ethnic identities, and how people live. Human beings grow and change in a complex environment of beliefs, attitudes, definitional frameworks, languages, and traditions known as culture. *Anthropological approaches* look at cultural development with a focus on community practices and different ways people live. These domains of development appear throughout the text as we explore human development through the disciplines that investigate it. Developmentalists seek to synthesize these contexts and disciplines as they work to achieve an integrated view of human growth and transformation.

The Organizing Frameworks of Grand Theories in Human Development

As you might imagine, the disciplines that inform developmental studies comprise dozens of theories. Generally, there are four organizing principles into which the theories can be divided, based largely on which of the contexts of development the framework addresses. They are the biological–maturation framework, the environmental–learning framework, the constructivist framework, and the cultural context framework. While there are a number of theories that would fall into these broad categories, certain theories within

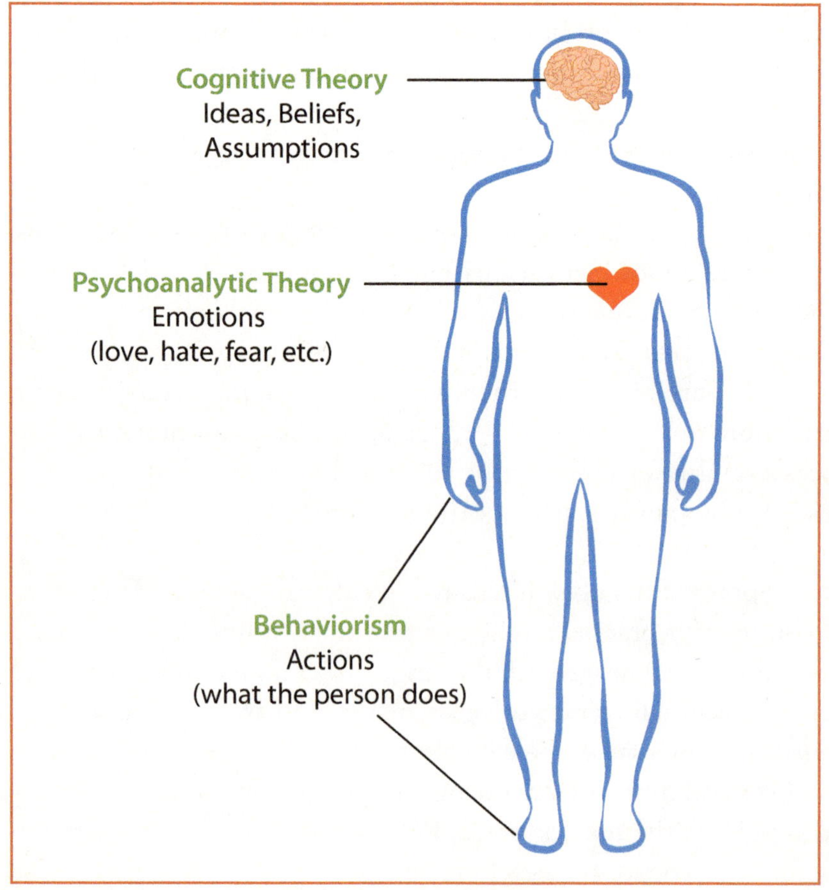

Major focus of the three grand theories.

each category are still considered fundamental because these powerful theories shaped what was, at that time, considered to be the framework for interpreting and understanding change and development in individuals. They also became the prototypes for many of the ideas that followed them. They were the creators of scientific movements that dominated the discipline for decades. There were the:

1. psychoanalytic movement, which was established by Sigmund Freud and advanced by Arnold Gesell and Erik Erikson;
2. behaviorist movement, led first by John Watson and Burrhus Frederic, also known as B. F. Skinner;
3. cognitive movement, whose founder was Jean Piaget; and
4. cultural constructivist movement, represented by Lev Vygotsky and Urie Bronfenbrenner.

Organizing Frameworks and Their Associated Grand Theories

FRAMEWORK	THEORY	THEORIST
Biological-Maturational Believes biology is the determining factor in human development. This means that biological growth and maturation determine a person's behavioral development.	Psychoanalytic	Freud
	Psychomaturational	Gesell
	Psychoanalytic ego	Erikson
Environment-Learning This theory considers behavioral changes as being a product of the immediate environment, which means humans change and develop behavior as their environment dictates it.	Behaviorist	Watson
	Social behaviorist	Skinner
Constructivist These theorists believe that cognitive maturity is the driving force in human development. The term "constructivist" refers to the fact that this theory believes knowledge is constructed, thus behavior changes based upon the newly constructed thoughts.	Cognitive constructivist	Piaget
Cultural Context The cultural-context theory takes into consideration the role of different contexts in human development. Contexts are defined by the totality of environments to which a person is exposed, which will determine human behavior and growth.	Social cultural	Vygotsky
	Social ecological	Bronfenbrenner

Biological–Maturation Framework

The organizing principle of the **biological–maturation framework** is that the sources of changes that characterize human development are **endogenous,** that is, changes that arise come from inside the organism as the result of the organism's biological heritage. The major cause of development is **maturation,** a sequence of changes that are strongly influenced by genetic inheritance and that occur as individual's age from birth to full adulthood. The major theorists include Freud and Erikson. These two developmentalists postulated theories that focus on physiological changes and maturation, which in turn lead to psychological and cognitive advancement. Both Freud and Erikson believed that emotional and mental growth are directly related to aging processes, which consequently cause development and maturation.

Psychoanalytic Theory

Psychoanalytic theory interprets human development in terms of motives and drives. The theory is based on the existence of mental processes of which people are not consciously aware. The central concept of its creator, Sigmund Freud (1856–1939), is that reason does not rule behavior, as scientists had

Sigmund Freud (1856–1939).

(Photo courtesy of Everett Historical/Shutterstock.com)

Freud's Developmental Stages

STAGE	AGE	EROGENOUS ZONE	DESCRIPTION
Oral	Birth–1 year	Mouth	Satisfaction comes through the mouth, beginning with nursing.
Anal	1–3 years	Bladder and bowel	Satisfaction comes through the elimination processes.
Phallic	3–6 years	Genitals	Satisfaction is centered in the genitals, but in an immature manner.
Latency	6–puberty	Dormant sexual interests	The unconscious drives are latent; sexual interests are secondary to developing thinking processes.
Genital	Puberty–end of life	Mature sexual interests	Satisfaction comes from mature sexual relations, through love and familial relations, and through the acceptance of adult responsibility.

believed; rather, unconscious psychological forces, which originate in childhood and continue to exert influence throughout adult life, powerfully affect human thought and behavior. For Freud, the mind comprises three structures. The **id**, based on the pleasure principle, seeks immediate satisfaction of biologically based drives. The **ego**, based on the reality principle, adapts to reality through the use of defense mechanisms. The **superego**, based on societal principles, represents internalized social restrictions. People differ in their ego **defense mechanisms**, which control the expression of the more primitive forces in their personalities. According to Freud, because mental health involves the ability to love and to work effectively and harmoniously, psychoanalysis provides a method for overcoming unconscious psychological conflict. **Psychoanalysis** is a method of talk therapy designed to uncover unconscious processes and release blockages (inner conflicts), which lead to anxiety and other psychological disorders. It is important to uncover the unconscious motives and drives because conscious experience often cannot be trusted due to distortions produced by unconscious defense mechanisms.

Freud did not incorporate social influences into his theory other than to say that all societies deal with universal human conflicts and lead to repression of individual desires. Freud pioneered this new movement because he was among the first thinkers to explain that in addition to biology, psychiatric symptoms such as emotions and mental states influence behavior.

Freud is considered a developmentalist because of his conviction that an individual's experience in the first five years of life is critical to his or her personality formation. Freud claims that tensions central to personality development can be represented in five stages: oral, anal, phallic, latent, and genital psychosexual stages. These stages mark an individual's progress through childhood. In Freud's mind adult personality changes very little.

Psychomaturational Theory

Arnold Gesell (1880–1961), also an advocate of stage theory, was concerned with early child development. A school psychologist and later a pediatrician, Gesell was fascinated by **dysgenic** factors, the accumulation and persistence of defective traits in the gene pools of certain populations, especially as hereditary differences may influence the level of sexual drive (libido) and the occurrence of disorders such as homosexuality. However, it is worthy to mention that psychologists today no longer consider homosexuality to be a disorder, but in Gesell's era it was considered a serious deviation.

He established a clinic in Wisconsin focused on children with disabilities to further study which genetic defects lead to impairment. His central theoretical principle was that heredity causes human development to unfold in a series of predetermined steps, with very little individual variation, on a biological clock or timetable. His major contributions include schedules of behavioral development, a timetable for when and how developmental sequences take place, especially in infants and toddlers. As a maturationist, Gesell was interested in identifying the onset of specific observable behaviors that he believed were common to all children, such as rolling over, sitting up unaided, and grasping

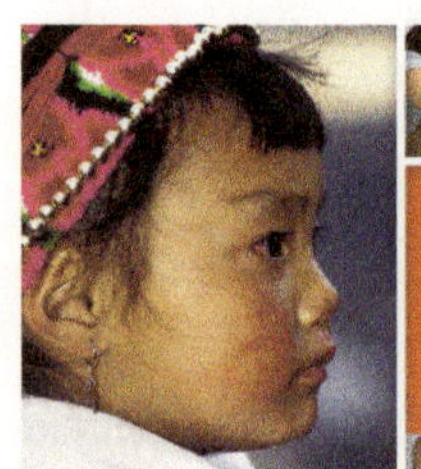

Arnold Gesell

Arnold Gesell (1880–1961) was active in adoption reforms in the early part of this century. *Eugenics*, or the idea that many children were not adoptable because of their bad genetics coming from impoverished or mentally ill parents, was popular with many professionals during the early 1900s (i.e., if you were poor you were biologically defective and had defective children). However, Gesell believed with proper psychological testing and screening that children who were of normal or above normal intellect could be placed with families. He worked with child agencies to reform adoption during this time. Children could be tested because he believed that children follow a set developmental pattern. This is an accepted idea today, but was a new idea in the early 1900s.

objects. Gesell even pioneered the Gesell dome, a dome of one-way mirrors in which children could be observed at play without interference from observers.

Psychoanalytic Ego Theory

The central focus of Erik Erikson's (1902–1994) psychosocial life span theory of development was identity formation or the development of a clear sense of who and what we are within our cultural and environmental framework. Instincts and needs are seen as important, as they are in all behavioral maturation theories, but how the person interprets and acts on them is chiefly important to Erikson. **Psychoanalytic ego theory** argues that a strong ego is the key to good mental health; however, individuals differ in their ego strengths. In addition, due to biological differences, the process of ego formation is different in males and females, thus leading to different personality characteristics.

Erikson developed his psychosocial concepts by observing the profound confusion and disorientation of World War II soldiers suffering from posttraumatic stress disorder (PTSD). He also witnessed similar psychological dysfunction in the Native American population of the Oglala Sioux, as a result of their treatment by the U.S. government. Based on these observations, Erikson concluded that ego strength and integrity are correlated to positive mental, emotional, and behavior functioning.

For Erikson, the ego realizes and recognizes itself as the "I." It is the source of a person's self-awareness, which allows an individual to develop a sense of continuity. The major task of human development is to establish and maintain a sense of personal identity, as the Individual makes conscious adjustments to interpersonal influences. Erikson further built on the instinctual theoretical framework—Freud's psychoanalytical theory, which is founded on the psychological and physiological aspects of human development. He added the element of psychosocial influences to human development, and believed these influences lead to the conception of personality development.

Ego strength comes from good resolution of the eight stages of ego development in which positive ego strengths predominate over the negative ones. One of the major contributions of this theoretical perspective is that people pass through developmental stages of the human life cycle from infancy to old age. Children develop through four psychosocial stages, each presenting a crisis in which a specific ego strength is developed. Adults and adolescents also develop through the four remaining psychosocial stages, each of which also presents a crisis in ego strength. These ego strengths manifest as virtues such as hope, will, purpose, and wisdom.

Each stage is represented as an **ego crisis**, a conflict between two opposing outcomes, one positive and the other negative. The first stage is basic trust

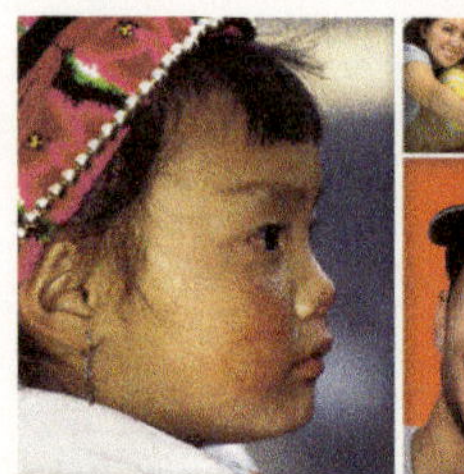

Erik Erikson

Erik Erikson (1902–1994) was born in Germany to Danish parents. He studied art and various languages rather than the sciences while in school. Before attending college he traveled around Europe for a year and then returned and attended art school in Germany. After a few years he began teaching art to children of parents that came to Vienna for Freudian training. He then was admitted to the Vienna Psychoanalytic Institute. In 1933, he came to Boston to become the first child analyst at Harvard Medical School. Later he came to California where he worked for the Center for Advanced Study in the Behavioral Sciences at Palo Alto, followed by working at Mount Zion Hospital in San Francisco, where he was a clinician and psychiatric consultant.

Erikson had wide areas of interests and work experiences during his life. He studied what is known today as Posttraumatic Stress Syndrome among soldiers of World War II. He also studied child-rearing practices among the Sioux in South Dakota and the Yurok along the Pacific Coast, and social behavior in India. Erikson was also interested in troubled and normal children's play and causes of juvenile delinquency. On a broader scale he was interested in the changing sexual roles of our society, the generation gap, and increasing racial tensions.

versus basic mistrust. The infant develops basic trust as his or her caregiver provides consistent, responsive, affectionate care in feeding, changing, comforting, and touching the baby. The child establishes a sense that the world is a reliable, predictable, and trustworthy place, and that he or she is good and valuable.

In the second stage, autonomy versus shame and doubt, the toddler learns a sense of independence by controlling physical activity, especially elimination functions. The third stage, initiative versus guilt, results from the child's increased mobility as a result of walking, and increased imagination as a result of talking. Successful and supported experiments with these new abilities allow the child to develop courage and perseverance as he or she pursues valued goals without experiencing crippling excessive fear of failure or punishment.

School-age children focus their attention on the fourth developmental stage, industry versus inferiority, building the skills that allow them to diligently and patiently complete their tasks. They learn that the completion itself, rather than mere praise, is intrinsically rewarding.

Erikson believed that the fifth stage, identity versus role confusion, involved a psychosocial suspension. The premise of this stage is to exercise identity exploration, which encompasses the evaluation of who we are and what we want our

Erikson's Psychosocial Stages

NO. OF STAGE	STAGE	ASSOCIATED AGES	EGO STRENGTH
1	Basic Trust vs. Basic Mistrust	Birth–1 year	Hope
2	Autonomy vs. Shame and Doubt	1–3 years	Will
3	Initiative vs. Guilt	3–6 years	Purpose
4	Industry vs. Inferiority	6–12 years	Competence
5	Identity vs. Role Confusion	12–19 years	Fidelity
6	Intimacy vs. Isolation	19–25 years	Love
7	Generativity vs. Stagnation	25–50 years	Care
8	Ego Integrity vs. Despair	50 years and older	Wisdom

final destination to be. Adolescents in this stage want to know what role they would be playing in society. Who do they identify with most? Is it their parents who define them most, or is it a prominent social figure, or some celebrity in the media? This psychosocial challenge and confusion allows the adolescent to explore a whole range of possible role opportunities. The identity challenge, if successfully achieved, will result in an identity decision made by the adolescent, which enable him or her to sustain a healthy psychosocial status and eventually have a successful transition to the next stage, which is young adulthood development. The identity versus role confusion could also result in role bewilderment, which means that psychosocially the adolescent has not been able to commit to a particular identity role and will remain in suspension, which could lead to identity role confusion.

The sixth through eighth stages present the challenges of adulthood, and are based on successful completion of the previous stages, even though no stage is ever one-hundred percent accomplished and individuals can revisit issues of previous stages as the complications and challenges of the current stage expose the need to do so.

Unlike Freud's theory, Erikson's theory is based on many concepts that can be easily tested. In his psychosocial theory, Erikson concluded that social, biological, and cultural variables are critical factors in human development, but he also believed that individuals were capable of choice within these constraints. His theory is based on biological and social forces (which encompass cultural factors) as being instrumental in shaping personality characteristics and human behavior.

Environment–Learning Framework

The **environment–learning framework** theorists take exception with the biological–maturation theorists. Environment–learning developmentalists believe that the source of changes that characterize human development are **exogenous**, that is, changes that arise come from outside the organism as the result of the environment, especially from adults who shape children's behaviors and beliefs. The major cause of development is learning, the process through which an organism's behavior is modified as a result of experience. Major theorists, including the behaviorists Watson and later Skinner, focused their attention on the complex processes of learning. They considered these processes to be far more powerful than heredity or maturation.

Behaviorism

Behaviorist theory begins by offering radical redefinition of the most basic terms we had heretofore used to define human behavior and functioning. For behaviorists, development is the result of a complex series of **learned behaviors**, which means **behavior**—anything an organism does that can be measured—is *learned* or *conditioned* through *experience.* What is experience? *Experience* is exposure to events that are capable of having a measurable effect on behavior; such events are called **stimuli.** Behaviorists believe that developmental processes are largely the result of learning.

This pronounced emphasis on learning does not eliminate the influence of heredity and biology. Behaviorism argues that this debate over nature versus nurture (environment–learning and biology) creates an artificial division between the contributions of heredity and experience. It wrongly implies that the answer must be one or the other. The ability to learn is itself the product of BOTH heredity and experience. They are merely different ways of adapting to change. In fact, behaviorists would argue that the ability to learn is itself the product of natural selection. **Natural selection** is the tendency for characteristics that contribute to the survival of a species to persist, and for those that do not contribute to disappear. Through learning, an organism can cope with changes in the environment for which its innate behavior is inadequate, allowing that organism to survive.

Much of the behavioral research on innate behaviors is done on newborns, because they have had relatively little contact with the social environment. There are essentially three types of innate or inborn behaviors. A *reflex* is a relationship between a specific event and a reactionary and physiological response to that event. An example of this behavior occurs when a parent touches the palm of a newborn with a finger. The infant will grab the finger tightly.

Fixed action patterns (FAPs) are a largely inherited series of interrelated acts, usually elicited by a particular stimulus (a releaser). Both smiling and yawning are FAPs that are easy to detect in newborns.

Inherited behavior traits consist of any general behavioral tendency that is strongly influenced by genes. These are the behaviors that would make a grandmother say that her granddaughter turns her head to the side just like her father or that her grandson walks with one shoulder slightly elevated, just like his mother. Another example of such inherited behavioral traits is that some people can curl their tongue and some people cannot. Can you curl your tongue? Try it.

How Do We Learn?

For behaviorists all learning is the result of conditioning, the process by which a particular behavior (response) is associated with a particular event (stimulus). There are essentially two types of conditioning—classical conditioning and operant conditioning.

Pavlov

There are some events to which organisms respond because of how that stimulus makes the organism feel. Behaviorism is based on the fundamental principle that any organism, including humans, will naturally avoid a painful event, and will seek pleasurable events. Events that naturally cause pain or pleasure responses are called **unconditioned stimuli**; we will react to them without training. For example, if we flash a bright light in a newborn's eyes, the child will instinctively shut his or her eyes tightly. The bright light suddenly flashed is the unconditioned stimulus; the tightly shut eyes are the unconditioned response.

Classical conditioning is a procedure in which a neutral stimulus, called a *conditioned stimulus,* can be made to elicit the same response as an unconditional stimulus. Ivan Pavlov (1849–1936) became fascinated by this process. In the early 1890s he began studying the chemistry of saliva in dogs, and therefore he would present the dogs with foods that caused them to salivate. But he noticed that after a while the dogs would salivate BEFORE they actually were presented with the food. He eventually discovered that, if he paired (presented) a neutral stimulus, like a whistle, with an unconditioned stimulus, like ground meat, after a short time the dogs would salivate whenever they heard the whistle, even when there was no meat presented. The whistle, called a **conditioned stimulus** (CS), elicited the same response as the meat, called the **unconditioned stimulus** (US). Once a *conditioned response* (CR) is established, it can be maintained indefinitely so long as the CS is sometimes followed by the US. If, however, the CS is repeatedly presented without the US, the CR will become weaker and weaker. The procedure of repeatedly presenting the CS without the US is called **extinction.** The sudden reappearance of a CR after extinction is called **spontaneous recovery.**

Watson

Although behaviorists would argue that behavior is attributable to reinforcement at any age, the study of child development from a behaviorist perspective is actually credited to Watson, an early twentieth century psychologist. He believed that babies could be better reared by parents who had received training in behaviorist theories and techniques. Building on Pavlov's work, Watson concentrated on children's reflexes in classical conditioning. He believed that, while parents should treat children with respect and care, they should not get too emotionally attached to their children, since it interfered with the parents' objective compliance with the demands of effective reinforcement. This view on child development could have been influenced by the earlier colonial concept on child rearing. Pre-industrial families' idea of raising children was to instill traditional values in children, emphasizing the role of adults as authority figures. This perspective did not allow for public display of affection, fearing that it would undermine the strict relationship between the authority and the subordinate figures.

Watson was able to offer proof of his theoretical position through his experiment with "little Albert," a baby whom Watson taught to fear little fuzzy stuffed animals by pairing their presentation (CS) with a loud gong (US). Watson was so convinced that his methods would prove successful that he once quipped that if he had twelve healthy babies, he could train them to be successful in whatever professions he chose.

B. F. Skinner

Social behaviorist Burrhus Frederic Skinner, also known simply as B. F. Skinner (1904–1990), expanded on Pavlov's and Watson's work. He focused on the fact that classical conditioning might result in actually increasing, or decreasing, behavior. He called his experimental form of behaviorism **operant conditioning,** any procedure in which a behavior becomes stronger or weaker (i.e., more or less likely to occur). Skinner realized that classical conditioning pointed to an important principle, the *law of effect* or that behavior is a function of its consequences. The strength of a behavior depends on the effect that behavior had on the environment in the past. The consequence is dependent on that particular behavior, which causes the behavior to increase. In other words, since the consequence does not happen until the behavior is demonstrated, the organism will repeat the behavior to receive the consequence. The procedure of providing consequences for a behavior that increases or maintains the strength of behavior is called *reinforcement*.

There are four types of reinforcement; two types *increase* the likelihood of a repeated response, and the other two *decrease* the likelihood of a repeated response. **Positive reinforcement** is an increase in the probability of occurrence of a behavior by *adding* a stimulus as a consequence. For example, a mother says, "Come here" to her baby, and the baby comes to the mother in response. If the mother then picks up the child and praises, cuddles, and applauds the baby, she is providing the baby positive reinforcement. The stimulus is the command "Come here," the response is the child's obedient move toward the mother, and the praise/cuddling/applause is the reinforcer. **Negative reinforcement** entails the *removal* of a stimulus as a consequence of a response, which increases the probability of that response. Assume that a ten-year-old child is having a hard time settling down to finish homework assignments. The likelihood of the child sitting and finishing the homework could be increased by saying, "If you finish your homework on time, you don't have to set the table tonight." This will encourage the child to finish the assignment for the benefit of not having to do the chore. Understanding positive and negative reinforcement can be confusing—it is tempting to think of positive reinforcement as "good" and negative reinforcement as "bad." Think instead in terms of their consequences. Positive reinforcement pairs behavior with the start of a pleasurable consequence, while negative reinforcement pairs behavior with the removal of a painful consequence. Suppose a father has promised his daughter that he will come to school with her if she does not study for her history exam. If she studies and passes her exam to keep him from coming to her class (presumably having dad in class with her would be embarrassing, i.e., negative), then her father is using negative reinforcement. His daughter is able to avoid a negative consequence by increasing her study behavior. Using either positive or negative reinforcement increase the likelihood that behavior will be repeated. At times, one reinforcer alone may not be as effective as desired; therefore, pairing a positive with a negative reinforcer will effectively increase the likelihood of the behavior to either cease or continue.

Punishment occurs when behavior is followed by a painful consequence. We have all had extensive experience with this form of reinforcement. A young toddler reaches for a forbidden object, and the parent says a loud, stern "No!" If the child pulls back and stops reaching for the object, then the parent's stern voice provides punishment. Punishment decreases the likelihood that a specific behavior will recur. *Extinction* will also decrease the repetition of a behavior by removing a positive consequence. Parental disapproval is a very effective reinforcer. Suppose the young adolescent lies to her usually pleasant and cheerful

Behaviorism (Learning Theory)	Classical conditioning is based on stimulus and response: Watson, Pavlov
	Operant conditioning is based on reinforcement: Skinner
Social Learning	Through observing, modeling, and imitating, which becomes copied behavior: Bandura

father and, as an expression of his disapproval, he refuses to smile at her. Many parents can successfully shift their children's behavior by the simple removal of their otherwise agreeable attitude.

Whether or not a particular reinforcer will actually increase or decrease behavior depends also on the schedule of reinforcement, the frequency and intensity with which the behavior is followed by the reinforcer. There are two types of frequency schedules. **Ratio schedules**, which are based on the number of responses for each reinforcer, involve a specific number of responses. If a child is given a jelly bean every time he or she raises his or her hand in class, assuming that the child likes jelly beans, then he or she will raise his or her hand at a steady rate of response. If the child is fed a jellybean on an unpredictable number of times he or she raises his or her hand, the child will raise his or her hand even more often. The first example is a **fixed ratio schedule** and the second is a **variable ratio schedule**. The other form of reinforcement timetable, *interval schedules,* depends on an interval of time associated with the reinforcer. A *fixed interval* offers the reinforcer only after a specific amount of time has passed. This pattern of reinforcement causes the actor to increase responses near the end of the interval, but to slow responses right after a reinforcer has been delivered, in the way that a student tends to study a lot near the time of the exam, but not so much just after the exam. *Variable interval schedules* offer the reinforcer after an unpredictable amount of time has passed; however, the response to this type of schedule is steady, but slow.

Skinner believed that our society shapes our personality development by providing the conditions of learning. Children learn which behaviors will lead to positive reinforcement and which lead to punishment, and they respond accordingly. These responses shape both childhood and adult development. Skinner also believed that any society could create better, more productive members by paying deliberate, close attention to the presentation of rewards and punishments. He concluded that psychology would be better served to focus not only on "illness" or "health," but on which behaviors should be increased and which behaviors should be decreased. Skinner did not believe in the study of mental processes, because they were too difficult to assess and measure. Instead, he sought to explain mental functions in terms of the behaviors that they manifested.

Constructivist Framework

Constructivists sought to resolve the dispute between the biological–maturational advocates and their environmental learning counterparts, which is basically the nature versus nurture debate. The constructivists argue that the major cause of development is neither heredity nor learning. It is the role that children themselves take as actors in their own development. **Constructivist framework** theorists believe that children play an active role in their own development, in opposition to the previous theoretical belief that either children are passive learners or, as the product of the immediate environment, easily conditioned. This school of thought firmly believes that children take information from the surroundings (parents, teachers, and environmental stimuli) and they actively construct their own perception of the world around them. This ability thus leads to the child making his or her own version of reality; therefore, the child's behavior is shaped based on personal understanding of the facts. This frame of mind explains that children construct successively higher levels of knowledge and the processes of development are universal in the species. These ever-increasing, ever-deepening ways of thinking are the central interests of the major constructivist theorists.

Piaget

Like the behaviorists, Piaget believed that human development entailed a growing relationship between the individual and the environment. But Piaget was convinced that mental processes were not only important, they were pivotal in understanding how humans grow and change. Piaget believed that humans *adapt;* they change based on their interaction with their environments. He argued that intelligence was the hallmark human experience, and that intelligence develops as a result of specific interactions between a person and the world in which the person operates.

Children begin their experience by experimenting with the environment through their own physical movements. As soon as a child moves in the world, he or she begins to form **schema** or mental–motor representations about the nature of the environment. For example, a child learns to grab a bottle and put the tip in his or her mouth. The child has a schema for objects—grab-and-put-in-mouth. If the child sees a pen, he or she will grab it and put the tip in his or her mouth. This is an example of **assimilation**, incorporating a new object into an old schema. This will continue to work until the child encounters an object that won't fit in the schema, such as a balloon. This object requires a new movement skill, like grab-and-turn. This is an example of **accommodation**, changing the schema because of a new object. The schemas are transformed through a series of successive assimilations and accommodations until the child reaches a state of equilibrium, which can be thought of as a good workable model of what reality is like.

Piaget proposed that cognition develops in four stages: the sensorimotor stage, the preoperational stage, the concrete operations stage, and the formal operations stage.

1. **Sensorimotor stage:** From birth until approximately two years of age, the infant focuses on controlling his or her own body through six successive substages. During the first substage, **simple reflexes**, the infant responds to the environment through his or her reflexes, for example, sucking and grasping. But in the **primary circular reaction** substage, the now one- to four-month-old child begins to repeat the simple reflex motions trying to get an enjoyable event to recur. In **secondary circular reaction**, the third substage, when the infant is four- to eight-months-old, the child will intentionally repeat certain behaviors in order to repeat pleasurable events. By the time the child is eight- to twelve-months-old, the young child intentionally combines series of behaviors to achieve a goal, such as sitting up and grabbing a string to bring a balloon nearer, largely due to the development of object permanence, which is the surety that an object exists even when it cannot be seen. This signals the fourth stage—coordination of *secondary circular reactions*. The fifth stage is called **tertiary reactions** and occurs when the child is one to one and one-half years old. In this stage the toddler repeats the same behaviors with new objects, like beating the bed with a spoon, beating the pan with a spoon, beating the babysitter with a spoon. In the last stage—**coordination of tertiary circular reactions**—the young toddler begins to internalize objects through symbols. Children of this age show signs of plans, symbolizing behavioral strategies before they carry them out. They are capable of **delayed imitation**, such as watching an adult use a cell phone and then putting the cell phone to their own ears.

2. **Preoperational stage:** At about two years of age children begin to represent the world symbolically through images and through language. Children can organize information but they still rely on fantasy to make sense of the world. Children of this stage are **egocentric**; they experience themselves as the center of the world. Everything refers to them. The toddler believes that inanimate objects are alive (**animism**) and that everything is made by humans. Preoperational children express a strong belief in **imminent justice**, that there is a system in the universe of reward and punishment and if something bad happens to you, it's

Piaget's Stages of Development

SENSORIMOTOR STAGE	PREOPERATIONAL STAGE	CONCRETE OPERATIONAL STAGE	FORMAL OPERATIONAL STAGE
The infant constructs an understanding of the world by coordinating sensory experiences with physical actions. An infant progresses from reflexive to instinctual actions at birth to beginning of symbolic thought.	A child begins to understand his or her world through words and images. These words and images show the increase of symbolic thinking and go beyond the connection of sensory information and physical action.	A child can now reason logically about concrete events and classify objects into different categories.	An adolescent reasons in more abstract, ideological, and logical ways.
Birth to 2 years of age	2 to 7 years of age	7 to 11 years of age	11 years of age through adulthood

because you did something wrong. The preoperational child still cannot fully conceptualize time, but is growing better and better at conceptualizing events and processes.

3. **Concrete operational stage:** A seven- to eleven-year-old child is able to mentally move concrete things around in his or her mind to organize materials and is interested in organizing things and information. The child is also committed to rules. In fact, the child's moral development does not include the underlying principles of moral behavior. The child is simply committed to understanding the simple do's and don'ts that authority figures reinforce. By age ten the child is capable of **metacognition** or the act of thinking about thinking. This child can make rational judgments about the world by thinking about it, without having to manipulate the objects and events. The child can understand that it is possible to change the way he or she thinks and can think about the way he or she is thinking. Gender play is polarized; boys play with boys, girls with girls. Peer influence increases. Children are urged to learn to be a girl or a boy by practicing gender-related activities and scenarios.

4. **Formal operational stage:** Between the ages of eleven to adulthood, specifically in the beginning of adolescence, Piaget explained that humans begin to understand and make meaning of abstract, what-if scenarios, which will lead to further cognitive maturity. This new-found cognitive ability enables humans to make complex decisions and

eventfully develop further meta-cognition (thinking about thinking). Formal operations is the final stage of Piaget's cognitive development. The adolescent can make fully rational judgments through symbolic representation and is able to perceive lengthy trajectories of behavior and consequence from a number of perspectives.

Cultural-Context Framework

All of the preceding frameworks are based in psychobiological perspectives because they represent theorists from the earliest history of developmental inquiry. But as the discipline itself developed, some theorists grew concerned about the narrow perspective that biological and psychological perspectives promoted. **Cultural-context developmentalists** assert that there is a third, equally powerful determinant of human development—culture. **Culture** is the direct, intervening variable through which biology and environment are interpreted. The inclusion of the cultural factors transformed the nature versus nurture debate because culture dictates how to interpret both heredity and learning. It also changes the focus of the discussion from the individual to the group.

Social Cultural Theory: Vygotsky

Lev Vygotsky's (1896–1934) **sociocultural theory** seeks to explain the growth of individual knowledge, development, and competencies in terms of guidance, support, and structure supplied by the society. This cognitive theory emerged from the scientific understanding that human development results from dynamic interaction between an adult (teacher) and the learner (child). Sociocultural theory focuses on the fact that development is embedded in a rich and multifaceted context—human culture and society. The child learns not only particular behaviors, but also mental habits and structures of meaning through intimate interaction with those who have mastered the culture's symbols or language and other symbolic systems. This process is often referred to as **cultural mediation.**

From Vygotsky's perspective, human development is the result of dynamic interaction between the child and his or her parents and teachers; the interaction, however, goes beyond the child's typical nurturing experience. This perspective is based on cultural and ritualistic interaction between a child and adults interacting with the child. Vygotsky believed that in every culture there are adults who act as mentors and tutors. He considers adults teachers. Therefore, due to the uniqueness of each culture and the environmental influences, each child will be subjected to particular environmental factors brought to the child based on his or her mentor's specific interaction. These mentors not only define and describe the next steps, they provide instruction and direct participation in

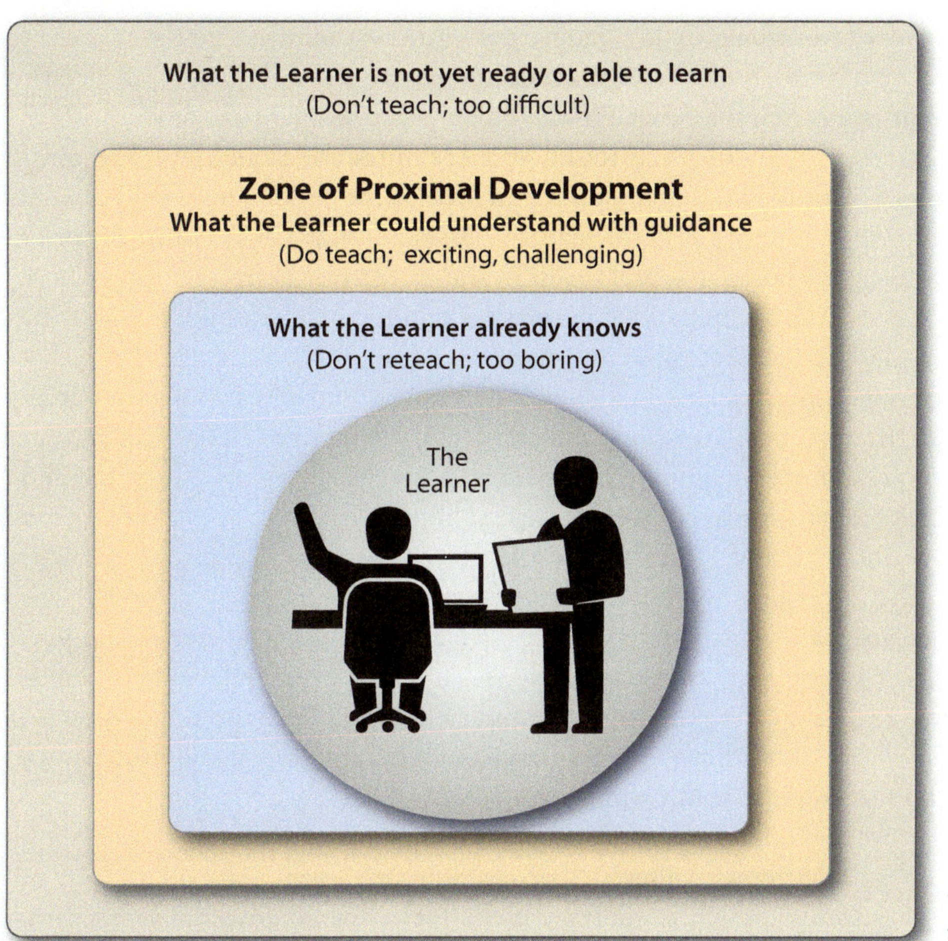

Vygotsky's cultural mediation process.

the learning process. The mentor guides the learner in joint activities, leading ultimately to the new task. This process, known as **scaffolding** (step-by-step teaching method), permits the young apprentice to join the mentor in the execution of the new task. A teacher is scaffolding a student when the teacher places his or her hand over the student's hand and together they write the student's name. This specialized assistance acts like a bridge in the **zone of proximal development** (ZPD), the place where the learner can perform the new task or behavior only with the help of the mentor. Through guided participations, adults offer children assistance, structure, opportunities, and strategies for learning new skills that modify their behavior. Guided participation is a process in which an adult collaborates with a child using specific teaching tactics, explicit modeling, and assistance to help a child learn a new skill. The guided participation must be done knowing the degree of the child's learning abilities, existing knowledge, and the child's capabilities to learn new concepts. Therefore, the ZPD is the difference between what a child can do with and without help. It is a gauge, a measuring tool used by the teacher to adjust the degree of teaching material. In order to use ZPD, an adult must be aware of the existing knowledge the child possesses, so that old lessons are not repeated, as this will lead to the learner's boredom and lack of interest. In addition, the tutor (adult) must have an idea of the child's (learner's) capacity for learning in order to prevent teaching concepts that are too difficult for the learner to grasp because it will result in the child's giving up.

Vygotsky also stressed the importance of play as the means through which children learn to separate abstract ideas from the specific objects in which these ideas can be embodied. Vygotsky's famous example of this phenomenon occurs when a three-year-old, unable to ride an actual horse, straddles a stick and pretends to ride a new imaginary horse. The stick's role as a *pivot* allows the child to mimic riding a horse without the actual object. This sort of play permits the child to internalize the meaning of the object. As the child grows to adolescence, the internalization continues to be part of the child's process of cognitive maturity, and making sense of the world around his or her to the point that these pivots grow to the level of symbolic and representational thoughts, actions, and behaviors. The symbolic and representational thoughts learned in the latter part of toddlerhood will continue to be used during adolescence and adulthood. Humans draw from these symbolic thoughts and behaviors to grow and mature cognitively.

Overall, Vygotsky believed that children are social learners and do not learn in isolation, which is contrary to Piaget's view. Vygotsky discussed that children need instruction and cultural teaching by adults in order to develop cognition, cognitive maturity, and appropriate behavior. Sociocultural theory is one of the first theories to give importance to culture as an agent of learning and as an important part of cognitive development. Vigotsky believed that culture acts as a mediator in shaping behavior; therefore, his theory is heavily based on adult/child interaction, guided participation, and learning. These concepts are critically important in the practice of formal education. A familiar example of adult participation occurs when a teacher helps students learn a new math concept. The teacher will first lecture on the new topic and its concepts, and, using practical examples, show how to solve a math problem using the material students have just learned. In the beginning, just a few students might get it and will start tackling their homework assignments and eventually solve the problem. At the same time, several students may need the teacher's help to understand and solve the assignments. In that case, the teacher will use different teaching tools to help the students learn the new math concept little by little. This example supports Vygotsky's view of development since the teacher uses guided participation to teach students new skills. This example demonstrates that children learn through scaffolding and guided participation in their ZPD.

Social Ecological Theory: Bronfenbrenner

The 1980s saw a significant shift in the perception of culture. The work of Stuart Hall, Michel Foucault, Angela Robbie, and Paul Willis demonstrated a concern for the political character of contemporary culture and the various media through which culture could be generated and apprehended.

Urie Bronfenbrenner understood that children are embedded in layers of culture, absorbing information from a number of cultural media simultaneously. He saw this interactive system of relationships as a sociocultural ecology.

In the **microsystem**, children learn through direct interaction with those people who populate their immediate environment such as their families, their classmates and teachers, their churches and other peer groups, sports teams, and academic clubs. When a child joins a soccer team, his or her associations with other team members, with the coach, with the team parents, and with the soccer officials are all microsystemic interactions. The **mesosystem** describes the connections and relationships between the various elements of the microsystem, such as the bonds between parents and children, between students and teachers, between priests and teachers, and so forth. The **exosystem** defines those institutions that regulate everyday public life—the courts, the school systems, mass media, as well as the various community systems. The decisions of the local school board about the number of teachers available for classes have an exosystemic impact on each child. Finally the **macrosystem** describes the national customs, economic systems, political structures, and ethnic customs that impact

Bronfenbrenner's Social Ecology

Chronosystem	▪ Biological: The dimension of time ▪ The patterning of environmental events and transitions over the life course
Microsystem	Family, classroom, church, peers
Mesosystem	Mesosystem provides connections between various aspects of the microsystem. Like links in a chain, the mesosystem binds children to parents, students to teachers, etc.
Exosystem	Community, public systems, mass media, school system
Macrosystem	Cultural values, social conditions, national customs, economic patterns When an economic recession produces high unemployment and thus increases child abuse it shows the effect of the macrosystem on the microsystem

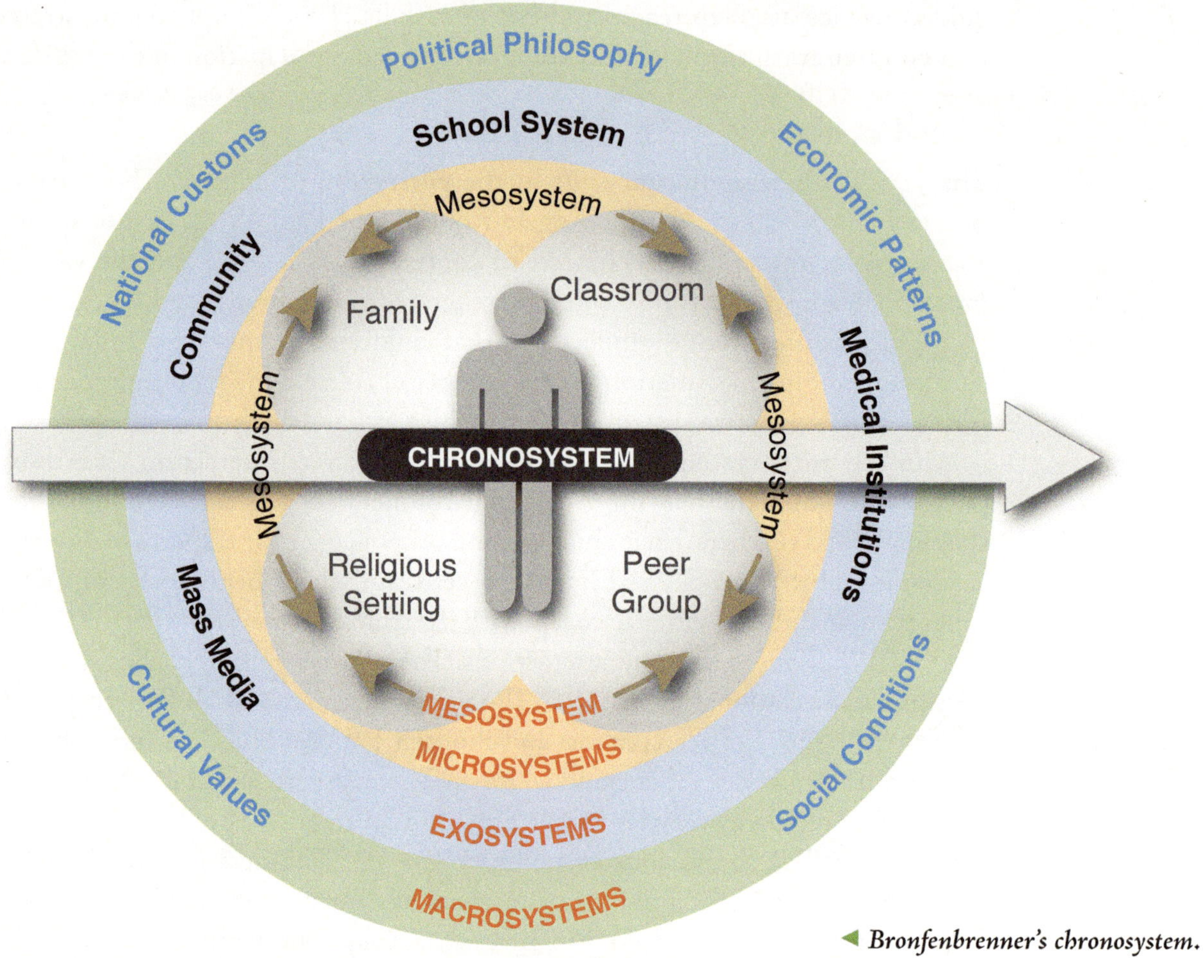

◄ *Bronfenbrenner's chronosystem.*

all children in a particular nation state. The final system—the **chronosystem**—involves the dimension of time, in terms of the biological life span, as well as the patterns of change that occur in all systems.

Comparing the Psychoanalytic, Behaviorist, and Cognitive Theories

Each of the psychoanalytic theories has stressed the importance of early childhood experiences. Behaviorism has shown the effects of the immediate environment on behavior. Cognitive theory has helped us understand how the intellectual process and thinking affect actions. Each of the major theoretical perspectives shares certain commonalities. These theories also share certain limitations. They are all too wide ranging and less comprehensive than they once seemed. The theories also ignore the fact that worldwide cultural differences and human experiences do not fit neatly into these theoretical categories. Ironically, all three perspectives also seriously underestimate the role of biological and genetic influences.

Comparing the Cultural-Context and Constructivist Perspectives

A distinguishing characteristic that separates these two theoretical views is whether development is qualitative or quantitative. In the **qualitative view**, theorists believe development is sudden, stage-like, step-by-step, immeasurable, and governed by discontinuity laws (development based on stages). A qualitative theoretical perspective would argue that, all of a sudden, toddlers learn to talk, going from crying, babbling, and making sounds to full sentences. The explanation given by this theoretical framework is that we know hearing is acute at seven months of gestation; therefore, unborn children can effectively hear the language spoken by their parents. This exposure to language will eventually lead to the child beginning to talk around twelve months of age. This is a sudden, but expected development emerging as a result of being exposed to language. The cultural-context and constructivist theorists agree that the individual undergoes qualitative changes during the course of development. They also argue that development is impossible without children's **active agency**, which means actively participating in their own learning and developmental processes. Piaget, as a qualitative theorist, believed that children are active learners, and that they purposefully participate in their own learning by discriminately developing their own perception and experiences from the environment they live in. On the other hand, a **quantitative theorist** explains that development is measureable, little by little, incremental, and continuous. This can be seen by the example that children learn to walk having gone through several other milestones such as rolling, sitting, crawling, cruising (using objects to hang onto to get from one point to another) before actually walking on their own. This example illustrates that development can be measured in each of these developmental milestones. One way to keep track of these developmental changes would be for the caregiver to start observing the infant's behavior, noting the number of times the child rolled over or tried to roll over in order to see the child's incremental development.

These two sets of theorists disagree on three critical points. First, the cultural-context theorists believe that children and caregivers are both active agents. Together they construct development. Children create their own reality through their own highly individual mental construction of concepts, which become more and more consistent with the paradigms of others as they interact with their caregivers. Second, cultural-context theorists do not look for stages. For them, children grow based on caregiver expectation and on the child's increasing capacity to perform tasks. Finally, the sequence of human developmental changes in the child's life depends not on the child's own inner construction and conceptual facility, but on the child's cultural and historical experience.

CHAPTER 3 SUMMARY

Generally, theory organizes how we collect and interpret data and facts. The multidisciplinary focus is based on anthropological, sociological, psychological, and biological approaches. The theories that arise from these approaches fall into four general organizing frameworks or perspectives on the characteristics of theory. The biological-maturational frameworks focus on the nature of human beings. The endogenous theories begin with the idea that the human organism changes because it matures. Freud, Gesell, and Erikson are representatives of this perspective. Watson and Skinner represent a different posture. Their exogenous perspective begins with the idea that the human organism changes because it learns. Their position, called environmental-learning framework, focuses on the nurture of human beings.

Piaget is almost in a class by himself. A cognitive constructionist, he believed that humans change as they construct reality in their minds. His theory is both exogamous and endogamous, focused on the nature of human cognition. *Exogamous* factors in development are the external factors leading to behavioral change and cognitive construct. An exogamous factor may be the media shaping and forming adolescents' views on how they see themselves and others based on the media images and cultural cultivation. On the other hand, an *endogamous* factor involves the child's predisposition to genetic influences. The tendency to develop addictive behavior or mental problems may be genetically linked, which makes the child susceptible to his or her own genetic makeup.

All of the preceding theories have a powerful flaw, according to Vygotsky and Bronfenbrenner. The cultural-context framework they represent focuses on the intervening environmental milieu, interactions, and collaboration with others—one's culture—as the factors shaping human experience on all levels. For cultural-context theorists the human organism changes because of its intense interaction with the culture that encompasses it.

Comparing these theoretical perspectives reveals the contributions made by each to the field of human development, each new framework added to the great puzzle of understanding human experience. These theories attempt to explain the plasticity and stability of human development; however, it is imperative to consider different disciplines, framework, and factors that contribute to humans' growth and change.

CHAPTER 3 VOCABULARY

Accommodation
Active Agency
Animism
Arnold Gesell
Assimilation
B. F. Skinner
Behavior
Biological Approaches
Biological-Maturation Framework
Chronosystem
Classical Conditioning
Cohort
Concrete Operational Stage
Conditioned Stimulus
Constructivist Framework
Coordination of Tertiary Circular Reactions
Cultural Mediation
Cultural-Context Developmentalists
Culture
Defense Mechanisms
Delayed Imitation
Developmentalists
Dysgenic
Ego
Ego Crisis
Egocentric
Endogenous
Environment-Learning Framework
Erik Erikson
Exogenous
Exosystem
Extinction
Fixed Action Patterns
Fixed Ratio Schedule
Formal Operational Stage
Id
Imminent Justice
Learned Behaviors
Lev Vygotsky
Macrosystem
Maturation
Mesosystem
Metacognition
Microsystem
Natural Selection
Negative Reinforcement
Operant Conditioning
Pavlov
Positive Reinforcement
Preoperational Stage
Primary Circular Reaction
Psychoanalysis
Psychoanalytic Ego Theory
Psychoanalytic Theory
Psychological Approaches
Qualitative View
Quantitative Theorist
Ratio Schedules
Scaffolding
Schema
Secondary Circular Reaction
Sensorimotor Stage
Sigmund Freud
Simple Reflexes
Social Behaviorist
Sociocultural Theory
Spontaneous Recovery
Stimuli
Superego
Tertiary Reactions
Unconditioned Stimuli
Unconditioned Stimulus
Urie Bronfenbrenner
Variable Ratio Schedule
Zone of Proximal Development

Chapter 4

PRENATAL DEVELOPMENT

(Photo courtesy of Sunny studio/Shutterstock.com)

Joy

By Margaret Goetz

Light in his eyes,
Laughter on her lips,
Hugs from a friend
Generosity
Kindness
Sunshine on a winter's day.
Music in their ears.
Smiles on their faces.
Love one another and
Joy to the world.

Prenatal Development and Delivery Based on Western Research Findings

Compared to other vast areas of study in the past century on human development, minimal research has been done in prenatal growth. Scientists have long debated the various psychological, cognitive, and social factors that contribute to the development of a child while in the mother's womb. Human development traditionally emphasizes different stages of development than the medical world. Prenatal development continues to fascinate, baffle, and intrigue scientists. More and more discovery in this area also adds to the fascination on how and why certain changes take place during prenatal development. In this section, we discuss and learn about prenatal development as researchers in the Western world establish it. In addition, we will look at the non-Western perspectives as they pertain to the beliefs on pregnancy and prenatal development.

Prenatal Development

This period of life is the development in the womb. In the twentieth century, researchers gained a tremendous amount of knowledge in this area, yet psychological, cognitive, and social prenatal development remains the least understood period of human development. Starting with a single cell and ending as a newborn infant is one of the fastest growing areas of study and one of the most fascinating. In the past, many scientist believed that prenatal growth is simply a matter of predetermined genetics, yet today we understand that the environmental factor along with genetics are at play as growth begins, continues, and ends in this period of life. Current research in the Western world has shown that prenatal development is divided into three distinct stages, which are further discussed in this chapter (these differ from traditional medical stages of development). The following sections discuss the physical development, the interaction between genetics and environment, fetal behavior, and many other interesting research findings regarding the development of the fetus.

Nature versus Nurture

One of the key questions for any stage of development including the prenatal period is the role of nature versus nature, and how each contributes to human growth. Research poses the burning question: How much of development is based on genetic disposition and how much of it is based on the environment? Scientists in the past believed that prenatal development is strictly the work of genetics; however, recent research has shown that environmental factors can very well change the course of Mother Nature. The interaction between genetics and environment has been the topic of many studies in the scientific world of Western researchers (Miller, 2011).

One issue in prenatal development is whether it is **continuous development** or **discontinuous development**. Scientists are interested in finding out whether prenatal development is gradual (little by little), or has sudden stages of development. In early studies, many experts firmly believed that the development of a fetus from the beginning to the end is a series of stages independent of each other, meaning that each stage will not impact the next one in any shape or form. Modern research has shown that a fetus might develop in a series of stages each influencing one another, leading to further fetal abilities and learning. This discovery poses the following two questions:

1. Is the fetus capable of learning and what event may lead to that capability?
2. In which stage of development does that learning occur and in what capacity?

Presently, these two questions are being investigated as well as many more questions regarding fetal capabilities and learning.

There are approximately 100,000 human genes that play a distinct role in the development of humans. The Human Genome Project, which was started in 1988, extensively explains the role of each of these genes and its impact on development (Mehlman & Borkin, 1998). Researchers who study the impact of the environment on genetic makeup believe that there may be several different influences. A person's genetic inheritance, which is the genes they receive from the egg and sperm, is called the **genotype**. The way the genotype expresses itself under the influence of the environment is known as the **phenotype**, which means environmental factors can influence biological development. For example, painful shyness may be the result of a genetic disposition that can be influenced by the environment. Alcoholism is also a good example of environmental influences on the genotype. Genetically, if a person has inherited the genetic predisposition for alcoholism, and is then put in an environment where drinking is common and encourages the person to drink, this may lead to alcoholism.

Prenatal Growth Begins

Stages of Prenatal Development

The physical development of a fetus is divided into three stages: **germinal** (0–2 weeks), **embryonic** (2–8 weeks), and **fetal**, (8 weeks to birth; Berger, 2004). These three stages are not the same as the trimesters used by the medical community. Stages of pregnancy signify the type of development, the amount of time it takes, and the characteristics of each developmental period the unborn baby goes through.

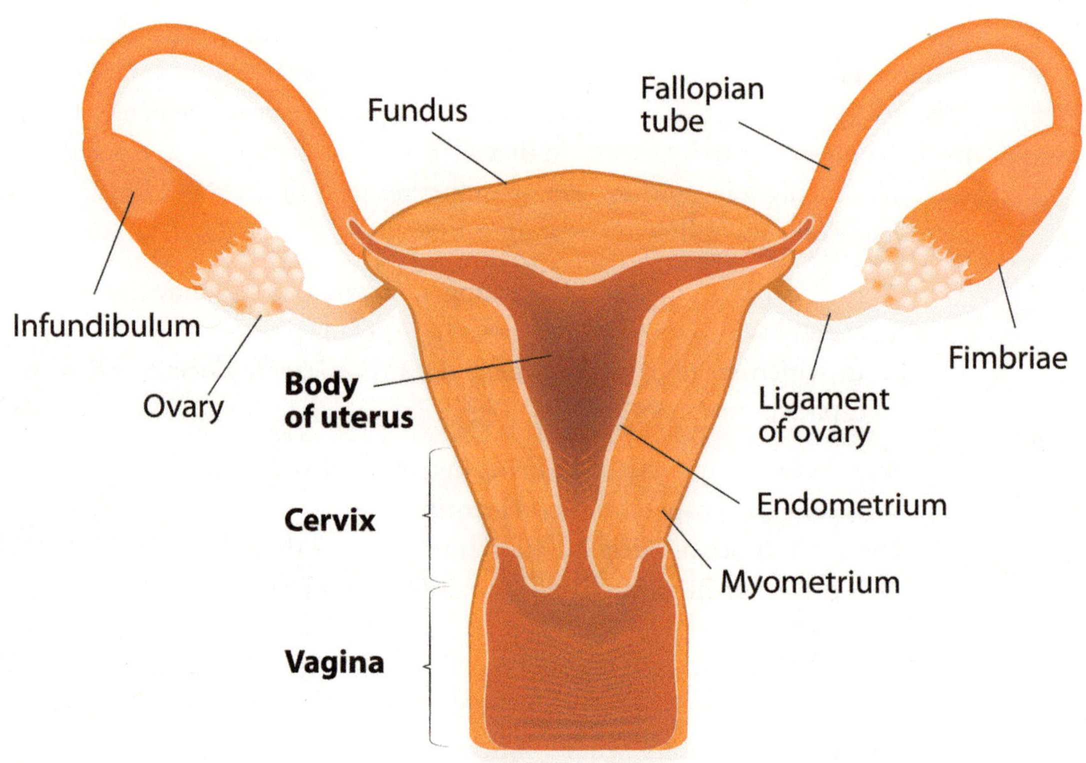

▲ *Female reproduction system.*

(Photo courtesy of Designua/Shutterstock.com)

First Stage—Germinal

When and how does human development start? Scientists consider human growth from the moment of conception. The human reproductive cells (sex cells) are referred to as gametes, which stand for both female egg (ovum), and male sperm (spermatozoa). The traditional way a woman's egg is fertilized by a sperm is through the act of intercourse between a man and a woman. Conception can only take place during ovulation; however, intercourse during ovulation does not always result in an egg's fertilization. Although, if the woman is ovulating and the sperm is of good quality, chances are the woman will get pregnant. The mature female egg is produced by the ovary once a month and stays alive for twelve to twenty-four hours, which is the crucial time for the sperm to travel up the fallopian tube to find and penetrate the egg, which is the act of fertilization. The fertilized cell or **zygote** then moves down the fallopian tube to the uterus, where it embeds itself in the lining of the uterus and will be housed for the next nine months. Normally, only one egg is released during ovulation, but in rare cases more than one egg is released, which could result in multiple fertilizations resulting in twins or multiple births (Pasquariello, 1999).

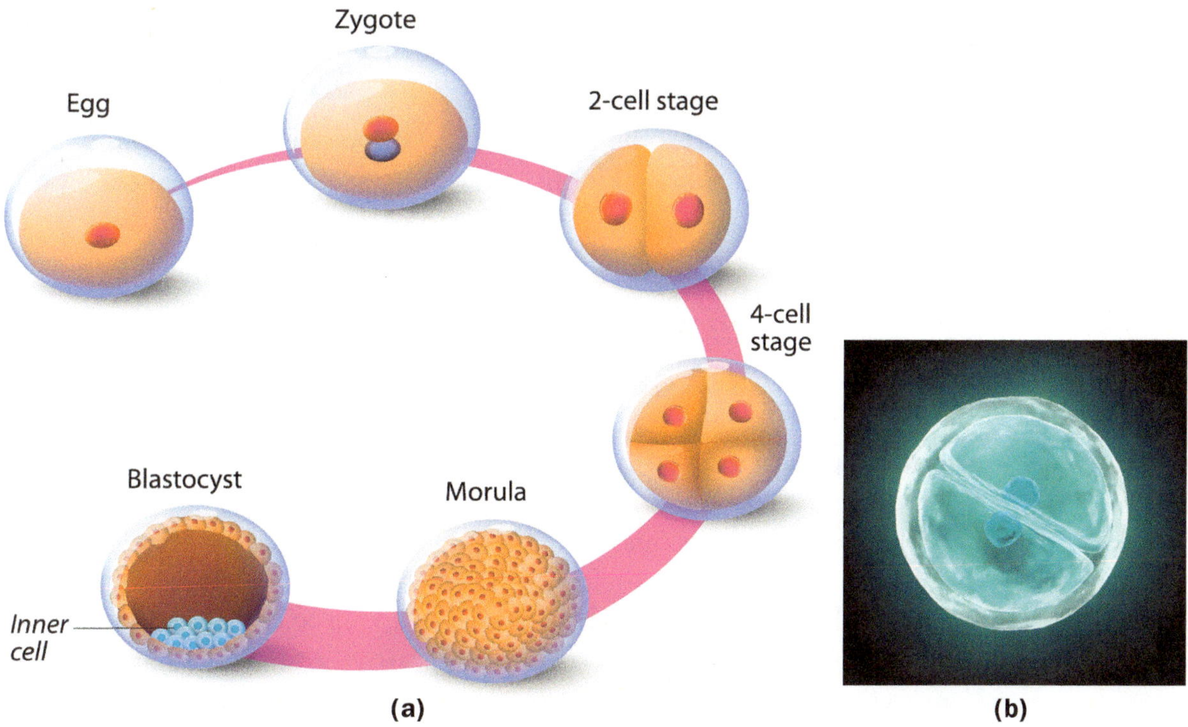

▲ (a) *Development of the embryo;* (b) *Zygote.*

(a. Photo courtesy of Designua/Shutterstock.com; b. Photo courtesy of Mopic/Shutterstock.com)

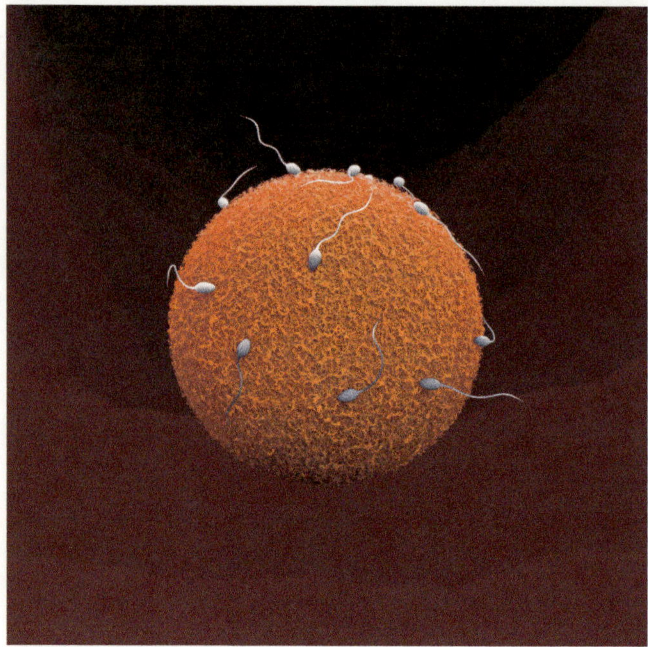

Egg and sperm: The egg is released from the ovary and then moves into the fallopian tube where it is fertilized by single sperm.

(Photo courtesy of EMcgiq/Shutterstock.com)

After ejaculation, sperm can stay alive in the cervical mucus for three to five days; however, the longer sperm stays in the cervix, the less likely it will fertilize an egg. The woman's egg carries half of a fetus's chromosomes, and the sperm contributes the other half. Each egg and sperm carries twenty-three pairs of chromosomes. The egg and sperm at the moment of conception combine together forming one cell (zygote) with forty-six chromosomal pairs. Chromosomes are tiny structures in the nucleus of a cell that contain the genetic material a child inherits from his or her parents. Chromosomes make up the genetic blueprint of a person (Berger, 2004). The germinal stage takes approximately two weeks (fourteen days) for the zygote to travel through the fallopian tube to the uterus. This journey is quite dangerous as the zygote is dividing, duplicating, and replicating itself.

Cell division starts approximately twenty-four to thirty-six hours after conception, which makes this period one of the most rapid growth of the fetus. The zygote's rapid cell division forms the **blastocyst** structure, which has three layers: (1) the **ectoderm**, which will form the skin and the nervous system; (2) the **endoderm**, which will become the digestive system; and (3) the **mesoderm**, which will become the muscular and skeletal systems of the fetus. Overall, the prenatal germinal stage includes: the creation of the zygote, continued cell division, and the attachment of the zygote to the uterine wall—called the implantation process.

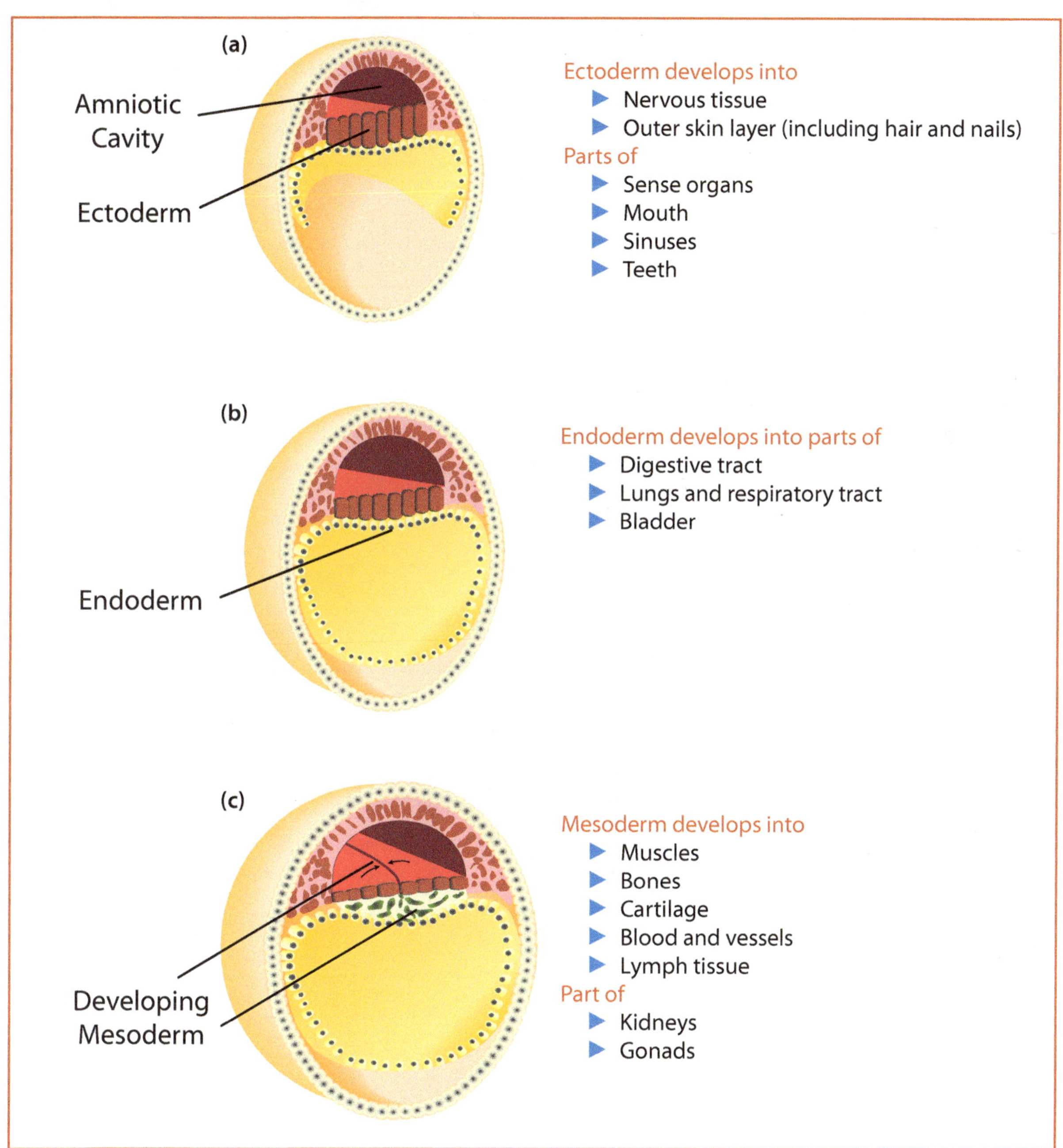

▲ *Early fetal development: The three primary germ layers.*

GENDER OF THE BABY: How is the sex of the baby determined? As previously discussed, the reproductive cells, the egg (**ovum**) and the sperm (**spermatozoa**) each carry only twenty-three pairs of chromosomes. At the moment of conception, the two gametes fuse and form a complete cell that will now have forty-six pairs of chromosomes. The twenty-third chromosomal pair contains instruction for the baby's biological gender determination. The twenty-third chromosome of a female egg always carries a pair labeled XX and the sperm carries XX or XY. When the chromosome carrying the XX pair of the female gamete coincides with a male gamete carrying the XX chromosome, the biological sex of the baby will be female. Similarly, if the twenty-third chromosome of the male gamete carrying the XY pair coincides with a female egg, which always carries the XX pair, the biological gender of the baby will be male. Indeed, it is the twenty-third chromosome that is the deciding factor in the determination of the biological gender of the baby. The development of the actual sexual organs will not start until the embryonic stage, which is around the sixth week of prenatal development (Rathus, 2006).

XX + XX = XXXX or female

XX + XY = XXXY or male

Second Stage—Embryonic

This stage of pregnancy starts when the zygote has implanted itself in the uterus, successfully completing the journey of traveling through the fallopian tube. Once the zygote has attached itself onto the uterine wall, the mass of cells will now be known as the **embryo**, which will now go through rapid growth of the major body systems and organs. The new embryo will now divide itself into the umbilical cord, the placenta, and the embryonic structure. The umbilical cord connects the baby to its mother and acts as the fetus's lifeline. It is through the umbilical cord that the baby gets its nutrition, oxygen, and other vital ingredients to grow. This cord is connected via an opening in the baby's stomach to the placenta where oxygen and food are passed through the mother's body, and consequently through the umbilical cord to the baby. The **placenta** is an organism that is attached to the lining of the mother's womb. It provides the blood supply for the newborn separate from the mother's, and functions in ways that the fetus is not capable of doing on its own yet such as eating, breathing, digestion, and so on.

The embryo resides inside what is called the **amniotic sac**, filled with amniotic fluid. The purpose of the amniotic sac, which is made of two membranes (the **amnion** and the **chorion**), is to protect the embryo and provide protection against environmental harm. The amniotic sac also acts as a thermal buffer and shock absorbent in the womb providing a protective layer for fetal development. Amniotic sac development is part of the initial differentiation of the embryo. This means that in the beginning of the embryonic stage, part of the differentiation process of the embryo structure is to develop a sac filled with **amniotic fluid**, a clear and pale, straw-colored fluid. The main function of the amniotic sac and the amniotic fluid is to protect the fetus from outside harm. The unborn baby floats and moves freely in the sac and the fluid cushions the fetus from bumps or injury. The fetus breathes in the amniotic fluid, which also provides a constant temperature for the baby.

In the next six to eight weeks, rapid growth continues mostly involving the development of the major organs and body parts. The spinal cord, the brain, and the heart are among the first organs to develop. Although the brain is one of the first organs to develop, it is also one of the last organs to complete its growth in the womb and growth continues long after birth, well into the twentieth year of human life. The heart is the first organ that starts to function and begins to pump blood even with only the initial two chambers. Any adverse behavior by the expecting mother, such as drinking, smoking, and using drugs, could very well interfere and impact the normal growth of the heart and brain. In most cases, these negative influences are irreversible and tragic.

The second stage of pregnancy is also critical because the environmental influences can and may interfere with the normal growth of the embryo. For example, if a pregnant women is exposed to German measles (rubella), it may put her baby in grave danger. If the mother contracts rubella, blindness, deafness, congenital heart disease, or mental retardation may occur in the unborn baby (Iconis, 1995). The growth during the embryonic stage is so rapid that by the end of this stage, fingers, mouth, eyes, and ears have begun to develop. Most

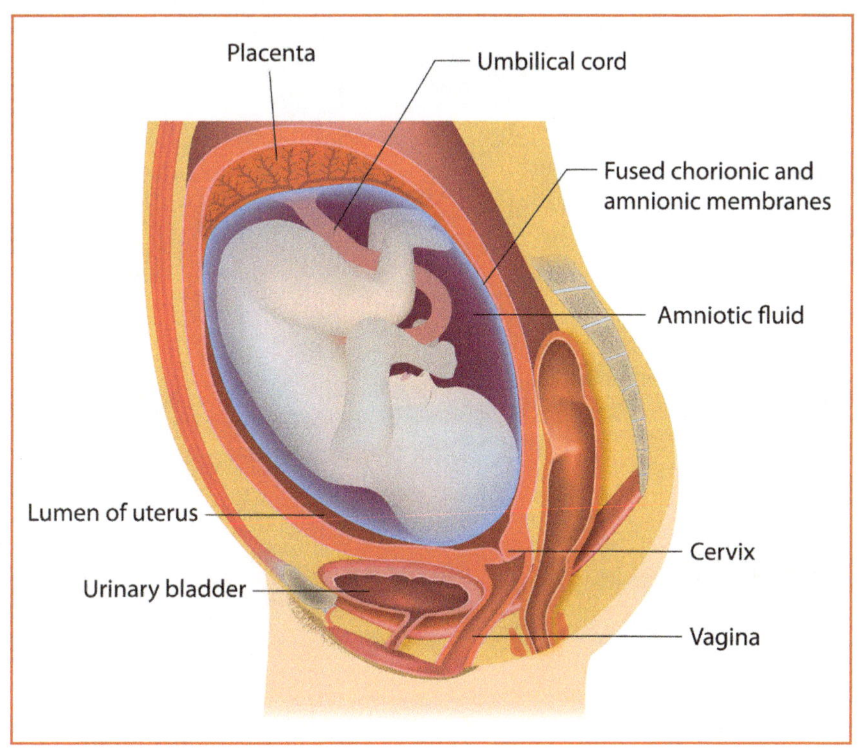

Human fetus.

(Photo courtesy of Alila Medical Media/ Shutterstock.com)

major organs begin development in the embryonic stage; therefore, there is a higher risk of spontaneous abortion (miscarriage) due to chromosomal defect or environmental factors. These factors, such as genetic malfunctioning, smoking, or drinking (to name a few), can play an important role in whether the pregnancy will continue or will result in a miscarriage.

Third Stage—Fetal

By the time the embryo reaches the end of the embryonic stage, most of the cell differentiation is complete. In the next and final stage, the embryo will be known as the **fetus**. The main structures that were laid down during the embryonic stage will be refined and completed. By the end of the fetal period, the unborn baby will be fully developed and ready for birth.

The fetal stage starts approximately two months after conception and continues for the next seven months. On average, the length of the fetus increases from 11¼ inches in the embryonic period, to 20 inches in the fetal period. Weight gain changes from 8 grams (0.28219 oz.) in the embryonic period to 3,250 grams (114.64 oz.) in the fetal period. Because the fetal period is all about finishing touches and the refining of incomplete organs, no new structure will be created except for the completion of body parts and gaining weight.

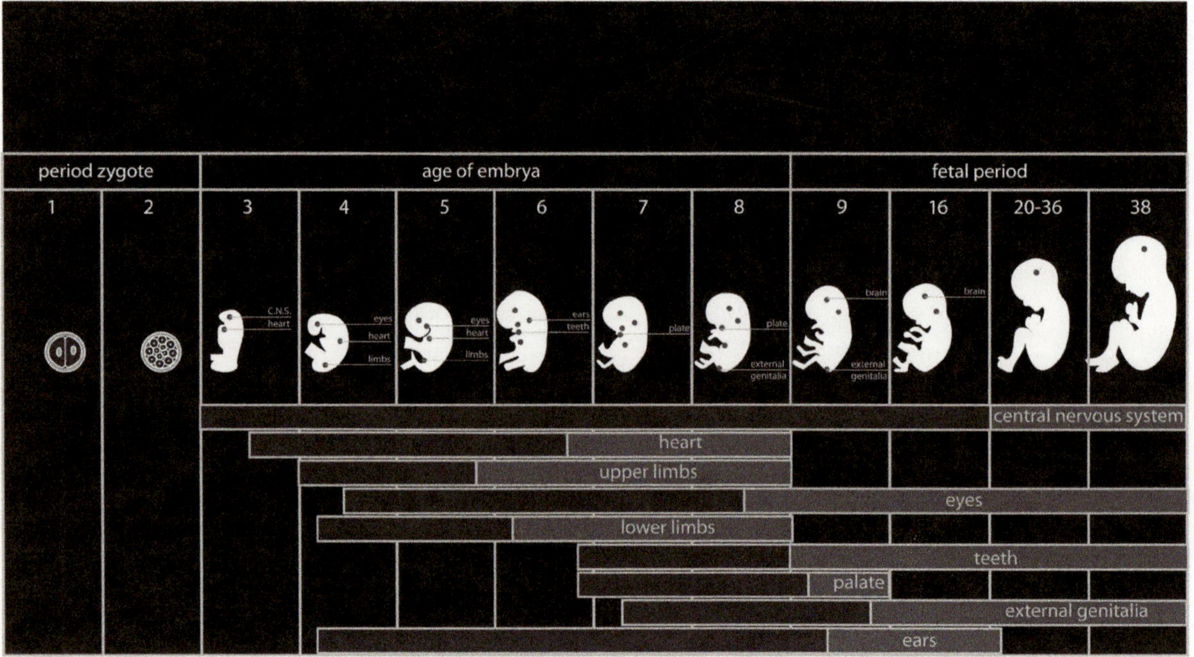

▲ *Fetal development from 1 to 38 weeks.*

(Photo courtesy of Dragana Gerasimoski/Shutterstock.com)

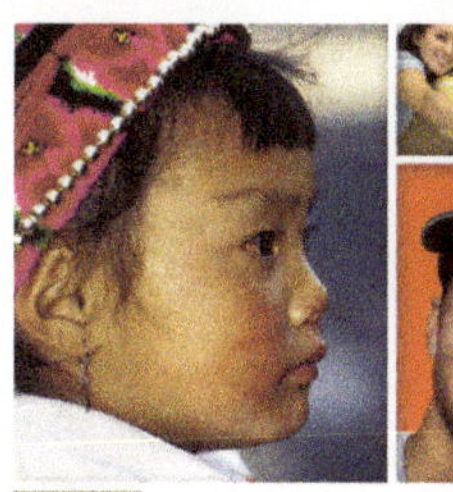

The Bari

What impact can one biological father for a child have on "family"? The Bari can have more than one biological father.

The Bari Indians live on the border area between Venezuela and Colombia. Though many aspects of their culture have changed because of contact with Western cultures, many of their traditional beliefs and their lifestyle have not significantly changed. One belief is that there can be more than one biological father for a child. In modern Western biology it takes one sperm and one egg to combine to result in a child. The Bari believe that it takes one sperm and egg to combine to start a child developing, but the fetus needs continual washes of sperm to grow and flourish. This can result in a child having more than one father. An elderly Bari woman explained this to anthropologist Stephen Beckerman:

> "My first husband was the father of my first child, my second child, and my third child. But the fourth child, actually, he has two fathers." He [Beckerman] states that: "A fetus is built up over time with repeated washes of sperm—which means, of course, that more than one man can contribute to the endeavor." (Small, 2004, p.186)

The Bari women often give the reason they take on lovers as that it takes a great deal of work for a man to have enough sex to nourish a developing child and they do not want to wear out their husband. Lovers can help. "Just look what the Bari say. Women grow fat during pregnancy, while men grow thin" (Small, 2004, p. 187). The Bari are not unique when it comes to this belief. Many indigenous groups in South America, New Guinea, and India believe this. The secondary fathers have some obligation for their child. They are expected to provide additional fish and meat as gifts to the mother and child. Secondary fathers do not live with the child but with their wife and the children their wife births. Interestingly when histories were taken of Bari women's births and children it was shown that children who had two fathers survived the pregnancy at a higher rate than children with one or more than two fathers.

Critical Thinking Question

The Bari have a different view of biology and family from that of Western culture. Would more open sexual relations work in our society and how would our society change?

Development of Senses

Research in prenatal behavior shows that early into fetal development, a fetus's various senses begin to function before birth, and even before the sensory systems are fully developed (Browne, 2008). These senses are touch, taste, smell, hearing, and sight. Through ultrasound waves, scientists have observed that fetuses respond to touch. For example, when a fetus experiences touch from the mother stroking her stomach, the fetus reacts by starting to suck the thumb.

In the uterus, a fetus can also detect and taste the flavors of the amniotic fluid. Premature infants born at thirty-three weeks of gestation (a full-term pregnancy is thirty-eight to forty-two weeks) were given nipples tainted with sweet, sour, and bitter tastes. They preferred the nipple with the sweet taste over bitter or sour. This indicates that babies' sense of taste at thirty-three weeks is at least partially or fully developed.

Some of the senses develop fully during the prenatal stages, yet some complete development after the neonate is born. Based on the fact that some senses are functional in the fetal stage, it can be concluded that the brain experiences activities in the womb even though it is not fully developed itself. As mentioned earlier, the brain is one of the first organs to develop in the embryonic stage, yet it is one of the last organs to complete its development. The early activity of the senses in the prenatal period helps shape the development of the brain and nervous system (Berger, 2004).

Sense of Smell

Human beings' sense of smell is through breathing and air, so how is it that an unborn fetus can smell while still in the mother's womb? **Olfactory cells,** which are necessary for smell, along with the nostrils are formed at about nine months of development of the fetal structure. As previously discussed, the fetus breathes the amniotic fluid; therefore, through this fluid it can smell what the mother eats or inhales. Newborns can distinguish between different smells and they do show preference toward amniotic fluid, colostrum, and transitional milk; however, they do not show the same reaction to a control substance (Lipsitt et al., 1963). The fetus also turns away from certain odors such as ammonia (Rieser et al., 1976). This discovery once again highlights the importance of prenatal care because the baby will become accustomed to what the mother eats and smells.

Sense of Hearing

From at least the sixth month of prenatal development, the fetus responds to the sound of the mother's voice, of others talking to the mother, to the mother's blood pumping, and to her breathing. Because auditory abilities are one of the senses that start developing early on, the sense of hearing is acute at birth; however, hearing maturation is gradual and level based. The fact remains that after birth, neonates prefer familiar voices (DeCasper & Fifer, 1980; Simon & Butterworth, 1998). Furthermore, scientists have used ultrasound images to observe a fetus's behavior while exposing them to sound. Through these images, researchers have seen that sounds outside of the womb prompt the fetus to move toward the direction of the sound.

Sense of Sight

Scientists have long suspected that the fetus's vision is not as well developed as some of the other senses, such as hearing or smell. During growth in the fetal stage, the fetus may react to a bright light shown against the mother's skin, but its visual experience is very slight and not yet matured. Studies have shown that by its twenty-eighth week of gestation, the fetus can open its eyes. The sense of sight is one of the senses that is not fully developed in the womb. This lack of fetus's visual maturity could also be due to the immaturity of the various aspects of the visual cortex. At birth, infants do not have clear vision, and they see with a blurry sight. Over the course of the first few months, stimulation of the visual cortex will lead to the maturity of this part of the brain, thus better vision will ensue, but it could take up to six months after birth for the neonate's vision to fully complete its development (Johnson, 1999). That explains why newborn's respond to objects that are within inches from their face. Poor vision prevents them from noticing objects that are far away.

Fetal Learning, Memory, and Behavior

Fetal Learning

As the fetus progresses in the final stage of prenatal development, scientists have observed evidence of fetal learning. Of course, there are limitations to fetal learning research, and these studies are in the primal stages. Several studies suggest that learning begins in the mother's womb and in the fetal stage. Scientific observations have also shown the ability of the fetus to learn and remember. Fetuses prefer the sound of the mother's voice to other voices. In other studies, mothers were asked to read the Dr. Seuss story *The Cat in the Hat* to their fetus twice a day, for at least 1½ months during the fetal stage of pregnancy. After birth, the same newborns were given a pacifier that was connected to a machine measuring the rate of sucking motions on the pacifier; similarly, the heart beats of the newborns were measured. Half of the mothers then read aloud *The Cat in the Hat* story, and the other half read another story aloud. Infants increased their rates of sucking when they heard the familiar story *The Cat in the Hat*

(Decaspar & Spence, 1986). This meant that every time the newborn heard the recording of its mother's voice, the rate of the sucking was increased as the neonate made more sucking motion. The increased rate in the sucking motion relates to the neonate's reaction to hearing a familiar voice and remembering an experience. Thus the familiarity of the mother's voice creates a preference for the newborn to recognize and prefer her voice over others, and this preference seemed to have been developed in the womb. The latest findings are that a fetus can sense motion at about five months of development. In another study, newborns stopped crying when songs were played for them that were from the shows their mother had watched during pregnancy. Even nutritional intakes that were kept consistent by the mothers during and after pregnancy produced a positive result with babies when mothers' breastfed them on the same cycle.

Evidence of Fetal Movement in Response to Music

Although the idea that exposing an unborn baby to music will somehow create a smarter child appeals to many mothers, there is little scientific basis for it. One of the challenges to studying this is obtaining objective measurements of what the fetus hears. This is typically done by measuring fetal movements or heart rate, and observing how these change in response to music or sounds that are played loudly. The results of this type of research indicate the sense of hearing does not become well developed until well into the late fetal stage of development (seven to nine months). Fetal movements and heartbeats typically increase in response to music, and this tends to be more pronounced for music with a fast tempo (Kisilevsky et al., 2004).

Evidence of Fetal Memory

The scientific world has long been fascinated by investigations into fetal memory, fetal learning, and other developmental senses that a fetus goes through. Scientists in the Netherlands used one hundred healthy pregnant women and found that by thirty weeks of pregnancy, fetuses had a short-term memory of sound and may have developed a long-term memory of a sound (Dirix et al., 2009). The researchers documented fetuses' memory by observing fetal movements through ultrasound waves as they played a particular sound. This sound was repeated until the fetus "habituated" to it or no longer reacted to that sound. Memory of the fetus was tested by playing the sound in intervals to see if the fetus recognized and remembered the sound until at one point it no longer reacted. Evidence from the study found that a fetus could remember a sound for ten minutes and by the thirty-fourth week of gestation may be able to remember the sound for several weeks.

The Critical Period Hypothesis (CPH)

The **Critical Period Hypothesis** was originally developed by Eric Lenneberg (1921–1975) and has been the subject of many debates and research. Lenneberg believed that human ability for language is genetically programmed. This hypothesis states that normal developmental events occur during a limited time, when human growth is most sensitive to certain environmental and contextual stimuli. A critical period is the time when an organism is likely to be influenced most by specific events (Lenneberg, 1967).

This critical period plays an important role in the embryo's exposure to **teratogenic** substances, such as alcohol, drugs, smoking, stress, and the mother's exposure to disease. This exposure can cause irreversible damage to the embryo's development. An example would be a mother contracting rubella (German measles) while pregnant that results in birth defects. During the embryonic stage (first twelve weeks), rubella can cause congenital heart disease, cataracts, deafness, and mental retardation.

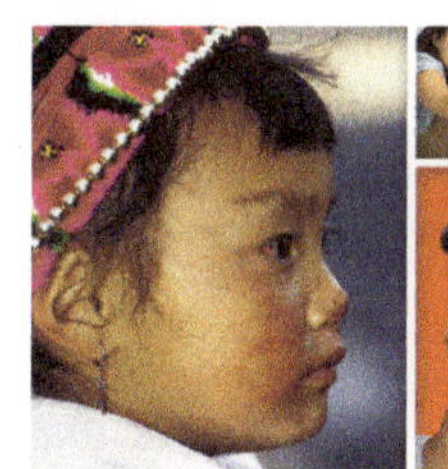

Pink Floyd . . . A Tale of Critical Period . . .

Up in the Seattle, Washington area lives a family who owns a small homestead farm housing 120 chickens, a cow, and 9 sheep. Recently, Hope, one of the female sheep gave birth to two lambs, a male and a female. The daughters of the family named the female lamb, Pink and the male lamb, Floyd. The male lamb looked healthy at birth, but it appeared that he was not getting enough milk. He seemed to try but his sister was more aggressive and looked like she was pushing him aside a bit. The next day or two, Floyd, the male lamb was lethargic and motionless. It was apparent that something was not right with him since the mother lamb vigorously kept licking and nudging him. The farmers knew something was wrong and set out to intervene. The farmers rushed Floyd inside the house, massaging his body and wrapping him with electric heating pads as a last-ditch effort to save the baby lamb. His rectal temperature when he was brought inside was 89.8, whereas the normal body temperature for a sheep is around 102.3°F, so his had dropped dangerously. It was crucial that his body temperature be raised avoiding death due to his body going through a hypothermic shock. A few hours later, his body temperature started to rise as he started to breath normally. Within four hours from his ordeal, the baby lamb seemed to have recovered showing normal physical signs. He was then taken back to his

(continues)

(continued from previous page)

mother; however, she rejected him! It seemed that even though Floyd had been cared for by his mother for one day before he became hypothermic at a day old, he was now a stranger to his own mother. Hope, was attached to him in the beginning, but gave him up for gone when she couldn't find him. It also seemed that having one of her babies taken away from her, she was now counting one lamb as her only baby dismissing ever giving birth to a second one! To save the rejected lamb from rejection and starvation, the farmers had to resort to other means to provide basic needs for his survival. From the beginning of his ordeal and by the time Floyd was taken back to his mother, four hours had passed. The mother lamb's refusal to accept and nurture him the same way she cared for Pink (Floyd's sister) means the Critical Period for Floyd's imprinting and early socialization with the mother had passed. He could no longer bond with his mother, and his mother no longer had attachment to him! Being faced with this dilemma, the farm owners had to resort to plan B! Floyd was once again brought back into the house to stay indoors until he was strong enough to be on his own in the pastor. His new living arrangement gave him an opportunity to bond with the family. This phenomena is explained under Sensitive Period, which is a more extended period of time, when a species (humans including) is more receptive to environmental influences and stimuli.

Update: Floyd is now 2 months old, has learned to act like a lamb, and spends his days with the other sheep, but unlike them, he is very friendly with the farmers and their daughters, and he is not afraid. He has now bonded with the family! Floyd responds to his name and likes to cuddle. He is friendly with all the other farm animals as well. He plays with the dog, is very friendly with the chickens, and shows no sign of aggression! Hope is still hostile toward Floyd and considers him a threat! What a difference a few hours makes!

Patterns of Growth

Cephalocaudal and Proximodistal Development

The patterns of growth have been divided into **cephalocaudal** and **proximodistal.** When growth takes place starting from the head and ending at the toes, it is called cephalocaudal. An example of cephalocaudal growth in the embryonic stage would be that of the development of the brain followed by the spinal cord. At any given time, based on the cephalocaudal principle, structures closer to the head are more developed than those closer to the feet.

Conversely, the terminology of proximodistal refers to the sequence in which development takes place starting at the center of the body and moves outward toward the extremities. An example of proximodistal development can be found in the growth of the shoulders all the way to the development of the fingers. The development of the shoulders leads to the development of the arm and consequently the hand, fingers, and nails.

Twins

During the first fourteen days of the germinal (conception) period, there is a possibility that the fertilized egg (zygote) may split in half; each half containing a separate set of identical genetic makeup. This occurs in about one third of all twin cases, and results in "identical twins" or monozygotic twins. Even though the identical twins have the same hereditary makeup, they may not share all of the same temperament characteristics. This is as close as we can get to cloning humans without doing it in a science laboratory!

Nonidentical twins are the result of two separate eggs being released in the ovary and two separate sperms penetrating the eggs. This means that two separate zygotes will continue the journey through the fallopian tube in order to reach the uterus, thus creating dizygotic twins. The commonality between dizygotic twins is that they were both conceived at the same time and share the uterus. Otherwise, "nonidentical twins" are no more alike than any other brothers or sisters. Recently, due to the increased use of fertility drugs or the method of conception, we have seen a greater increase in nonidentical twin occurrences than ever before.

Alternative Methods of Conception

One way for a human female to get pregnant is to have intercourse, which is the most common method. There are times that medical problems may hinder pregnancy or prevent it. When infertile couples seek professional help, they will be seeking the methods of assisted reproductive technology (ART). In such cases, the couple may be getting help from available medical solutions for the process of a zygote's fertilization.

Among such methods of ART is in-vitro fertilization (IVF). In this procedure, the egg is separately fertilized by a sperm (creating a zygote) in a laboratory dish, which is consequently inserted into the women's uterus. Sometimes the egg or the sperm that is used in the IVF process may be a donor's, either from a sperm bank or a female donating the egg. Overall, the IVF process may be risky. At times, the fertilization of the egg (the making of the zygote) may not take place, or the process could be expensive for the couple, or it could be emotionally strenuous for prospective parents. The success rate of IVF depends on the age and the health condition of the woman, but overall, IVF has a relatively low success rate. In modern days, for women under the age of thirty-five, some doctors claim to have 30 to 35 percent success rate. Generally, the success rate may even be as low as 20 percent; therefore, due to the financial burden as well as the emotional challenge, couples usually attempt the IVF procedure only once or twice.

One reason for multiple pregnancies through an IVF procedure is that in order to increase the chances of a successful zygote implantation in the uterus, multiple fertilized eggs (zygotes) are transferred. This practice increases multiple births in mothers who use the IVF procedure. In many cases of successful IVF, we have seen the birth of many twins, triplets, quadruplets, and even sextuplets. Recently, some of these multiple births have prompted many ethical questions and moral issues regarding how many fertilized eggs is too many to be used in such procedures.

Western Medical Research on Stages of Delivery

Just as there are three stages of prenatal development, there are three stages of the delivery process. The first stage is the dilation and effacement of the cervix. Dilation is the opening of the cervix and effacement is the thinning of the cervix. After both dilation and effacement are complete, the birth canal will open to begin allowing the baby to move down. The point of full dilation of ten centimeters and full effacement is called transition, and at this point the woman may begin to push during a contraction. The first stage will usually last about twelve hours for a first birth and about six hours for later births.

The second stage of the delivery process is the delivery of the baby. The mother will begin to push with her abdominal muscles down into her pelvis. First to appear is the top of the baby's head followed by the emergence of the whole head. After the baby's entire body is pulled out, the umbilical cord is cut and the baby takes its first breath and cries. A quick assessment is taken by the obstetrician and the nurse practitioner to ensure good health and physical normalcy of the newborn, and finally the baby is given back to the mother. The third and final stage is the delivery of the placenta. This is the shortest stage in giving birth, lasting approximately ten to thirty minutes, in which the mother will push out the placenta just as she pushed out the baby (Bjorklund & Hernandez, 2012).

Baby during Labor and Delivery

While the baby is going through the birth canal, the head may be misshapen due to squeezing through the birth canal and the overlapping of the skull plates. The soft spots on the baby's head are called fontanels and will be squeezed activating the production of a hormone that regulates oxygen intake. Also, the squeezing of the baby's body helps to force out the amniotic fluid that is in the lungs, preparing the lungs for oxygen intake once the baby is out of the womb.

Screening and Assessment

In the United States, immediately after birth, all infants undergo assessments to test for special medical needs. This test is called the APGAR scale and is scored 0, 1, or 2 on five dimensions: Appearance, Pulse (heart rate), Grimace (reflex, irritability), Activity (muscle tone), and Respiration (breathing or respiratory effort). A perfect score is a 10, good physical health is a 7, medical support is 4 to 6, and urgent medical care needed is a 3 or below and usually predicts infant mortality. Another screening that is done on infants is a series of blood tests. These tests screen for phenylketonuria (commonly known as PKU, an inherited disorder), congenial hyperthyroidism, sickle cell anemia, and galactosemia (Hotchner, 1995).

Medical Techniques during Labor and Delivery

Fetal monitoring is used to detect fetal heart rate, respiration, and other vitals and is usually used at higher rates when an instrumental labor will be conducted such as a cesarean section, also known as a C-section (Goldberg, Brinkley, & Kukar, 1998). A C-section is a surgical procedure using anesthesia to deliver the infant through an incision in the mother's abdomen and uterus. It is a very popular procedure in the United States, with 26 percent voluntary C-sections done in 2002, and increasing to 29 percent in 2004. Some medical issues that are taken into consideration that may result in a C-section are maternal age, obesity, diabetes, and high blood pressure.

Another medical technique that may be done to help the birthing process is conducting an induced labor. An induced labor should only be done for medical reasons, not for convenience, and is seen in about 20 percent of U.S. births. Having the amniotic sac broken manually by the doctor and providing a hormone called pitocin to stimulate contractions induce labor. This is usually a more difficult delivery than a natural birth and more pain medication is needed. Instruments

Zambia

In Zambia there are many beliefs held by women associated with childbirth and prenatal care. For example a pregnant women should not have extramarital relations with other men during pregnancy because it could lead to an abortion or problems during labor. The reasoning behind this is that different men have different blood and therefore cause problems. Women are also advised not to eat certain foods during pregnancy. It is believed that if a pregnant woman eats eggs the baby will be born without hair and this will be embarrassing to the family. They are also advised not to eat fish because it could cause infant abnormalities (Maimbolwa et al., 2003).

▲ ***Zambian women and their children.***
(Photo courtesy of Anton_Ivanov/Shutterstock.com)

may also be used to aid in the delivery of the baby, such as forceps, which clamps around the baby's head to pull it out of the birth canal. Also, a vacuum extractor may be used to suck the baby out of the mother. Instrumental deliveries consist of less than 10 percent of the live births done in the United States.

Birth Complications

Some complications that may occur during birth are anoxia and cerebral palsy. Anoxia is the separation of the placenta from the uterine wall too soon and results in a lack of oxygen to the fetus. This separation could also result in maternal hemorrhaging, which may be lethal to both mother and fetus. Anoxia during or just before birth can cause cerebral palsy, which is a disorder of lack of muscle control, leading to speaking and motor-control inability (Paneth, 1986).

PRETERM AND LOW BIRTH WEIGHT INFANTS. Preterm or premature infants are babies that are born earlier than thirty-eight weeks of gestation (conception) and may also be low birth weight (LBW) babies. LBW infants weigh less than 5½ lbs at birth, very low birth weight (VLBW) weigh less than 3 lbs at birth, and extremely low birth weight (ELBW) infants weigh less than 2 lbs at birth. Low birth babies encounter a great deal of tribulations such as immature digestion problems and heart problems.

Harmful Environmental Factors

In the Greek language, "tera" means monster, basically meaning giving birth to a monster. Scientifically, any substance that interferes with the normal development of a human being is considered to be a **teratogen**. As previously discussed, current research has shown that prenatal development can be hindered by environmental factors. The impact of environmental factors may be devastating to any of the prenatal stages. Remembering the Critical Period Hypothesis, the devastation depends on the timing and the degree of exposure of any of these environmental factors. The end result may be permanent or life-altering consequences for both the baby and the parents. These factors may also be direct or indirect, meaning the mother may knowingly or unknowingly expose her unborn child to environmental factors that would change the course of the normal development. For example, consumption of alcoholic beverages during pregnancy, smoking, and using both legal and illegal drugs are among some of the environmental factors that may cause harmful damage to the unborn baby's development.

Teratogens

As previously mentioned, any substance or environmental factor that could harm or alter the course of normal development is called a teratogen. The impact of the teratogen depends on the timing of its exposure and interaction with other factors. The nature and impact of some teratogens, some of which are well-known substances, are discussed further in the following sections.

Alcohol

The impact of alcohol on the fetus's development is irreversible and devastating. If the mother consumes alcohol while pregnant, especially in the first few weeks of pregnancy, the impact is most grave. Babies born with **fetal alcohol syndrome** (FAS) have an abnormally small head, eye abnormality, facial malformation, underdeveloped brain, eye abnormalities, congenital heart disease, and other irregularities. Alcohol is the most frequently used teratogen during pregnancy. Even though each year in the United States 12,000 FAS babies are born carrying FAS syndrome, the number is feared to be even higher (Nevitt, 1998).

Prescription Drugs

Most drugs are considered harmful if taken during pregnancy, but some may have a more pronounced impact on the fetus's development than others. Prescription drugs such as Valium (tranquilizer), Thalidomide (nausea), Accutane (acne), and antibiotics can cause devastating developmental abnormalities (Gillio,

1999; National Library of Medicine, 1997). Of course, the amount of drugs and the timing of the consumption is the determining factor in the degree of abnormalities caused in prenatal development.

Caffeine

Drinking caffeinated beverages or consuming caffeine during pregnancy can lead to an increased rate of spontaneous abortion and low birth weight (Signorello et al., 2001). Mothers are advised to avoid caffeine altogether or limit it to very small amounts. Caffeinated beverages such as tea or coffee are considered to be unbeneficial and at times harmful to the full growth of the unborn. Mostly, caffeine consumption may impact the germinal stage as it poses the danger of spontaneous abortion or the fetal stage because it interferes with the fetus's gaining the appropriate amount of weight. Nutritionally, it is not advised for pregnant women to consume caffeinated beverages or food items that contain caffeine.

Cigarettes

Mothers who smoke when carrying a baby increase the risk of having an infant born prematurely or with low birth weight, which could cause complications for the newborn (Lieberman et al., 1994). Any baby born before full gestation (thirty-eight weeks) is considered to be premature, and may lack fully developed organs and necessary weight. A premature newborn lacks the necessary stamina to survive in the outside world because it did not have the full period of prenatal development necessary for a healthy start. Smoking at any stage of pregnancy poses harm and irreversible damage to the unborn baby. In particular, smoking during the second stage of pregnancy, which is the embryonic stage, poses greater threat in terms of spontaneous abortion. Even if the fetus survives, once it reaches the fetal stage, smoking will hinder its ability to gain the proper weight in order to survive outside the mother's womb. Not having completed the full term, a baby who is born prematurely is more susceptible to neonate illnesses or diseases. While pregnant, mothers should stop smoking at all costs!

Illegal Drugs

If taken during pregnancy, marijuana adversely impacts the fetus and causes low birth weight and premature delivery. Infants born to mothers who smoked marijuana are more readily startled, they have tremors, and may demonstrate problems in their sleep cycle. Cocaine is another drug to be avoided particularly during pregnancy because it has been linked to stillbirth and premature birth.

Babies born to mothers who used cocaine during pregnancy may be born with low birth weight syndrome, or have strokes and birth defects. These babies may also show more irritability and incoordination as well as mental disorders such as learning disabilities. Mothers who use methadone and heroin are also risking their babies' well-being because there is a very high possibility that the infant will be born addicted to these drugs. In addition to an addiction possibility, the newborn is more likely to be underweight, be born prematurely, and show respiratory problems, irritability, and poor coordination (Tronick et al., 1996).

A Non-Western View on How Conception Takes Place

Every culture around the world has a theory or belief of how conception occurs and of the developmental needs of the fetus. Many of them vary significantly from the modern Western medical model. As modern medicine becomes more accepted around the world, traditional belief systems are often maintained and combined with modern treatments. In the following sections we discuss a variety of different belief systems.

Bali

In the Balinese culture if you are a healer or *Balian*, you do not separate physical body illnesses from mental well-being. They treat what Westerners consider physical conditions, such as infections, as well as invisible conditions caused by spirits, witches, and sins of ancestors or actions of gods. They believe that when a woman is pregnant the intermingling of the mother's and father's souls created their child and the child will be the reincarnation of an ancestor's spirit. This spirit will also remain present in the household garden shrine as well as in the child's fetus (Deloache & Gotlieb. 2000).

The Balinese believe that for every positive force there is a counter negative force. As a result a person must take extra precautions by making frequent offering to their ancestors and gods in order to protect the developing baby from "'**leyek**" or witches. A pregnant woman will also often wear a magic charm on her belt or hang one on the front household gate to protect the fetus against witchcraft. These charms are purchased from the local healer. Leyek or witches can transform themselves into different forms late at night. As a result a pregnant woman should not venture out of the house late at night, particularly around

◀ ***Balinese women.***

(Photo courtesy of dmitry_islentev/Shutterstock.com)

midnight (Deloache & Gotlieb, 2000). The fetus is believed to have four sibling spirits that protect it. At the time of birth these four spirits are present in the blood, amniotic fluid, placenta, umbilical cord, and waxy coating of the infant at birth. The job of these four spirits is to protect and nourish the fetus during development (Deloache & Gotlieb, 2000).

A pregnant woman also needs to be somewhat cautious about what she eats and must maintain a balance between foods that are considered hot or cold. For example octopus, eggplant, mango, and roasted pig are considered hot foods. If a pregnant woman eats too much hot food then this might cause her to become ill. Also expecting women should never accept food from a person who is considered ritually impure, such as another women who is menstruating or someone who has recently had a death in the family (Deloache & Gotlieb, 2000). When a pregnancy is about six months along, a traditional ritual is preformed that will help anchor the fetus firmly in the womb. This ritual involves offerings, use of holy water, and keeping evil spirits away from the home (Deloache & Gotlieb, 2000).

Samoans

If a child is born with physical deformities or genetic defects it is often considered punishment for past bad behavior. This negative behavior can be by the husband during pregnancy, unacceptable behavior by the mother or a family member while she was pregnant, or eating food that is considered taboo during pregnancy (Lipson et al., 1997).

Vietnamese

Pregnant women should eat lots of healthy food and getting enough rest is very important. Strenuous activities are restricted during the whole pregnancy, but particularly during the last trimester. Expecting mothers must also take special care with their hygiene, for example, using only salt water to brush the teeth and gums. Generally sex is not recommended throughout the whole pregnancy (Lipson et al., 1997).

West Indians: Trinidadians, Jamaicans, Barbadians, and Other Caribbean Islands

Often West Indians believe a child born with physical defects is "God's will" and is sometimes seen as punishment from God for the parents' or family's sins (Lipson et al., 1997).

Russian

When a Russian women thinks delivery time is near she is traditionally encouraged to take castor oil in the belief that the birth of her baby will be easier. Many births are overseen by doctors; however, if a doctor is not available then midwives are commonly used. The lighting should not be too bright in the room where the birth takes place because of the belief that the baby will develop poor eyesight (Lipson et al., 1997).

Ethiopians and Eritreans

The nine months that a woman is pregnant is considered a dangerous state. The mother could miscarry or a deformity could occur because of someone giving the "evil eye" or as the result of sorcery. The pregnant mother is given lots of attention by her family and is supposed to avoid excesses in everyday activities. This includes avoiding lifting heavy objects, climbing lots of stairs, exposure to very emotional situations that include funerals or fights, or hearing bad news. Mothers-to-be are encouraged to eat well and get plenty of sleep. Food cravings are important because if they are not given attention, it may cause a miscarriage.

A week before the due date the mother is encouraged to drink a hot mixture of flax seed, water, and honey, which is believed to ease labor and act as a mild laxative (Lipson et al., 1997).

The Na, from the Yunnan and Schuan Provinces in China

The Na (also often called the Mosuo) is a minority group in China that lives in the Yunan and Schuan provinces. Brothers and sisters generally live in their mother's home for their whole lives. Men and women do not get married, but instead men visit the women in their household, primarily at night. Any adult female or male are able to have sex with each other as long as they both agree. Technically these visits are done in secret but often the family is aware of them. When children are born they remain with their mother and her family. The women's brothers act as the father to the children. The Na do not recognize fatherhood and the fathers have no obligation to their children. They believe that the fetus exists in the women's womb before intercourse and that all the men do is "water the fields of the womb," which enables the baby to grow and develop. It makes no difference to the Na women who does the "watering" (Cherlin, 2008).

Na or Mosuo woman in traditional dress.

(Photo courtesy of Yu Zhang/Shutterstock.com)

Zambia

In Zambia there are many beliefs associated with childbirth and prenatal care. For example, a pregnant woman should not have extramarital relations with other men during pregnancy because it could lead to an abortion or problems during labor. The reasoning behind this is that different men have different blood and therefore the mixing of blood can cause problems. Women are also advised not to eat certain foods during pregnancy. It is believed that if a pregnant woman eats eggs the baby will be born without hair and this will be embarrassing to her family. They are also advised not to eat fish because it could cause infant abnormalities (Maimbolwa et. el. 2003).

Hmong

The Hmong live in the hills of Laos. Many immigrated to the United States after the Vietnam War and number over one million today. They believe in Animism, which is the belief in different spirits that inhabit a person, animals, and plants. This belief system impacts their perceptions of Western medicine and care during childbirth.

A young Hmong woman in traditional dress.

(Photo courtesy of Muellek Josef/Shutterstock.com)

The Hmong believe that surgery allows the spirit to leave the body when the body is opened and results in deformities and illness that may be carried into the next life. If an organ or body part is removed then part of a person's soul is removed. A person is believed to have a limited supply of blood. Withdrawing blood is believed to sap strength and could result in the loss of the soul or spirit. Many of Western medicine's common practices associated with prenatal care are seen as dangerous to the Hmong and could cause the loss of the mother's and possibly the child's soul. These include cesareans and common diagnostic blood tests. They believe the dilating of the vagina may allow "wind" to enter a women's body, which is a common cause of disorders (Jambunathan & Stewart, 1995).

CHAPTER 4 SUMMARY

Traditionally, human development describes prenatal development in three distinct stages: germinal, embryonic, and fetal. Both medicine and the social sciences view development in a scientific and structured pattern using a data-based approach. This perspective included the belief that prenatal growth is simply a matter of predetermined genetics, Russian roulette style! However, some of these beliefs have changed due to continuous research studies in this field and newfound evidence. For example, the nature versus nurture debate has shed some light on the role of environment and contexts as it pertains to child development. Arguments include genotype, the original genetic makeup and how environment can impact its growth producing phenotype, which is the modified expression of genetic makeup. This new discovery has given today's scientists a great deal of ideas when it comes to prenatal stages of development. However, there is still a great deal to understand about this subject, and prenatal development continues to fascinate, baffle, and intrigue scientists.

Another baffling phenomenon is the development of identical and non-identical twins. Scientists do not all agree on how this happens and there remain ongoing debates.

One key issue in the prenatal development is the nature versus nurture debate, which poses a burning question as to "How much of development is based on the genetic disposition and how much of it is based on the environment?" Other evidence shows that in the fetal stage, the fetus develops learning and memorization. The scientific world has long been fascinated by investigations into fetal memory, fetal learning, and other developmental stages that a fetus goes through. However, according to the Critical Period Hypothesis, this learning and other prenatal development may only take place during a certain time frame, when human growth is most sensitive to certain environmental and contextual stimuli. The nature versus nurture debate also brings attention to environmental harms labeled "teratogens," which are substances that interfere with the normal development of a human being.

This text has outlined the Western scientific data and findings on prenatal development; however, as demonstrated, these views are not shared by all traditional and non-Western cultures. Either as scientific finding or cultural belief, humans are fascinated by the nature of prenatal development. This fascination is the motivation that drives scientists to continue to do research and document their findings.

CHAPTER 4 VOCABULARY

- Amnion
- Amniotic Fluid
- Amniotic Sac
- Blastocyst
- Cephalocaudal
- Chorion
- Continuous Development
- Critical Period Hypothesis
- Discontinuous Development
- Ectoderm
- Embryo
- Embryonic
- Endoderm
- Fetal
- Fetal Alcohol Syndrome
- Genotype
- Germinal
- Mesoderm
- Olfactory Cells
- Ovum
- Phenotype
- Placenta
- Proximodistal
- Spermatozoa
- Teratogen
- Teratogenic
- Zygote

Chapter 5

INFANT AND TODDLER
Physical Development

(Photo courtesy of Wendy Lopez)

Introduction

Physical development in infancy and early childhood is a noticeable and rapid process. When looking into the physical development of this age group, it is important to understand that childhood experiences and genetics both play a huge role in a child's development. Within the first year of life, children demonstrate significant physical growth, for example, from not being able to hold their heads up at birth to being able to walk within one year. Additionally, it is during this first year of life that many connections in the brain form and for many years continues to grow. Various stimulations, brain activities, and experiences help make these brain cell connections. In the meantime, many of these brain cells may be lost due to the lack of stimulation, poor nutrition, or appropriate experiences.

Sensory and Perceptual Development

During infancy and early childhood, body growth, sensory and perceptual development, motor skill development, and brain development are all undergoing major changes, resulting in more growth during this age period than any other time in a child's life. An infant's growth is extremely rapid, and it is important to

A young child playing with a ball is an example of proximodistal development.

(Photo courtesy of tankist276/Shutterstock.com)

A child learning to walk is an example of cephalocaudal development.

(Photo courtesy of Elena Efimova/ Shutterstock.com)

understand all of the different ways in which an infant grows. As mentioned earlier, there are two terms that describe the type of growth patterns: **cephalocaudal** and **proximodistal**. Cephalocaudal refers to growth happening from head to toe, while proximodistal refers to growth from the core (center of the body) outward to the extremities. Cephalocaudal development is apparent first as babies learn to lift their heads, and later on when they learn how to walk. An example of proximodistal growth would be the fact that children learn basic movements and gross motor skills first, and then eventually fine motor skills (i.e., directing a ball through cones with their feet). It is also important to understand that different systems grow and change at different rates. For example, the nervous system develops quickly, while sleep patterns and overall growth develop at a much slower rate and over a longer period of time (Patterson, 2008).

Within the first six months of life, infants often double their birth weight, and by one year have nearly tripled their birth weight. Within the first 1½ years of life, babies generally gain a foot in height. This development is discontinuous as it happens in bursts. Babies usually reach their chubbiest around seven to nine months (Patterson, 2008). During the preschool years, children tend to grow between 2½ to 3½ inches in height a year and generally gain four to five pounds per year. At this age, children begin to lose their body fat and tend to get taller and slim down. During this growth, muscle tone improves and arms and legs get longer. One more thing to note is the presence of teeth. Within the first two years of life, primary teeth begin to emerge, and during the preschool years the upper jaw widens to create space for permanent teeth.

Sensory Perception

Sensory and perceptual development is an important part of growth during infancy. Vision is the least developed sense at birth. Newborns prefer looking at patterns versus looking at solid colors. However, they have the ability to know where one object ends and another begins, also known as object segregation. Even though newborn babies can see color, often they have difficulty recognizing different shades; therefore, they prefer black and white or patterns. The ability to see color rapidly develops in babies. Even as early as four months old, babies start to have color preferences; however, during early visionary growth, babies pay attention to bold patterns, strong differences in light and dark, and contrasts in color. Infants do not obtain adultlike vision until six months of age.

An infant's hearing is well developed at birth. We know this because infants turn their heads toward unexpected loud noises, show awareness of sounds, and are able to discriminate among many different sounds. Speech perception is shaped by experiences. Researchers have found that infants prefer the sounds of human conversation versus other sounds, and that infants also prefer to listen to child-directed (baby language) speech. In the process called perceptual tuning, infants respond less to stimulation that is not familiar or used in their typical environment.

▲ ***An infant looking at a mobile.***

(Photo courtesy of Sokolova Maryna/Shutterstock.com)

Toilet Training

Toilet training in today's American culture usually takes place between the ages of two and three years. Parents are often advised to begin toilet training when their child is ready, that is, when they start to express themselves and show dislike of wet or messy diapers. Boys often toilet train at a slightly later age than girls. Toddlers are in a stage of development where they are seeking autonomy and more independence. They are just discovering they are separate people with their own ideas and wills. This is often expressed by the answer of "NO!" whenever they are asked to do something. Since the toddler is seeking independence, toilet training can become a battle of wills between the parents and the child. As a result, rewards are often used to encourage participation when a toddler successfully uses the toilet. If a child does not seem ready to potty train then it is often wise to try again in week or two. If a child is ready then the child toilet trains during the day rather quickly, in a matter of a couple of months. Night training usually comes after daytime training. However, this toilet training philosophy is certainly not universal (see "The Cultural Conflict Over Toilet Training" and "Fulani: Parent Guide for Toilet Training").

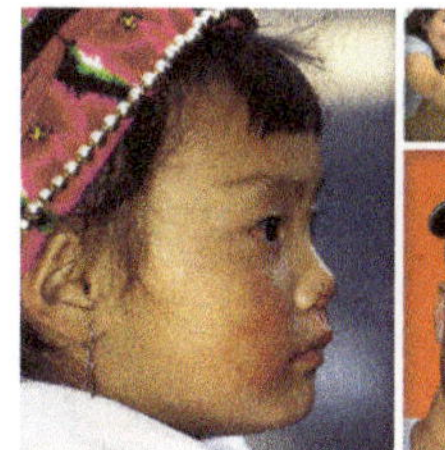

The Cultural Conflict Over Toilet Training

By Mary Exton

"These will get really stiff and uncomfortable and take hours to dry," my mother said, poking suspiciously at the very expensive ducky-printed Velcro-closing cloth diapers my mother-in-law had sent across the Pacific. Bicultural marriage was not that easy. It seemed that we always had a lot to figure out about which way we should live. Before my daughter Elizabeth was born, my husband told me about disposable diapers. But China did not produce diapers, disposable or otherwise. At the fancy hotel drugstore, imported Pampers or Huggies sold for the equivalent of one dollar each. At that rate, we calculated Elizabeth would be going through $4,000 worth of disposable diapers a year. Our salaries were only half that amount.

One month after Elizabeth was born, my mother suggested we toilet train her. My husband suspected this early toilet training wouldn't work. Having read several parenting books sent from America, my husband mumbled something incoherent about the emotional scarring of overly early toilet training. My mother often bragged to me that I was done with my toilet training when I was 6 months old. She was confident she could toilet train Elizabeth. Motherhood was a new experience for me, so my mother became my first supervisor.

(continues)

(continued from previous page)

Chinese toilet training means to hold a baby gently by the hips over a potty or by the edge of the road and whistle softly to imitate the tinkle of urine. Chinese babies and toddlers don't wear diapers at all, not even cloth ones. Instead, they always wear open-crotch pants. Cotton, water, and soap are all scarce items and someone is always available to be with a Chinese baby to supervise toileting. Parents begin to toilet train their children as early as 1 month of age. Incredibly, most babies are toilet trained by 6 months of age, at least during waking hours. By the time children can walk, usually at 12 to 14 months, they know to squat down in their open-crotch pants whenever they feel the urge.

▲ *Pants with an open crotch are common for children being toilet trained in China.*

(Photo courtesy of Augapfel, Christopher, Baby's Butt. 1 May 2007. https://www.flickr.com/photos/491316054_9cfa545df5_b.jpg)

Just as my mother said, Elizabeth was toilet trained when she was 7 months old. Even though she had some accidents, most of the time she knew to tell us she needed help to use the potty.

An American friend, Barbara, who was trying to toilet train her own son, watched in amazement once as teachers prepared fifteen toddlers for a turn on the trampoline in a playground. "The teachers went around and said, 'pee, pee, pee,'" said Barbara. "I thought, how could they all have to go at the same time? But they all squatted down." A lot of American people were shocked by Elizabeth's well-done toilet training at that early age. I was also shocked by some American 3-year-olds still using diapers.

I had my second child in America. I tried to use the Chinese way to train him to use the potty, but it didn't work!! He is one and a half years old now, and he still uses diapers. My mother called me a lazy mother because I am relaxed about training the American-born baby. Living in a different culture and having heard much varying information about this issue, I stuck to my guns.

Cultural conflicts can create quite a challenge; however, in many ways, they can be considered assets. You cannot only gain strength and skills as you work your way through them, but you can gain new knowledge as well (Gonzalez-Mena, 1997). Toilet training is an issue that is heavily laden with emotion for most people, and there seems to be no obvious right or wrong answer. I was embroiled in a cultural conflict.

Part of the problem resides in the definition and goal of toilet training (Gonzalez-Mena, 1997). If the caregiver defines toilet training as teaching or encouraging the child independently to take care of his or her own toileting needs and the goal is to accomplish this as quickly and painlessly as possible, the caregiver will regard 12 months of age as too early to start. Children under 12 months need adult help. However, if toilet training is regarded as a reduction of the number of diapers used and the method is primarily to form a partnership with the child to do just that, the caregiver will start as soon as he or she can read the children's signals and "catch" the child in time. This method focuses on interdependence or mutual dependence.

> "Americans, who value independence and individuality, see the baby as dependent, undifferentiated . . . the Chinese, who prize close interdependence between a child and adult, regard the infant as having a small component of autonomy . . . believe they must tempt the infant into a dependent role, rush to soothe a crying infant, respond quietly to the baby's excited babbling, and sleep with the young child at night in order to encourage the mutual bonding necessary for adult life" (Kagan, 1984).

Chinese babies are held so much of the time that there is an immediate response from caregivers to the need for urination and bowel movements. Hence from an early age, there is an association in the infant's mind between these functions and actions from the mother. Consequently, when the baby wants to urinate, his or her whole body participates in the preliminary process. The Chinese mother, holding the baby in her arms, learns to be sensitive to the minute details of the process, and to hold the baby away from herself at exactly the critical moment. Eventually, the infant learns to ask to be held out. In contrast, the transition is more difficult for middle-class American infants whose bodily functions typically occur alone. The mother begins to interfere with bowel and bladder activity after many months of only cursory attention.

I visited the teacher, Althea Goundry, who works in the Plymouth State College Development and Family Center; she told me American people won't start to toilet train their children until the children show an interest in using the toilet and are physically ready (personal Interview). A toddler should have the verbal and conceptual skills to be able to understand what is expected during toilet training. He or she should know that certain things belong in certain places. Goundry was very interested in what I said about Chinese toilet training. She said most Americans don't try behaviorist strategies, and maybe it is easier to stay the way it is than to change it. American research also shows children won't stay dry and clean much before 24 months of age. "On the other hand," Goundry told me, "I think it is better to pull more than to push." She also feels it is necessary to provide the child with a treat after successful use of the toilet, to reinforce the learning that has occurred. Two behaviorists (Azrin and Faxx, quoted in Shimoni, Baxter, & Kugelmass, 1992) suggest that children over 24 months of age can be taught to use the potty by imitation and reward.

"There is no shame with accident," Goundry told me. This is also different from Chinese toilet training. One characteristic of Chinese culture is honor and "saving face." I punished my daughter's feelings. Chinese toilet training implies that the focus is on what the adult does, rather than what the child does. Research shows that children have their own feelings about toilet training. They are being asked to do something that they often cannot see any

(continues)

(continued from previous page)

reason for. Their compliance will depend on their readiness (Shimoni et al., 1992). If a child is not ready, toilet training can become a battle of wills. Toilet training is regarded as a highly individualized process in America. Children should be trained without pressure.

Culture is never static; it continues to evolve. When one culture rubs up against another, both are transformed (Gonzalez-Mena, 1997). A challenge for many parents in the United States is to maintain their cultural identity and pass it on to their children in the face of this inevitable evolution.

Cultures are not superior or inferior; they just are. Toilet training is the issue that made me learn more about and appreciate human diversity. Because I live in America now, I would say "help the children to learn" rather than "train them." Toilet training should be thought of as a combination of skills that the child will acquire with guidance and assistance from parents and teachers.

Adapted from http://jupiter.plymouth.edu/~megp/webct/culturalconflict.htm

Motor Skills Development

Motor skills significantly improve during infancy and early childhood. The amount of improvement is apparent when realizing that children go from barely being able to lift their head to being able to run and jump by the end of early childhood. When looking at motor skill development in infancy, it is important to understand that infants are born with **instinctive reflexes**, which are involuntary reactions/impulses to situations, people, and environmental stimuli. For example, newborns know how to suck, will grab onto your finger with their hands, will hold their breath underwater, and will move their legs back and forth when held up in a simulated walking movement. Some of these reflexes seem to disappear during the first year of life due to the maturation of muscles and to brain development. For example, reflexive walking movement seems to disappear within a few short months because the legs grow too heavy to be moved back and forth. However, if children are held upright in water, they instinctively start to move their legs back and forth. As brain development progresses, infants are gradually able to adjust the involuntary actions to voluntary reflexes as needed to respond to stimulus. An example would be controlling the speed of sucking on a bottle or pacifier.

By three months old, babies can usually hold their heads up and prop themselves up on their own. By three to four months old, infants are able to reach and make contact with an object. Around seven to eight months of age,

Fulani: Parent Guide for Toilet Training

The Fulani are one of the largest ethnic groups in West Africa. They number about ten million and are located across the east-west belt of the savannah. This includes grassland, interspersed with woodland. Most Fulani are Muslims.

For the first two years of life a mother spends a great deal of time carrying her child around on her back and as a result needs to know what the child's excretory needs are. A mother may find it easiest to give her baby an enema twice daily, once in the morning and once in the evening. Eventually the child will slip into a regular routine and it will be easier to toilet train him or her.

An enema is given by filling a rubber bulb with water and laying the child across the lap, belly down. The mother then gently squeezes the water into the child's anus. Then the child is put into a sitting position and gently jiggled to encourage a bowel movement. In the past before rubber bulbs were available, mothers used their mouths to administer the water into the anus.

▲ *Fulani women at a market.*
(Photo courtesy of Attila JANDI/Shutterstock.com)

Once the child can walk, the child can be trained to go into the bush to relieve him- or herself. Remember that the bush can be a dangerous place and mothers accompany children until around the age of six.

Breast Feeding

Mothers should breastfeed their children into their second or third year of life. Mothers will of course start introducing supplement food after about one month of age. This is seen as a very important part of the development of a child's personality.

When Fulani breastfeed their children they are not only giving them nutrients and food but also their personality traits. The Fulani have the following sayings:

> "One can understand another's personality by knowing the breast from which one sucked."
> And "The milk that is nursed is the milk that comes back" (Johnson, 2000, p. 190).

Remember breastfeeding is a sign of devotion and affection. Babies who are breastfed for the first two years of their life are more likely to be intelligent and have a closer relationship with the mother when the mother grows older.

Adapted from Johnson, 2000.

infants have usually learned to crawl on hands and knees. Fear of heights is one of the fundamental human emotions that develops very early on. This useful emotion is considered instrumental in preventing humans from falling to their deaths. Human babies' fear of height and awareness of depth perception was shown in an experiment known as the "visual cliff" (Gibson & Walk, 1960)). In this experiment, researchers were interested in finding out whether infants are naturally afraid of heights or if this fear is a learned behavior due to life experiences.

Visual Cliff Experiment

Psychologists Eleanor J. Gibson and R. D. Walk at Cornell University were interested in researching depth perception in animals and human babies. In order to conduct such research, an apparatus called the **visual cliff** was created to show both optical and tactile perception; it simulated the illusion of a cliff without posing danger to babies under experimentation. It used a table divided into two halves, with its entire top covered by acrylic Plexi-type glass. One half of the table has a checkerboard pattern, which lies immediately under the Plexiglass. The other half of the apparatus is transparent, imitating a sharp drop of about forty inches (a meter or so). At the bottom of the transparent Plexiglass is also a checkerboard pattern to demonstrate continuity with the other half. During the visual cliff experimentation, the mother or the caregiver stands on the "deep" side, but the infant is placed on the opposite side where the Plexiglass has a checkerboard pattern immediately under it. The infant is then enticed and encouraged by the mother to crawl to her. In these experiments, the mother also uses a toy or an interesting item to coax the infant to cross over the simulated height. The visual cliff experiments have shown that younger infants of around seven months of age will crawl over without hesitation to reach the mother on the other side. However, older infants, over eight months, will hesitate and avoid making the journey. These infants refuse to crawl to the other side, and since they are being enticed by the mother's encouragement to come to her, they visibly become upset and often cry showing anxiety over their inability to move farther to reach the mother. The emotional response these eight-month-olds display when facing this dilemma shows two important developmental phenomena. On the one hand it shows that the infant understands that in order to feel secure, they need to sit on a solid surface. On the other hand, the infants' anxiety and crying show that they understand depth perception and fear, preventing them from crossing over (Berk, 2008).

Further development of the nervous system and cognitive maturation will help the infant overcome this fear. Eventually, during the toddler years, children

Toddler visual cliff experiment.

become increasingly experimental and curious about the world around them. The curious and the explorative nature of toddlers often creates dangerous situations for them. As a result of the overwhelming need to explore, toddlers often put aside fear and forge forward into situations where their safety is compromised. Statistically, household accidents, mainly falling from high surfaces, are the main cause of death in toddlers. The same infant who once had a fear of heights, is now ready to explore and jump from furniture and tabletops.

Learning to Walk

By around twelve months of age, American infants learn how to walk: first through crawling, then cruising (standing and holding onto objects while moving their bodies—simulated walk with assistance of objects), and eventually walking on their own. Human development is universal, but the order of developmental processes may not be the same and some steps may be skipped. For example, not all children go through crawling, cruising, and then starting to walk. Some may skip some of these developmental stages; however, all healthy children will eventually learn to walk. In Africa, children start to walk at around ten months; in France, toddlers learn to walk around fourteen months of age; in the United States, pediatricians expect babies to master the ability to walk by the time they have reached their first birthday (Berger, 2004). The ability to walk is a developmental milestone, which is influenced by cultural practices. In Africa, caregivers practice walking exercises with babies as young as six months old; therefore, African babies learn to walk very early on (Patterson, 2008). These

Beng Guide to Parenting Toddlers

The Beng are a small group of about sixty ethnic groups located in West African country of the Ivory Coast. Their population size is about 12,000 and lives in a geographical area between the rain forest to the south and the savanna to the north.

Teething—Baby's first teeth development starts with the lower tooth. It is a bad omen if your baby's first tooth comes from the top down or if it is born with teeth. In the past if this happened a female elder would be asked to drown such a baby or someone in the family would die. Today we do not do this because we would go to jail for murder. We now just worry and wonder who in the family may die.

Walking—It is a proud moment when your child starts to crawl, however they should not walk before the age of one. You may have to keep the child strapped to your back or spank the baby for trying to walk too early. Babies are reincarnations of our ancestors and have souls that cross over daily between these worlds and beyond. As a result babies and elders are closely connected and only have a fragile hold on life. An infant that walks too early treads on the spirit of their grandparents and may cause them to pass on to the other world.

If your child is over a year and has not started to walk yet you should do everything you can to encourage them. This may mean that you have started to have sex with your husband too early and may cause "split leg," which may result in your child never being able to walk. Remember that having sex before your child can walk is forbidden. You do not want to become pregnant before the first baby learns to walk and you stop breast-feeding. If you do your new baby in your belly will steal your breast water from your older child and they will eventually die. It is better that your husband has sex with your co-wife, if you have one or have him visit a prostitute than to have sex with you.

Talking—When your child learns to talk they should first learn all the words to refer to their relatives and all of the proper greetings. Then your child must learn how to tease certain relatives by tossing out dirty names at them. Relatives will tease your baby boy by calling him jokingly dirty names such as, "shit prick," "Red prick," "Raw shit scrotum" and your daughter names like, "Shit cunt," "Black cunt," or "Baby cunt."

Your child should learn to laughingly return the insults. For example, it is adorable to see a two-year-old yell to their grandmother, "you black asshole" or their grandfather "you red balls." It will be a comfort to your children as they grow older to have such a relaxing relationship with their grandparents and aunts and uncles.

Adapted from Gottlieb, 2000.

cultural differences, as well as the infant's biological growth, will lead to differences in timing and the infant's readiness to walk. As can be seen, the age and the method by which an infant learns to walk are different depending on the culture and traditional practices.

Play Time

Once infants reach early childhood, they thrive on active play time as they are working on improving and using their newfound motor skills. Boys tend to be more active than girls, and there is also evidence that genetics has an influence on activity level. In early childhood, boys can "jump higher, run faster and throw a ball farther than girls" (Patterson, 2008, p. 260). During early childhood, children are also learning and practicing their fine motor skills. As previously stated, large motor skills develop the use of the larger muscles of the body, such as for

▼ *Pictures of art done by children.*

Age 2½

Age 4

Age 5

Age 7

walking or grabbing. Fine motor skills are the ability to use the smaller muscles, such as for holding a pencil correctly or grasping an object. The acquisition of large or gross motor skills is evident in watching a child kick or throw a ball, and fine motor skill development is evident in the child's learning to hold a pencil or use scissors. The development of fine motor skills is also obvious when looking at children's art. Children start off by drawing scribbles, and as they get older they learn to draw detailed people and objects.

Brain Growth

Brain growth during infancy and early childhood is significant and largely based on experiences. Compared to all other organs in the body, the brain is the closest to adult size at birth; however, major changes occur during the first two years of life. Neurons in the brain begin to function by creating **synapses** (connections). It is through these synapses that neurons are able to communicate and send signals to one another. By two years of age, as many as 10,000 synapses have formed. If synapses are not stimulated by the environment, these connections eventually die. This is known as synaptic pruning and is a normal part of brain development (Patterson, 2008).

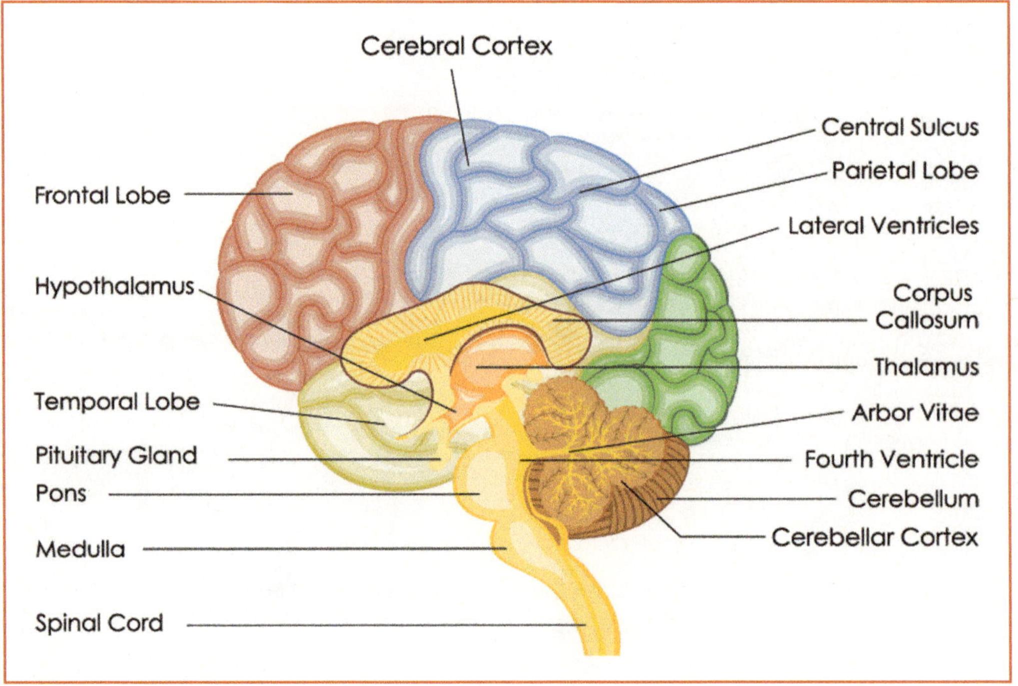

▲ *Parts of the brain.*

(Photo courtesy of stockshoppe/Shutterstock.com)

Overall, there tends to be an overproduction of synapses, followed by selective pruning. Throughout growth, the brain may also be influenced by uncommon situations and create new connections based on these experiences. This is known as **experience-dependent plasticity**. Synapses also form at different rates in different parts of the brain. For example, in the visual cortex, the peak of **synaptogenesis** (the forming of synapses) is reached at around six months of age (Patterson, 2008).

The cerebral cortex, the part of the brain that controls multiple human functions (such as seeing, hearing, reading, and writing), is separated into lobes and develops at different speeds. The cerebral cortex is divided into two hemispheres, and each hemisphere controls different functions. The left hemisphere generally controls logic and language and math. The right hemisphere generally controls special visual, artistic, and music skills. Between the ages of three to six years, the left hemisphere shows great activity and development, while the right hemisphere shows more activity between the ages of eight and ten years (Patterson, 2008).

Myelination is the process whereby neural axons (or nerve fiber) become coated with a fatty sheath of myelin. This occurs at different rates throughout the brain and is not complete until the end of adolescence. Picture a bunch of wires that are placed inside a cable in order to protect them from harmful elements.

Temperament of Infants and Toddlers

Temperament is the general way in which a person responds to different experiences in the world around him or her. There are different emotional styles that different people use when responding to these experiences; we call these temperaments. Temperaments include such opposing characteristics as shy/outgoing, active/calm, and aggressive/passive. We are born with these different temperament characteristics; however environment, can strengthen or weaken the trait.

Alexander Thomas and Stella Chess (1977, 1984) have been influential in the modern studies of temperament. They have developed nine temperament characteristics and three main temperament types. The nine temperament characteristics are: activity level, adaptability, approach or withdrawal, attention span, distractibility, intensity of reaction, quality of mood, rhythmicity, and threshold of responsiveness. The three temperament types are easy child, difficult child, and moderate child (or slow to warm up). The *easy child* generally has a positive mood and a positive approach (rather than withdrawing) when presented with new people, low or moderate intensity to reactions, high adaptability to new situations, and regularity in body functions and sleep. The easy child generally makes up about 40 percent of the American population. The *difficult child* is generally not regular in his or her bodily functions or sleep, usually has intense reactions, tends to withdraw in the face of new people, is not very adaptable to new situations, and is generally more negative in mood. About 10 percent of the American population is made up of the difficult child. The *moderate or slow to warm up child* has a low activity level, tends to withdraw in new situations and with new people when first exposed but warms up over time, and tends to respond with low intensity to new situations. This temperament type makes up about 15 percent of the American population. About 35 percent

Chess and Thomas's Temperaments*

DIMENSION OF TEMPERAMENT	EASY (40%)	MODERATE OR SLOW TO WARM UP (15%)	DIFFICULT (10%)
Activity Level: Proportion of active periods to inactive ones	Varies	Low to moderate	Varies
Adaptability: The ease with which a child adapts to changes in environment	Easily adaptable	Slow to adapt	Slow to adapt
Approach or Withdrawal: Response to new object or person	Positive approach	Initial withdrawal, then approachable	Withdrawal
Attention Span/Persistence: The amount of time devoted to an activity, and effect of distraction on the activity	Variable	Variable	Variable
Distractibility: The degree to which extraneous stimuli alter behavior	Variable	Variable	Variable
Intensity of Reaction to Event: The energy of response, regardless of the quality or direction	Mild	Mild	Intense
Quality of Mood: Amount of friendly, pleasant, joyful behavior as contrasted with unpleasant, unfriendly behavior	Positive	Slightly negative	Negative
Rhythmicity: Regularity of hunger, excretion, sleep, wakefulness	Very regular	Varies	Irregular
Threshold of Responsiveness: The intensity of stimulation required to evoke a discernible response	High or low	High or low	High or low

* Thirty-five percent of American children do not fit into any of these categories.

of the American population of infants and toddlers do not fit into any of these three temperament categories.

It is also important to remember that the labels and terms used by Chess and Thomas were designed for the American culture. They are highly culture specific, and have positive and negative connotations. The easy child implies traits that are desirable, and the difficult child implies undesirable traits. Many of the characteristics deemed desirable or undesirable can vary from culture to culture.

According to Chess and Thomas (1999) what is most important about these three temperaments is goodness of fit between the child's personality and the environment. For example, if a child does not do well with new environments with lots of people around, it is wise to try and avoid these kinds of situations unless the toddler is well rested and fed.

Do babies and toddlers maintain the temperament they are born with? This depends on many factors. Many children do maintain their temperament throughout their whole lives, while others do not. Environment and life events can play an important role. For example, if a child is shy, his or her life experiences can reinforce this shyness, making the child more shy. Life experiences can also encourage the shy child in new situations so he or she becomes less shy as he or she grows. Temperaments usually do not change drastically throughout life.

Temperament and Survival in the Maasai Culture

An unusual study (de Vries, 1987) was conducted with the Maasai people in Kenya, south of Tanzania. It looked at temperament and discovered that the more "difficult" child (versus the more "easy" child) had a much higher rate of survival in times of famine. Originally they tested twenty Maasai newborns for temperament. At this time a ten-year famine was in progress and worsened substantially after the infants were born. As a result many of the Maasai left the area or relocated. When the newborns were six to eight months of age the researchers could only locate thirteen of the twenty babies. Of the thirteen that they could locate, seven of them had been classified as "easy" babies and six as "difficult" babies. Five of the seven easy babies had died and only one of the difficult babies. To understand these results one needs to look at the Maasai culture.

The Maasai are traditionally nomadic and live in extended family groups; men often have several wives. They also have a prized warrior class. The Masai

The Maasai.

(Photo courtesy of nelik/Shutterstock.com)

mother also feeds her infant on demand. The more demanding and fussy a child is the more the child gets fed. The culture also values aggression and assertiveness and encourages this behavior in their children. M.W. de Vries (1987) concluded that the "difficult" child therefore got fed more often than the "easy" child and resulted in a higher survival rate in times of famine. Remember that the terms "difficult" and "easy" are very culture specific. They were determined by White middle-class social scientists studying American children.

The Maasai live in extended family groups and they all participate in raising the children together. Therefore, it is easier for a Maasai family group to raise a more demanding, difficult child than in the United States where there are generally only nuclear families and where the mother has to deal with a demanding child by herself. As a result American mothers prefer a less demanding, less fussy child than Maasai.

Maasai Pregnancy

On the average most Maasai women have six pregnancies in their lifetimes. Once a woman finds herself pregnant she is not to have sex until that child is weaned from breastfeeding at 1½ to 2 years of age. Her husband can only have sex with his other wives. This acts as a form of birth control and increases the likelihood of child survival because it spaces out pregnancies.

What is also interesting is the eating beliefs of pregnant women. Generally the diet of the Maasai consists of meat, milk, and blood from their herd animals.

Their vegetable intake is minimal. During the last three to four months of pregnancy the women goes on a "starvation diet" of drinking protein broth made from boiled lungs, livers, or kidneys mixed with bitter bark. The last month she generally only drinks milk. The reason for this diet is so that the birth "can proceed normally," possibly to ensure that the child is born smaller and therefore easier to birth than a larger baby.

CHAPTER 5 SUMMARY

In infancy and early childhood, physical development follows a general guideline and in most situations stays on the predicted path. When looking at body growth, cephalocaudal and proximodistal growth make it clear as to the order and predicted path in which children grow. On top of this, sensory and perceptual development, motor skill development, and brain development are all largely shaped on a child's experiences. If the child's environment does not provide certain experiences, those connections in the brain will eventually deteriorate. Conversely, constant exposure to certain situations will strengthen connections in the brain, therefore having an impact on development and improvement in these specific areas. There are variations in physical growth among children of the same age. These variations may be due to genetics, order of birth, the child's eating habits, the parenting style, and many environmental factors. As an example, Lily, a second child to her parents was born a half-pound heavier and one inch taller than her sister was at birth. This variation continued even in toddlerhood and later though adolescence. Lily was always physically bigger than her sister. This may have been due to Lily's genetic makeup, eating habits, choice of food, amount of activities, and other environmental influences. No two children are alike, and as mentioned, even in twin studies researchers have found 20 percent overall differences in identical twins.

CHAPTER 5 VOCABULARY

Cephalocaudel
Experience-Dependent Plasticity
Instinctive Reflexes
Myelination
Proximodistal
Synapses
Synaptogenesis
Temperament
Visual Cliff

Chapter 6

INFANT AND TODDLER
Cognitive Development

(Photo courtesy of Teresa Kasprzycka/Shutterstock.com)

Teddy Bear

By Margaret Goetz

He entered my life on my third birthday.
A big brown stuffed bear with shiny eyes
and real joints. I adored him.
Definitely a he, he never had a more sophisticated
name, Teddy Bear he remained.

He slept beside me every night, sat on my bed by day.
I told him stories, dressed him, fed him. I dragged
him along on many an adventure, even convinced Mom he could
not stay home when we drove around Europe for three
months when I was 7. He spent weeks in the hospital
with me when I was 10, and helped me be brave.
He cheerfully endured endless sessions of playing school,
watching childish performances and heard my fears and woes.

I took him to college when I moved away from home.
A mascot on my bed, though I had stopped talking to him
and thinking of him as real, it seemed he had to come along.
Alas, now he sits almost forgotten in a closet.
His fur is worn, his growler long silent, pads of his feet mended.
So faithful a friend, he needs a new place of honor.
But few will guess his history.

Introduction

Research about the cognitive development of infants and toddlers has taken many twists and turns as different theorists and research findings have presented many views. Earliest research in infant and toddler development has been traced to the seventeenth century when in 1601, the oldest son of the King of France was born and his childhood was observed and documented in a diary by his physician, Dr. Jean Heroard. This lengthy journal continued until the physician's death in 1628, which marks one of the earliest studies in infant and toddler behavior. In the eighteenth century, Dietrich Tiedemann, a German philosopher, kept a baby diary upon the birth of his son, and he recorded detailed observations on the behavior and development of his child. Tiedemann's detailed diary of his son is often referred to as the first scientific documentation of infants' and toddlers' development. In the nineteenth century, Charles Darwin, the greatest naturalist of all times, started his own observations of his son who was born in 1839, and later compared him to his other children. Darwin's publication of this baby diary gave the scientific world yet another powerful look into the world of children. Although these baby diaries mark the beginning of child development as a science, they were still lacking in details and individual differences because they were accounts of one particular child's development.

It was not until the twentieth century that scientists started to have a closer look at the cognitive development of infants and toddlers. For example, the famous cognitive theorist Jean Piaget started by making very detailed observations of his own three children. He extended his observations by also trying to understand their behaviors. He actively started to manipulate different cognitive tasks, and noted any changes that occurred as a result of these manipulations. Piaget's observations and cognitive experimentation with his own three children led him to develop the **discontinuity theory**, which is still influential in how scientists view human development today.

During the past fifty years, many observations and experiments about child development have been made by researchers to determine the cognitive abilities of infants and toddlers. Consequently, researchers have realized that, cognitively, children are capable of much more at a younger age than ever imagined. There are many theorists who have laid the framework for cognitive development, the most well-known being Jean Piaget and Vygotsky. Even though recent researchers have found some errors in Piaget's time frames, overall his concepts and theories laid the groundwork for cognitive development. Vygotsky also demonstrated that the context in which learning takes place is an important factor in the development of the child.

Jean Piaget's Cognitive Development Theory

Jean Piaget (1896–1980) was instrumental in laying the groundwork for what we know today about children's **cognitive development**. He described children as little scientists, as he believed that children explore their surroundings and environment to "figure things out." Through exploration, children go through the process of assimilation and accommodation, both of which are vital in the process of cognition growth.

Assimilation and Accommodation

Jean Piaget uses the term **assimilation** to describe infants, children, and adolescents' use of new and existing information or experiences. Assimilation is when a child uses newly gained or existing knowledge in new situations. For example,

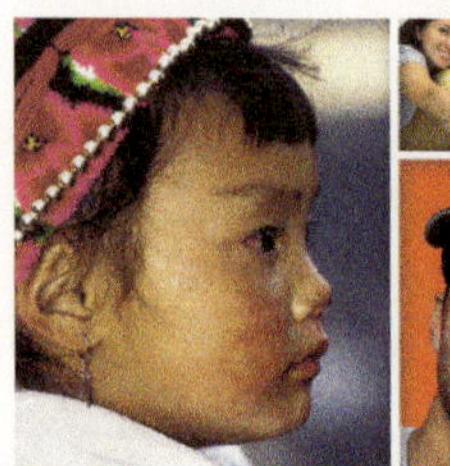

Jean Piaget

Jean Piaget (1896–1980) was born in Switzerland. His father was a professor of medieval literature. His mother he would refer to as neurotic later in life. His mother's behavior would eventually lead to his interest to the field of psychology. He received his doctoral degree at the age of twenty-two and was known as a developmental psychologist. In 1923 he married and had three children. He informally studied the development and behavior of his own children, which led to some of his most important and renowned work. Piaget believed that children are not less intelligent than adults, but just think differently.

an infant is born with the knowledge of sucking on his or her thumb while in the mother's womb. At birth, the newborn uses this existing experience of sucking the thumb in the situation of learning to suck on the mother's or a bottle's nipple. The knowledge of sucking the thumb being used on a different type of nipple is called "assimilation."

The modification the infant has to make in order to make the existing information fit into a new situation is called **accommodation.** In the same example, the newborn may find that the two types of sucking (on the thumb and on the nipple) are not quite the same. The infant may find that sucking on the nipple perhaps takes more work and energy. At this time, the infant starts to make adjustment to the method of sucking in order to be able to use an existing knowledge in a new situation.

Piaget asserts that through assimilation and accommodation children develop their own perception of the world. This means that children may change or alter their perception of the outside world in order to fit their internal view of the world. According to Piaget, children use an internalization process to understand and make sense of their world. Through assimilation, children use their external perception in new situations and through accommodation, they internalize what they have learned and make it into a new experience (Patterson, 2008).

Piaget also developed the concept of "schema." Children take old experiences and use them in new situations, and thus consequently develop new thoughts or experiences. These new thoughts and experiences are called **schemas.** Piaget describes schemas as organized concepts and patterns in the brain. For example, when two-year-olds experience a new event, they store it in their brain in a perceptional manner. This phenomenon indicates that two-year-olds have developed their own unique concepts and perceptions of the world around them and are able to put their thoughts into a **conceptual pattern.** These concepts are used as references for later actions and application of thoughts, and the child will be able to access these experience or schemas in later applications. For example, when a mother tells her two-year-old son that it is time for a bubble bath, the child knows the schema of a bath, because the experience is familiar to him.

Similar schemas are organized and stored together in the brain. As a result of this compartmentalization, new collections of related experiences are formed. Children use existing experiences (schemas) to make new ones all the time. The rapid development of schemas and consequent compartmentalization of these schemas allow a child to access information when faced with a similar situation. This process allows the child to constantly build new schemas and add to his or her cognitive abilities. Piaget believes that this process starts at birth when a child first starts using his or her reflexes.

Cognitive Functioning

Jean Piaget believed that children go through four main stages as they grow into adulthood:

1. The **sensorimotor stage** from birth to age two has six substages. In this stage, babies and toddlers mainly learn through sensory experiences and manipulating objects.
2. The **preoperational stage** from ages two to seven is the prelogic development of cognition. Children in this stage learn through pretend play, but have difficulty with logic and how others view things.

Piaget's Four Stages of Childhood Development

Sensorimotor	Birth–2 years	Babies and toddlers mainly learn through sensory experiences and manipulating objects.
Preoperational	2–7 years	Kids learn through pretend play but have difficulty with logic and how others view things.
Concrete Operational	7–11 years	Kids start to use more logic in their thinking but still struggle with more abstract concepts.
Formal Operational	11–adulthood	Teens' logical thinking continues to develop, along with more deductive thinking and understanding of the abstract.

3. The **concrete operational stage** from ages seven to eleven is the time children develop logical thoughts and learn to socialize. In this stage, children start to use more logic in their thinking, but still struggle with more abstract concepts.
4. In the **formal operational stage** from age eleven to adulthood, teens' logical thinking continues to develop, along with more deductive thinking and understanding of abstract concepts.

In this chapter, we discuss the sensorimotor and preoperational stages in greater detail; the other stages are discussed in later chapters.

Piaget's Six Sensorimotor Substages

Jean Piaget is also responsible for a major breakdown of expected levels of cognitive functioning, as he created **six sensorimotor substages** in his theory of cognitive development. Piaget determined that children go through these sensorimotor stages from birth to two years. The first two years of an infant's life is mostly spent discovering the surrounding environment. Infants know very little about the world around them; however, their curious nature kicks in and they enter the zone of discovery wanting to explore their environment. In the first substage, babies use their **reflexes**, which are innate, involuntary, and automatic responses to environmental stimuli, to make sense of the world. These reflexes enable the infant to survive and make connections with the environment. For example, babies use crying to make a connection and communicate with their caregiver; therefore, crying as a reflex serves babies to get their needs met. This substage takes place from birth to one month old.

In the second substage, between the ages of one and four months of age, babies explore different movements of their body, and how their body relates to them. During these times, infants' own motor activity creates experiences that result in pleasure for the baby. This is called **primary circular reactions**. It is called "primary" because the focal point of the baby's attention is his or her own body. "Circular reaction" indicates that the baby finds pleasure in doing these movements, continues to repeat them, and is fascinated by them. These are babies' first outside experiences that will build schemas for further cognitive development. In this stage, children are focusing on using their reflexive behavior and repetition of these movements, but have no understanding of cause and effect. These repetitive motions, such as shaking a rattle, excessive sucking on their thumb, and putting their toes in their mouths, allow infants to use their bodies to get physical gratification.

Baby sucking on his/her toes is an example of primary circular reactions.

(Photo courtesy of Shyamalamuralinath/ Shutterstock.com)

In substage three, children between the ages of four and eight months repeat actions in order to create an interesting effect. At this point, children are beginning to control events outside of their bodies. This is referred to as **secondary circular reactions**. Similar to primary circular reactions, in the secondary circular substage, the baby's main objective is to explore the outside world and to build further schemas. For example, a baby's attempt to hit the mobile above the crib is an indication that the baby's focus has now extended from his or her body to items separate from him- or herself. As the baby touches the mobile, it moves and the baby discovers how this object is part of something else, thus recognizing his/her own existence separate from the environment.

Baby reaching for mobile is an example of secondary circular reactions.

(Photo courtesy of wavebreakmedia/ Shutterstock.com)

Piaget's Six Sensorimotor Substages (Birth–2 years)

Babies and toddlers mainly learn through sensory experiences and manipulating objects.			
Substage 1	Reflexes	Birth–1 month	Explore innate and involuntary physical responses to environmental stimuli.
Substage 2	Primary circular reactions	1–4 months	Explore different movements of their body, and how it relates to them. This results in pleasure.
Substage 3	Secondary circular reactions	4–8 months	Repeat actions in order to create an interesting effect. Babies are beginning to control events outside of their bodies.
Substage 4	Coordination of secondary circular reactions	8–12 months	Coordinate their actions and are more goal directed. Understand cause and effect.
Substage 5	Tertiary circular reactions	12–18 months	Use trial and errors to problem solve.
Substage 6	Symbolic thoughts	18–24 months	Work on mental combinations and are able to pretend play and imitate the actions of others.

Another example would be when a baby is sucking on his or her toe and notices the parent's favorable reaction. After all, to an adult it is funny to see a baby with a toe in his or her mouth, sucking away. The baby's noticing of the adult's positive reaction encourages the baby to continue to suck his or her toe and even join in the parent's laughter.

Substage four is the **coordination of secondary circular reactions**, which is a cause-and-effect relationship. Infants begin to coordinate actions according to what purpose or goal an action will lead to. For example, if an infant notices his or her security blanket is nearby and can reach a corner of it, rather than crawling to grab it, the infant will pull on the corner of the object to gain possession of it. This is a goal-oriented action that combines existing knowledge and previously learned experiences. At this substage, which takes place between eight and twelve months, children begin to have some understanding of cause and effect. In addition, the acquisition of object permanence develops during this substage, which is the realization that objects can still exist even if they cannot be seen. The saying, "out of sight" does not always mean "out of mind."

Object Permanence

Object permanence is yet another important concept that Piaget brought to cognitive development. Early in the sensorimotor development, out of sight to an infant means out of mind; however, development of object permanence enables the child to understand that objects still exist even after disappearing. Piaget believed that due to lack of representational thoughts, an infant does not have a mental picture of items; therefore, it cannot relate to its continuous existence. The understanding of object permanence enables an infant to understand the continuity and the co-existence of things. The idea that objects or people do not just disappear when they are out of sight is a very important concept for children to understand.

Piaget (1963) believed that children's understanding of object permanence starts around the age of eight months; however, this is not universally agreed upon. Researcher Renee Baillargeon challenged this idea and discovered that it is possible for children as young as four months old to show some understanding of object permanence. An example of this is playing peak-a-boo with an infant. The baby realizes that you are simply hiding your face and that it will reappear, and might even attempt to find your face again by forcing your hands open.

In substage five, children are exploring their **tertiary circular reactions**, and are starting to use trial and error to problem solve. This takes place between twelve and eighteen months of age. Infants at this stage show a lot more creativity and association between items and ideas. For example, they will use more perseverance to look for items or to figure toys out in order to

Mom and child playing peak-a-boo is an example of object permanence.

(Photo courtesy of Dejan Ristovski/ Shutterstock.com)

gain better understanding of the functioning of objects. Piaget often experimented on his own children to develop his cognitive theory. Here's an example of Piaget explaining tertiary circular reaction by observing his own daughter Jacqueline at fourteen months old:

> Jacqueline holds in her hands, an object which is new to her; a round, flat box, which she turns all over, shakes, rubs against the basinet, etc. She lets it go and tries to pick it up. But she only succeeds in touching it with her index finger, without grasping it. She nevertheless makes an attempt and presses on the edge. The box then tilts up and falls again. Jacqueline, very much interested in this fortuitous result, immediately applies herself to studying it . . .
>
> Jacqueline immediately rests the box on the ground and pushes it as far as possible (it is noteworthy that care is taken to push the box far away in order to reproduce the same conditions as the first attempt, as though this were a necessary condition for obtaining the result). Afterward, Jacqueline puts her finger on the box and presses it. But as she places her finger on the center of the box she simply displaces it and makes it slide instead of tilting it up. She amuses herself with this game and keeps it up (resumes it after intervals, etc.) for several minutes. Then, changing the point of contact, she finally again places her finger on the edge of the box, which tilts up. She repeats this many times, varying the conditions, but keeping track of her discoveries: Now she only presses on the edge! (Piaget, 1952, p. 272)

The sixth substage takes place between the ages of eighteen and twenty-four months, and is the development of **symbolic thoughts**. In this substage, children work on combining mental processes of pretend play, and imitating the actions of others. The symbolic thoughts substage involves children's ability to use their thoughts in a symbolic and representational manner. This means that a child will use his or her thoughts in terms of understanding the object and what it represents in terms of their own internal and mental existence. For example, a two-year-old may be playing with her older sister, who is pretending to be a princess. The two-year-old also dresses up as a princess, copying her older sister. The fact that the two-year-old has the capacity to remember, copy, and imitate others' behavior shows the child's capability in using representational thoughts. This newfound cognitive ability enables the child to understand that thoughts represent an action or object. Of course, Piaget believed that the ability to copy and imitate in this age is limited and still needs to be improved and advanced.

We use these sensorimotor substages as we grow and mature, well into our adulthood. Even as adults, we continue to shape our behavior using perceptual and representational schemas that we learned as infants. These early stages of cognitive development and the skills we acquired as infants continue

◄ ***Girls playing dress-up is an example of symbolic thought.***

(Photo courtesy of Cindy Donham)

to help us figure out new situations and perform trial-and-error experimentations in new situations.

Preoperational Thought Stage (Ages 2–7)

Jean Piaget believed that once children left the sensorimotor stage at two years of age they then faced the stage of **preoperational thought**. While in the stage of preoperational thought, children start to become more capable of representational thought or pretend play. Based on Piaget's cognitive theory, during this stage children face three main limitations. First, children face **egocentrism**. They have trouble seeing things from any view other than their own. Like Lev Vygotsky, Piaget believed that a child uses language primarily to communicate to him- or herself in order to address his or her own needs and wants. During play, egocentric children use language merely to reflect their own thoughts and ideas. Talking to themselves is just a way of reassuring their internal thoughts to themselves and others. Therefore, the egocentric nature of children directs them towards concentrating only on what they want, using language to communicate with adults about things that interest them.

Piaget's Preoperational Thought Stage (Ages 2–7)

Characteristics of Limitations of Logical Thinking: Kids learn through pretend play but have difficulty with logic and how others view things.	
Egocentrism	Children are starting to become more capable of representational thought or pretend play. They have trouble seeing things from any view other than their own.
Conservation	Children perceive some properties of objects remain the same, even while other properties are changing.
Logical Inferences	Children are unable to put objects/people within an ordered series.

The egocentric view also prevents children from seeing others' views. This means that children believe that what they know about a subject is exactly what the adults know. That is why it is hard to argue or make a point with a three-year-old. In the egocentrism stage, a child's own opinion and thoughts about people and things are the most important and most valid to him- or herself. What others think about the matter is not important or even considered at all.

Distinguishing between subjective and objective matters is also very difficult for this age group; it is a skill that is to be learned in the next developmental stage. Children in the preschool years have not yet developed the ability to differentiate between the external world and their own internal world. In other words, egocentrism is still interpreting the world around them, based on their terms.

An example of egocentrism would be when a child's toy is broken, and the child becomes visibly upset about it. The adult may be reassuring the child that it is not a big deal or that the toy can be fixed. It would be unlikely for the child at this age to believe the reassurance of the adult because at the moment what the child sees and knows is his or her favorite toy is broken and nothing can fix it. Another example would be if you ask a three-year-old what would be a good birthday present for Mommy, most likely the child would pick an item that is a favorite of his or hers, such as a truck or a doll or something similar. It would be hard for a three-year-old to understand that other people have different likes and dislikes because the child's world is constructed based on his or her own opinion and perceptions.

Second, children face the issue of **conservation**. This is when children in the preschool stage believe that some properties of objects remain the same, even after the properties change. Children in this stage do not yet understand concepts that involve area, amount, numbers, and length. Toward the end of preoperational thought, some children are starting to grasp these concepts; however, only in the most basic way. Third, Piaget believed that children are not able to have adult-like conversations and dialogue, as they are unable to

Summary of Developmental Milestones in First Few Years of Life

AGE	MILESTONE
3 Months	▪ Begins to babble ▪ First smile ▪ Brings hand to mouth ▪ Starts to see some colors
7 Months	▪ Babbles strings of sounds ▪ Can see all colors ▪ Responds to name ▪ Transfers objects from hand to hand ▪ Responds to emotions by tone of voice spoken to them ▪ Starts to crawl
1 Year	▪ Bangs two objects together ▪ Starts to walk by holding onto objects ▪ Cries when parent leaves ▪ Finds objects even when they are hidden under blanket ▪ Starts to sit on their own ▪ Starts to talk
2 Years	▪ Begins make-believe play ▪ Begins to run ▪ Begins to show defiant behavior; says "NO" a great deal ▪ Begins to sort by shapes and colors ▪ Says two to four word sentences ▪ Turns over containers to pour out contents ▪ Begins to walk up and down stairs holding onto support
3 Years	▪ Can ride a tricycle ▪ Expresses affection openly ▪ Sorts objects by shape and color
4 Years	▪ Starts to cooperate with other children ▪ Uses scissors ▪ Walks up and down stairs without support
5 Years	▪ Dresses and undresses on their own ▪ Learns to tie shoes ▪ Uses a fork and spoon to eat

put objects/people within an ordered series. The age that young children understand conservation and logical inferences is being challenged in modern research. There are indications that it may start at a much younger age than two years.

Lev Vygotsky: Sociocultural Learning Theory

Unlike Jean Piaget, Lev Vygotsky had more of a sociocultural approach to cognitive development, as he believed that the context in which learning takes place is extremely important. He formulated the sociocultural learning theory that believes younger children develop lower mental capacities first, including simple perceptions and involuntary attention. Children eventually build on their basic thought processes and mentally become more sophisticated, through interaction with adults and social interaction with others.

Lev Vygotsky also realized that parents and other role models in children's lives play a very important part in guiding and assisting children so that they are able to develop to their fullest potential. One of Vygotsky's most important concepts is the idea of **scaffolding**, which is the step-by-step guidance and teaching that adults provide to help the child participate and learn. Examples of scaffolding may be found when children are allowed to participate in family activities. In this way, adults teach, set limits, and provide lessons for the child to learn (Plumert & Nichols-Whitehead, 1996). In this concept, adults help the child only when necessary and help just enough to allow the child to complete the task. Over time, adults gradually withdraw the support they have been giving to let the child master the task independently and on their own.

Zone of Proximal Development

Lev Vygotsky (1978) also generated the idea of the **zone of proximal development** (ZPD), which refers to the difference in what the child can do with and without help. This concept implies that there is a gap between what children can do independently and the degree of adult supervision needed to complete the task. Because adults play the important role of guidance counselors in helping children grow and develop through the ZPD, adults can gauge how much a

Lev Vygotsky

Lev Vygotsky was born in Russia and died at age 37 in 1934. He had a cultural/psychological approach to child development. His findings were not translated into other languages until decades later, which delayed the scientific world's access to his significant findings. It is widely believed that the scientific field of human development would have taken a more sociocultural direction if his body of work had been translated earlier.

child has learned and how much learning the child can handle for the next wave of teaching. In summary, in Vygotsky's theory, the adult becomes the teacher and the child becomes the apprentice. An effective teacher is constantly looking for opportunities to teach and to test the pupil's level of understanding. When the pupil is ready to move to the next level, the adult or the teacher will provide the learning material. Vygotsky determined that children's development is based on what they know and how well the adult teaches them. In this theory, an important and heavy responsibility is put on adults to constantly look for teaching opportunities and at the same time engage the child. This type of development is called **sociocultural learning** because it relies heavily on the child's environment, particularly the adults to decide what the child needs to learn. Vygotsky's theory on sociocultural learning has been criticized for having children rely solely on adult guidance and for not including the fact that children at times want to learn on their own.

Lev Vygotsky was also intrigued by children's use of **private speech** or when children talk out loud to themselves. He found that children use the method of talking out loud to review, plan, and reevaluate their thoughts. Looking at a preschool classroom setting, one will see four- and five-year-olds talking out loud as they are playing. It is obvious that they are not talking to a particular audience, but merely talking to themselves as they are planning their moves. Young children are more likely to use private speech when working on something challenging, using it to help direct them in their activity. The use of private speech by young children usually takes the form of a loud conversation, but as they grow older and during school years, their private speech becomes quieter and more whisper like. Adults also use private speech; however, this strategy is mostly done quietly.

Lev Vygotsky believed that children benefit from **cooperative learning** or learning that takes place through group interaction. Through working in groups and being able to talk it out with others, children are more likely to be able to solve a problem that they could not have solved alone. In cooperative learning, children learn from each other while learning new tasks. Through ZPD, a child can accomplish tasks on his or her own as well as learn from adults and peers. In other words, ZPD requires the use of a cooperative learning strategy. Children can accomplish tasks on their own and also learn from others. Cooperative learning is an important part of a child's social learning.

CHAPTER 6 SUMMARY

All of these theories and researchers laid the groundwork for everything known today about cognitive development. Through the researchers' search for understanding cognitive development, people today are able to understand and appreciate the process/stages of cognitive development. Early on, researchers such as John Watson believed that children are passive learners and they can be conditioned easily. This philosophy led adults to believe that children are not capable of developing thoughts on their own and are dependent on adults for their cognitive development. Scientists such as Jean Piaget and Lev Vygotsky revolutionized the field of research on children's thought processes. Through extensive research, both scientists brought awareness to the scientific world that children are capable of thinking, developing thoughts, building experiences, and using their schemas. Due to Piaget's research, today we know that children are active learners and they are capable of deductive reasoning and thinking on their own. Soon after birth and through the processes of building schemas, assimilation, accommodation, and adult-guided participation, children learn to think for themselves.

CHAPTER 6 VOCABULARY

Accommodation
Assimilation
Cognitive Development
Conceptual Pattern
Concrete Operational Stage
Conservation
Cooperative Learning
Coordination of Secondary Circular Reactions
Discontinuity Theory
Egocentrism
Formal Operational Stage
Object Permanence
Preoperational Stage
Preoperational Thought
Primary Circular Reactions
Private Speech
Reflexes
Scaffolding
Schema
Secondary Circular Reactions
Sensorimotor Stage
Six Sensorimotor Substages
Sociocultural Learning
Symbolic Thoughts
Tertiary Circular Reactions
Zone of Proximal Development

Chapter 7

INFANT AND TODDLER Psychosocial Development

(Photograph courtesy of Cynthia Donham)

Introduction

When Lily was first born, she seemed to be an easygoing child. Her eating and sleeping habits were consistent, easy, and on schedule. She was not a fussy baby and she seemed to be happy most of the time. Her needs did not disrupt the rest of the family's daily routines, including the busy schedule of her four-year-old sibling. This meant that Lily's mom Kathy would be taking the older sister to dance class, gymnastics, and karate classes while Lily was in tow, either in her stroller or in her little car seat. Up to eight months of age, Lily seemed to be a friendly and happy infant. Around nine months, Lily's personality started to change. This change was drastic to the point that when Lily was out and about with her family, she would cry at the sight of a stranger or when in an unfamiliar place. At times, if Lily could not see where her mother was or could not get a glimpse of her, she would start screaming or even shrieking. She would not be comforted until her mom picked her up and talked to her. At times, Lily would not give up easily and would continue to cry even after she had been picked up.

At home, if Kathy left Lily even for a minute, she would show the same reaction of anxiety. This was particularly hard on Grandma and Grandpa who would visit often, but would have to face Lily's reaction as if she had never met them before. Lily would still cry or shriek if Grandpa or Grandma tried to hold her or even talk to her. So, what happened to that easygoing, happy-go-lucky infant? Well, it is safe to say that these types of reactions to strangers are all part of normal development. Two developmentally important concepts happen as infants grow up physically, their social interactions increase, and they are introduced to more new situations or new people. Self-concept development and stranger wariness are what developmentalists expect infants to experience as they grow older.

Development of Emotions

Emotions are heightened human feelings that are apparent at birth, which once expressed allow us to externalize internal and physiological states of being. A study by Carroll Izard (1991, 1992) concluded that these physiological reactions are innate and apparent at birth as newborns show an array of discrete emotions.

Basic Emotions

Basic emotions are strong feelings that one experiences or expresses in accordance to facing an event, remembering a memory-thought, or encountering a challenge. Parents will learn to distinguish the emotions of their child and this helps the infant to communicate more effectively with his or her caregivers. Researchers use facial expressions to study an infant's emotional being. In infants, emotions are usually related to the state of physical comfort. An infant whose physical needs have been met most likely will be happy. As cognition develops and infants gain further mental capacities, their happiness depends more on psychological reasons rather than physiological causes. The emergence of fear is believed to take place around the time the infant is believed to gain self-awareness (around four to six months old).

Primary Emotions

Emotions fall into two categories: primary (basic) and secondary (complex) emotions. There are six **primary emotions**: sadness, happiness, surprise, fear, disgust, and anger. These feelings are reactions to situations or experiences. In

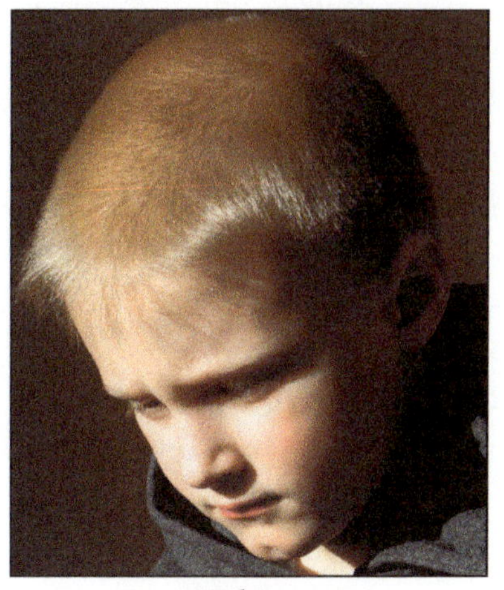

Sadness

Happiness

Surprise

Fear

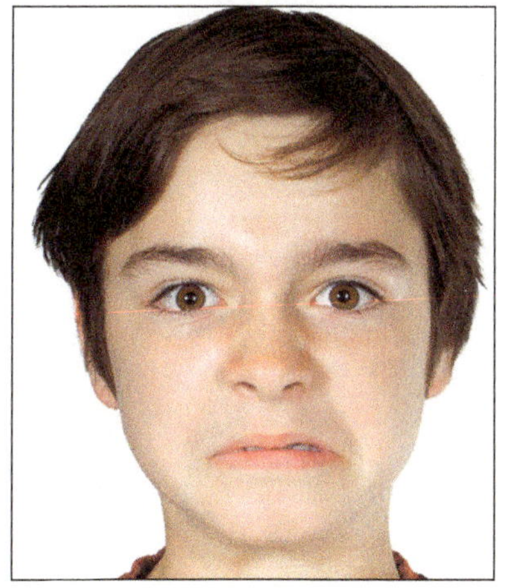

Disgust

Anger

Photos courtesy of Shutterstock.com

the case of a newborn, altered behavior—crying or fussing or screaming—may be a response to stress. In an experimentation by Izard (1983), the facial expressions of newborns were studied for signs of stress, anger, surprise, sadness, happiness, and contentment. The study showed that, universally, infants and adults show the same facial expressions to convey basic emotions. All human babies are born with the ability to show basic emotions.

Primary emotions are culturally universal. For example, across the globe everyone laughs when they hear a funny joke; however, what is funny varies among different cultures. Laughing or smiling indicates the emotion of happiness and is expressed the same way in all cultures. Universally, crying usually indicates sadness or extreme happiness.

Secondary Emotions

Secondary or complex emotions are subjective and culturally bound feelings such as shame, guilt, or embarrassment. This type of emotion is based on cultural teaching, the do's and don'ts taught to children, what is proper and what is not proper both socially and culturally. Due to the development of self-awareness, at about eighteen to twenty-four months of age the child gradually grasps the ideas of externally set standards or what is considered emotionally appropriate. Because secondary emotions are based on learning societal and cultural norms, what one can be proud of in one culture may not be the same in another, and what one should be ashamed about is different in various cultures and societies.

Secondary emotions are more complicated and the projection of these types of feelings requires a more in-depth knowledge of the culture and the environmental setting. For example, in order to project pride or be embarrassed, one needs to rely on contextual and environmental beliefs rather than depending on physical needs. These emotions require a more in-depth understanding of what is expected of oneself. That is why secondary emotions develop about the same time that self-concept emerges.

Development of Self-Awareness

Self-awareness is a developmental stage where children learn that their existence is separate from others and the environment; this usually happens around three to four months of age when a child will start to notice his or her environment and show reactions. Development of self-awareness helps infants to establish relationships with the environment and the people who surround them. For example, when a six-month-old baby starts to point at objects and simultaneously look at the parent for reaction, it shows the child has self-awareness. The child now notices objects and people as separate beings not part of the child.

MILESTONE	DESCRIPTION OF MILESTONE	TIMING OF MILESTONE	EXAMPLE OF MILESTONE
Development of Emotions	Primary or basic (physiological) and later secondary or complex (cultural)	Primary: Soon after birth Secondary: 18–24 months	Basic/primary: Fear, happy, sad Secondary/complex: Pride, shame, guilt
Development of Self-Awareness	Knowing and understanding that you exist separate from others	3–4 months	Infants will start smiling only at people they know. This new change in behavior indicates that infants have moved from social smiles (indiscriminate smiles at everyone) to only smiling at people they know, thus being aware that they are independent beings and part of the environment.
Stranger-Wariness	Fear of strangers	4–6 months	Cries when approached by a stranger.
Separation Anxiety	Infant fears being separated from the primary caregiver	6–9 months	Emotional meltdown as parents/main caregivers leave.
Self-Concept	The perception a person develops of him- or herself, and the process of gathering information from others and forming a view of him- or herself. As a result children start to become more aware of their immediate environment.	18–24 months	I am a girl/boy; I like ice cream; my favorite color is red
Self-Identity	This is having a clear and definite cognitive understanding of who you are and how you fit into the world around you.	Starts in the first year and continues into the adolescent years, where it is finalized.	I want to be a firefighter, a dancer, a teacher; I am like my mother, aunt, or grandpa

Stranger-Wariness

Stranger-wariness is the fear of a stranger. Stranger-wariness is a sign that the infant is developing self-awareness and becoming aware of his or her environment. Self-awareness allows infants to recognize and be aware of what is going on around them, thus differentiating between what is familiar and unfamiliar to them. This usually occurs at about four to six months.

Separation Anxiety

Separation anxiety is also part of a baby's first year of developmental growth. At around six to nine months, infants start to react to being separated from their primary caregiver. During the first six months of their lives, infants show very little reaction to being left with a stranger or a new babysitter or someone other than their main caregiver. However, around six months of age and older, many children start to show a great deal of objection with an unfamiliar person. Separation anxiety is a developmental stage that supersedes development of stranger-wariness in a series of developmental stages of growths.

Self-Concept

Self-concept is the process of gathering information about yourself from others around you and then applying this information to your own understanding of yourself. This newfound knowledge about themselves makes infants more aware of others (Cole, Maxwell, Martin, Peeke, Seroczynski, Tram, & Maschman, 2001). Infants develop their first ideas about "self" between eighteen and twenty-four months of age. People are continually updating and changing their self-concept throughout their whole lives. The ability to develop self-concept stems from the biological maturation of the brain combined with the environmental influences that teach children the expectations of people around them. The **"mirror and rouge" experiment** demonstrates the developmental process of children's self-concept (Butterworth 1990; Schneider-Rosen & Cicchetti, 1991).

Mirror and Rouge, the Development of Self-Concept

A marking of lipstick was put on a nine-month-old baby's nose and the child brought to a mirror. Researchers were looking to see whether the infant would notice the red marking on his or her nose. They found that nine-month-olds were interested in investigating the reflections in the mirror but did not notice anything different about their appearance. The conclusion the researchers made was that in order for a nine-month-old to notice the marking on his or her nose, the infant first needs to have an idea of what his or her face looks like. The infant's lack of understanding of his or her own facial characteristics prevents the infant from noticing the red marking on his or her face and recognizing that it is not a normal part of his or her face. This same procedure was repeated with toddlers who were twenty months old, and as soon as they were brought to the

◄ ***A child around eighteen months old starts to recognize the red mark on their nose.***

(Photo courtesy of Your image/Shutterstock.com)

mirror, they immediately noticed the red mark on their nose. This demonstrates they had developed a self-concept and knew what they looked like.

Self-Identity

Self-concept development will later lead to self-esteem and self-identity development. **Self-identity** is having a clear and definite cognitive understanding of who you are and how you fit into the world around you. This starts in the first year and continues into adolescent years.

Erikson's Theory: Infants' and Toddlers' Development of Personality

Erik Erikson was one theorist that developed a comprehensive theory explaining human development from infancy throughout the life span. Erikson's psychoanalytical theory has expansive views on each stage of life, particularly the first few years, which are marked with many important milestones. Let us review some of these milestone that infants and toddlers face in the first few years of development.

The importance of Erikson's psychosocial theory is the fact that he considers social settings and personal experiences as part of human development. On the other hand, Sigmund Freud, who pioneered the psychoanalytical theory, believed in psychological and biological drives and forces as having the sole part in child development. He believed that these biological and psychological drives were instrumental in emphasizing early life's experiences and had an impact on later development. Freud's and other early views on human development did not consider contextual, environmental, and cultural experiences as being important in development. Erikson's theory is important because it was one of the first theories that offered an extensive view of a child's personality development from personal experiences and the social environment.

Erikson's psychoanalytical theory is based on eight stages of development starting in infancy and ending with late adulthood. Each stage is based on a series of challenges and crisis. According to Erikson, during each stage of development, the child tries to meet the challenge within that stage. If the challenges are successfully met, the child can move to the next stage. However, if the child fails to meet these challenges successfully, then the child will encounter a crisis. Children who face a crisis in any given developmental stage will not be able to successfully enter the next stage and consequently will have to carry the burden of the previous stage into the new stage. In this chapter we look at the first three of Erikson's developmental stages: trust, bonding, and attachment (Charlesworth, 2011 & 2008).

Trust

The first stage of Erikson's psychoanalytical theory is **trust versus mistrust**, which means the challenge the infant faces is to establish trust between him- or herself and the environment; the crisis would be mistrust if caregivers somehow failed to meet all of the infant's needs. Erikson's first stage also explains that it is the quality of care that establishes trust between the newborn and its caregivers. His outlook is similar to Freud's view on the importance of feeding and biological needs during the infancy period. Establishment of trust between the infant and the caregiver means taking time to attend to the newborn's every need. Socially, infants need to gain the trust between themselves and the environment. This trust is helped by a two-directional relationship between the infant and the caregiver. As the needs of the newborn are met, the level of trust between the infant and its environment increases.

Bonding

The second stage is the concept of **bonding**, which is a physical relationship between an infant and its caregiver. Bonding is an immediate and physical relationship that develops soon after birth. In today's hospitals, right after birth, the newborn and mother are reunited so that bonding can start to take place. As time passes and the trust between the infant and the mother is built, the bonding grows stronger. The infant knows whom to trust for basic necessities such as food, getting picked up, and other needs. Gradually, as bonding takes place, this developmental stage will give way to the development of attachment.

Attachment

Attachment is the third stage and is an emotional, invisible, and bidirectional relationship between the toddler and the main caregiver. This stage usually takes place between nine and twenty-four months of age. Attachment is the ability to trust and use the main caregiver as security, particularly when a child is faced with stressful situations. Infants use this emotional tie to seek out the proximity of the main caretaker in times of stress. They learn to explore the environment in the presence of that caretaker.

Harry Harlow (1905–1981) performed a series of experiments on the impact of attachment on baby monkeys, experiments that were later instrumental in understanding the relationship between humans and their offspring. In pursuing and challenging Freud's (1856–1939) earlier claim that human babies' only care about food and any substance that feeds their internal hunger, Harlow set out to show that love is more important than food. He believed that, ultimately, humans value love and security above all other basic needs. Of course, ethical codes forbid this type of experimentation to be performed on human beings; therefore, monkeys were used.

A set of baby monkeys were separated from their mothers and consequently raised by two types of mechanical mothers; a cloth monkey with no milk, and a wire monkey that had milk. During the course of the study, it was shown that the baby monkey spent seventeen hours on the cloth mother and only spent time with the wire monkey during feeding time, thus indicating that comfort was more important than food. A mechanical device was used to scare the monkey and consequently to raise the level of its stress. The wire mother with food is brought into the environment to see whether the baby monkey will use it as a base for security (no cloth mother is available). The baby monkey did not use the wire monkey, and did not even acknowledge its presence. This demonstrates that the wire monkey represents a source of food, not comfort. The second time around, the baby monkey's level of stress was increased by the presence of the mechanical device, but the cloth mother monkey was brought in instead of the wire mother. Upon seeing the cloth mother, the baby monkey ran to it for comfort and shortly after started to explore the unfamiliar environment and play.

Attachment is an important milestone that takes place from nine to twenty-four months of age. Children who originally bond with a primary caregiver will eventually move on to develop other attachments. This milestone is important as it teaches children to create an invisible and emotional tie with a human figure who provides security. Most of the studies done on attachment and infant–parent bonding focus on the mother–child relationship as the main characteristics of attachment. Studies by Freud, Harlow, Ainsworth, and Bowlby see the mother–infant relationship as being the focal point in the development of attachment. Cross culturally, these studies also lay the foundation for a mother–infant orientation when it comes to researching attachment. Historically, theorists have always believed that a mother–infant relationship that is trusting and contains unconditional love sets the proper foundation for secure attachment. This type of thinking does not leave much room for the father to play a role in establishing secure attachment. After his experiments with monkeys, Harlow claimed that attachment develops between an infant and a caregiver. This is usually the mother, but can be the father or other caretakers.

Following Harry Harlow's study of attachment, Mary Ainsworth and John Bowlby continued researching types of attachment. In their experiments, Ainsworth put toddlers in new or stressful situations to see whether or not they follow the same actions as established by Harlow's monkey experiments. Bowlby and Ainsworth found early on that parent and child establish a two-way reciprocal relationship. In response to the child's behavioral reactions in different situations, parents will modify their behavior in order to better respond to their child's emotional needs.

Attachment Types

Ainsworth and Bowlby found that human infants tend to develop secure attachments, and in cases where this does not happen then insecure attachments result. Secure attachments are vital to future developmental stages. Children who have established secure attachments early on will benefit later during school and adolescent years. Insecure attachment has been categorized as four different types: avoidant, ambivalent, disorganized (disoriented), and resistant. Each one of these insecure attachments demonstrates specific characteristics that clearly explain a negative reciprocal relationship between the child and parent.

Secure Attachment (Type 1)

Secure attachment requires that the child has already accomplished the development of self-awareness and self-concept. During the second year of life, self-awareness and self-concept will eventually lead to the development of attachment. Mothers who are sensitive and responsive to their children's needs in addition to having a healthy reciprocal relationship with them, have connected in a securely attached manner with their children. Children of these mothers get upset when the mother leaves the room, but upon seeing her, will go to their mother to get comfort. They use the mother as a secure base to receive comfort and to explore the environment in her presence. About two-thirds of American children have established a secure attachment with their mothers. The ability to establish secure attachments in the early stages of development will be instrumental during the school and adolescent years because it teaches children from the start the art of establishing a bi-directional, reciprocal, and trusting relationship. Securely attached children are more successful in making social ties with others and in maintaining a healthy connection.

Insecure Avoidant Attachment (Type 2)

In stressful situations, when the child does not seek the proximity of the mother, the insecurity is identified as **insecure avoidant attachment**. When left in an unfamiliar environment these children may show distress; however, when the mother returns to comfort them, they show no interest in using her as a secure base. This phenomenon is an indication that the children do not see the mother as a secure base and do not seek comfort in her presence. This connection between parent and child is not a healthy relationship. Researchers theorize that there is a lack of trust or perhaps anger that prevents the child from making a connection with the mother. In the future, these children may have problems making connections to others and, therefore, may suffer from inabilities to form secure relationships. It is thought that 20 percent of American children may fall into this category.

Ambivalent Insecure Attachment (Type 3)

Ambivalent insecure attachment is when infants are faced with a new and stressful situation, and show both a positive and negative aggressive reaction to the mother when she tries to comfort them. For example, even though the child shows great distress when the mother leaves and upon her return seeks her out, once the child is hugged the child tries to kick her and get away. Children with ambivalent insecure attachment are not sure of how to react to their mother. It is believed about 12 percent of children in the United States suffer from this type of insecurity.

Disorganized (Disoriented) Insecure Attachment (Type 4)

Children who fall into **disorganized insecure attachment** suffer from inconsistent behavior toward the mother. For example, upon the mother's arrival the

Types of Attachments

TYPE OF ATTACHMENT (9–24 MONTHS)	CHARACTERISTICS OF RELATIONSHIP	CHILD'S BEHAVIOR IN A STRANGE SITUATION	CATEGORY
Secure	Trusting, exploratory, and confident	▪ Seeks proximity of mother ▪ Approachs mother upon her return ▪ Uses the mother as a secure base when threatened	Two-thirds of children are in this category
Insecure Avoidant	Angered but avoidant	▪ Does not seek the proximity of the mother ▪ Does not use the mother as a secure base ▪ Does not acknowledge the mother's presence before, during, and after a strange situation	20% of children are in this category
Ambivalent Insecure	Positive and negative reactions	▪ Displays both negative and positive reactions to mother's departure ▪ Shows distress when mother leaves ▪ Upon mother's return, seeks close contact but also hits and kicks her	12% of children are in this category
Disorganized (Disoriented) Insecure	Contradictory behavior	▪ Child shows inconsistent, contradictory behavior ▪ Approaches mother upon return, but will not look at her	Least secure
Resistant Insecure	Angered and persistently upset	▪ Angry when left in a strange situation ▪ Upon mother's return, still angry ▪ Will not be comforted or consoled by caregiver	5% of insecure children are in this category

child approaches her, yet when the mother hugs the child, the child pushes the mother away. The main difference between insecure ambivalent attachment and disorganized insecure attachment is that ambivalent insecurity is more aggressive and anger oriented. These children demonstrate the highest degree of attachment disorder.

Resistant Insecure Attachment (Type 5)

In **resistant insecure attachment**, the child shows great distress when faced with a new or stressful situation and the child is unable or unwilling to seek comfort from the mother. For example, a baby is left with the babysitter and becomes very upset. The mother returns to comfort the child; however, the child will not be consoled by her. This is an indication that the baby does not seek comfort from the mother, and does not consider her to be a pillar of trust. It is theorized that these children are holding on to their anger of being abandoned by their mother and are not willing to let go of their strong emotions. It is thought that about 5 percent of American children fit into this category. The main difference between resistant insecure attachment (type 5) and insecure avoidant (type 2) is the anger component. The insecure avoidant child is not angry.

In Western culture traditionally, scientists who study child development look at the mother as the main figure who establishes attachment with the child. Western fathers are seldom considered to be a prominent figure in establishing a bond or attachment with the child. One of the reasons for this may be actually two separate functions. Western mothers are traditionally looked at as the primary caregiver; the interesting part is that the infant also recognizes this distinction and acts accordingly. Infants bond faster and stronger with their mothers than they do with their fathers. On the other hand, fathers in the Western culture are traditionally considered to have the role of the entertainer. Soon after birth infants recognize their father as the source of play and fun. Infants react to their fathers in a more fun-loving way than they do to their mothers.

Theoretically a child is placed in only one of the attachment categories and does not fit into several of them at the same time. Of course any child has good or bad days but overall a child fits into one category only. Insecure attachments can result in a child growing up with attachment issues, although this does not mean it is inevitable. Children can learn to attach at a later age. Also a child may have a secure attachment to his or her mother growing up but because of life circumstances, develops attachment issues later on in life.

Cross-Cultural Issues and Attachment

Bowlby's (1907–1990) report to the World Health Organization on "Maternal Care and Mental Health" took his results from data he had collected from France, Holland, Sweden, and the United States. As a result of this report, good maternal care and attachment became important and internationally accepted. It is important to note that all of the cultures studied by Bowlby were Western cultures and did not include non-Western cultures. More recently more researchers have started to look at attachment cross-culturally.

Mary Ainsworth (1913–1999) completed her first study of attachment in Uganda her second study, done on American babies, was a replica of the first study. She found that attachment behaviors were the same between these two diverse cultures with some differences in expression of attachment behaviors. For example, American children hugged and kissed their mothers and Ganda babies clapped their hands when their mothers returned.

However, it must be remembered that the strange situation test that Mary Ainsworth used was developed to study American children and therefore may be culturally biased or ethnocentric. This test reflects the norms and values of the American culture. It uses the idea that attachment is based on anxiety and separation. It also assumes that the same behavior in different cultures has the same meaning. The social conditions and norms in different cultures vary a great deal. One example is Japan, where infants are rarely separated from their mothers and, as a result, when a Japanese child is separated from their mother it will represent a larger threat than to an American child. In the study on Japanese babies, Mary Ainsworth interpreted this behavior as insecure attachment. This demonstrates that the strange situation test and its usefulness cross-culturally may be limited. Also, when Van Uzendoorn and Kroonenberg (1988) completed an extensive analysis of cross-cultural studies in attachment they found there were more variation within cultures than between cultures (1.5 times).

A study that looked at attachment in the Nigerian Hausa culture looked at the affect multiple mothers had on infants' attachment behaviors (as cited in Pior & Glaser, 2006). The children formed positive attachment relationships with many of the maternal figures but usually demonstrated a preference for one mother over others. The preferred mother was the one who held and interacted with the baby most frequently.

What is evident in the body of research on **cross-cultural attachment issues** is that research is in its infancy and a great deal more needs to be done. More notice needs to be made of any cultural bias that may exist in how research is carried out in cultures significantly different from Western culture.

CHAPTER 7 SUMMARY

Emotions are part of early development. Basic or primary emotions are what humans are born with, which makes them a physiological development. Newborns have shown signs of fear, contentment, or anger in response to physiological changes. On the other hand, complex or secondary emotions are cultural; therefore, they are contextual and part of the child's environmental upbringing. As part of psychosocial growth, toddlers develop self-awareness. They now notice objects and people as separate beings not part of themselves. Consequently, this newfound discovery about self leads to stranger awareness. Children at this age understand that there are objects and people who exist, separate from them. This understanding and awareness brings anxiety as if the child realizes that others matter and are instrumental in their being. This anxiety is normal and it is part of their survival technique. Separation anxiety soon follows, where the child shows emotional distress when separated from parents or the main caregiver. Self-concept develops when the child realizes facts about him- or herself such as what he or she likes to eat, to wear, to play with, and so on. It is an understanding about self and the perception of one's own being. Self-awareness, stranger and separation anxieties, and self-concept are all milestones of this age. Self-concept development will later lead to self-esteem and self-identity development. All of these are part of normal milestones of development and parents need to be aware of the cumulative impact of growth necessary for a healthy psychosocial development in young children. Bonding occurs at birth, which is a physical tie between the newborn and the primary caregiver; however, proper bonding will lead to attachment. An important milestone in psychosocial development, attachment is an invisible emotional tie assuring the child that he or she can trust the environment. This security leads to the child discovering the environment and if threatened, feeling assured that support is available when needed.

CHAPTER 7 VOCABULARY

- Ambivalent Insecure Attachment
- Basic Emotions
- Bonding
- Cross-Cultural Attachment Issues
- Disorganized (Disoriented) Insecure Attachment
- Insecure Avoidant Attachment
- Mirror and Rouge Experiment
- Primary Emotions
- Resistant Insecure Attachment
- Secondary or Complex Emotions
- Secure Attachment
- Self-Awareness
- Self-Concept
- Self-Identity
- Separation Anxiety
- Stranger-Wariness
- Trust versus Mistrust

Chapter 8

PRESCHOOL AND PLAY YEARS
Physical Development

Happy school children from Nigeria.

(Photo courtesy of Lorimer Images/Shutterstock.com)

Children's Center

By Margaret Goetz

Sweet Thabisa, Longo,
Mbale, dark cherub faces
shrieking with joy with
your friends in the play yard.
I wish I didn't know what lurks
in your blood and that you will
grow up in this orphanage because
no one wants a child with HIV.

Western Research Findings

Biological Development

Early childhood, also known as the preschool or play years, is the time of discovery, independence, and learning. Physical development continues, but it is at a slower pace than that of the first two years of life, and the most noticeable physical growth is on the child's torso, arms, legs, and the tummy area. During this stage of biological development and biological maturation, children are capable of doing more physical activities and become more involved in adults' social activities. Parents are now excited about the fact that their child has gained more mobility; however, adults should also know that the rate of physical growth is not the same for every child. Parents need to consider their child's individuality when they compare their child to other children. It is important for parents to know what establishes normal physical growth. This awareness helps parents understand the expectations they should have of their preschooler and to look for any abnormality. **Normative development** is the rate of growth that is average or typical for this age group. There are differences in the rate of growth among individual children.

Normative Development

Arnold Gesell (1880–1961) was one of the pioneer scientists to set the first standards for normative rate of growth in young children. Many researchers consider Gesell to be the father of child development in the United States. He believed that child development is mostly biological not environmental, which, according to his theory, means that children develop based on their genetic inheritance. The Gesell maturation theory dismisses any environmental factors, such as personal experiences or injuries, as playing only a small role in the child's overall development. In which case, the role of parents on the behavioral modification of a child also becomes insignificant. Gesell notes that as long as parents are sensitive to the child's needs, it will be sufficient. Considering that Gesell's theory relies heavily on the biological maturation of the child, it may not be up to date; however, his contribution to the advancement of child development as a science cannot be denied.

Considering normative development described by scientists such as Gesell, it is safe to say that any scheduled or rigid developmental expectation should be looked at as average and generalized. Most children grow approximately two to three inches a year and gain four pounds a year. Female and male children share a similar physical growth pattern. On average, a two-year-old child weighs twenty-eight pounds and is thirty-four inches in height. At about the age of five or six years, primary teeth start to fall out and permanent teeth start to come in. Today, the American Academy of Pediatric Dentistry (AAPD) has new guidelines for parents in adopting the proper care of dental hygiene for their young children. The AAPD recommends a first visit to a pediatric dentist to take place as soon as the first primary tooth emerges and a bi-annual visit from then on. Children need to be taught the ritual of teeth cleaning at a very young age. Even at eighteen months old, a toddler can be taught the habit of tooth brushing using a soft bristle toothbrush.

Early Childhood Brain Development

Basic Brain Structures

The brain of a toddler goes through rapid growth, which continues to around five years of age when the brain has reached 75 percent to 90 percent of its adult size. Basic brain structure contains neurons, axons, dendrites, and glial cells. **Neurons** are thin, long nerve cells that constrict the nervous system. A neuron consists of a cell body, an axon, and dendrites. The main function of a neuron cell is to receive and transmit information from the rest of the body to the brain as well as within the brain. **Axons** are nerve fibers that extend from the neurons and send impulses away from the cell body toward other neurons. **Nerve fibers** extending from the neurons are called **dendrites**, which receive input from neurons. Axons send information from other dendrites. The cells that support and protect neurons are called **glial cells**. A synapse is a gap between nerve ends, where the tip of a nerve fiber almost touches another nerve cell in order to transmit signals.

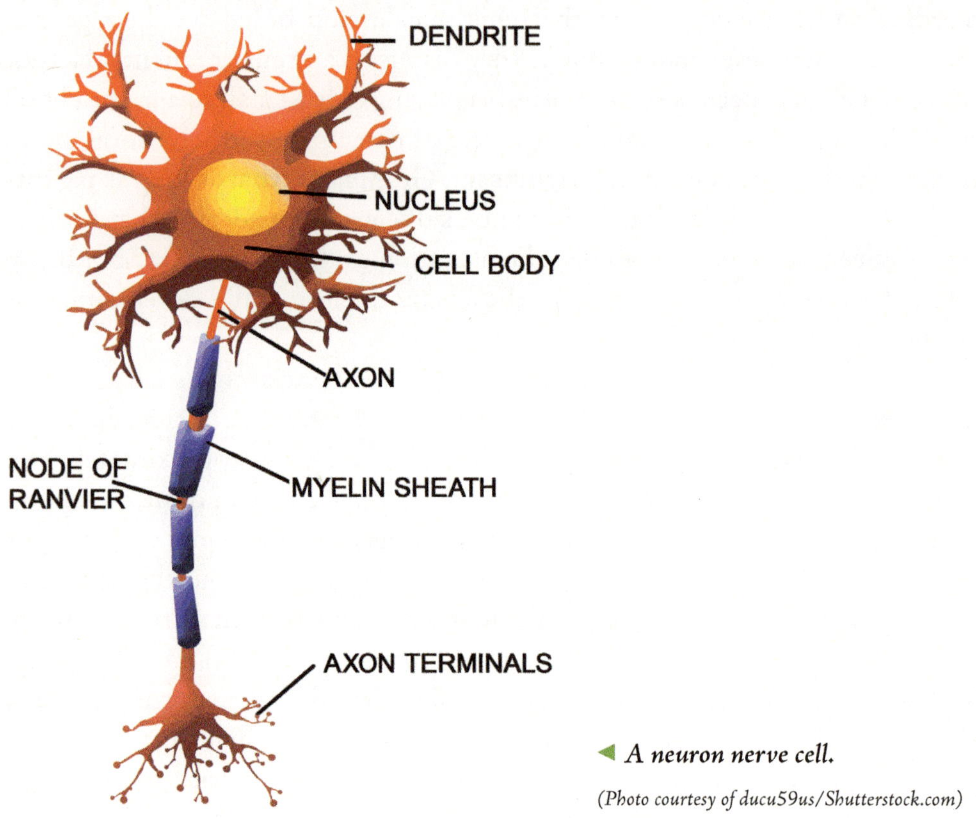

A neuron nerve cell.

(Photo courtesy of ducu59us/Shutterstock.com)

Myelination

A process that improves connections and communication within brain cells is called **myelination. Myelin** is a fatty sheath that wraps around axons in order to protect the transmission of information. The myelination process not only speeds up the process of information transmission, but it also provides for a more efficient way of processing these electrical signals. Proper nutrition and care of young child contributes to the development of a healthy myelination process. Myelination increases as the physical growth of the child increases, which in turn allows for information to move quickly between cell bodies in the brain. The myelination process is at its fastest during the first year of an infant's life. An infant who is experiencing a normal myelination process will have normal motor development (Johnson, 1999).

Cerebral Cortex

The **cerebral cortex** is a creased gray outer layer of the front parts of the brain's cerebral hemispheres. The cerebral cortex functions to control higher thought processes such as problem solving, consciousness, and language abilities. Damage to the cerebral cortex could lead to memory loss, mental retardation, visual impairment, and other types of brain disorders. Due to the cerebral cortex's slow growth, it is the last part of the brain to be completed. There is a rapid increase in this area during the teenage and young adult years. The cerebral cortex is also very sensitive to damage from environmental influences such as teratogens.

Right and Left Hemispheres

The cerebral cortex is divided into two halves called the **left and right hemispheres**; each hemisphere specializes in certain functionings of the brain. The left hemisphere specializes in analytical thinking, auditory, and language, which all develop around the age of two years, enabling the child to better communicate and speak more efficiently. This is not to say that these preschoolers magically begin to apply logic or to reason with their caregivers. What this newfound skill does for them, however, is prepare them for logical thinking, which will become stronger later through brain maturation and by acquiring experience. The age of logic according to Piaget's theory does not set in until the school years or between seven and eleven years of age. The right hemisphere specializes in visual, spatial position, novelty, and comprehension of meanings, which all develop around the age of five years in a normative development. The two hemispheres continue to grow, and around the age of two years, the connection between the hemispheres increases and functions more efficiently.

Motor Development

Motor Skills

For most children, new skills emerge rapidly in the third year of life. Both gross and fine motor skills develop remarkably during the early childhood years. With little training, children learn to run, walk on their toes, walk backward, throw balls, and jump. Important factors associated with children's motor development are the development of children's visual systems. Areas of the brain associated with the ability to focus the eyes and with eye movements continue to develop through early childhood. The development of visual pathways combined with improving communication between the hemispheres result in advances in eye–hand coordination and allow preschoolers to become better at left–right directions. The development of balance, and practicing, imitating others, and the caregiver's expectations and encouragement also play important roles in motor development. Development of motor skills enables a helpless infant to become more independent and self-sufficient. There are two types of motor development: gross and fine motor skills.

Gross Motor Skills Development

Gross motor skills develop when a child develops the ability to control large movement of the arms, legs, and feet, or the entire body. Using the larger muscles will result in the child's development of gross motor skills such as sitting, walking, running, kicking, jumping, and throwing. Arnold Gesell was the first scientist to publish the developmental milestone catalogue for small children (Gesell & Thompson, 1938). A normative gross motor development would consist of some of the following movement in early childhood:

- **2-year-olds:** Scribble, turn pages in a book, and construct towers consisting of six to eight blocks.
- **3-year-olds:** Eat with a spoon, copy a circle, and pour from a pitcher.
- **4-year-olds:** Dress themselves, cut on a line with scissors.
- **5-year-olds:** Fasten buttons, draw letters, unzip a zipper, and string beads.

A boy learning to kick a ball. This is an example of a gross motor skill.

(Photo courtesy of Rob Hainer/Shutterstock.com)

◄ *A little girl learning to cut with scissors. This is an example of a fine motor skill.*

(Photo courtesy of MNStudio/Shutterstock.com)

Fine Motor Skills Development

The ability to use and control the smaller muscles is known as fine motor skill development. **Fine motor skills** involve the coordination of the smaller muscles of the body such as the face, hands, and fingers. Examples of fine motor skills include movements such as holding a pencil to write, buttoning a shirt, turning pages of a book, and successfully cutting paper with scissors. Children's fine motor skills improve remarkably in early childhood, and are more apparent during the preschool years (Papalia, Cross & Feldman, 2003).

Determinants of Biological Growth Rate

Various factors contribute to children's physical growth such as genetics, healthy nutrition, the environment, nurturing, and various other factors. Cultural factors such as child-rearing practices and the interaction between cultural and biological factors can also be important determinants in a child's biological and physical growth. African American children genetically seem to be taller than Caucasian American children. At the same time, both African American and Caucasian American children tend to be taller than Asian American children. Healthy nutrition also plays an important role in the rapid rate of growth in children. Children who are exposed to proper nutrition and life style habits are inclined to suffer from fewer physical problems.

Genetic Factors in Growth Rate Variations

Children with African origins typically are more advanced in motor development than children with European origins; they throw farther, balance better, and are better able to run. Cultural factors in growth rate variations include parenting practices, nutrition, and the perceived importance of motor skill development. Babies who are massaged and have physical contact with the caregiver show greater physical development than infants who are not cuddled and held. There is also the impact of cultural and biological interactions that could result in growth rate variations. For example, African American infants show early motor precocity and are especially reactive, which may, in turn, contribute in a transactional way to caregivers' encouragement of their motor skills.

Opinion Piece: *Little Miss Perfect*—Good or Bad?

By Cindy Steinhaus-Donham, Ph.D.

Two of the reality TV shows broadcast are *Toddlers and Tiaras* and *Little Miss Perfect*. They focus on families and kids that are involved in fashion shows and beauty pageants mainly for little girls. What are these programs teaching our little girls today? How do they affect little girls when they grow up and become young adults? Parents of these little girls spend a large amount of money to have their young children participate. Dresses and costumes can cost hundreds of dollars. The girls have fake teeth, spray-on tans, adult makeup, fake nails, hair styles like adults, and are taught sexy provocative moves for their dance routines. Basically little girls are being taught how to act and look like "sexy young adults." They are being taught that to win they have to be sexy. Advocates of these shows say that it is not all about looks but about talent. Come on; when was the last time an unattractive, very talented little girl won? When one watches this reality show one sees these kids pulling tantrums, and being prima donnas. These

(Photo courtesy of Zagorodnaya/Shutterstock.com)

girls likely grow into teenagers and young adults with low self-esteem, believing that to attract a boy or to have anything else they want involves looking very sexy or acting that way. They often constantly need approval by their peers and will do almost anything to get it.

Many people ask why parents put their children in these shows. Some women were in these shows themselves as little girls and want their children to have the same experiences. Some parents want to dress their little girls like dolls, or to live their own dreams through their children. Parents will say they believe their daughters are learning self-confidence, to talk and act in front of audiences, to be less shy. On some level the little girls are learning these things but at what cost? Do the positives outweigh the negative? In my mind, no—the negatives far outweigh the positives. There are many other ways less damaging for little girls to learn self-confidence and to speak in front of others. Little girls already grow up getting the message through media that they need to be sexy, thin, and attractive, and that if you do not look or act in a certain way you are a loser. They do not have to have it pounded into them by little girl beauty pageants.

Also what are these kinds of reality TV shows telling our youth? On one level, the reason they are popular television shows and are interesting to the general public is because it is not the norm and there is a multimillion-dollar industry involved in children's pageants. Adults and older teens may look at these shows and think how shocking, funny, or dumb they are. However, young teens and children watching these shows are not as sophisticated and mature. These shows tell them to be a princess, be pretty, and win prizes. It is teaching boys that this is how girls should look and act. Younger children do not understand the long-term effects and implications these shows have. If it were up to me I would vote to take these shows off the air because they are so damaging to our youth.

Critical Thinking Questions

- What are these pageants teaching these girls?
- Why are parents putting their girls in these pageants?
- How does it affect them as they grow into the teenage years?
- What is your personal view on these pageants and would you put your daughter into one?
- What would you do if your spouse wanted you to?

Links to access program show examples:

http://www.highglitz.com/gallery/index.html

http://tlc.discovery.http://www.wetv.com/little-miss-perfect/index.hhttp://www.youtube.com/watch?v=ORcBTC7TiVY&feature=channeltmlcom/videos/http://tlc.discovery.com/tv/toddlers-tiaras/toddlers-tiaras.htmltoddlers-and-tiaras/

Early Childhood Problems

Nutrition and Health

During the play years, children are not growing as fast as they did as infants. Most children lose their healthy appetites, which often worries parents. Of course, parents have a legitimate reason for being concerned about their children not getting enough nutrition to continue healthy biological growth. It is not rare to see some children suffer from malnutrition even though they consume enough calories. These children fill up on "empty," nonnutritional calories (such as those found in cookies and potato chips) and fail to eat enough healthy foods. Biological growth and the development of motor skills may be delayed if a toddler experiences undernutrition. There is also risk for cognitive disabilities such as slow levels of attention, learning impairments, and poor academic and school-related problems. Nutrition and health are extremely important during the preschool years. Good nutrition is crucial to the brain's biological and physical development. Early childhood nutrition helps normal growth and consequently the functioning of the brain, which is an important part of subsequent developmental stages.

Accidents

In general, preschoolers are healthy; however, because they are now more active and curious about their surroundings, household accidents make up the leading cause of death for this age group. In other words, the early childhood age group is more accident prone in this time of their lives due to increased mobility, ease in getting around, their curious nature, and their overall lack of experience. Due to their lack of cognitive maturity, preschoolers do not put too much thought into their decision making and actions. This leads to taking more risks and not being aware of the consequences.

As children go through fast physical growth in early childhood, they gain new and improved skills and abilities. They become more active and consequently try to do more, which results in more independence. The role of parents also changes as children become older. With an infant, a parent's role is to give care. Eventually, this role changes to protector because the young child is now capable of more actions and can do more. As a result of doing more, the occurrences of accidents and injuries also go up. Parents need to become teachers for this age group, so that the preschooler learns to do new things, but at the same time is protected from harm and mishaps. A parent's job is never easy!

CHAPTER 8 SUMMARY

Preschoolers are fun to be with. They are now more independent than children of a younger age, and the string of new vocabulary they have now developed makes them good partners for interesting conversation. However, all may not be as easy as it seems. This age group is known for their egocentric and one-sided views. It seems that they can only think of themselves and be concerned with their own affairs. All the cognitive skills they learned in their first two years of life now help them expand and improve. Brain activity such as the growth of brain cells and axons, and myelination are all part of the biological development of this age group. This age group's physical development is more complex and sophisticated than younger children. Preschoolers become more skilled in their use of gross motor skills along with experiencing more sophisticated fine motor skills. Activities such as running, climbing, pinching, picking up and holding objects will become easier for them. Although there are specific areas of biological growth that scientists have earmarked for preschoolers, parents and caregivers must remember that there is variation in development among children—that is, not all children develop at the same rate. Genetic and environmental factors may lead to a variance in growth rate for each individual child. While toddlers are picky eaters, preschoolers may develop a wider taste in foods and what they like to eat; adults should introduce a variety of food choices to their young children making sure they receive the necessary nutritional intake.

Preschoolers are notorious for getting into trouble; as they become more independent it is expected to see them wanting to try new things. This newfound discovery could therefore lead to accidents, which are the number one cause of death for this age group. Parents and caregivers must exercise caution at all times making sure their children are safe.

CHAPTER 8 VOCABULARY

- Axons
- Cerebral Cortex
- Dendrites
- Fine Motor Skills
- Glial Cells
- Gross Motor Skills
- Left and Right Hemispheres
- Myelin
- Myelination
- Nerve Fibers
- Neurons
- Normative Development

Chapter 9

PRESCHOOL AND PLAY YEARS
Cognitive Development

A child's drawing of a tank in war.
(Photo courtesy of s_oleg/Shutterstock.com)

How Was Your Day

By Margaret Goetz

Just the usual, said the child with old eyes.
They killed a few in the marketplace
A young man, and old woman
Someone got one of the snipers
The second missile only hit a house
We had to take cover during math
So we didn't have the quiz, the girls
Didn't want to go outside in the heat.
I saw a body on my way home.
Just an ordinary day.

Western Research Findings

Language Acquisition in Early Childhood

Language development is a process that occurs in conjunction with the biological growth leading to the neuromuscular coordination of the vocal organs. It is a tool that is necessary for social interaction and psychological growth. Children use language to organize their thoughts and to adapt to their environment, all the while improving their linguistic abilities by mastering the sounds and the associated meanings in the language. Early childhood language development is a combination of words and gestures. A child's first attempt at communication may be using single words combined with a gesture, such as a nine-month old baby saying "bye bye" with a hand wave or saying "daddy" while shaking his head indicating that dad is not here. The time of language explosion and rapid growth in the ability to comprehend and use language is between the ages of two and six years. In early childhood, children learn several new words per day and by six years of age, a child's vocabulary expands to between 8,000 and 14,000 words. This transformation causes their mental and social life to explode.

24 Months

Around the second year of development, children use language common to their surroundings, and such use of language will be limited to naming objects common to their environment. Children at this age learn to combine words and prepositions such as "in," "on," "under," and so on. However, this use of elaborate language by toddlers is basically to create short sentences, often lacking a verb or correct grammatical structure, to mimic adult language. This phenomenon shows the sophisticated manner in which children learn to speak their native language. An example of this type of sentence would be "Want up," "Dad not here," and "Sissy gone." The number of comprehensible vocabulary for this age group is between 150 and 300 words, while rhythm and fluency is still poor due to the lack of cognitive abilities. Children in their second year are able to use some pronouns correctly such as "I," "me," and "you," and can respond to such commands as "Where is the dog?"

36 Months

The correct use of more pronouns becomes apparent. A child in the third year of development can name simple body parts easily with an increased vocabulary up to 900 to 1,000 words; the use of plurals and past tense becomes easier. This poses the question: How is a three-year-old (who has not yet taken grammar lessons) able to use past tense correctly (in most cases)? It is common for a child at this age to make grammatical sentences such as, "I goed to the store with mommy today," which although not perfect grammar, does convey the message. In addition, a three-year-old understands most of the simple commands dealing with his or her environment such as "Where did you go with mummy this morning?" However, due to the lack of logical reasoning at this age, adults should not expect full or elaborate answers to all questions. Adults can also expect a three-year-old to know the names of some familiar animals with the exception of overextensions and underextensions. An **overextension** is when a child applies a verbal label too broadly (e.g., "rabbit" to all four-legged animals that resemble a rabbit); conversely, an **underextension** is applying the label too narrowly (e.g., "dog" only to the family's dog).

48 Months

Imagination and make-believe thoughts and ideas flourish during this time of development. Around four years of age, children use more words, phrases, sounds, and vowels (a, e, i, o, u), to describe events and stories. A child at this age should have developed an understanding of opposites such as long–short, big–small, far–near, and should have learned all the vowels and the consonants.

60 Months

By the time children reach five years of age, they have developed language and communication skills; however, logically they are still maturing. At this age, children have obstacles in understanding reasoning and logical sequences. This lack of logical understanding is due to the brain's biological deficiency in proper synapse connectors and lack of experience; however, the child's own curiosity will lead to higher cognition and eventually logic will develop.

Cognitive Development

No other cognitive theory has had as much influence in the child development field as that of Swiss child developmentalist, Jean Piaget (1896–1980). He studied the thought process of children believing that an egocentric perspective limits a young child. This view shocked the scientific world because previously, most scientists thought children's thinking processes to be passive and nonparticipatory. In his cognitive theory, Piaget developed a new concept that children are eager to interact with and make sense of their world. Development is a combined method of biological maturation of the brain and the nervous system along with experiences to which the child adapts. Piaget, who developed the four stages of cognitive development, believed children are active learners, which means they actively construct their own perception and thought in regard to their environment. The thought process and the cognitive development of a child are based on his or her biological maturation along with the stimulating interaction with the child's surroundings. Piaget divided cognitive development in four stages: sensorimotor, preoperational, concrete operational, and formal operational. Previously, we discussed the sensorimotor stage, which involves infancy through early toddlerhood. In this section, we discuss the preoperational stage, which explains the early childhood development of thought and cognitive maturity.

Baby Sign Language

Some experts believe that teaching babies sign language will help expedite their language development. According to a long-term study at the University of California at Davis, funded by the National Institutes of Health, signing babies speak sooner and have larger vocabularies. The study also showed that these infants have stronger parent–child bonds; have less frustration, crying, and tantrums; show more interest in books; engage in more sophisticated play; and

▲ *Children doing sign language.*

(Photo courtesy of Kate Shannon/Shutterstock.com)

have increased IQ scores. Researchers believe that signing also increases a baby's self-esteem and gives parents a window into their child's mind and personality (Briant, 2004).

Preoperational Characteristics: Obstacles to Logical Thinking

Piaget describes **centration**, as the young child's inability to recognize multiple sides or the logic of the situation. They tend to focus on one aspect of the situation ignoring all other relevant aspects. The centration characteristic of preschoolers may be the reason why they have difficulty understanding the complexity of human beings' relational dynamics such as the relationship between aunts, uncles, and cousins. Centration can also be described as having tunnel vision. Another hindrance for this age group is **egocentrism**. In early childhood,

Your Child's Language Development Timeline

From that first coo to the full play-by-play of their day at school, children's language skills usually develop in an orderly fashion. Here's an idea of what to expect when—but it's perfectly normal for a child to hit these milestones a little early or a little late.

BABY	
Birth to 3 months	Makes quiet cooing sounds when pleased. These are typically a single vowel, like *ahhhh.*
2 to 3 months	Cries differently in different situations. As you get to know your baby, you may be able to distinguish a hunger cry from the cry he or she makes when tired, for example.
3 to 4 months	Vocalizes mostly vowels, but cooing becomes a little more sophisticated, with more varied sounds.
5 to 6 months	Practices intonation by making his or her voice rise and fall, often in response to baby talk and your facial expressions.
	RED FLAG: If your child isn't making vocal sounds by six months old, talk with the doctor.
7 to 12 months	Begins to babble with greater diversity, making new sound combinations and intonations. Tries to imitate your speech, putting consonants and vowels together (like "bah-BAH-bah" or "dee-dee-dah"). Has pretend conversations with you; taking turns "talking."
TODDLER	
12 months	Has said his or her first word. Knows one to five words well enough to use them.
14 months	Uses inflection (e.g., raises his or her voice at the end of a question, like, "more?") and makes hand gestures to complement speech.
	RED FLAG: If your child isn't saying any words by the time he or she is fifteen months old, bring it up with the doctor.
16 months	Talks to someone much of the time as opposed to just babbling out loud. Calls you to get your attention ("Mommy!"), nods and shakes head for yes and no. Makes many common consonant sounds, like *t, d, n, w,* and *h.*
18 months	Has a vocabulary of five to twenty words, including names ("Mama"), verbs ("eat"), and adjectives ("cold"). Uses common phrases ("want doll") to make requests.
18 to 24 months	Starts putting two-word phrases together for more novel purposes ("Daddy go," "milk mess").

PRESCHOOLER	
24 months	Knows 150 to 300 words. Uses short, two- or three-word sentences with lots of pauses ("Baby . . . fall down!" "Me go . . . school?").
2 to 3 years	Can carry on a simple conversation about something in the immediate environment. Asks simple questions frequently. Expands phrases from three- to six-word sentences and develops a vocabulary of 450 words, including lots of verbs. Uses past tense by tacking on a "d" sound to verbs ("runned") and plurals by adding an "s" sound to nouns ("mans"). Uses pronouns (I, she, we) correctly.
	RED FLAG: If your two- or three-year-old echoes your questions rather than answering them, tell the doctor about it. This could be an early sign of a language delay.
3 to 4 years	Is able to talk and play at the same time. Knows about 800 to 1,000 words. Favorite words often include "why," "what," and "who." Can be understood most of the time. Can tell you what happened if you were out of the room.
	RED FLAG: Your child may sound as though he or she is stuttering if the child gets tripped up on words in his or her excitement to communicate. This is perfectly normal. If it continues for more than six months, though, or if the child tenses the jaw or grimaces while trying to get the words out, ask your child's doctor for a referral to a speech pathologist.
BIG KID	
4 to 5 years	Communicates easily and boasts a vocabulary of about 2,000 words. Can retell a simple story with a beginning, middle, and end while looking at pictures. Can use four to five sentences to describe a picture, with most of the grammar elements in place. Pronounces most sounds correctly (but may still have trouble with *th, r,* and *l*). Uses lots of descriptive words, including time-related words like "yesterday."
6 to 7 years	Can describe how two items are the same or different, retell a story or event without the help of pictures, and recount past conversations and events. Uses some irregular plural nouns ("men," "teeth").
8 years	Has mastered all speech sounds as well as the rate, pitch, and volume of speech. Uses complex and compound sentences correctly and is capable of carrying on a conversation with an adult.

Source: Baby Center.com, 2014.

the cognitive ability of preoperational characteristics is the ability to see only one's own personal perspective. An example of egocentrism is when three-year-old Joey wants a cookie before dinner and does not understand why Mom is telling him that soon they will be having dinner, and that if he eats a cookie now, he will spoil his appetite. Joey's egocentric perspective is that he wants a cookie and, to him, whether dinner is going to be ready soon is irrelevant. This is called seeing only one side of the story, which in this case is Joey's point of view. **Animism**, also part of the preoperational stage, is when a young child believes that inanimate objects are real, such as a character in his favorite cartoon or the fact that his beloved teddy bear is tired and needs to take a nap. At preschool age, young children treat their favorite toy as if it is alive and capable of functioning just like they are!

Focus on Appearance

During early childhood, children ignore all unique human attributes except appearance, which means they understand their environment based on how it looks to them. For example, a four-year-old child sees her mother put on a witch Halloween costume and becomes frightened, refusing to go anywhere near her mother. The child's sudden fear of her mother, whom she normally loves to be around, is best explained by the child's **focusing on appearance** as reality. The child at this point does not recognize his or her mother, and visibly gets upset with the strange and unfamiliar figure in front of him or her.

Static Reasoning

Children in the early years assume the world is unchanging and all things will stay the same. During this stage of cognitive growth, a three-year-old child's thinking pattern is that everything is static and nothing changes. The place they live in, toys, friends, parents, and the overall environment around them will always stay the same. In the mind of a three-year-old, the street where they live is the world, and will always stay the same. Nothing ever changes! **Static reasoning** prevents children from thinking and analyzing beyond their own little world.

Irreversibility

In children age three to five years, **irreversibility** is the failure to recognize that reversing a process can restore whatever existed before the transformation occurred. Piaget used "conservation" experiments to see whether children realized that characteristics of objects remained the same despite changes in physical appearance. According to Piaget's theory, "conservation" is the principle

Types of Conservation Tests Used

TYPE OF CONSERVATION	INITIAL PRESENTATION	TRANSFORMATION	QUESTION	PREOPERATIONAL CHILD'S ANSWER
Liquid	Two glasses of same size with equal amounts of water	Pour one into a taller narrower glass	Which glass contains more?	The taller narrower glass
Number	Two lines of equal length made up of six checkers	Increase spacing of checkers in one line	Which line has more checkers?	The longer one with more space between the checkers
Matter	Two equal ball of clay	Squeeze one ball into a long thin shape	Which piece has more clay?	The long one
Length	Two sticks of equal length	Move one stick	Which stick is longer?	The one that is further to the right

that the amount of a substance is unaffected by changes in appearance. There are many versions of the conservation experiment; for example, in one type of testing for conservation in young children, a child is shown two equal lines of checkers and after one line has been spread out, the child is asked which line has more checkers. In conservation problems, preschoolers will be fooled by the appearance because they ignore the transformation that has taken place. They think that the new longer line has more checkers than the shorter line. This is called conservation test failure.

Criticism of Piaget

Piaget's theory was criticized for underestimating a child's ability to learn. His methods were flawed and too hard to understand by his subjects of study. He also underestimated the role of culture in a child's cognitive development, thus, experts in the field of child development believe his theory to be culturally biased. He did not take into consideration the impact of schooling on further cognitive learning. Further criticism of his theory included the fact that he proposed a rigid developmental chart for children, which generalizes child development and ignores individual differences.

Sociocultural Theory

Lev Vygotsky (1896–1934), a Russian theorist, also debated the cognitive development of children, yet unlike Piaget, he argued that *"learning is a necessary and universal aspect of the process of developing culturally organized, specifically human psychological function"* (Vygotsky, 1978, p. 90). In other words, social learning tends to precede (i.e., come before) development. Vygotsky's theory of social development regards children as apprentices who learn through social interaction and adult interaction. Unlike Piaget, who believed children actively experience and shape the world around them, Vygotsky emphasized the importance of adult interaction on children's optimal learning experiences. Lev Vygotsky's untimely death at the age of thirty-eight has left his theory incomplete, yet some of his writings are still being translated from Russian into other languages. Although Vygotsky died too soon, his theory tremendously impacted the ideas of child development. His main contribution to the science of child development are the:

- importance culture plays in children's upbringing;
- role adults play in shaping a child's behavior; and
- role of language as a mediator of a child's cognitive development.

These are important factors that some of the early child development scientists such as Piaget, Watson, and Pavlov had not taken into consideration.

Many of Vygotsky's ideas were in accordance with Piaget's. However, his emphasis on the cultural and social aspects of a child's learning set him apart (although, it is noteworthy to mention that both Piaget and Vygotsky believed in a child's discovery and exploration learning as well).

A contemporary application of Vygotsky's theory in today's world is the use of "reciprocal teaching," which is collaboration between student and teacher.

The reciprocal teaching strategy is in the form of a dialogue between a teacher and a student. This strategy can also be used in pairing up students, and the goal is to learn through a collaborative effort. This method teaches children to work together by discussing the problem, summarizing, questioning, clarifying, and predicting the outcome. It is a great learning tool that teaches children to use critical thinking and analysis. Vygotsky emphasized the role of adults with children who are learning, because he believed that children learn through interaction with adults. This is contrary to Piaget's explanation, arguing that development is entirely based on the ability of the child and genetic predisposition dismissing any environmental influences. Through this interactive, collaborative, and reciprocal strategy, the teacher's role decreases as learning increases until the student has gained the desired knowledge. Vygotsky described this gain of knowledge and cognitive maturity as the **zone of proximal development (ZPD)**, and **scaffolding**.

ZPD is the difference between what a child can do with and without help. It is the amount of assistance, the gauge of help, the degree in which the adult interacts with the child making sure the new skill or behavior is learned. The degree of help varies from one child to another. Some children are fast learners or are cognitively more mature. Using ZPD allows the adult to take into consideration the child's individual ability in learning new skills. Scaffolding is the step-by-step method by which the degree of help is given to the child. The method of teaching or scaffolding is also unique to the child's way of learning. An adult will take into consideration the way an individual child learns, then will customize an effective method of teaching for that particular child. ZPD and scaffolding are two important tools that adults use in their interactions with a child. They are the important factors of teaching adults use to help the child develop new skills.

Cognitive development in the early years is intense and rich. The combination of the brain's biological maturation along with external experiences enables children to reach their cognitive potential. Experts such as Piaget and Vygotsky offer insights into the workings of a young child's mind and cognition. It is also important to understand the capabilities and the inabilities of a young child's cognitive development. This valuable knowledge helps adults, teachers, parents, and caregivers look for areas where they can help the child improve cognition or help recognize a child's abnormalities and shortcomings. Knowing the developmental milestones and norms helps parents detect developmental problems early on. Some of these cognitive disabilities that can be recognized by parents during this stage of development are **Attention Deficit Disorder** (ADD), **Attention Deficit Hyperactivity Disorder** (ADHD), and **Autism**.

Attention Deficit Disorder (ADD)

The symptoms of ADD and ADHD are very close; however, the two are not quite the same. Individuals suffering from ADD demonstrate problems with concentration and focus; however, it is important for adults to note that the lack of attention is not due to lack of logic or cognitive ability in ADD children in this age group. Furthermore, due to the active nature of children, the majority of them are diagnosed as having ADHD versus ADD, which adds to the misconception and misdiagnosis. That is why it is crucial for caregivers to be cognizant and aware of ADD symptoms (Dickerson, 2014).

Attention Deficit Hyperactivity Disorder (ADHD)

The symptoms of this disorder are lack of concentration, hyperactive behavior, and lack of focus. Preschoolers are active by nature, especially boys; however, as they reach the end of early childhood, parents should notice an improvement in their child's attention span and interest in finishing projects. Toward the end of early childhood, a four-year-old should be able to sit through preschool sessions and behave in a cooperative manner. The lack of concentration and the inability to focus on tasks may be a sign of ADHD. Traditionally, more boys are diagnosed with this disorder than girls. Perhaps the reason for the higher number of boys being labeled with ADHD is that boys are biologically more aggressive and less mature than girls of the same age. In recent years, some psychologists and educators have voiced their concerns over lack of specific criteria for diagnosis of such borderline disabilities, meaning that ADHD could easily be overdiagnosed (Simonson & Glenn, 2001).

Autism

Otherwise known as Autism Spectrum Disorder (ASD), this disorder can be diagnosed as early as the second year of life, when a child might show signs of autism. This neurological disorder impairs the social and communication ability of the individual. Early detection is key leading to treatment that could eventually enable the child to fully function in social settings. As discussed earlier, at around six months old, infants should engage in social interaction with adults and the surrounding environment. This connection starts with s**ocial referencing**, which is when an infant points at things while looking at the adult as a way to communicate or seek guidance. According to research (Klinnert et al., 1983) infants use social cues from adults (information received through interaction

The Effects of Music Therapy on Autism

By Nicole Jafari

Autistic Spectrum Disorder (ASD) is a developmental disorder with impairment in three main areas: (1) social/emotional interaction; (2) communication; (3) restricted and repetitive behavior and/or interests (Ball, 2004; Gold, Wigram, & Elefant, 2006; Mandy & Skuse, 2008). The *Diagnostic and Statistical Manual of Mental Disorders (DSM-IV)* was developed to assess children with potential autism spectrum display of characteristics in the areas of a child's interaction with others, delayed language or process of social cues, and repetitive behavior such as preoccupation with objects or abnormal obsessions with particular items or concepts (as cited by Gattino et al., 2011).

ANALYSIS

Music Therapy

Music therapy is a clinical health care intervention, which uses music and musical instruments as the basic tools for treatment. The individual's ability in different areas such as physical, emotional, social, and cognitive would be strengthened through several musical interventions such as listening to music, singing, creating, and moving to music. This type of intervention is especially helpful for clients who are not able to express their feelings through words or articulation. The Australian Music Therapy Institute recommends "Music Therapy" for the purpose of cognitive and social development (Doostar, 2009).

Correlation between Music and Autism

Rafei (2006) stated that autistic children rarely respond to common psychiatric therapy and occupational therapy because of their specific limitations in language, communication, and social skills. Many other studies have shown that autistic children prefer auditory stimuli to other stimuli (Blackstock, 1978; Kolko, et al., 1980 as cited by Simpson & Keen, 2011) and according to Thout (1992), Snell (1968), Euper (1968), Edgerton (1994), and Demyer (1974), children with ASD prefer musical stimuli to other auditory and/or visual stimuli and respond better to a musical climate and instruments (as cited by Dezfulian, 2007).

(continues)

(continued from previous page)

Wigram and Gold (2005) conclude that children with ASD who have fundamental difficulties in conventional and common methods of communication and social interactions respond positively to music and music therapy. Music and musical instruments attract the autistic child's attention and the music therapist would be able to interact with the child through music in the first step and thus provide an opportunity to maintain the child's interest in this kind of interpersonal communication, which is not direct (Gold, Wigram, & Elefant, 2006; Holck, 2011).

Effects of Music Therapy on Autistic Children's Communication Skill

A communication difficulty is one of the core problems of autistic children (Gattino et al., 2011; Gold et al., 2010) and one of the main therapeutic targets of music therapy is communication skill in ASD (Wigram & Gold, 2006). Verbal and nonverbal communication skills would be established through music therapy interventions. Music therapy interventions significantly improve verbal and nonverbal communication skills in children with ASD (Gattino, Riesgo, Longo, Leite, & Faccini, 2011; Gold, Wigram, & Elefant 2006). Similarly a significant development of imitation, joint attention, and language was found in ASD children who received music therapy interventions (Mundy, Sigman, & Kasari, 1990; Schuler, Prizant, & Wetherby, 1997 as cited by Holck, 2011).

Music therapy is reinforcement for autistic children because it does not force children to use typical verbal interaction and direct communication (Bhatara, 2009; Judd, 2007 as cited by Austin, 2009) and the nonverbal aspect of this intervention facilitate therapeutic relationship (Simpson & Keen, 2011). The therapist and the child would have a nonverbal and or preverbal language and communication through musical interactions and this kind of relationship helps the child to learn social skills and engage with others through musical experiences and musical-emotional communication . . . (Alvin, 1987 as cited by Simpson & Keen, 2011; Ball, 2004; Farmer, 2003 as cited by Austin, 2009; Kim et al., 2009).

Gold, Wigram, and Elefant (2010) through a systematic Cochrane review, showed that music therapy is preferred over other therapeutic interventions. The research results investigated that gestural and verbal communicative skills improve significantly through music therapy compared with other treatments not including musical elements.

RESULTS

The majority of research-based evidence indicated that music interventions would be beneficial for individuals with ASD and would lead to social, behavioral, and/or communicative improvement. According to the National Research Council (2001), autistic children would respond to interventions, which have a focus on social skills, nonverbal communication; behavior function and language (as cited by Levy, Kim, & Olive, 2006) and music therapy's techniques address these specific needs in ASD. Music therapy provides an alternative way for interpersonal interactions through musical elements (Gattino et al., 2011; Gold et al., 2010; Wigram, 2006) and as Kim et al. (2008) stated: "Musical attunement would open and maintain a channel of communication with the child."

The literature on music therapy reports the positive effects of music intervention and its efficacy on different impairments of ASD, and supports the belief that music therapy techniques offer and provide ability of development for autistic children (Gattino, 2011; Gold et al., 2006, 2010; Holck, 2010; Kim et al., 2008). Although many studies support the hypothesis that music therapy has positive effects on autistic children, many of these studies lack sufficient analysis. Additional information is needed to provide clear and accurate evidence for the effectiveness of music therapy for people with autism. Future studies should consider the limitations of previous studies including sample size, therapy condition, assessment tools, research design and methodology, control groups, duration of the therapy and follow-up results to increase the accuracy of music treatment effects on autism spectrum disorder.

References

Alvin, J. (1966). Music as a means of communication. In: *Introduction to Music Therapy.* London: Society for Music Therapy and Remedial Music.

American Music Therapy Association, 2013. Retrieved from: Austin, R. 2009. *Growing Through Music: How Music Therapy Increases Development in People with Autism.*

Ball, C. M., 2004. Music Therapy for children with Autistic Spectrum Disorder. *STEER, 4*(1).

Dezfoolian, L. (2007). *The Positive Impact of Arf Technique's Music Intervention on Autistic Children.* Dissertation: University of Tehran, Department of Psychology and Social Sciences.

Doostar, H. (2009). *Music Therapy.* Publisher: Department of Public Health, Tehran, Iran.

Edgerton C. L. (1994). The effect of improvisational music therapy on the communicative behaviors of autistic children. *Journal of Music Therapy, XXXI*(1), 31–62.

Gattino, G. S., Riesgo, R. S., Longo, D., Leite, J. C. L. & Faccini, L. S. (2011). Effects of relational music therapy on communication of children with autism: A randomized controlled study. *Nordic Journal of Music Therapy, 20*(2), 142–154.

Gold, C., Wigram, T., & Elefant, C. (2010). *Music therapy for autistic spectrum disorder (Review).* The Cochrane Library, Issue 1. Retrieved from: http://www.thecochranelibrary.com

Holck, U. 2011. Music Therapy Research—children with an autism spectrum disorder. English translation of the peer reviewed article; "Forskning i musikterapi-børn med en Autisme Spektrum Forstyrrelse," published in *Tidsskrift for Dansk Musikterapi, 8*(2), 27–35.

Kim J., Wigram T., & Gold C. 2008. The effects of improvisational music therapy on joint attention behaviors in autistic children: A randomized controlled study. *Journal of Autism and Developmental Disorders, 38*(9), 1758–66.

(continues)

(continued from previous page)

Kim J., Wigram T., & Gold C. 2009. Emotional, motivational and interpersonal responsiveness of children with autism in improvisational music therapy. *Autism 13*(4), 389-409.

levy, S., Kim, A., & Olive, M. L., 2006. Interventions for young children with autism: A synthesis of the literature. *Focus on Autism and Other Developmental Disabilities, 21*(1), 55-62.

Lim, H. A., 2010. Effect of "Developmental Speech and Language Training Through Music" on Speech Production in Children with Autism Spectrum Disorders. *Journal of Music Therapy.* XLVIt (1), 2-26.

Mandy, W. P., & Skuse, D. H. (2008). Research review: What is the association between the social-communication element of autism and repetitive interests, behaviors and activities? *Journal of Child Psychology and Psychiatry, 49*(8).

Rafei, T. (2006). *Autism: assessment and treatment.* Publisher: Danezheh, Tehran, Iran

Simpson, K., & Keen, D., 2011. Music interventions for children with autism: Narrative review of the literature. *Journal of Autism Developmental Disorders, 41*(11), 1507-1514

Wigram T., & Gold C. 2006. Music therapy in the assessment and treatment of autistic spectrum disorder: Clinical application and research evidence. *Child Care, Health and Development, 32*(5), 535-42.

with others), assess the action, and consequently form their own behavior. Social referencing has two components: The first part is when a cue or information is received, and the second part involves the use of that information in a conduct or behavior. A caregiver's facial expression observed by a baby enables the infant to regulate his or her own actions, eventually leading to emotional development. The use of social referencing allows the child to regulate behavior and adapt to social norms and conventions. Failure to make this connection or use social referencing along with other communicational inabilities such as lack of eye contact may be an indication of ASD. Also, autistic children have severe self-absorption, as they seem aloof or not interested in social interaction.

The medical field today has made tremendous progress in diagnosing autism at an early age; however, a child's lack of communication does not always mean autism, and may be related to other cognitive/emotional problems. Today, diagnostic tools have been greatly improved, yet the causes of autism are still under a cloud of ambiguity. Scientists have referenced the possibility of pregenetic disposition, childhood immunization (although an extremely controversial argument), and even the quality of the male's sperm that fertilized the egg as possible causes.

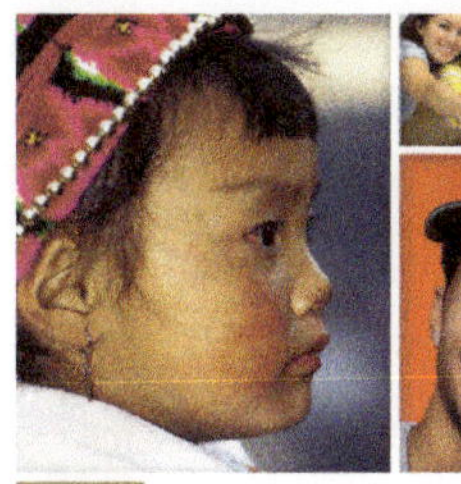

Unwanted Children in Korea

In a country that prizes physical perfection, Pastor Lee Jong-rak had his eyes opened after caring for his own disabled son and has begun taking in unwanted infants. These infants would be left in the street if it were not for his drop box. The drop box is attached to the side of a home in a ragged working-class neighborhood. It is lined with a soft pink and blue blanket, and has a bell that rings when the little door is opened. This depository isn't for books, it's for babies—and not just any infants. These children are the unwanted ones, a burden many parents find too terrible to bear.

One is deaf, blind, and paralyzed; another has a tiny misshapen head. There's a baby with Down syndrome, another with cerebral palsy, still another who is quadriplegic with permanent brain damage.

But to Pastor Lee Jong-rak, they are all perfect. And they have found a home here at the ad hoc orphanage he runs with his wife and small staff. It is the only private center for disabled children in South Korea.

(Photo courtesy of Jaren Jai Wiklund/Shutterstock.com)

"This is a facility for the protection of life," reads a hand-scrawled sign outside the drop box. "If you can't take care of your disabled babies, don't throw them away or leave them on the street. Bring them here."

Since 1998, Lee, now 57, has taken in nearly three dozen children and raised them, loved them, sent them to school. He has changed their diapers, tended to their cries in the middle of the night. Today, he has 21 wards: the youngest a 2-month-old, the oldest 18.

His motivation is painfully personal. Twenty-five years ago, Lee's wife, Chun-ja, gave birth to a baby so disfigured Lee kept the boy from her for a month until he could figure out a way to tell her the unthinkable, explaining only that the child had a serious illness and was rushed to another hospital.

The baby was born with cerebral palsy. A mammoth cyst on his head choked off the blood flow, slowly rendering him brain damaged. Doctors gave him months to live.

Today he lies on a bed in Lee's home, his legs splayed at impossible angles, his feet turned back inward. Eyeing the room impassively, he occasionally lets out a snort or sigh, as his parents regularly vacuum his saliva through a tracheal hole in his throat. They call him Eun-man, which means full of God's grace.

(continues)

(continued from previous page)

He plays the role of emotional touchstone for an orphanage in peril: Health officials have ordered Lee to close his drop box, saying it encourages parents to abandon their babies.

Authorities also say Lee has no formal training and not enough space for his wards, only two of which are not handicapped; they were left by single mothers. Lee has no license, but for years he had operated underneath the radar. Now he worries he will lose the government funds he receives as the children's legal guardian; the money keeps him in operation, along with donations from local firms and private benefactors.

Orphanage supporters say authorities are missing the big picture. Though there are other institutional facilities nationwide for disabled children, they say, no salaried caregiver could match Lee's compassion and paternal touch.

"Rather than look at what he can bring, they focus on what he doesn't have," said Peter A. Dietrich, an orphanage volunteer. "The enormity of his mission hits you between the eyes. I don't know anyone who goes there for the first time and doesn't tear up."

Eun-man's birth caused a religious man to question his faith.

"I asked God, 'Why would you give me a handicapped child?' I wasn't grateful for this baby," Lee recalled.

He soon came to regret those words. Looking down at his son, helpless and beyond hope, he says he witnessed the preciousness of life. He and his wife decided to work desperately to keep the boy alive.

In the mid-1980s, Lee said, the disabled in South Korea were often viewed as embarrassing curiosities—more creature than child. Even today, he said, babies with physical deformities are seen as a national shame in a culture that prizes physical perfection, where cosmetic surgeries have become as common as haircuts.

Given his limited brain function, Eun-man needed constant care. He spent his first 14 years at a hospital. To help pay for his care, Lee sold his family food market, borrowed money, and took up odd jobs to bring in more cash.

He spent months at the hospital and began visiting the rooms of other disabled children, encouraging their parents not to give up on them. Many began calling him "the pastor."

Strangely, the boy Lee once blamed on God ended up bringing him closer to his faith. In 1992, when Eun-man was 6, Lee entered theology school to become a Christian minister.

One day, an elderly woman at the hospital asked Lee to take her paralyzed granddaughter. The bargain: If Lee said yes, the woman said, she would agree to convert to Christianity. He accepted the child, named Sang-hee, who still lives with him. Months after making the deal, the woman was dead.

A social worker then asked Lee to accept the brain-damaged daughter of a 14-year-old girl who drank and did drugs during her pregnancy. The social worker assured Lee the infant, named Hannah, wouldn't live long.

Lee fed her through a tube, amazed at the child's hunger to survive. Hannah lived 6 more years: "When she died, I cried so much, more than even when my own parents passed away."

That's when Lee vowed he would never turn away a challenged child. He has officially adopted several as his own and gained temporary legal guardianship of others. In 2009, he installed the drop box. Immediately, the babies began appearing, some with their umbilical cords still attached. The child welfare people visited Lee in the spring. They had seen a TV report on his orphanage. The drop box had to go.

Child abandonment is a crime in South Korea and they said Lee provided parents an easy out. They said the orphans also deserved to know the identity of their biological parents eventually, a service Lee could not provide with the anonymous drop offs.

Although they acknowledge that Lee is well meaning, officials believe he may be doing more harm than good. "Just accepting an infant without going through the proper verification steps is wrong," said Lee Woon-gyu, a child welfare officer.

Social workers who recently visited the orphanage say that 21 children are far too many for a four-bedroom home; some called the conditions unsanitary. They added that the law requires a doctor to be on hand around the clock in case of an emergency.

Pastor Lee insists that his orphanage has been running safely and efficiently, but acknowledges that he wants to raise the money to build a larger facility. He says the drop box offers salvation for babies who might otherwise be deserted in trashcans or public restrooms. He refused to remove the box, but agreed to turn over any children left there. Since February, eight infants have been placed there.

On a recent day, he hurried around the orphanage, kissing each baby on the cheek and forehead as four donated washing machines hummed in the background.

The walls are covered with pictures of his brood, some of which are named for the time they appeared in the drop box, such as Midnight and Autumn. Of the 32 children he has taken in, three have died, three went back to live with their parents, and five were adopted.

Lee says he loves them all equally, but there's one he cannot forget. Little Hannah is buried under a tree just outside Lee's front door. "I just couldn't let her go," he said. "It comforts me to know she's still here" (Gilonna, 2011).

Adapted from article written by John Gilionna.

Children, who suffer from Asperger's, a milder form of ASD, show tremendous interest in one subject, but significant difficulties in social interaction and nonverbal communication. This over-the-top interest in one object or topic could be characterized as obsession, yet a child with Asperger's may almost be oblivious to other situations. Children with Asperger's display a high IQ mark in artistic testing, but in cognitive assessment perform as low as children with mental disability. As early detection may lead to better prognosis, there is still no cure for autism; however, cognitive behavioral therapy (CBT) has shown some promise in enabling children with Asperger's to lead a relatively high functioning life.

Parenting a child with any form of disability is challenging, and at times too difficult to bear. Children who suffer from developmental malfunctioning require hours of therapy, rehabilitation, and around-the-clock care. The degree of help that these children need may be overwhelming for parents; therefore, effective social assistance becomes vital and crucial to these caregivers. In the United States, and in most Western countries, child experts and the medical field have always aspired to learn more about the abnormality and the shortcomings of development. Socially, the Western world has also made tremendous efforts in accommodating children with disabilities such as offering additional assistance or providing accommodation in school, so that a child with disabilities can enjoy a productive and happy life similar to his or her peers. This is not always the case in non-Western countries. (See "Unwanted Children in Korea.")

CHAPTER 9 SUMMARY

Cognitive development in preschoolers is more noticeable and appreciated by parents. Children of this age group can easily strike up a conversation and have an interesting dialogue. Language acquisition is rapid and plentiful. What makes a conversation fun with preschoolers is their attempt to use the vocabulary they have developed but do not quite yet understand the specific use for it. They use overextension, using a word beyond its meaning or at times use underextension, not understanding the complete use of the same vocabulary. This will then lead to fast mapping, which is another way of expanding one's own bank of vocabularies. Young children often use words they hear in unfamiliar situations using it in a familiar context. Cognitively, young children lack the sense of logic. This is due to the fact that they have obstacles to logical thinking. The egocentric and one-dimensional views of a preschooler limit them in seeing other people's views; therefore, their reasoning is one sided and from the point of view of a self-centered person. They also have trouble understanding that other people may have views different from theirs. This lack of realization makes preschoolers stubborn, selfish, and one sided, which could lead to power struggles and a lot of frustration for parents and children alike.

CHAPTER 9 VOCABULARY

Animism
Attention Deficit Disorder
Attention Deficit Hyperactivity Disorder
Autism
Centration
Egocentrism
Focusing on Appearance
Irreversibility
Overextension
Scaffolding
Social Referencing
Static Reasoning
Underextension
Zone of Proximal Development (ZPD)

Chapter 10

PRESCHOOL AND PLAY YEARS
Social Development

Two young children in Turkey.
(Photo courtesy of thomas koch/Shutterstock.com)

Western Findings

As discussed earlier, the concept of "self" develops early in life. This phenomenon is the understanding, the attitudes, and the beliefs that one learns about self throughout the life span. In early childhood, children not only have a sense of who they are, but they also have developed a sense of what their capabilities are, what their relationship is in comparison to others, and the social environment they are in. Is self-concept development a matter of biological and cognitive interaction combined with maturity? Or is self-concept development an innate ability that all children possess?

This again reminds us of the nature versus nurture co-construct debate. Perhaps both nature and nurture are at work helping the child develop a sense of self in relation to his or her surroundings. Most scientists believe that both nature and nurture play an important role in the development of self-concept; however, it is hard to determine the exact degree of involvement each contributes to this development. Self-concept is domain specific, which means a child will develop self-concept based on different criteria such as sports, abilities, gender, physical appearance, and other childhood-related events.

Self-Esteem

Self-esteem is the ability to recognize one's own worth. It is a Westernized concept that was theorized by William James, an American psychologist, in 1890. The concept grew more popular in the 1960s as self-worth and self-evaluation became points of interest in the Western culture's world of psychology. Self-esteem is the measurement of self-worth and self-evaluation that individuals place on their own capacities and abilities. It has also been linked to individuals' view of their competencies, ability to perform tasks, personal worth, and understanding of the world around them. Healthy self-esteem is instrumental in normal life span development; however, the degree, intensity, and measurement of self-worth vary for each age group.

As self-esteem fluctuates during life span development, the highest degree of self-worth is considered to be during preschool years. This can be explained by considering the egocentric view in early childhood, which brings self-esteem to its highest level in this age group. The fluctuation and decline of self-esteem starts later as the child approaches school age. A child's view of his or her own self-worth between the ages of five and eight years develops much more dramatically as the child begins to pay more attention to physical appearance, social acceptance, scholastic ability, athletic ability, artistic skills, and behavior (Harter & Pike, 1984). As children gradually become skillful, they initiate new conduct such as becoming further independent with more competencies; they start to evaluate their own self-worth and self-accomplishment.

According to Erikson's second stage of development, children in this age group face the challenge of gaining "autonomy and independence" versus the crisis of "shame and doubt" in failing. Having successfully completed the second stage, the challenge in the third stage is to initiate learned behaviors versus the crisis of "guilt" due to failure. Successfully finishing tasks will enable the child to further become confident in his or her own ability, thus leading to a healthier self-esteem. However, since the child is being compared to others (due to social comparison), failing the initiative may turn into feelings of inadequacy and incompetency, thus leading to a lower self-esteem measurement.

Erikson's Theory Third Stage

Initiative versus Guilt

Mastering new skills, desiring to perform new tasks, seeking independence, and taking initiative to do things on their own are all part of early childhood development. The desire to do things for themselves develops very early on as children seek independence and freedom from adults. Erikson's (1963) theory explains that children develop a sense of self as they become initiators rather than being told what to do. The degree of success in performing these tasks leads to a child's sense of self and self-worth. Children whose parents are criticizing or restrictive may be led on the path of failure and lower self-esteem. It is important to give this age group opportunity to perform tasks they have been taught. Parents, caregivers, and educators must be cognizant of the fact that while the child learns new skills, the child needs to be given an opportunity to practice what he or she has learned. Adults must provide and give ample opportunities for children to use their newly learned skills.

Gender Development

Gender awareness and gender role specification are early childhood developments that some theorists believe take place as early as the toddler years. Gender development is a process that takes place between two and six years of age; however, it entails different stages of understanding of one's gender and gender role expectations. Gender refers to the social referencing of one's biological status of being a male or a female. Gender role expectation refers to the cultural view on one's gender type, expected behavior, thought patterns, feelings, and action.

Traditional cultures view the female's gender role expectation as working alongside the mother and having increased restriction in socialization. In a traditional culture, as girls approach puberty more restrictions are imposed on them, which leads to narrower socialization. Girls in such cultures face even more social restrictions as they are expected to become more home oriented and work alongside the mother. This lesser degree of freedom contracts a girl's world. On the other hand, boys in traditional cultures have more freedom given to them, expanding their socialization. Boys in this type of culture are given newer opportunities to socialize, network, and develop relationships outside the family. This newfound freedom allows their world to expand.

Freud's Psychodynamic View on Gender Development

Sigmund Freud (1856–1939) introduced **predetermined sequences of five stages or erogenous zones** that, if completed successfully, can result in completion of a healthy personality. However, failure to successfully complete these stages can lead to an unhealthy personality. Although Freud's theory on gender development and gender issues has been greatly criticized at times, nevertheless, he has been credited with highlighting the importance of early childhood gender development. Freud's third stage in development refers to the greatest degree of sexual conflict. In Freud's theory, gender identity develops sometime in the "phallic" stage between three and six years of age, where the male child develops the "Oedipus" complex and the female child develops the "Electra" complex. The conflicts for both male and female children involve the unconscious desire to possess the opposite-sex parent and to eliminate the same-sexed one.

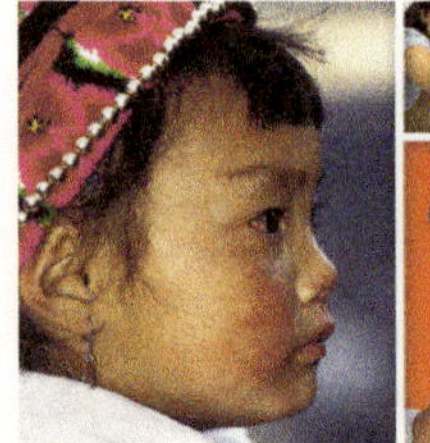

Oedipus Complex

Oedipus, a mythical Greek king and the son of Jocasta and Laius, king of Thebes, unconsciously killed his father and married his mother. He put out his own eyes when he discovered what he'd done. Although dismissed by many theorists, Freud believed that every boy secretly desires to marry his mother.

Phallic Stage

During the phallic stage, known also as the jealousy phase, a young child develops sexual feelings toward the opposite-sex parent comparable to a jealous lover's feeling of obsessive possession. Freud believes that a male child develops sexual desire for his mother; however, out of fear of being punished or castrated, he eventually decides to identify with his father rather than go against him. Through identifying with the masculine features and characteristics of the father, and by differentiating from the mother, a boy eventually takes on the gender role expectations of a male. Freud explains a male child's gender identification as a process that involves differentiation (separation) from the mother and affiliation (association) with the father.

A female child in the phallic stage develops gender identification through affiliation (association) with the mother. It was suggested that the female child goes through a similar experience of developing an attraction to her father. The "penis envy daughter" secretly desires to posses her father sexually; however, the fear of retribution from the mother represses her impulses, thus creating the Electra complex.

According to Freud, the gender development process for females (affiliation with the mother) deprives women from ever differentiating. This lack of experience could therefore lead to a feeling of emotional dependence. He believed that because women never experience differentiation (separation), their psychological makeup never becomes independent of its emotional component, as do men's. Freud theorized that a child might be fixated on any of the psychosexual stages if their normal urges are frustrated. Not being able to become emotionally independent would then turn into a fixation or complex of this phase. In lieu of not experiencing this emotional detachment and not having learned to

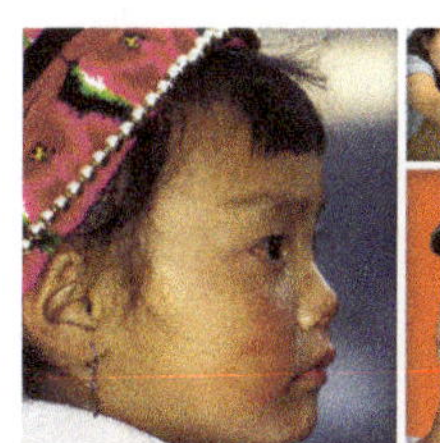

Electra Complex

Carl Jung (1875–1961), a Swiss psychologist and rival of Freud, identified the "feminine Oedipus attitude," deriving the name from the Greek myth about Electra, who wanted her brother (Orestes) to avenge the death of their father Agamemnon by killing their mother, Clytemnestra. The Electra complex describes a female child's affectionate feeling toward the father and her anger toward the mother.

emotionally separate themselves makes women frustrated with the sexual urge of the phallic phase. Thus, girls may end up with a fixation in the phallic stage; such a fixation may result in either over or under sexual indulgence once she becomes an adult.

Piaget's Theory of Gender Development

Piaget's (1896–1980) gender theory focuses on the structure and development of thought processes, which shape perceptions, attitudes, and actions. Children use these active cognitive processes to acquire gender-related behaviors. Based on Piaget's stages of cognitive development, during the "preoperational" phase (two to four years), the child relies on gender schema to develop gender identity. **Gender schema** is an explanation of how children's sexual identity develops, which includes elements of social-learning theory and cognitive-developmental theory. Gender schema is very similar to the concept of gender stereotyping, which is grouping individuals based on a certain attributes. Socially, a child learns gender schemas from family, culture, religion, media, and other social observations. Gender schemas help shape the way individuals notice, interpret, and remember information according to social expectations about genders. These expectations form and shape human beings' thought processes. These expectations could be as simple as pink being feminine and blue being masculine, or as complicated as career choices or limitations on social behavior, or the degree of independence one may have in making these choices.

Kohlberg's Theory of Gender Development

Building on Piaget's cognitive development theory, Lawrence Kohlberg (1927–1987) believed that gender identity takes place in several stages. The first stage is **basic sex-role identity**; at around three years of age, children can label themselves as "boy" or "girl" and therefore look for opportunities to behave in gender-appropriate ways. By the time a child reaches age four or five, the child can also identify things as appropriate for either males or females as the child develops gender stability. During the stage of **gender stability**, a child acquires the understanding that sex roles are stable over time, and that the child will remain a boy/girl over time. However, it is not until six or seven years of age that children finalize their perception of gender, which means they develop **gender constancy**. Gender role development is accomplished in the gender constancy stage, when a child realizes that his or her gender stays the same regardless of the situation; for example, growing long hair does not change a boy into a girl (Martin & Ruble, 2004).

Bandura's Theory of Gender Development

Albert Bandura is best known for his work on the importance of observation and imitation. Adults provide the role modeling and children imitate the behavior as they observe it. Because social learning theory has its foundation in classical and operant conditioning, Bandura believed that adults' use of reward for sex-appropriate behavior and punishment for cross-sex behavior encourages

THEORIST	THEORY	AGE	STAGE	GENDER
Freud	Psychoanalytical	3-5	a) Differentiation	Male child: Differentiates from mother and identifies with father.
			b) Affiliation	Female child: Differentiates from father; affiliates with mother
Piaget	Cognitive	2-3	Develops gender schema	Boy: Receives social cues and mental pictures on being a male
				Girl: Receives social cues and mental pictures on being a female
Kohlberg	Cognitive	3	Identity labeling: Child labels him- or herself as being boy or girl	Labeling: Boy/girl
		4-5	Stability of gender: Child realizes that he or she will probably stay at this labeled gender	Stability: Gender labeling will stay the same
		6-7	Constancy of gender: The labeled gender will never change	Constancy: Gender labeling will not change
Bandura	Social Learning	Birth onward	Child observes the role model and imitates sex-appropriate behavior, receives reinforcement for role modeling the right behavior, and gets punished for inappropriate gender behavior	Reinforcers for sex-role appropriate behavior will lead to gender identity and behavior

children to behave based on gender expectation. In accordance with other behaviorists, social learning theorists believed that behavior is learned. Examples of this type of role modeling are when parents punish a male child who is crying by saying, "Boys don't cry," or tell a female child that "Little girls sit up straight," referring to social roles.

Aggression

Aggression is committing acts of violence with the intention to hurt others. There are different types of aggression such as instrumental, hostile, and relational. **Instrumental aggression** refers to the use of force in order to obtain something or to fulfill a personal goal. An example of instrumental aggression is when a two-year-old hits another child to obtain a toy. Some experts believe the reason for this type of aggression might be due to the child's lack of ability to communicate, reason, and negotiate. The major part of this inability is that language skills are not yet fully developed, and children at this age face many obstacles to logical thinking. Instrumental aggression may be part of a normal development; however, it needs to be addressed and corrected (shortly we discuss ways to prevent aggressive behavior). **Hostile aggression** refers to hurting another person with the purpose of establishing dominance; therefore, this type of aggressive behavior is more male oriented such as bullying, which is very common among school-age children particularly toward sixth grade. Using words such as "I hate you" to hurt others is called **relational aggression**, and it is more female oriented; however, in later childhood, any hostile aggression may lead to relational aggression.

Changes in Aggression

Aggressive behavior in children between the ages of one and two may increase because of the development of self-awareness and self-concept. As previously explained, self-awareness is a developmental phase where children learn that their existence is separate from others and that they co-exist with their environment. Between seven and nine months and upon development of self-awareness, stranger wariness and separation anxiety follow; however, these developmental events are precursors to developing self-concept. Around sixteen months of age, children begin to recognize their own perceptions, impressions, and thoughts regarding themselves and others, which will develop into self-concept. Due to this new sense of self, between the ages of one and two, there may be a rapid increase in instrumental aggression. Around two years of age and with the development of early language, this instrumental aggression may be slowly changing to relational aggression, which means a combination of teasing and usage of words to hurt rather than the physical aspect of aggression. This type of relational aggression will be more common in female children than it would be in males, such as "You can't play with MY toys!" This type of aggressive behavior can be explained by the fact that children are learning about ownership rights and how they would protect what they consider to be theirs. As for aggressive behavior in male children, the instrumental aggression that was used to gain and attain will turn into more physical tussles over possessions and will change into hostile aggression, and eventually bullying.

Causes of Aggression

Bandura's social learning theory is based on observation of the behavior and the role modeling of the observer (Bandura, 1977). Social learning theory believes aggression develops as a result of a child observing then role modeling the aggressive behavior. Bandura has also done extensive studies on aggression as an observed and imitated behavior. Violent behavior observed by children may lead to the imitation of the violence by the child. Through a series of experiments, Bandura and his colleague filmed adults kicking, hitting, and inserting aggressive behavior towards a Bobo doll. Later, children were shown these films of adults demonstrating violent behavior toward the Bobo doll. Children who had observed this aggressive behavior toward the doll had more tendencies to repeat the aggressive behavior. In some cases, children showed additional violence toward the doll even though that particular act had not been role modeled by the adult subject. On the other hand, children who had not observed the aggressive behavior were less likely to show aggressive behavior.

Bandura may have demonstrated by his Bobo doll experiment that aggressive behavior is learned and role modeled, but are there other reasons for aggressive behavior? When aggression is rewarded either by the victim giving in or retreating, the aggressor will claim victory and thus be rewarded for the aggressive behavior. In other cases, the adults might provide the positive reinforcement that encourages aggressive behavior by paying more attention, laughing, signaling approval, or simply by coercing the aggressor child. Therefore, the approval or the lack of criticism on part of adults may also result in aggressive behavior. In some cases, the adults might inadvertently provide an environment for a child's aggressive behavior by role modeling the behavior. Adults who use physical punishment particularly with anger as a way of disciplining a child's misbehavior may be teaching that this type of behavior is accepted. Research has shown that the aggressive behavior of children who had observed adult aggression was substantially higher than that of children who had watched nonaggressive interactions. It made little difference whether the adult models were live or filmed.

Controlling Aggression

Develop a Hierarchical System

Aggression can be controlled in several ways, one of which is developing a hierarchical system of control. Through this method, the aggressor understands his or her position in the hierarchy and challenges only those whom it is safe to challenge, leaving others alone and thereby reducing the amount of aggression within the group.

Venting Method

Another method to control aggression is to let the aggressor "blow off steam" in a safe environment before he or she explodes violently. This method may enable the aggressor to talk about the problem; however, research has shown little evidence to support the effective use of this method.

Punish Aggressive Behavior

Aggressive behavior can be punished in order to suppress the behavior, but only when the child strongly identifies with the person who administers the punishment. The punishment method may be effective only when the aggressor looks up to the punisher as an authority figure. This relates to the hierarchical

◀ ***Children using aggressive behavior.***

(Photo courtesy of Maxim Blinkov/Shutterstock.com)

system that was previously introduced. In a hierarchical system, authority is established; therefore, the aggressor has a clear understanding of the authority figure. The key to the punishment method is to be consistent; however, this punishment itself may provoke additional aggression and this method must be used with great caution. Furthermore, this method may be ineffective if physical punishment is used as a way of discipline. Research has also shown that physical punishment itself may encourage children to demonstrate aggressive behavior.

Reward Nonaggressive Behavior

Because young children sometimes become aggressive in order to gain attention, one strategy is to ignore it and to pay attention to children only when they are engaged in cooperative behavior. For example, an adult may step in between the children involved and pay attention only to the victim (i.e., comfort the child, give the child something interesting to do). Side benefits are that other children who may have observed the situation learn that it is appropriate to be sympathetic to the victim of aggression.

Cognitive Training

Cognitive training involves short, individual discussion with the aggressor focusing on the fact that aggression hurts another person, or aggression makes the victim feel sad, or aggression does not solve problems. This method may be an effective way to train the aggressor's mind in handling a violent situation in a more civilized manner. Teaching children to communicate and discuss problems with others will equip them with effective communication tools, and will provide them with necessary skills to resolve conflict in a nonviolent way.

Parenting Styles

Diana Baumrind, who studied developmental, clinical, and social psychology at the University of California, Berkeley, earned her MA in 1951 and her PhD in 1955. By 1960, she became affiliated with Berkeley's Institute of Human Development, where she conducted extensive studies of family socialization, developmental competence, adolescent risk-taking, and ethics. She is the recipient of many awards and grants for her extensive studies on family issues, ethics, and moral values. Her published research on parenting styles is still the protocol for human development views on Western styles of parenting. Diana Baumrind's prototypical parenting style was first published in 1966, where she introduced three types of parenting styles: authoritative, authoritarian, and permissive. Later on, researchers added a fourth parenting method to Baumrind's existing styles—indifferent. Most parents fall somewhere in the continuum or fit into at least one of these categories.

The Four Basic Parenting Styles

Most parenting styles can be labeled as one of the four basic styles that have been researched and categorized by human developmentalists. There are parents who are heavy on rules and discipline, yet do not particularly cater to the child's needs. Also, there are parents who are more child-centered and extremely responsive without a whole set of rules in place. Recognizing which category of parenting couples use will help them to recognize their weaknesses and to improve on the areas that need attention.

Diana Baumrind's categorization of parenting styles was based on studies she did at the child center in the University of California, Berkeley. She studied thirty-two preschoolers, ages three to five years, in order to observe the relationship between each child and their parents. The study focused on the type of practices parents adopt when it comes to their child-rearing methods, and the behavior children exhibit in response to those practices. Baumrind's study mainly focused on the dynamics and interaction between parent and child. In order to establish a connection between the two, the rigidity of demands, rules, and structure set by the parent and the degree of responsiveness and attentiveness by the said parent were observed and analyzed.

The main criteria she was looking for were the demandingness (control) of the parents in comparison to responsiveness (warmth). The study defined demandingness in terms of control and structure that is fair and reasonable based on the child's capabilities. Responsiveness was based on the degree of sensitivity that parents show toward the child's needs and expectations, such as warmth, love, and affection. Based on these two dimensions, the four basic parenting styles are categorized as authoritative, authoritarian, permissive (also known as indulgent), and indifferent (also known as neglectful).

Authoritative Parenting Style

According to Western scientific studies, the authoritative parenting style is considered to be the best parenting practice because it offers rules, structure, and discipline in addition to affection and responsiveness in a balanced and moderate degree. Parents who use the authoritative parenting style tend to be high in demandingness and high in responsiveness. Most middle-class American families use this method of parenting, and they tend to be more educated and accomplished individuals themselves. This type of parenting style involves reasonable directives that are combined with issue-oriented situations. For example, if there are rules to be followed and the authoritative parent is faced with resistance from the child, the parent is willing to communicate, negotiate, rationalize, and compromise in order to not only teach the child the art of communication, but also to persuade the child to conform to the set rule. Authoritative parents are demanding and high in responsiveness, maintaining a healthy balance between structure, rules, communication, and negotiation.

Qualities of the Child Raised with an Authoritative Parenting Style

Children who are raised in an authoritative parenting environment tend to be lively, happy, and self-confident. They have confidence about mastering tasks, are independent, and have secure attachment disposition. They have developed healthy emotional regulation techniques and appropriate social skills. There is less gender bias in this type of parenting method because girls are more independent and boys are more sensitive. These children learn to take responsibility for their actions and face the consequences.

Methods Used in Authoritative Parenting Style

Parents reward children for positive behavior and discipline them for inappropriate behavior. Discipline and consequences are discussed and understood by the child. The discussion and explanation of consequences is at the level that makes sense to the child. These parents use consistency in their rules and consequences, so the child knows exactly what to expect. Rules are firm, yet there is

A child in "time out," a commonly used method to discipline a child.

(Photo courtesy of Viacheslav Nikolaenko/ Shutterstock.com)

room to compromise. Guidelines and expectations are appropriate, reasonable, and gauged to the behavior and circumstances of the situation.

The age and abilities of the child also play an important role in setting the rules and structures, which are explained to the child in advance. Children raised via this method learn to become effective communicators, negotiators, and learn to compromise. For example, if a child has a school project to finish and at the same time wants to go outside and play, an authoritative parent would say: "If you finish your school work by 5:00 P.M. today, you can play outside for an hour." In this method of parenting, the child knows the expectations and the consequences. The choice is now up to the child, whether he or she wants to meet the standard that was just set for the child or not. These parents value autonomy, offer their perspectives, yet solicit the child's input. They also teach values and use the child's objections to rules as a teaching opportunity to instill individuality and independence.

Authoritarian Parenting Style

In this method of parenting, rules are firm, rigid, and there is no room for negotiation or compromise. Authoritarian parents often tend to set unreasonable rules and expectations. If the child does not meet the expectation, the punishment is usually harsh or even physical. In this style of parenting, parents use physical punishment to assert rules and instill conformity. Control of children's behavior is a priority among authoritarian parents who want to make sure the rules are followed and their authority is recognized. Often, guidelines are enforced with harsh consequences for compliancy, and little or no explanation is given to explain the rules. These parents are highly critical of their children and any infraction, whether small or big, may result in harsh punishment. In the authoritarian parenting style, parents often shout, yell, or use aggressive behavior to make a point instead of calmly explaining the situation or getting the child engaged in a conversation. "Because I said so," seems to be the mantra of these parents with no explanation of why the decision was made by the parent. Authoritarian parents are high in demandingness and low in responsiveness.

Qualities of the Child Raised with an Authoritarian Parenting Style

Children who are brought up in this kind of environment may become aggressive due to the parents' use of physical punishment. They also seem to be unhappy, have low self-esteem, and often use aggressive behavior when faced with problems. Children in an authoritarian parenting environment are conformers to rules and they do not necessarily engage in antisocial behavior; however, it may be that during the adolescent years they may become nonconformists. Adolescents from this type of parenting style have shown a tendency to be rebellious and prone to excessive risky behavior. Because obedience to authority is a must in this type of parenting method, children in this parenting category may do well in academic performance as do the children in an authoritative parenting style. Girls in this type of parenting tend to be more submissive as boys become more hostile. In general, children in this group are faced with no choice but to abide by the rules set for them and to follow authority without question.

Methods Used in Authoritarian Parenting Style

Authoritarian parents set rules and expect complete obedience. They do not reward positive behavior as it is expected of children to do well and behave wisely, so there is no reward given for good behavior. Ethnic groups such as Latino Americans and Asian Americans have been labeled as using this type of parenting, where authority is highly regarded and structures are firm. Parents control and shape the behavior of their child in accordance to rigid and absolute standards, typically structured by a higher authority, which are not compromised or modified. The authoritarian parent is restrictive; autonomy is discouraged and consequently the parents do not want the child to become independent of family and hierarchical structure. These parents value obedience and practice forceful punitive measures to curb undesired behavior. "Father knows best" is the motto of these parents.

Permissive Parenting Style

These parents are the opposite of authoritarian parents, which means they conform to their child's wants, desires, and whims without having a great deal of expectations. Without control and demands, the parent does not hold the child responsible to any externally defined standards. These parents allow the child to set his or her rules and regulations as much as possible, which makes the parent frustrated because the child may behave out of control. Permissive parents set few demands or rules, and give very few firm guidelines for what is supposed to be appropriate behavior. The permissive parents make themselves the source from which the child can get anything he or she wishes, but they do not represent themselves as role models for the child to emulate, or learn guidance or any social skills necessary for the child's future growth. The child has free rein without any control; therefore, there is no opportunity to learn to exercise control or to uphold any externally defined standards. Permissive parents use low demandingness and high responsiveness (Baumrind, 1967).

Qualities of the Child Raised with a Permissive Parenting Style

Permissive parents raise children who have poor emotional regulation as well as who lack the ability to read and understand social cues. These children are defiant and noncompliant when challenged because they are not in the habit of hearing "NO." Because they have no expectations or demands placed on them, these children have low persistence when faced with a challenge or project. Their parents have not taught them how to set boundaries, follow standards, or have limits, which causes frustrations when facing challenges. Not having had to abide by any externally formulated standards, children who were raised by permissive parents demonstrate antisocial behavior and do not have many friends.

Methods Used in Permissive Parenting Style

In order to keep the child from getting upset, the usual method used by permissive parents is to give into their child's every whim and want. Allowing children to have their way creates an atmosphere that is frustrating because at times, when the parents try to avoid giving in, it may cause tantrums and excessive crying by the child in order to get what he or she wants. At this time, parents may resort to screaming or getting overly upset to counteract the child's tantrum. This does not create an effective nurturing environment as a role model for teaching the child emotional regulations, social cues, or dealing with anger.

Indifferent (Neglectful) Parenting Style

As mentioned, in addition to Baumrind's three parenting styles, indifferent parenting style is a method often used by dysfunctional parents. It is noteworthy that the indifferent parenting style is not always considered a true parenting method because it usually involves parents who suffer from mental disorders, low socioeconomic status (SES), a traumatic event, or illness. SES is defined by categorizing a population into three levels of: (a) education, (b) income, and (c) occupation. Families with low SES who lack proper education, income, and occupation often fall into this category of parenting. Indifferent parenting style has low demandingness and low responsiveness.

Qualities of the Child Raised with an Indifferent Parenting Style

Latch-key kids are often labeled as children who have indifferent or neglectful parents. These children are often home alone and are responsible for their

Effective Parenting Style in the 21st Century: Post-Industrial (Information) Age Western Culture

SCENARIOS OF THE FOUR BASIC PARENTING STYLE	
AUTHORITATIVE	**AUTHORITARIAN**
Parent: You can't go to the mall with your friends because we have to go to grandma's house for a visit. **Child:** But that is not fair, I have made plans with my friends. Can I please go with them? **Parent:** Let's see what we can do. You'll have to visit grandma; however, later we can drop you off at the mall, but you will only have one hour to spend with your friends. **Child:** Thanks, Mom and Dad. I love you.	**Parent:** You can't go to the mall with your friends. It is Sunday, and we are having a family dinner. **Child:** But why can't I go??? **Parent:** Because I said so. This is my house and I make the rules.
INDIFFERENT/NEGLECTFUL	**PERMISSIVE**
Child: My mother is working tonight. Again! I have to take care of my little brother and sister. I am a latch-key kid!	**Parent:** Joey, don't worry if you ruined your brand new iPod, you can have a new one. Don't cry. I will pay for a new iPod! **Child:** But I want this iPad too like the one Billy has. I want it all. **Parent:** OK, dear. You got it! Just stop crying!

own care and sometimes other siblings. The absence of a parent provides no standards or structure that could provide guidelines for behavior. The lack of control often leaves the child with decision making that requires an adult's cognitive ability; therefore, the end result may be disastrous. Children who are left to fend for themselves can easily get in trouble, be injured, or even die. A child's cognitive ability is not the same as an adult's. Children always need guidance, supervision, and teaching. These children frequently end up in the custody of the legal system, either as a criminal or as a fugitive.

Methods Used in Indifferent Parenting Style

Indifferent parents are the opposite of permissive parents. They put their own needs ahead of their child's, as if the child does not exist or poses an inconvenience. Because the indifferent parent is usually from a low SES, it may be the lack of education or income that prevents these parents from practicing an effective parenting style. A child simply does not have the skills, the cognitive ability, or the psychological ability to take care of him- or herself or siblings. Even though Western culture encourages independence and freedom to be expressive in child rearing, children still need supervision and adult intervention in order to develop and flourish as best as they can. In severe cases of neglect, various social agencies will get involved to mediate the situation, especially in cases of child abuse, child endangerment, and child abandonment.

Parenting Style Diversities in Various Cultures

Authoritarian parenting style is a traditional technique of raising children, and for the most part is considered to be a rarity in the Western world. The traditional cultural values dictate that authority is to be obeyed without question, and parents with this type of belief inherently have more authority over children. Parents using an authoritarian style do not feel they need to explain, compromise, or communicate rules to children; children will face harsh punishment if they break the rules or disobey authority. Due to this traditional parenting style, the likelihood of adolescents' rebellion and risky behavior is very high. Research has shown that a rigid structure and too many rules may be met with objection once the child has reached the adolescent years.

This may be more true for adolescent males who are the subjects of strict authoritarian parenting style. The phenomenon of globalization has also made this type of behavior more common universally. Due to globalization and the Internet, adolescents across the globe are identifying with more individualistic cultural values, as opposed to their traditional collectivistic view. The authoritarian type of parenting style also coincides with the collectivistic cultural value that traditional cultures adhere to, such as considering the well-being of the family as a priority versus individual needs and wants.

Asian American Parenting Style

The one parenting style that best fits traditional cultures is the authoritarian technique, where rules are to be obeyed without explanation, compromise, or communication. Asian culture being a traditional one should therefore be categorized under authoritarian; however, not all researchers agree with this categorization. Chao (2001), an Asian scholar, disagrees with the Western researchers' classification of Chinese parents' classification in that taxonomy. According to Chao, Asian adolescents by tradition obey and abide authority; therefore, there are none of the negative effects that other traditional parenting styles may face. Adolescents who are raised under an Asian parenting style for the most part are high academic achievers, show very little or no rebellious behavior, and are conformist to authority beyond middle childhood. This shows that there is a fundamental difference between non-Western authoritarian parenting styles, where children are expected to follow rules without question, versus the Asian parenting style, where rules are followed without objection. It is then noteworthy to mention that such objection could mean that because obedience to authority is a cultural inheritance in the Asian community, comparing it to the Western authoritarian style may not be an accurate portrayal of their parenting techniques. Furthermore, culturally it is not required to explain rules because in the Asian culture authority is obeyed out of respect and without question; therefore, it should not be compared to Western authoritarian style, where authority is demanded. Asian adolescents do not ask for an explanation or compromise of the rules because there is no need for such communication; therefore, when there is no objection to the rules as a matter of cultural inheritance, there is no defiant or insubordinate behavior as a consequence.

Latino American Parenting Style

Generally, Latino parents have been categorized as authoritarian parents. The obedience to authority in the Latino culture is somewhat different than that of the Asian population. The belief of "*respecto*" is a Latino cultural belief deeply set in the idea that parents and elders—especially fathers—are to be respected without question. In addition, the cultural belief of "*familismo,*" which is love, closeness, and family obligation, leads adolescents to conform to authority. The collectivistic cultural value is also very much practiced and observed by the Latino family emphasizing more the importance of family and group mentality versus the individualistic view with which Western adolescents are more familiar.

Divorce

The impact of divorce can be devastating regardless of the age of the child; however, some age groups may have a significantly harder time dealing with divorce than other age groups. Adolescents particularly do not do well when their parents divorce. There may be behavioral problems or academic, psychological, emotional, or other developmental difficulties. It is imperative for parents who are thinking of divorce or who are going through divorce to be cognizant of the impact of divorce on their children. These parents may see their children demonstrate difficulties in some or all of the following areas:

- Risky behavior or misconduct such as breaking the law
- Decline in grades or academic achievement
- Signs of stress, depression, or psychological distress
- Tendency toward substance abuse
- Early sexual behavior, promiscuity, or even teen pregnancy
- Lower chance of pursuing higher education

Divorce can also create or increase already-existing financial distress, which could have an inverse effect on children, especially adolescents, who are going through a crucial time in their development. Amicable divorce (may be hard to achieve, but necessary) could decrease some of the problems inherent in divorce proceedings. Parents must be mindful of the harms of divorce and try not to expose their children to conflict, changing parenting style, or economic distress. Exposure to conflict between parents during divorce is especially damaging and harmful. Children are not equipped nor do they have the proper cognitive maturity to handle conflict arising between parents at the time of divorce. Research shows that children exposed to parental conflict should not be expected to take sides nor should they be expected to choose one parent over the other. Choosing one parent over the other is unfair and is detrimental to the child's psyche, which could have long-term adverse effects. Children love their parents equally, and it is hard for them to choose between them. This degree of clash and struggle is detrimental to children's normal development and sometimes the psychological consequences are irreversible.

During times of conflict and divorce, most parents change their parenting techniques. It is expected to see the parent who leaves become more permissive of children's conduct as a way of dealing with guilt brought by their desertion. In that case, it is also common to see the other parent applying more rules in order to compensate for the lack of structure from the other partner. This uneven way of parenting will adversely impact the child.

Another harmful result and consequence of divorce is the negative economic impact on the whole family, particularly for women. Females who experience divorce will have 40 percent to 50 percent less income; with custody of the children given to mothers 90 percent of the time, the scenario is stressful and financially gloomy. Consequently, the decline in income will most likely impact the children—if nothing else, it will change some of their routines, adding to the level of stress they are experiencing.

Impact of Remarriage

Overall, young children and adolescents do not do well when a parent remarries. The impact of a new partner in their parent's life is a heavy psychological burden for which children most likely are not ready. In particular, female children will have a harder time with their mother's remarriage, and the concept of a stepfather is especially difficult for them to handle. Similar to children of divorce, a parent's remarriage could lead to adolescents participating in problematic behavior in the following areas:

- Psychological malfunctioning such as depression, anxiety, distress, or emotional problems
- Lack of adjustment to the new family dynamic
- Decrease in academic performance or failure
- Misconduct such as breaking the law or disorderly conduct

Problems associated with the impact of living with a stepparent and/or stepsiblings are similar to those that a family break up will produce; however, the gender of the adolescent may make a slight difference in the degree of impact.

CHAPTER 10 SUMMARY

As children of this age group become more articulate, able, skilled, and independent, their social activities and interpersonal development grow. They start making new friends and act more sociable, thus making them friendlier. The development of self that started during toddler years becomes more sophisticated at this stage of development. Self-esteem develops and, due to the egocentric view of themselves, their self-worth is at an all-time high. Children in the preschool or play years want, seek, and demand more independence, which means they want to do more on their own! This newfound desire and willingness to initiate is helpful in teaching this age group to take initiative to start tasks, and to want to be successful in accomplishing them. Simple tasks such as pouring juice from a bottle into a glass, or wanting to button his or her own jacket shows that the child is now entering a more independent stage of self. However, failure at doing these simple tasks may also lead to a feeling of guilt. Adults' handling of a child's failed activity, such as making a mess while pouring milk into a glass, could be a very crucial determinant in how the child faces failure.

Other important milestones for this age group are gender identity development that occurs in phases as more maturity occurs with each advanced stage. Social stereotypes and gender role expectation are also important factors for the shaping of gender identity. Due to the difference in male and female gender identity, certain characteristics may ensue, such as the presence of more aggressive behavior in male versus female children. Some of the causes of aggressive behavior could be genetic and some may be environmental or social. Parents faced with such behavior can refer to a method of controlling aggressive behavior, preventing it from becoming a set behavior in their child's characteristics.

CHAPTER 10 VOCABULARY

Aggression
Authoritarian Parenting Style
Authoritative Parenting Style
Basic Sex-Role Identity
Cognitive Training
Electra Complex
Erikson's Theory Third Stage
Five Predetermined Sequences of Stages or Erogenous Zones
Gender Constancy
Gender Schema
Gender Stability
Hostile Aggression
Indifferent Parenting Style
Instrumental Aggression
Oedipus Complex
Permissive Parenting Style
Phallic Stage
Punish Aggressive Behavior
Relational Aggression
Reward Aggressive Behavior
Self-Esteem
Social Learning Theory

SCHOOL-AGE YEARS
Physical, Psychological, and Cognitive Development

School children eating at school in Namibia.
(Photo courtesy of thomas kock/Shutterstock.com)

Food Glorious Food

by Margaret Goetz

Children dance to celebrate
school lunch, rice and
ground meat stew
cooked over a fire by a
village woman, every plate
emptied clean. They dance
rhythm on bare cement
floors, school uniforms
askew, mended desks
pushed aside, windows
metal framed with lumpy
paint pushed open, naked
rafters clean with song.
Every day a meal with meat,
a luxury, provided by a
village in another world
where children
throw food away.

Introduction

Nicholas, a young twelve-year-old male, is propped up in the hospital bed in the emergency department, throwing his soccer ball keychain into the air. He tripped walking into his classroom and broke his left foot, which is swollen and red. As he was waiting with his soccer coach for the x-rays to be developed, his parents frantically hurried in to see him. His mother hugged him tightly and asked, "What were you doing? How did you break your foot?" "I don't know, Mom," Nicholas replied sheepishly. "I guess my foot wasn't where I thought it was."

Young "tweens" like Nicholas often have the problem of faulty **proprioception**, the body's inherent knowledge of its geographic positioning, because their limbs grow so quickly that they literally do not know where their limbs are. The physiological changes that accompany the middle childhood years are not as dramatic as those in adolescence at the onset of puberty, but they are nonetheless remarkable considering a baby boy begins life at 8½ pounds, 20 inches and reaches 180 pounds, 6 foot 2 inches at maturity. In this section we examine the physical, cognitive, and psychological changes that comprise the middle childhood years.

Physical Development

After the relatively powerful growth spurt of early childhood, children aged roughly six to twelve years grow at a rate of approximately two to four inches and five to seven pounds per year (Kuczmarski et al., 2000). In middle childhood,

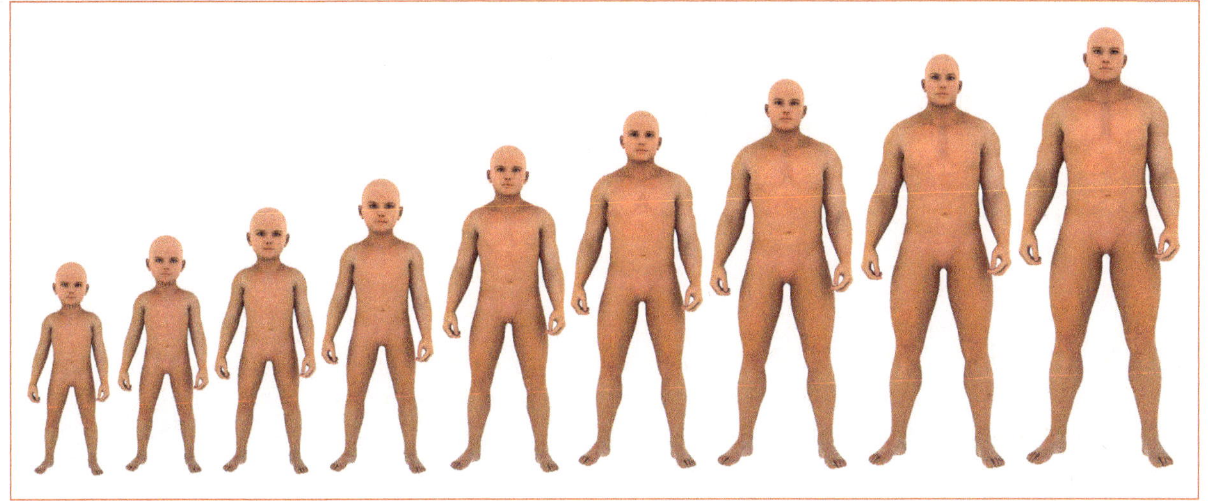

▲ ***A child growing up to adulthood.***

(Photo courtesy of designersl/Shutterstock.com)

the child's body generally slims, as the torso and legs lengthen and strengthen. This is accompanied by the loss of temporary teeth that are replaced by permanent teeth. Children in this age group need ten or eleven hours of sleep to accommodate their growth (National Sleep Foundation, n.d.).

There is a complementary increase in both gross and fine motor skills. Gross motor skills improve as children engage in jumping, skipping, climbing, and running. These changes are correlated with a child's participation in team sports in which the child learns organized play, taking turns, role responsibilities, and rule obligations. As children play in more and more complex situations, their timing and hand–eye coordination increase, and these new abilities qualify them for more and more complex play conditions.

School-aged children also demonstrate an increase in fine motor skills (Education Encyclopedia, State University). This is indicated by the capacity to play musical instruments, to draw details, and to manipulate computer controls, for example. The elementary school child's increased fine motor skills are also associated with growth in brain development. At approximately six to eight years old there is an increase in the protective covering of the nerves—the **myelin sheath**. As the process called **myelination** develops, the electrical transmission from the brain to the nerves increases. Faster nerve processing increases muscular dexterity. As the reflexes get faster, the brain gains more control over them. There are some gender differences in muscular control and development. On average girls outstrip boys in fine motor skills, such as writing and drawing, while boys excel in gross motor abilities, such as running and jumping.

Middle childhood children are also prone to injury. Their increased muscular development coupled with their generally poor judgment make these children susceptible to numerous injuries from sports and other physical activities, such as skateboarding, go-kart racing, and break dancing. These threats can be countered by good safety measures—helmets, elbow and knee pads, and other protective gear.

Health and Nutrition

The average four- to six-year-old needs about 1,800 calories a day, while the average seven- to ten-year-old needs around 2,000 calories a day (Ekvall, 1993). One of the central concerns of middle childhood is children's nutrition, which has resulted in an epidemic of obesity. In 2011/2012, more than 4.4 percent of children in the United States ages two to five, 17.7 percent of kids ages six to eleven, and 20.5 percent of children ages twelve to nineteen years old are obese (Centers for Disease Control and Prevention, 2014). Obesity is associated with heart disease and diabetes, and obese children are more likely to remain obese as adults. They are also at risk in social interactions, as they face ridicule and alienation as a result of our culture's negative attitude toward excess weight.

A child eating junk food, a very high calorie, high-in-fat diet.

(Photo courtesty of Decha Laoharuengrongkun/Shutterstock.com)

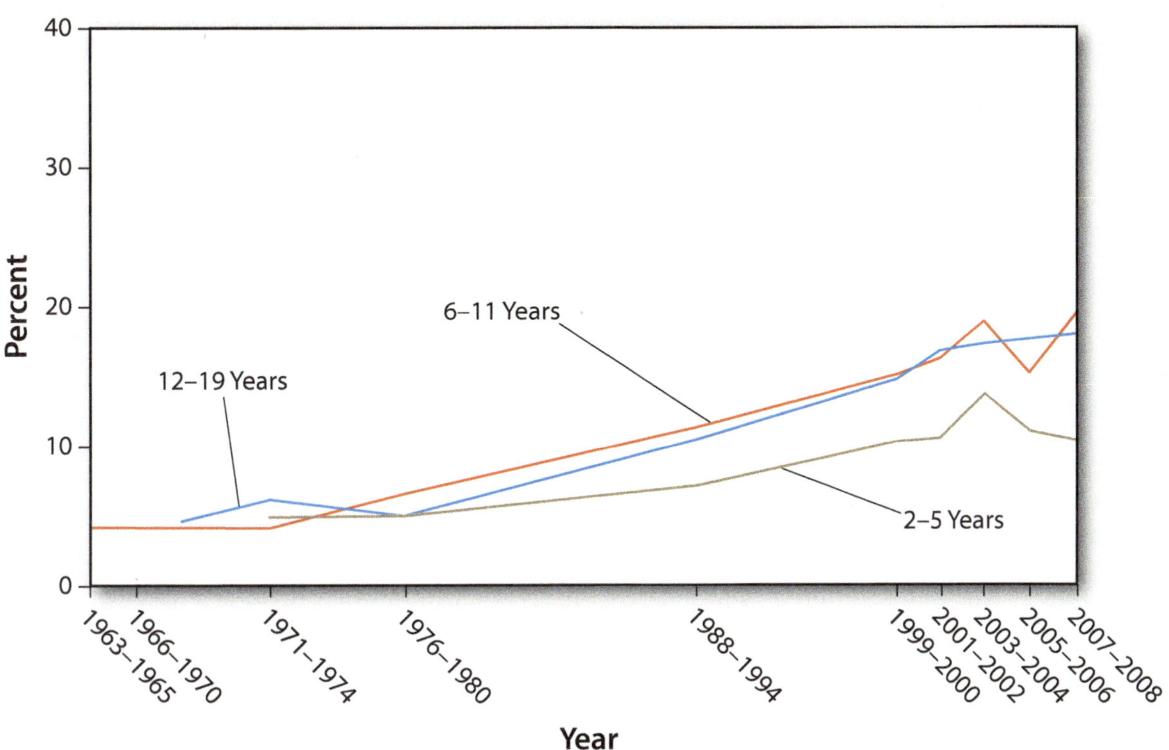

▲ ***Trends in obesity among children and adolescents: United States, 1963–2008.***

NOTE: Obesity is defined as body mass index (BMI) greater than or equal to sex- and age-specific 95th percentile from the 2000 Centers for Disease Control and Prevention Growth Charts.

Adapted from Centers for Disease Control and Prevention, 2010.

This results in obese children suffering from a higher rate of depression and low self-esteem, as well as other emotional and psychological distresses compared to average-sized or thin children. The tremendous prevalence of fast food and junk food promoted through commercials aimed at children, coupled with the presence of junk food in school cafeterias and vending machines, encourage children to eat empty calories, sugars, and fats to excess. Good nutrition is associated with optimal physical growth, as well as with strong cognitive, social, and emotional development.

Physical fitness is the key to positive development in all arenas, as it is in every stage of life. Physical fitness decreases children's susceptibility to heart disease, diabetes, and other degenerative diseases. According to the Centers for Disease Control and Prevention (2014), children need at least one hour of physical activity a day. Physical fitness also decreases the tendency toward depression and social alienation.

Prevalence of Obesity Among U.S. Adolescents Aged 12–19, for Selected Years 1988–1994 hrough 2007–2008

	NHANES 1988–1994	NHANES 1999–2000	NHANES 2001–2002	NHANES 2003–2004	NHANES 2005–2006	NHANES 2007–2008
Boys, All	11.3	14.8	17.6	18.2	18.2	19.3
Boys, Non-Hispanic White	11.6	11.8	16.6	19.1	15.5	16.7
Boys, Non-Hispanic Black	10.7	21.1	16.7	18.4	18.4	19.8
Boys, Mexican American	14.1	27.2	21.8	18.3	25.6	26.8
Girls,[1] All	9.7	14.8	15.7	16.4	17.3	16.8
Girls,[1] Non-Hispanic White	8.9	11.0	13.7	15.4	13.5	14.5
Girls,[1] Non-Hispanic Black	16.3	25.2	22.0	25.4	29.8	29.2
Girls,[1] Mexican American	13.4	19.3	20.3	14.1	25.4	17.4

[1] Excludes pregnant females.

How Much Physical Activity Do Children Need?

- **Aerobic Activity:** Aerobic activity should make up most of your child's sixty or more minutes of physical activity each day. This can include either moderate-intensity aerobic activity, such as brisk walking, or vigorous-intensity activity, such as running. Be sure to include vigorous-intensity aerobic activity on at least three days per week.
- **Muscle Strengthening Activity:** Include muscle-strengthening activities, such as gymnastics or push-ups, at least three days per week as part of your child's sixty or more minutes.
- **Bone Strengthening Activity:** Include bone strengthening activities, such as jumping rope or running, at least three days per week as part of your child's sixty or more minutes.

Source: Centers for Disease Control and Prevention, 2011.

Psychoanalytical Development

There are three well-known theories that expansively explain, analyze, and define development during middle childhood. Freudian theory identifies the period from six to twelve years old as the **latency period**. During the latency period, **libidinal** (sexual) energy is channeled toward skill mastery. Sexual tendencies are suppressed during this period. The latency period is critically important as physical development advances toward puberty. Today's middle childhood children are moving out of the latency period at earlier and earlier ages due to the pervasive and obsessive cultural focus on sexuality. This is resulting in some middle-school children having sexual relations; however, they lack physical readiness as well as psychological preparedness for such an advanced undertaking. As a result, these children are at even greater risk for sexual abuse, sex trafficking, and sexually transmitted infections (STIs) than their adolescent peers.

Erikson proposed that middle childhood is characterized by **industry versus inferiority**. Children of this age are naturally industrious and are focused on learning and mastery of adultlike skills. Unlike early childhood, children in this age groups are generally focused on activities outside of the family, reaching for skills within and beyond their former peer groups. Effective parenting during this period consists of enthusiastic support of activities and reinforcement of improved mastery. Children need parents to support their industriousness. When parents are involved, children gain the capacity to develop the organization and structure necessary to succeed. When parents are not involved, children become fearful and suspicious of their own competence, which undermines their confidence in themselves and in the world around them (Diessner, 2008).

Children aged seven to eleven fall into the third stage of Piaget's cognitive theory, the stage of **concrete operations**. In this stage, the child is able to move concrete things around in their minds to manipulate and organize materials.

Summary of Psychoanalytical Development Theories

Freudian Theory (ages 6–12)	**Latency period:** Libidinal (sexual) energy is channeled toward skill mastery.
Erikson Theory	**Industry vs. inferiority:** Children of this age are naturally industrious and are focused on learning and mastery of adult-like skills.
Piaget's Cognitive Theory (ages 7–11)	**Concrete operations:** The child is able to move concrete things around in their minds to manipulate and organize materials.

Elementary school children are interested in organizing objects and information. They also become actively invested in rule-based constructs, like games and clubs. Children in this stage also develop **metacognition**—the ability to think about thinking. Metacognition requires well-developed mastery of thought processes and cognition using past knowledge and learned skills. By age ten, children can understand that they are able to change the way they think about things, a major developmental step in the path to abstract thinking, which is the next stage of development.

Intelligence

What Is Intelligence?

There are no universally accepted answers to this question. People do not even agree on how much environment affects intelligence. Are people born with a certain amount of intelligence or can you increase intelligence as a child grows up? Can intelligence be increased once you reach adulthood? What is generally known as IQ (which stands for intelligence quotient or intelligence) is determined by tests that usually predict how well a child will do in school relative to other children. The tests are not good predictors of how successful a person will be once he or she leaves school and goes into the workplace or in other aspects of life. Most intelligence instruments are developed and tested on White middle-class children, which results in biases for many minorities. A general definition of **intelligence** is "the capacity to understand the world, to think rationally and to use resources effectively when faced with challenges" (Feldman, 2008).

Generally IQ is thought to be constant across the life span. However, new light has been shed on this from a study conducted by researchers at the University College in London that used neuroimaging to track changes in IQ and how they correlate to changes in brain development during teenage years (Ramsden et al., 2011). They found that small changes in the brain during adolescence correlate to intellectual abilities, but were unable to determine direct cause and effect. They tested thirty-three healthy teenagers whose initial IQ scores varied from 80 to 140, and then they tested them again four years later. They found that the IQ scores could vary as much as 20 points, which is a significant variation (Ramsden et al., 2011)

Most experts believe that intelligence is culture specific, that is, that what constitutes "intelligent" behavior in one culture may not necessarily represent intelligent behavior in another culture. Cross-culturally defined intelligent behavior could include the capacity to adapt readily to new situations, to apply prior knowledge to new situations, or to learn how to quickly perform a new task.

Intelligence Testing

History of IQ Testing

In 1905, Alfred Binet (pronounced bee-*ney*), a French psychologist, developed the first IQ or intelligence test. Binet attended law school and graduated in 1878, and then decided to pursue his interest in psychology. He was mainly self-educated in this area.

In the early 1900s many French school children were not benefiting from French school instruction. The Ministry of Education approached Binet about developing a way to identify at a young age children who would benefit from special instruction.

What is interesting is that Binet did not use any theoretical concept of intelligence. He used instead a very pragmatic, trial-and-error approach. He grouped two sets of students that teachers had identified as "smart" or "dull." He then asked the two groups of students to perform different tasks. The tasks that the "bright" students could complete but the "dull" ones could not were retained and the questions that both groups could complete were thrown out. He eventually was able to devise a test of about thirty questions that identified fast and slow learners.

In the 1920s, Louis Terman of Stanford University, started to make revisions to Binet's intelligence test. The *Stanford-Binet Intelligence Scale* is one of the

How much does a child's IQ score correlate with their education opportunities and socioeconomics?

(Photo courtesy of Sergey Nivens/ Shutterstock.com)

most widely used intelligence tests today in the United States; however, revisions still continue to be made. The test includes four content areas:

1. verbal reasoning,
2. quantitative reasoning,
3. abstract/visual reasoning,
4. and short-term memory.

It has become significantly more sophisticated and accurate for children of different ages (Arnet, 2001). The test is given orally and has a list of age-appropriate questions that increase in difficulty until the child is unable to proceed.

Many of the intelligence tests used today can trace their roots to the tests Binet developed. For example, the *Wechsler Intelligence Scale for Children,* fourth edition (WISC-IV) provides separate measures for verbal and performance (or nonverbal) skills. The *Kaufman Assessment Battery for Children,* second edition (KABC-ll) takes a different approach. Children are tested on their ability to integrate different kinds of stimuli given at the same time and integrate systematic thinking. It minimizes verbal questions and responses. It allows test administrators to use different languages, wording, or gestures when administering the exam. This helps to make testing more equitable for students who speak English as a second language (Feldman, 2008). Often, if a student is having difficulties, he or she is administered a variety of different tests to evaluate abilities.

Intelligence testing has vastly improved and changed since Binet's day; however, intelligence testing is still linked to school success. In short, people who do well in school test as smart, and those who do not do well in school are likely to test as less intelligent. As a result, these tests do a fairly good job of predicting how successful a student will be in school, but not how successful they will be at other tasks outside of school or in the work place. It says nothing about social skills, personality, and other abilities and talents a person may have. These tests do not necessarily test real intelligence. If a child does well in school this may or may not have a direct relationship to intelligence.

Ethnic Differences in IQ Scores

How a person scores on intelligence tests is related to a combination of genetics and environmental factors. How to separate the role of genetics and environmental factors is problematic and has led to considerable debate among scientists. Studies have shown that children from middle- and upper-class backgrounds score higher on IQ tests than children from lower-middle and poor backgrounds, no matter what their ethnicity is. Also, African American and Hispanic children have an overall lower average score than White children. Earlier studies of IQ testing of African American children showed that they scored on the average about fifteen points lower than White children. However, this score varied significantly depending on what tests were used. In one study that looked at differences in test scores between Blacks and Whites and that controlled for class level and various differences in parental background, the differences between the two groups disappeared (Brooks-Gunn, Klebanov, Duncan, 1996). The question is, "Are differences in score really showing differences in intelligence?"

An interesting set of IQ studies has been done on children from **transracial adoptions**. These are children who have been adopted by parents of a different ethnic or racial background. These children have been raised in a White majority cultural environment and are not genetically related to their parents. Many of these studies have looked at Black children that were adopted by White parents (there are a lack of studies of this type done with other ethnic minorities). These studies showed that the Black adopted children scored on the average as high or higher in IQ than the White children (Arnet, 2001). This shows that the differences that have been found between African American children's and White children's IQ scores are due to cultural and socioeconomic differences. What is also interesting are that studies have shown that people's IQ scores change as they age to some degree. If intelligence were only genetically based then it would be fixed at birth or set once the brain was fully developed. Today, it is still very controversial in scientific circles how much of a role both genetics and environment play in intelligence. Furthermore, it is important to keep in mind that the results would also be biased if a child grows up in a disadvantaged environment.

Other cultures, such as China and Japan, do have intelligence tests that they use. There is scarce information available on how these tests differ from the Western-based culture IQ tests and how American kids compare to kids in these other countries. This is one area where a great deal more research needs to be done.

Other Conceptions of Intelligence

Many of the traditional IQ tests used today are based on the theory that intelligence is one-dimensional or a unitary mental ability, which results in a single score (Lubinski, 2004; Spearman, 1927). Many psychologists dispute this and believe that intelligence is multidimensional. Some developmentalist theorists believe intelligence is two-dimensional and made up of fluid and crystallized intelligence. **Fluid intelligence** refers to information processing capabilities, reasoning, and memory. This type of intelligence is the person's ability to think in a logical and independent way in novel situations. Fluid intelligence works independent from acquired knowledge or past information. It uses the skills of analyzing, making sense of patterns, relationships, and mathematical and technical problem solving. It uses inductive and deductive reasoning skills to solve problems in novel circumstances. In other words, fluid intelligence requires the person to come up with innovative and new ways to solve problems whatever the situation may be. A good example of this is when a student is asked to learn how to spell a list of words. This would require the use of fluid intelligence, where the person uses processing capabilities in an effortless and systemic fashion. Learning to spell a list of words requires the person to figure out a way to combat this problem, not necessarily needing past experiences or previously stored information.

Crystallized intelligence is the use of life-long accumulation of information, learned skills, and different strategies that people have learned in the past and can apply to problem-solving situations (Alfonso, Flanagan, & Badwan, 2005). It should not be confused with memory or accumulated knowledge, merely the ability to effectively access and utilize one's stored information from long-term memory. Because crystallized intelligence is a life-long process, it is therefore expected to improve with age and longevity. An example of crystallized intelligence is when a student is asked to analyze the meaning of a poem or to come up with solutions, for example, to how to get teenagers to use protection when having sex. To solve such a problem, the person must rely on what they know and use the general knowledge they have acquired on the subject of analyzing a poem or finding a strategy to teen's use of protection while having sex. It is expected that in both cases, the answers would differ depending on the age and the amount of acquired knowledge on the subjects.

Howard Gardner's Eight Levels of Intelligence

Howard Gardner was born in 1943 and was the "father" of the eight levels of intelligence. He proposed that there are eight distinct intelligences:

1. linguistic;
2. bodily kinesthetic;
3. logical mathematical;
4. musical;
5. spatial;
6. interpersonal
7. intrapersonal; and
8. naturalist.

Howard Gardener's Eight Levels of Intelligence

	**Intrapersonal Intelligence:** Self-awareness. The knowledge of one's interpersonal self, one's own emotions, feelings, and thoughts.
	**Spatial Intelligence:** These are the abilities associated with images and space. Artists, interior designers, architects, and one who can navigate without maps or instruments are people who often have good spatial intelligence.
	**Linguistic Intelligence:** The abilities associated with speaking and writing well, and mastering languages. Effective writers, poets, and speakers usually have a high linguistic intelligence. This form of intelligence is highly valued in our educational system.
	**Logical Mathematical Intelligence:** The abilities associated with thinking logically, problem solving, mathematics, and scientific thinking. Engineers, computer programmers, math teachers, scientists, and researchers are examples of people who usually have a high level of logical mathematical intelligence.
	**Musical Intelligence:** The abilities involved in producing music, rhythm, and sound. This includes abilities that singers, musicians, and composers have.
	**Body Kinesthetic Intelligence:** The ability to use one's body (or parts of it) to solve problems and to use one's mental abilities to coordinate body movements that result in products or displays. This includes abilities that good dancers, gymnasts, surgeons, actors, and athletes have.
	**Interpersonal Intelligence:** The ability to interact and work effectively with others. The ability to understand moods, personalities, motivations, intentions, and desires of others. Often therapists, teachers, social workers, and sales people have high interpersonal intelligence.
	**Naturalist Intelligence:** The ability to recognize patterns in nature and differences among natural objects and life forms. Identifying members of particular plant or animal species. Examples of this type of intelligence are: ▪ Classifying natural forms (e.g., rocks, types of mountains) ▪ Applying one's knowledge of nature in such activities as farming, landscaping, or animal training.

Based on Gardner 2000, 2003. All images courtesy of Shutterstock.com

Each of these elements operates individually as well as together in different combinations depending on the situation or activity (Gardner 2000, 2003; Chen & Gardner, 2005). Our American educational system emphasizes linguistic intelligence and logical mathematical intelligence and downplays other forms. However, how successful a person is in life and in work is often related not just to these two forms of intelligence emphasized by our school system, but all of the ones listed by Gardner.

Robert Sternberg, Triarchic Theory of Intelligence

Robert Sternberg was born in 1949 and is currently a provost at Oklahoma State University. He earned his BA in psychology from Yale and then earned his PhD from Stanford in 1975. Robert Sternberg's research interests lie in the areas of intelligence, creativity, wisdom, thinking styles, leadership, ethics, love, and hate, and he is considered one of the top psychologists today.

Sternberg (1990, 2003) thinks intelligence should be thought of in terms of abilities to process information; that is, the way people store learned information and then use it to solve intellectual tasks. While Gardner emphasized the various parts or components that make up intelligence, Sternberg is more concerned with the process that one goes through when carrying out intelligent behavior (Floyd, 2005).

Sternberg's **Triarchic Theory of Intelligence** suggests that intelligence is made up of three main elements:

1. componential,
2. experiential, and
3. contextual.

Componential is the part of intelligence that is used to analyze and solve problems using previously learned information. For example, it is the part of a person's

Three Components of Sternberg's Theory of Intelligence

Componential	The part of intelligence used to analyze and solve problems, using previously learned knowledge.
Experiential	How knowledge from prior experiences are related to new situations and experiences that they have not encountered before.
Contextual	How intelligence is used to face real-life situations and demands. It is also referred to as practical intelligence.

Adapted from Sternberg, 1985, 1991.

intelligence that they may use to solve a math problem, or a Sudoku puzzle. Experiential refers to the relationship between one's past experiences and intelligence. It is often referred to as the insightful part of intelligence, where people relate what they already have learned from past experiences to new situations that they have not encountered before. An example of this may be when someone has a romantic relationship that does not last and the person applies what he or she learned about self and others to a new romantic situation. People's contextual intelligence is seen as how successful they deal with the demands of real life situations, such as at work or as a student at school (Sternberg, 1985, 1991). Contextual intelligence is also known or referred to as practical intelligence. IQ tests traditionally focus on componential intelligence. Interestingly, research indicates that one's contextual intelligence is a much better predictor of how successful a person will be as an adult in work and everyday life than componential intelligence.

Practical and Emotional Intelligence

Practical intelligence is behavior primarily learned from observing and modeling other people's behavior. Traditional IQ tests are relatively good at predicting one's success in school but are not as good in predicting how one will do in other kinds of achievements, such as work. Of course educational success does correlate to the types of jobs a person may get and then this relates to income level. However, one can be average in their success in school but have a very high practical intelligence that will allow them great success and advancement in their career. Look at President George W. Bush who was an average student at Yale University, but in part probably has a great practical intelligence, which led him to become president of the United States (Miller Center, 2014). People with high practical intelligence involve knowledge drawn from observing others. They can deduce and extract broad principles and norms from these observations and apply them in appropriate settings.

Emotional intelligence is often referred to as a component of practical intelligence. It utilizes skills that involve the accurate understanding, evaluation, expression, and reading of emotions. This relates to how well a person gets along with others and how sensitive a person is to other people's emotions and feelings and responding appropriately. Children and adults with a high level of emotional and practical intelligence have a high rate of success in their social lives.

So what is intelligence? There is no one answer to this question. It is related to what you think success is and in what area it is important to be successful. This is very culture specific. In Western culture being successful in school and having a good career are important. So we look for aspects of thought and learning that make this possible and call it intelligence. In a culture that does not value formal education but how to hunt for food and survive in the wilderness, a different kind of intelligence is important and these people would probably define intelligence very differently. There is virtually no research that looks at different cultural views of what intelligence is or how it is defined by that culture.

Achievement and Aptitude Tests

Many children are not given an IQ intelligence test but are given aptitude or achievement tests while going through school. **Achievement tests** measure a person's level of knowledge in specific subject areas. Students are required to take these tests at the end of each school year by the state in which they live. Also, many times high school students may take an achievement test in a specific area to get credit for a college course or are required to pass a high school graduating exam before graduating from high school. When entering college many students will be required to take an achievement test in Math or English to determine how well they will do in college in these areas or in other areas for which they may need remedial work.

Aptitude tests are designed to predict an area that a person is good at or to predict the person's performance. There are aptitude tests that people take that identify what kind of jobs they would be good at and enjoy. SAT and ACT are tests required by many colleges before a student can attend. These tests predict how well a student will perform in high school and in college.

The differences between achievement tests, aptitude tests, and IQ tests seem theoretically clear, but in reality the distinction is much less clear cut. Almost all forms of testing have been a source of great controversy. Many critics will argue that our education system is putting too much emphasis on the results of one test and needs to look at the bigger picture. How much do the results of these exams really predict how well a person will do in the real world?

CHAPTER 11 SUMMARY

After the relatively powerful growth spurt of early childhood, children age six to twelve years grow at a rate of approximately two to four inches and five to seven pounds per year. There is a complementary increase in both gross motor and fine motor skills and there are some gender differences in muscular control and development. On average girls outperform boys in fine motor skills, such as writing and drawing, while boys excel in gross motor abilities, such as running and jumping.

One of the central concerns of middle childhood is children's nutrition, which has resulted in an epidemic of obesity. Obesity is associated with heart disease and diabetes, and obese children are more likely to remain obese as adults. They are also at risk in social interactions, as they face ridicule and alienation as a result of our culture's negative attitude toward excess weight.

There are three well-known theories that expansively explain, analyze, and define development during middle childhood:

1. Freudian theory identifies the period from six to twelve years old as the latency period. During the latency period, libidinal (sexual) energy is channeled toward skill mastery.
2. Erikson proposed that middle childhood is characterized by industry versus inferiority. Children of this age are naturally industrious and are focused on learning and mastery of adultlike skills. Unlike early childhood, children in these age groups are generally focused on activities outside of the family, reaching for skills within and beyond their former peer groups.
3. The third is Piaget's cognitive theory, the stage of concrete operations. In this stage, children are able to move concrete things around in their minds to manipulate and organize materials.

A general definition of intelligence is "the capacity to understand the world, to think rationality and to use resources effectively when faced with challenges." Most experts believe that intelligence is culture specific, that is, that what constitutes "intelligent" behavior in one culture may not necessarily represent intelligent behavior in another culture. In 1905, Alfred Binet, a French psychologist, developed the first IQ (intelligence quotient) test. Many of the intelligence tests used today can trace their roots to the tests Binet developed. These tests do a fairly good job of predicting how successful a student will be in school, but not how successful they will be at other tasks outside of school or in the work place. Results are also biased if a child grows up in a disadvantaged environment.

Many of the traditional IQ tests used today are based on the theory that intelligence is one-dimensional or a unitary mental ability, which results in a single score. However, many psychologist dispute this and believe that intelligence is multidimensional. Some developmentalist theorists believe intelligence is two-dimensional and made up of fluid and crystallized intelligence. Howard Gardner has proposed that there are eight distinct intelligences: linguistic, bodily kinesthetic, logical mathematical, musical, spatial, interpersonal, intrapersonal, and naturalist. Robert Sternberg's triarchic theory of intelligence takes another approach and thinks intelligence should be thought of in terms of abilities to process information; that is, the way people store learned information and then use it to solve intellectual tasks. Sternberg suggests that intelligence is made up three main elements: componential, experiential, and contextual.

So what is intelligence? There is no one answer to this question. It is related to what you think success is and what you think it is important to be successful in.

CHAPTER 11 VOCABULARY

Achievement Tests
Aptitude Tests
Concrete Operations
Crystallized Intelligence
Emotional Intelligence
Fluid Intelligence
Industry versus Inferiority
Intelligence
Latency Period
Libidinal
Metacognition
Myelin Sheath
Myelination
Practical Intelligence
Proprioception
Transracial Adoptions
Triarchic Theory of Intelligence

Chapter 12

SCHOOL-AGE YEARS
Social and Cultural Development

(Photo courtesy of Margaret Goetz)

Introduction

Eleven-year-old Aliyah is seated in the waiting room of Dr. Phyllis Metcalf's office. Dr. Metcalf is a well-known psychologist in Los Angeles. Aliyah's parents have brought her for counseling because she is struggling with several issues in school. Aliyah is quite bright. She was accelerated into the sixth grade, and her achievement scores placed her well beyond many of her peers in the gifted category. Aliyah is articulate, but she has been spending a great deal of her time reading. She has a limited circle of friendly acquaintances, but no really close friends and is content to spend her time with her family members, which include her parents and five younger brothers. Aliyah is devoted to her brothers and enjoys babysitting them three times a week while her parents manage additional work. Aliyah's behavior has changed over the past three weeks. She has become more withdrawn and increasingly angry. She complains of headaches, especially before school. Her grades have fallen from straight A to the B to C range. In school, she is listless and distant. Her parents are worried and do not understand what the causes of Aliyah's recent behavior changes are. In addition, she is going through many physical changes that may have resulted in her recent depressive mood and change in attitude. However, at the same time, these changes could be the result of social problems, being bullied, starting to experiment with drugs, or even being physically abused. Aliyah's parents are concerned and anxious to find out from Dr. Metcalf the possible causes of her mood and attitude changes.

History of Family and Children and How It Has Changed

Children in the Colonial Family

The concept of family is always changing. It changes in response to societal norms and the need for family members to survive and flourish. If you were to transport yourself back in time to 1776 to the Colonial period in the United States, you might find it hard to recognize the **Colonial family** when you compare it to today's modern family. These differences in time periods become very noticeable when one looks at values, roles, and behaviors of family members.

During the Colonial period the dividing line between the average, middle-class, White family and community was more blurred than it is today. Today the domain of the family is separate from the surrounding community—what goes on in the privacy of family is generally not the community's concern. In the Colonial era, what went on in the family was the community's concern. The family and the home were the economic centers of survival for most middle-class families. People generally did not work outside the home.

A White, middle-class, married Colonial woman's role was to be wife and mother and to run the household. She had responsibility for the children's schooling, making the family's clothing, cooking, cleaning, making soap and candles, taking care of the farm animals, and helping to harvest crops when needed. She played a central role in the economic survival of the family. Once women were married any property she owned became her husband's.

It was a male-dominated society, and a middle-class husband was the head of the household and oversaw the family's needs. The men were the ones that were in charge of growing and harvesting the crops, raising the animals, and/or running the family shop.

Everyone in the family, including children, were put to work and expected to contribute to the family's survival. Children were given tasks appropriate for their ages. Boys, once they reached school age, would help their father and girls their mother. To some extent children were seen as miniature adults and were expected to act like adults. Kids were seen as economic assets and extra pairs of hands to help the family survive (Aries, 1985). This did not mean that their parents did not love and care for their children. Parents loved their children then, just as they do today.

Couples were expected to begin having children as soon as they were married. Birth control was generally unavailable and unreliable, and the average middle-class, White family saw the birth of eight or nine kids. However, infant mortality was high and resulted in the average household having four or five children that lived to adulthood (Aries, 1985).

In many ways teenagers were seen as young adults, as there was no concept of adolescence as a developmental period. Young men in their teens who were not going to learn their fathers' trades would often be sent away to be apprentices to learn a trade or skill in exchange for their work. They were expected to live under their masters' rules or accept the consequences. During these years of apprenticeship they often became members of their masters' households.

Children were brought up to respect and obey their parents. They were expected to do what their parents asked without question. Authoritarian parenting was the expectation in most White, middle- and upper-class households. Unruly behavior was unacceptable and would have been dealt with harshly in most households. Physical punishment such as spanking with a belt or switch, which is not acceptable today, was often the norm for misbehavior. Children were said to be dominated by the three Rs: Repression, Respect, and Religion (Aries, 1985).

Love and affection in most marriages was less important than it is today. Women often married in their late teens, men in their early or late twenties. Though marriages were not arranged, they needed to be approved by their parents. The Colonial period was a very class-ridden society so, not surprisingly, when parents were looking at marriage for their children, proper class and economic welfare were very important. People almost always married within their own social class. If a parent did not like whom their child wanted to marry then they would withhold their approval and often any inheritance if the children proceeded with the marriage.

Blended families were very common in the Colonial period, but for different reasons than they occur today. A **blended family** is a family that has a stepparent, and/or children from a previous marriage. Today most blended families result because of divorce. In Colonial times, divorce was not generally allowed and blended families were usually the result of a spouse's death. People often remarried after a relatively short time following the death of their spouses. It made survival easier and was almost a necessity. The average length of a marriage was twelve years. By the time they reached the age of twenty-one, one half to one third of all children had lost at least one parent. Blended families in Colonial times had many of the same problems as blended families today when it comes to getting along. This has probably always been true as demonstrated by the Cinderella fairy tale, written by Charles Perrault in the late 1600s.

Divorce under most circumstances was not allowed in the colonies. However if a couple did not get along, and one of them left for a far away state or territory it was unlikely he or she would be followed and could marry again without much fear of prosecution, even though polygamy was illegal. Also, if death occurred while a spouse was far away from home, the family may never hear or know what happened to him or her. One of the circumstances in which divorce was allowed in many of the colonies was when a spouse was "abandoned." After a respectable period of time (different in different colonies), they would be allowed to marry again.

Industrialization and Its Effect on Family and Children

Industrialization in the United States began in the late 1700s and continued throughout the 1800s. It resulted in factories and mass production of goods. More products became available at a lower cost to the average person than ever

A Victorian family from the 1890s.

(Photo courtesy of Donna Beeler/ Shutterstock.com)

before. Industrialization helped create jobs that were located in cities and large towns. As the demand for labor expanded quickly, people began to move from the countryside to the cities to live by wage labor. Many poor (a high number of immigrants) worked in factories for long hours and low wages.

The family home was no longer the center for the **Industrial Revolution family's** economic survival. Many of the institutions that used to be home based were becoming community based, such as schooling, production of goods, and businesses. The Industrial Age was also a time of very rapid change in the middle- and upper-class family structure. Women were no longer an integral part of the family's economic survival. Women were to uphold the family's moral standards by being pure, moral, and submissive to their husbands. The husband now worked away from the home and became the major wage earner. As a result his importance to the family increased. In middle-class families, children's work was no longer needed for the family's survival, though in poorer families children remained a critical part of the family's survival.

What resulted was the emergence of the modern concept of childhood. Children should be protected and supported; they should go to school and be able to play and be kids. Of course this was only possible for children of middle- and upper-class families. All family members of lower class and poor families had to work doing whatever they could to bring in money to the family. It was not until the early 1900s that the concept of adolescence as a developmental period emerged. The first parenting pamphlets and magazines started to be more commonly published at this time.

Comparison of Family Systems in the Pre-Industrial, Industrial, and Post-Industrial Eras

Family Era	Colonial	Industrial/Victorian	Rise of the Modern Family
Family Motto	"Family rules."	"One for all and all for one."	"Everyone for him- or herself!"
Family Size	Large because children were looked upon as an economic asset and helped family to survive.	Smaller size because children no longer aided in family economic survival (except in poor families).	Much smaller size. Children become more expensive to raise.
	High infant/child mortality.	Better infant/child mortality but still fairly high.	Lowest infant/child mortality.
	Average life span: 40s	Average life span: 60s	Life span of adults and children increases even more (70s and 80s)
Family Economy	Family-based economy. Integration of family and community.	Wage-labor economy. Families and community become more separate.	Wage-based economy. Families and community separate.
	Most families live on farms.	Families move into cities for better jobs.	Families start to move to suburbs.
	Family members depend on each other to survive.	Families starting to rely on available services in the community more than family members.	Families dependent on community-based services.
	Mother and father work together at home to survive.	Father works outside the home and mother stays home and cares for kids and household. Only poor women work outside home.	Both parents work.
	Patriarchal—father in charge.	Father still in charge but mother takes a more active role in raising and disciplining the children.	Both share more equally in responsibilities of raising children and disciplining.

Family Society	Family entertains itself.	Family gets its entertainment from both inside and outside sources.	Family relies on outside sources for entertainment.
	Divorce not allowed.	Some divorce is surfacing but not culturally accepted.	Divorce common and socially accepted.
	Health issues handled in the home by family and community.	Public hospitals established.	Health care formalized and community based.
	Alternative lifestyles not accepted.	Alternative lifestyles/ behaviors "in closet" but still seen as social outcasts.	Alternative lifestyles coming "out of the closet" and more socially acceptable.
	Community and home life intertwined.	Community and nuclear family separate spheres.	Community and nuclear family still separate spheres.

During the Industrial Age, the concept of autonomy of the family became a part of the American value system. The family was no longer as intertwined with the community as it had been in the Colonial era. The nuclear family became private and what happened in the family stayed in the family.

Rise of the Modern Family and Children

After 1900 the **modern family** began to emerge, and the idea of romance and love became a major component of marriage. People started to expect emotional satisfaction in their marriages. The number of children families had started to drop, along with child mortality. The mortality rate of children dropped significantly with the development of new medical advances, such as antibiotics in the 1940s and the polio vaccine in 1955. The development and approval of the first birth control pill in 1960 also had an impact on the number of children a family would have. For the first time women could now more easily control how many children they wanted.

In the early and mid-1900s divorce was still not socially acceptable, but the divorce rate started to rise. In many ways, as the emotional satisfaction from a marriage became more important, marriages became more fragile and divorce rates rose. Divorce then started to become commonplace and accepted. The divorce rate doubled in the 1960s and 1970s compared to previous

Orphan Trains

Elliot Bobo was taken from his alcoholic father in New York City and put on an "orphan train" bound for Arkansas when he was a young boy. His mother had died when he was two years old. He was given a small cardboard suitcase and a change of clothes. He never saw his father again (Graham and Gray 1995). He eventually found a loving home with a new family.

Elliot was one of the many destitute and homeless children of New York City that were put on trains to be given to families who wanted children. What was to become a controversial program began in the mid-1850s as a way to get homeless and very poor children off the streets of New York where they sought food and shelter. Many stole or sold matches, rags, or newspapers to survive (Graham & Gray, 1995). Police were at a loss of what to do with these children and often arrested and locked them up with adult criminals. These children were known as "Street Arabs."

Charles Loring Brace came to New York City in 1853 to finish his seminary training and was horrified at the lives of these children. He wrote that his goal was "to get [the children] utterly out of their surroundings and to send them away to kind Christian homes in the country" (Graham & Gray, 1995). He founded the Children's Aid Society that raised funds and gained legal permission to relocate destitute children to families in rural America. Over 100,000 children were relocated on what was to become known as the orphan trains, which operated from 1854 to 1929.

Brace recognized that farmers needed labor and believed many would welcome another child that could help around the farm and would treat them as their own. This was the beginning of the foster care system in the United States.

The children were placed on trains that would stop at towns where fliers had been sent out advertising the homeless children. They would be lined up and prospective parents would come and pick the children out of the lineup. The prospective parents were to be screened by the local communities. The result of these placements was mixed. Some like Elliot found loving, caring parents; however, many children were taken in by families simply as a source of cheap labor. They were not treated with love and were sometimes abused. Some of the children were rejected by their new families and in other instances the kids simply ran away. Many did find a new loving home but the exact numbers of how many successes and failures are unknown because follow-ups were scarce and not well monitored. Brace had good intentions but also understood his solution was not perfect. He stated: "When a child of the streets stands before you in rags, with a tear-stained face, you cannot easily forget him. And yet, you are perplexed what to do. The human soul is difficult to interfere with. You hesitate how far you should go"(Graham & Gray, 1995).

In the beginning Brace was praised for his work with the street children and other large cities copied his model. However, as years passed he came under heavy criticism, particularly in cases where children were taken from parents just because they were poor. The last train was sent out in 1929.

Questions for Thought and Discussion

- Brace came under severe criticism in later years for the orphan trains. Was it better to leave kids on the streets or with very poor parents in the city, or place them in an uncertain future with rural families?
- Would a version of this system be appropriate today in the United States? In other countries?
- Imagine what it would be like to live on the streets in a big city, hungry and trying to survive.

More information is available at:

http://www.pbs.org/wgbh/amex/orphan/

Source: Crichton, J. (Producer), & Graham, J. G., Edward (Director). (1995). *American experience: The orphan trains* (WGBH Boston). [Video/DVD] Edward Gray Films Inc.

generations. People were starting to leave unhappy marriages. Ronald Reagan was the first president (1981–1989) to have been divorced, demonstrating how accepting people had become of divorce.

In the late 1940s and 1950s, after World War II, there was a large jump in the number of children being born. This became known as the baby boomer generation. In the 1960s and 1970s these children were starting to grow up and many social changes took place. We had the women's movement, civil rights movement, environmental movement, anti-Vietnam War movement, and sexual revolution movement all taking place. This resulted in family structure and value changes. For example, the double standard was being challenged, and premarital sex became common, mainly because of the ease of birth control. Cohabitation without marriage also became more accepted and more common. More and more women were going to college and then working, resulting in marrying and having fewer children later in their lives. Two-income families were now the norm.

This modern period also marked the beginning of the cultural development and extension of adolescence and young adulthood. People were not getting married as young as they once were. The average age for marriage today for women is twenty-five and twenty-seven for men. More and more people are going to college and establishing themselves in a career before marrying. Because couples are putting off marriage, they are also putting off children. It is not uncommon for couples to have their first child well into their thirties today.

Children in Immigrant Working-Class Families

So far we have been discussing middle- and upper-class families. Working-class families, which include immigrants such as the Irish, Italian, and African American people, had a different family structure to some extent than White middle-class working-class families. In 1850 immigrants made up 10 percent of the total population in the United States. In 1900 more than 15 percent of the population was foreign born. Interestingly, it fell to 9 percent in 1960 and then went up again to 12 percent by 2003 (U.S. Bureau of the Census, 2004).

During the Industrial Revolution thousands of immigrants arrived and many working-class people came from the countryside to work in factories in the cities. They often worked ten-hour days, six days a week. One of the main differences between the working-class families and the middle-class was that the working class needed to pool their incomes for the family to survive (Golden, 1977). Everyone that was able needed to contribute to the family income, including the children. Unmarried children contributed their wages to the family fund. When children married and left home, a bed became available and families often took in a boarder. This helped replace the income the child was bringing in. The early Industrial Age was the time when many children were exploited and worked long hours in factories. Factories often liked to hire women and children because they could pay them less than men. Because teenage children often needed to go to work to help with the survival of the family, they quit school at an early age (Cherlin, 2008).

◀ ***Young Raoul Julien had already worked for two years before this photo was taken at the mule-spinning room in Chace Cotton Mill, Burlington, Vermont.***

(Photo courtesy of Everett Historical/Shutterstock.com)

History of African American Families and Their Children

Historians generally date the arrival of the first slaves in the Colonies to 1619 when a Dutch ship docked at Point Comfort, near Jamestown. The crew of the ship was starving and traded twenty African slaves for food. There may have been slaves earlier than this but this is the first known written record. Most African Americans at this time came to the colonies as indentured servants. They were mainly poor, young, and unmarried Whites and Blacks that could not afford their fare over to the new world. They worked a number of years for a family, usually five to seven years, to pay for their passage. By the late 1600s as the number of indentured servants declined, slavery in the colonies increased (Vox, n.d.). Slavery ended in the United States at the end of the Civil War (1861–1865).

One of the characteristics of the Black family, today and in the past, is its "fluidity" compared to White Americans. Middle-class White Americans are more conservative about who is "included" in their family. Most often White families are made up of people who are related by formal adoption, blood, or marriage. Blacks often informally adopt members into their family who are not necessarily related by blood. The roots of this go back to slavery days when families were torn apart by the slave master, who sold off family members, and had children with women slaves. When parents were sold off children were taken in and adopted by other families, though young children were usually sold with

Nicodemus, Kansas. A colony of free African Americans. Homesteaders ca. 1880–1890s.

(Photo courtesy of Everett Historical/ Shutterstock.com)

their mothers. Who the biological parents of Black children were was not as important as it was in White families of the time. This is even true today in the African American community. Many families will take in children from relatives or friends that are in need. Many times this will be on an "informal" basis—meaning they do not use formal government programs (formal adoption or custody) because of mistrust of the system—depending on the circumstances. An example of Black families "fluidity" would be Mrs. Jane Houser who is fifty-five years old and has five children. Her first two children, ages thirteen and fifteen, were from her first husband from whom she has been divorced for years and who is in prison. Her second husband, Mark Houser, is the father of her third child, age eleven. Jane and Mark also have two other children living with them. One is a thirteen-year-old boy whose mother is having many problems so they have taken him in to live with them. Another is a girl, age seven, who is Jane's younger sister's child; Jane's sister could not take care of her and Jane and Mark have agreed to raise her. The couple considers all five of them to be their children and treats them accordingly.

History of Asian American Families and Their Children

The first Asian immigrants were mainly from China and arrived in the mid-1800s to the western coastal area of the United States. The majority of the Chinese immigrants were men that came because of the gold rush and to help build the Central Pacific Railroad. Many tried their hand at gold mining at mines already abandoned by White miners (the only ones they were allowed to mine) or started small businesses. They were not allowed to become citizens or to own land. The railroad employed thousands of Chinese men workers and actively recruited in China for them. They were found to be more reliable workers than Whites. About half of these men left wives and families in China and sent money home (Glenn, 1983). Some brought wives over but many never married or had children. In 1882 Congress passed the Chinese Exclusion Act, which restricted most new Chinese from entering the United States until after World War II (Glenn, 1983).

The Japanese began to immigrate in the late 1880s to Hawaii and the western coastal states. Many opened small businesses, farmed, or worked as inexpensive labor. A more equal number of men and women came to the United States, so more families formed and children were born. As with the Chinese, Japanese immigrants were not allowed to become citizens or to own land. After

The toy peddler—Chinese immigrants in San Francisco China Town in 1896.

(Photo courtesy of Everett Historical/ Shutterstock.com)

the bombing of Pearl Harbor during World War II, because of discrimination and fear, the Japanese on the West coast (not Hawaii) were put into internment camps. This included citizens and noncitizens, men, women, and children. These Japanese lost everything they had as a result and were incarcerated for an average of four years. Ironically, many of the young men elected to volunteer for the military to prove their loyalty and get out of the camps.

In traditional Asian culture the father is the head of the household and has the final say. Wives were expected to care for children and husbands. Sons, particularly the oldest son, was valued over daughters because the sons carried on the family name and cared for their aging parents. Daughters went to live with their husband's family, where their new obligations as daughter-in-law, wife, and mother took precedence over the family of origin. They generally lived in extended family homes. What was best for the whole extended family or clan was more important than what was best for a person or nuclear family. Because many immigrants left families behind, they often formed family-like bonds with people from the same province or area of the homeland.

One of the results of the internment of the Japanese during World War ll was the disintegration of the traditional Japanese household. In the camps the children and adults usually ate with their cohorts instead of family groups. The children within the camps had more freedom and the parents, particularly the father, had less say over their actions. After leaving the camps many of the families did not go back to the same Japanese traditional family structure.

In 1965 Congress passed the immigration act that ended restrictions that blocked most Asians from immigrating to the United States and started the quota system. This allowed the number of Asians immigrating to American to expand rapidly. The United States pulled out of the Vietnam War in 1973. Large numbers of Vietnamese and Hmong immigrated under refugee status.

History of Mexican American Families and Their Children

In the early 1800s people from Mexico settled parts of what is now the western part of the United States. This was before many White migrants from the eastern United States arrived. These early Mexican settlements generally included large landowners who often grazed large numbers of cattle or sheep and poorer farmer-laborer settlers (Cherlin, 2008).

After the Mexican American War and a series of land grabs and revolts by U.S. troops in the 1830s and 1840s, many of the Mexican elite lost much of their land and the majority of the remaining Mexicans were working class. By the mid-1900s many Mexican immigrants came to the United States (legally and illegally) for jobs and a better life. As a result of their large numbers and some having illegal status many are paid low wages. Many Mexicans and other Hispanics have been in the United States for generations.

The Mexican American culture values family. Family members will help and support each other in times of happiness and in need. The father is traditionally the head of the household, and the mother raises the children. Often it is economically necessary for all members of the family to contribute to the family's survival, including the children. As in many working-class families many teenage and young adult children work part or full time to help their families.

Relationship with Peers

Play

In the middle childhood years, children become increasingly gendered. As peer influences increase, children learn how to be boys and girls by practicing, usually in polarized play where boys play with boys and girls play with girls (Fagot, 1994). In early research on play and gender differences, boys were observed participating in sports and organized game activities, while girls were observed in passive stances, watching the boys. The studies concluded that girls were passive and boys were active. Later studies on play emphasized different dynamics. They did confirm that the boys were indeed playing more active games and the girls were standing or sitting around more. However, the girls were standing and sitting around talking about relationships, their parents, siblings, and families. Girls were extremely active in the realm of interpersonal relationships. Boys were less relational and more instrumental in how they played.

Play Among School-Age Children

Research supports that play for all ages of children is beneficial (Berger, 2004). However when you review recent history, children's play has decreased dramatically. According to University of Michigan researchers, the average school-age child had 40 percent of the day for free time in 1981, with free time defined as hours remaining after sleeping, eating, studying, and engaging in organized activities. This time had decreased to 25 percent by 1997 (Cole et. al., 2005). Kids today spend more time in organized activities, less time playing outdoors, and more time watching TV, on the computer, or playing electronic games.

Before the mid-1800s the idea that a child should have a childhood and playtime was really not a concept shared by the average American family. It was only after this time that this concept first developed in middle- and upper-class families. As a result the study of play is relatively a recent phenomenon in the academic world and limited research is available.

Girls playing on a basketball league. Organized sports available for girls have greatly increased in the last thirty years.

(Photo courtesy of Cindy Donham)

Today many parents over schedule their children. Play makes a child happy, healthy, and probably smarter. Play refreshes and stimulates the mind (Cole, 2005). Einstein was known as a notorious dreamer who earned poor grades. Could over structuring of our child's lives and decreases in playtime lead to "crushing" kids who are like Einstein?

Play is a natural arena for children to further their development of language. They use language to plan, explain, and execute play. It facilitates cooperation and interaction. Playtime is when children learn which behaviors and interactions are socially expected and acceptable and which are not. It permits children to adjust to expected social norms (Azar, 2002).

Today children in many areas play less and less outdoors. Some of this is due to parents' fear of letting their children play outside or at the nearby park because of crime and the fear their children will be hurt. This can be a legitimate fear if the family lives in crime-ridden neighborhoods; however, we even see this with parents who live in safer neighborhoods. Parents hear of abductions and crimes and even if these did not occur in their neighborhoods, parents want to be "safe rather than sorry." Many parents do not know many of their neighbors and as a result do not trust them. For example, allowing younger children in elementary grades to walk to school alone without parents is becoming more and more unusual; however, a generation ago this was the norm. Kids are also being directed to more and more structured activities after school and on the weekends, such as sports, dance, art classes, music lessons, and so on. This is understandable with both parents working becoming the norm. In past generations, more mothers were home and knew all the children in the neighborhood. Walking around middle-class neighborhoods after school these days it is less and less common to see children playing. Another factor is the introduction of video games, television, texting, and computers. These activities keep children inside and less physically active. Childhood obesity is on the rise and one of the contributing factors is that children do not get enough physical exercise (Centers for Disease Control and Prevention, 2012).

Gender Differences in Play

Boys and girls generally have different play patterns. Boys tend toward more physically active play. On the playground at school boys tend to play games that are more team and rule oriented than girls. Boys who are skilled at an activity usually took on the leadership roles and often directed the other less skilled boys (Crombie & Desjardins, 1993).

Girls tend to interact in smaller groups and had more conversations with other girl friends (Crombie & Desjardins, 1993; Van Burnschot et.al., 1993).

▲ ***Boys and girls generally have different play patterns. Boys tend to play more physically active activities. Girls tend to interact in smaller groups and have more conversations with other girl friends.***

(Left photo courtesty of Dragon Images/Shutterstock.com; Right photo courtesy of nata-lunata/Shutterstock.com)

Girls in elementary school grades tended to spend most of their recess time at school talking with one another. Any games they played generally required close proximity, which allowed for conversations. When girls play games the leaders were not limited to the skilled players as with the boys. Often several girls would share the leadership role. Interestingly, the girls were more likely to exclude other girls from their play than the boys.

Another aspect of boys' and girls' play is they prefer to play with children of their own gender. Boys preferring to play with other boys, and girls preferring to play with other girls starts very young, around the age of two years (Fagot & Hagan, 1991; Hay, Payne, & Chadwick, 2004).

Bullying

Tyler Clementi, a freshman at Rutgers University, committed suicide by jumping off the George Washington Bridge in New York after his roommate and another student secretly web cammed an intimate encounter Tyler had with another boy by streaming it onto the Internet (Foderano, 2010). Tyler is only one example of how bullying caused such grief that the result was suicide. Bullying has become a recognized, widespread problem in schools and in the community. Children can be bullied for their religion, ethnicity, disability, sexual orientation, or just being different in any way. Some people may see bullying as just part of growing up but for the children that are bullied the pain is real and has devastating consequences. Schools and communities need to maintain a zero-tolerance policy and must teach tolerance toward children that are different.

What exactly constitutes bullying varies, but usually contains three main components (Department of Health and Human Services, 2014):

1. **Imbalance of power:** Bullies usually pick persons who are physically or psychologically weaker than they are and who have a hard time defending themselves.
2. **Intent to cause harm to another:** The bully's goal is to cause harm to another person. If harm is caused by accident it is not considered bullying.
3. **Repetition:** The bully causes harm to the same person over and over again.

There are several recognized categories of bullying commonly seen today—verbal, social, physical, and cyber bullying. **Verbal bullying** involves things related to teasing and name-calling. **Social bullying** involves actions such as spreading rumors, isolating someone, breaking up friendships, or leaving someone out on purpose. **Physical bullying** involves hitting, pushing, forcefully taking

Warning Signs of Children Being Bullied

- Coming home with damaged belongings, such as clothes, books, and so on.
- Reports losing items such as calculators, iPods, jackets, lunch money, etc.
- Has injuries that the child cannot explain or the explanation seems unrealistic.
- Does not want to go to school.
- Complains of physical ailments such as headaches and stomach aches so the child does not have to attend school.
- Has trouble sleeping or has bad dreams on a regular basis.
- Are very hungry after school because they did not have lunch.
- Loses interest in friends or suddenly has fewer friends.
- Starts running away.
- Seems depressed or unusually angry.
- Is reluctant to participate in activities at school or to go certain places.
- Talks about suicide.
- Feels helpless.
- Low self-esteem, thinks he or she is not good enough.
- Blames him- or herself for all his or her problems.
- Acts differently than usual.
- Loses interest in school work or has a rapid change in school performance.

Source: Adapted from the Department of Health and Human Services, Stop Bullying, 2014.

things, or any other physical act along these lines. **Cyber bullying** includes the use of computers, email, Facebook, Internet, phones, or other devices to harm or intimidate others. This form of bullying and intimidation is becoming more and more common with the advancement of new technologies.

Grave consequences can result from bullying. Children's self-esteem and feelings of worth can be affected, resulting in depression and, in severe instances, suicide. If you know someone who is being bullied, take it seriously and put a stop to it.

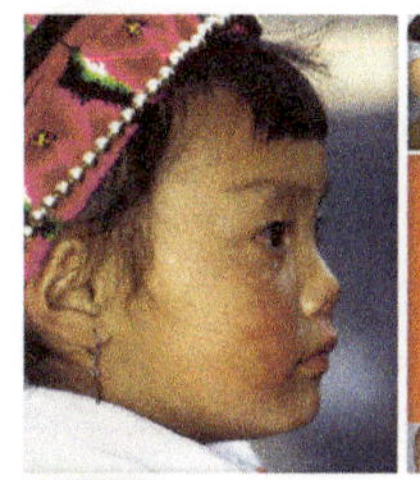

Street Children in Iran

By Nicole Jafari, California State University at Fullerton, USA
and Newsha Badiesabet, Baha'i Institute for Higher Education, Iran

INTRODUCTION

Street children, whose early developmental basic needs such as a formal education are not met, may later develop psychological, cognitive, and social incompetencies. Receiving a formal education is instrumental in children's development of cognition, reasoning, and overall perception. Consequently, lack of education may affect a child's cognition and may later lead to social incompetency and delayed psychosocial ability (Nurrenbern, 2001). According to Le Roux and Smith, "Street children fear being harmed, incapacitated, arrested (most report being subjected to police intimidation or brutality), and getting sick. They also are concerned about loneliness and being unloved" (Le Roux & Smith, 1998, p. 2). Another complexity these children face is that lack of education deprives them from learning and developing the necessary skills for social competency and capabilities. Recently, a comparative study on child labor in Africa was conducted in an attempt to understand causality and to influence policy in order to promote the school enrollment of at-risk African children (Canagarajah & Nielsen, 2001). Other research analyzing the effects of child labor on overall health of street children showed that lack of education is problematic for street children (Salary, 2005). Because they are forced to work during the critical period of their lives, these children miss the stages

▲ *Street children.*

(Photo courtesy of Anton_Ivanov/Shutterstock.com)

(continues)

(continued from previous page)

of normative development. Indeed, early childhood healthy development will lead to higher cognitive abilities and intelligence, and lack of such may lead to substandard intelligence. One article written on long-term effects of early childhood programs on cognitive and school outcomes indicated that early childhood education programs effect the cognitive development of children (Barnett, 1995).

RESULTS

Specific Results—Research by Salary revealed that 56 percent of children engaged in child labor are illiterate; as well, 61 percent show signs of speech problems (2005). This lack of formal education is due to the fact that these children relinquish education for the sake of earning an income to help their families' financial survival. Even those who receive a minimum education via nongovernment organizations are not allowed to practice or do homework, which makes their learning inefficient (Canagarajah & Nielsen, 2001). Collectively, the children participating in this study showed signs of inadequate speech and problems articulating their answers effectively. This finding was combined with participants' lack of understanding of questions or inability to fully express their feelings or thoughts. Data collected in this study showed that some participating children receive one hour a day of off-site schooling. These pseudoclassrooms are run by nonprofit, nongovernmental agencies, and only serve a minimum function; however, children mistook these classrooms as proper schooling. If they have not received any formal classroom teaching, they accept this minimal educational intake as normal. Also, their understanding of friendship is completely different from what children of the same age group possess. They considered their co-workers as their friends, which means these children shared a distorted understanding of friendship.

Unanticipated Results—The analysis of the questions given by children revealed that all participants have illegal status with most being immigrants from Afghanistan. Although some were born in Iran, due their parents' illegal status, they are not granted citizenship. Prior to the study, it was anticipated that due to the fact that working on the streets is dangerous (Christian Science Monitor, Web, 2014), the majority of children might be male; however, the study revealed that there was an equal number of girls and boys as child laborer. The type of work was similar for both genders and did not differentiate based on gender role expectations as female child labor did not necessary portray domestic duties or sibling care. Older children that were interviewed predicted that most likely they would continue street work, and were hoping to have their own ring of child labor once given the chance. Almost all children regardless of age had difficulty expressing feelings or articulating answers regarding emotions.

Significant Findings—Further analysis of the data showed that the level of cognition in all participants was below grade level. The majority had difficulty understanding the questions, which required further expansion of the meaning of the question; however, this may have been due to anxiety, delayed language, or certain learning disability issues.

DISCUSSION

Street children experience trauma such as psychological, social calamity, and emotional distress. Research indicated that maltreatment of street children is related to the increased risk of a variety of problematic behavior. Children of labor are prone to depression and anxiety, developing Post Traumatic Stress Disorder (PTSD), consumption of alcohol and drugs, personality-psychotic-eating disorders, aggressive behavior, cognitive problems, sexual dysfunctions, obesity, suicide attempts, criminal activities, and prostitution (Maciel et al., 2012). In addition, lack of economic and social development opportunities for these children may lead not only to physical issues, but to risk of mental and social abuse and neglect (Babaee, n.d).

In Iran, a minimum of seven million of the population lives below the poverty level, while children, who are the most vulnerable citizens, do not have health insurance or access to mental health care (Babaee, n.d.). The increase in Iran's street children in recent years has become a social phenomenon. Unfortunately, there is not a great deal of scientific research in this area, but the unofficial reports indicate that there may be approximately 20,000 street children just living in Tehran, the capital city of Iran. Professional criminals use street children for gangs of robbers and drug dealers, so their chance to hold decent jobs is low and lack of educational opportunities compromises their possibility of ever learning with other children (Ahmadi Khooie, 2004). Street children are in dire situations of social vulnerability especially in poor countries, and these social damages distinguish them from other children.

Furthermore, street children who have to work will miss their period of basic needs development such as formation of skills, resiliency, playing, and having relationships with friends. Children of labor, who work like adults, will miss the critical period of childhood that could later lead to forming irreversible defects in the developmental process (Salary, 2005). Reviewing previous research showed that chronologically, children involved in child labor often seem to have a less mature cognition and social perception than that of their peers. This phenomenon may be due to the fact that they are deprived of required nutrition and normal life activities, which may lead to certain cognitive or emotional dysfunction (Le Roux & Smith, 1998). Lack of formal education deprives street children from learning and developing necessary skills for social competency and capabilities. Even in cases of some limited literacy opportunity such as attending occasional school, their lack of attention span and attentiveness in the classroom due to extreme fatigue or physical and mental exhaustion is counterproductive to their learning (Canagarajah & Nielsen, 2001). One of the irrefutable rights of a child is to receive a basic education. Street children are deprived from this basic right, and the living conditions they are forced to endure greatly impacts their critical period of life (Demartoto, 2012). According to the investigation by Barnet, "Age at entry to or years of experience in child care during the preschool years influenced the reading and math achievement of children at ages five and six" (Barnet, 1995, p. 3).

(continues)

(continued from previous page)

Barnet's findings correlate to this study as they emphasize the importance of early childhood education and its impact on later development. Clearly, it can be concluded that early education deprivation and lack of basic needs in the early years of development can and may greatly influence later developmental stages.

CONCLUSION

Assessment of economic and social development requires consideration of not only the physical issues of street children, but also their mental and emotional well-being. These children are at risk of mental and social abuse and neglect especially in Iran (Babaee, n.d). Moreover, street children are in situations of social vulnerability especially in poor countries; these social damages distinguish them from other children. The longer this deprivation lasts, the greater the risk of mental dysfunction (Le Roux & Smith, 1998). This research study established a correlation between the existence of numerous risk factors to psychological cognition and social incompetency of children exposed to child labor hardship in Iran. Furthermore, findings mirrored a certain degree of lack of grade level cognition and lack of social competency in children who are exposed to hardship. Responses among participants to questions posed in the interviews were consistent and similar to findings in the literature review reflecting the validity of data collected along with interrater reliability of the study itself. Data collected showed that, overwhelmingly, children of labor have a confused understanding of the concept of regular school, playmates, and friendship. They also have difficulty expressing thoughts and discussing goals and dreams for their future.

Note: To read the entire research article go to: http://www.seekdl.org, ISBN Number 978-1-62348-007-1.

Child Abuse

Historical Perspective of Child Abuse

When you look at acceptable methods of discipline used in the past by parents and adults, many of them would be considered abusive today. Being whipped with a belt or switch on your legs, back, or buttocks was considered acceptable forms of punishment not that long ago in our history. Over the last 100 years, the American culture has changed its views on what is considered child abuse. For example, paddling was commonly seen in schools, and even stronger forms of physical punishment were not that uncommon. Stories of the schoolmaster whipping a child a few times because the child had not learned his or her lessons are commonly found in family histories and literature. However, there were still boundaries to what constituted abuse, such as if a child was so severally hurt that it caused permanent disability or died from the injuries. There was one case in a small town in Mississippi where the schoolmaster whipped a young girl for not learning her lessons. She died as a result of her treatment. The family of the girl decided that they would take matters into their own hands and proceeded to hang the schoolteacher on a nearby tree (Donham, 2014). No one was ever prosecuted for his murder, even though everyone knew who did it. Today there are discussions whether spanking a naughty child is acceptable or a form of child abuse.

The Society for the Prevention of Cruelty to Children (SPCC) was established in the United States as a result of the rescue of a severely abused child named Mary Ellen in New York in 1874 (American Humane Association, 2014). Ironically, the Society for Prevention to Cruelty to Animals was established before the SPCC and Mary Ellen was rescued because of its help. The original focus of the SPCC was to remove the child from the abusive home environment, but it originally only focused on families living in poverty and minorities. It was not until 1935 with the establishment of Social Security that the United States government started to track the number of abuse cases.

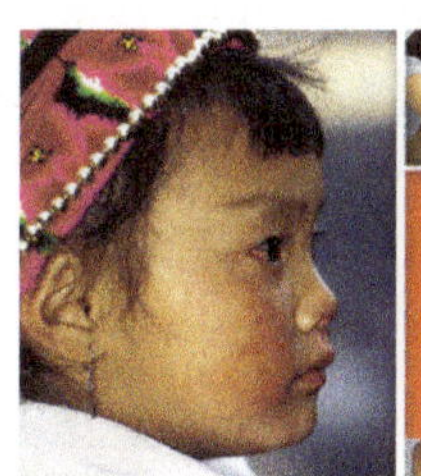

The Story of Mary Ellen

The Beginnings of a Worldwide Child-Saving Crusade

The sufferings of the little girl, Mary Ellen, led to the founding of the New York Society for the Prevention of Cruelty to Children, the first organization of its kind, in 1874, through the efforts of Henry Bergh, Eldridge T. Gerry, and John D. Wright.

The following account is by Mrs. Etta Angell Wheeler, the humanitarian who first discovered and reported the case.

Late in the year 1873 there was brought to me by a poor working woman, the story of a child whose sad case inspired the founding of the first "Society for the Prevention of Cruelty to Children." . . . The story was that during the two previous years, there had lived in the rear tenement, . . . a girl of five or six years old; that during these two years the child had been a close prisoner having been seen only once by the other tenants; that she was often cruelly whipped and very frequently left alone the entire day with the windows darkened, and she

(continues)

(continued from previous page)

was locked in an inner room; that the other occupants of the house had not known to whom to make complaint, the guardian of the house, who lived on the premises, refusing to listen.

A week before, this family had moved to the rear tenement 341, on the same street. Later in the day I went . . . and heard a like story from others; then, hoping to see the child, I went to 341. . . . I was there only long enough to see the child and gain my own impression of her condition. While still talking with the woman, I saw a pale, thin child, barefoot, in a thin, scanty dress so tattered that I could see she wore but one garment besides.

It was December and the weather bitterly cold. She was a tiny mite, the size of five years, though, as afterward appeared, she was then nine. From a pan set upon a low stool she stood washing dishes, struggling with a frying pan about as heavy as herself. Across the table lay a brutal whip of twisted leather strands and the child's meager arms and legs bore many marks of its use. But the saddest part of her story was written on her face in its look of suppression and misery, the face of a child unloved, of a child that had seen only the fearsome side of life. These things I saw while seeming not to see, and I left without speaking to, or of, the child. I never saw her again until the day of her rescue, three months later, but I went away determined, with the help of a kind Providence, to rescue her from her miserable life.

How was this to be done? . . . I had more than once been tempted to apply to the "Society for the Prevention of Cruelty to Animals," but had lacked courage to do what seemed absurd. However, when on the following Tuesday, a niece said: "You are so troubled over that abused child, why not go to Mr. Bergh? She is a little animal, surely." I said at once, "I will go." Within an hour I was at the society's rooms. Mr. Bergh was in his office and listened to my recital most courteously but with a slight air of amusement that such an appeal should be made there. In the end he said: "The case interests me much, but very definite testimony is needed to warrant interference between a child and those claiming guardianship. Will you not send me a written statement that, at my leisure, I may judge the weight of the evidence and may also have time to consider if this society should interfere? I promise to consider the case carefully." . . .

Mr. Bergh called upon me to ask if I would go to the Court House, the child having been already sent for. . . . After we had waited a short time in the Judge's Court, two officers came in, one of whom had the little girl in his arms. She was wrapped in a carriage blanket and was without other clothing than the two ragged garments I had seen her in months before. Her body was bruised, her face disfigured, and the woman, as if to make testimony sure against herself, had the day before, struck the child with a pair of shears, cutting a gash through the left eye-brow and down the cheek, fortunately escaping the eye. . . . The investigation proceeded. The child's appearance was testimony enough, little of mine was needed, and, thus, on Thursday, April 9, 1874, her rescue was accomplished. This Mr. Bergh had effected within forty-eight hours after first hearing of the case.

The prosecution of the woman who had so ill-treated her, followed soon. One witness was a representative of the institution from which the woman had taken the child, then less than two years old. No inquiry as to the child's welfare had been made by the institution during the intervening seven years. Record of her admission to this institution had been lost in a fire. The testimony of fellow tenants, and the damaging witness of the woman against herself, under cross-examination, secured her conviction and she was sentenced to the penitentiary for a year. When leaving the Court House I tried to thank Mr. Bergh for the rescue of the child, and asked if there could not now be a Society for the Prevention of Cruelty to Children, which should do for abused children what was being so well done for animals? He took my hand and said very emphatically: "There shall be one." Today all the world knows how well that promise was kept. The time has come for a forward movement in the welfare of children and little Mary Ellen's hand had struck the hour.

The child was rescued, but what was to be done with her?. . . soon after put Mary Ellen at my disposal. I took her to my mother near Rochester, New York, to my mother whose heart and home were always open to the needy. Here began a new life. The child was an interesting study, so long shut within four walls and now in a new world. Woods, fields, "green things growing," were all strange to her, she had not known them. She had to learn, as a baby does, to walk upon the ground, she had walked only upon floors, and her eye told her nothing of uneven surfaces. She was wholly untaught; knew nothing of right and wrong except as related to punishments; did not know of the Heavenly Father; had had no companionship with children or toys. But in this home there were other children and they taught her as children alone can teach each other. They taught her to play, to be unafraid, to know her rights and to claim them. She shared their happy, busy life from the making of mud pies up to charming birthday parties and was fast becoming a normal child.

I had taken her to my mother in June. In the autumn following my mother died. She had asked that, after her death, my sister, living nearby, should take Mary. This she did and under her care were passed years of home and school life, of learning all good household ways; of instruction in church and Sunday school, and in gaining the love of many and the esteem of all who knew her.

When twenty-four she was married to a worthy man and has proved a good home maker and a devoted wife and mother. To her children, two bright, dutiful daughters, it has been her joy to give a happy childhood in sharp contrast to her own. If the memory of her earliest years is sad, there is this comfort that the cry of her wrongs awoke the world to the need of organized relief for neglected and abused children.

Source: American Humane, 63 Inverness Drive East, Englewood, CO 80112-5117.

Child Abuse in The United States

Child abuse can be divided into four categories:

1. physical,
2. sexual,
3. psychological, and
4. neglect.

Physical abuse can take the form of hitting, beating, whipping, shaking, breaking of bones, burning with cigarettes, addicting children to a drug, restricting children physically, withholding of food and/or medication, and many other related actions. It is any abuse that is intentionally done to cause physical harm to a child or person. **Sexual abuse** is a form of physical abuse but is usually considered a separate category. It is a term that is hard to define but generally includes fondling of children's genitals, kissing them in a sexual manner, or having sexual intercourse with them (Haugaard, 2000). **Psychological abuse** can take the form of threats to kill or harm the child or loved ones; telling the child on a regular basis that he or she is worthless, dumb, or worse; or any kind of behavior that makes the child's self-esteem crumble and causes the child to give up hope. It is often hard to prove in legal settings without the presence of physical abuse. **Neglect** is a separate type of abuse in which a child is neglected. Parents do not supervise their child adequately for their age, feed their child on a regular basis, or provide adequate clothes or shelter. Often child abuse cases have elements of all four kinds of abuse.

An estimated 6.3 million cases of child abuse were reported in the United States and Puerto Rico in 2012 and 1,640 children died due to abuse and neglect (U.S. Department of Health and Human Services, Children's Bureau, 2012). If a person has been abused as a child or an adult, it is extremely important the person seeks help from a professional mental health expert. Abuse can cause a wide variety of severe psychological problems, or may cause the person to abuse other children when they themselves become adults. Unfortunately people are often afraid or unwilling to seek help because they blame themselves or are afraid of the stigma attached to it. Studies have found that 1.3 percent of juvenile delinquents, 40 percent of sexual offenders, and 76 percent of serial rapists report they were sexually abused as youngsters (American Humane Association, 2014).

Child Abuse from a Cultural Perspective

Child abuse is a term used in Western culture to refer to bringing intentional harm to a child. What constitutes acceptable harm is culturally determined and has changed over time. **Infanticide** has been practiced in many cultures throughout the world and throughout history. It is the hastening or directly causing the death of an infant. The way it is carried out and under what circumstances are culturally determined. For example, we can go back to Aristotle's and Plato's time when killing of defective children was considered a wise custom (Gracer & Alexandria, 2003). Infanticide has been reported in the past by anthropologists in the Eskimo, Polynesian, and many African and South American cultures. In China, female infanticide was legal until about 1837. Even in the history of England and Europe infants were left to die or were killed because parents did not have the money to feed them. It was not until industrialization and more modern times when views on how children should be treated that the idea of "child abuse" came into being.

Infanticide does differ in some respects to modern child abuse in that the motives behind the abuse are different. Cultures that practiced infanticide see it as a higher being's will or a necessity for the survival of their society. The personal responsibility of the action is not in their hands but in "God's hands." The Yanomamo of the Venezuelan Amazon region practice infanticide when two children are born too close together and the belief that the survival of the older child would be threatened. Napolean Chagnon (1968, p. 37) states:

> Kaobawa's eldest wife, Bahimi is about thirty-five years old. She is his first cross-cousin. Bahimi was pregnant when I began my fieldwork, but she killed the new baby, a boy at birth, explaining tearfully that it would [have] competed with Ariwari, her nursing son, for milk. Rather than expose Ariwari to the dangers and uncertainty of an early weaning, she killed the new child instead.

Dancing Boys of Afghanistan—Bacha Bazi Boys

A group of older men sit around in a circle watching a fourteen-year-old boy dance dressed in woman's clothes. His job is to dance for the men and sometimes hand out drugs to the guests. Afterwards the boy often goes home with one of the older men for the night and they have sex. Sometimes several Bacha boys are "owned" by one man and he prostitutes them out; other times one man will own his own private Bacha boy. It is common to hire dancing boys to dance at weddings and other celebrations.

The term **Bacha Bazi**, commonly used by people in Afghanistan to refer to this practice, literally means "playing with boys" (Qobil, 2010). Bacha boys are recruited into the dancing boy profession out of economic necessity. The streets of Afghanistan are full of children working and begging, helping their families to survive. Most of the boys are orphaned or from very poor families. An example would be Omid (not real name), fifteen, whose father died when he stepped on a land mine. He was the eldest son and it was his responsibility to provide for his mother and two younger brothers. His mother begs on the streets. He started dancing when he was around ten years old. His family was hungry and this was the only option open to him to help feed his family (Qobil, 2010).

After a boy becomes too old to be a Bacha Bazi, around the age of eighteen, he often becomes a pimp or prostitute. There is no place in mainstream Afghan society for someone that has been raped or abused (Londoño, 2012). Authorities are well aware of Bacha Bazi but choose to ignore the problem. It seems to be widespread in rural conservative areas as well as in some cities. No one knows exactly how many boys are involved in the abuse because no statistics are kept. Even though it is illegal, prosecution is very rare. Bacha Bazi has been around for generations, but it had a resurgence after the fall of the Taliban in 2001. During the Taliban's rule the practice went underground because men suspected of having sex with boys were executed. By-and-large the problem is ignored today by authorities. It's generally a taboo topic and is not discussed openly (Londoño, 2012).

Child Labor in India

Child labor under the age of fourteen is illegal in India and education is free and compulsory until age fourteen. Child bondage and servitude has been illegal since 1893 (Schmitz, Traver, & Larson, 2004). However, the exploitation of child labor is widespread around the world today and India has the largest number of children under the age of fourteen working. Children in India are commonly used in the glass-blowing, fireworks, and carpet industries. It is estimated that over fifty million children are employed by such industries in India today.

A boy sewing in a booth in the market, Nagaur, India.

(Photo courtesy of Claudine Van Massenhove/ Shutterstock.com)

It is commonly accepted by local populations as a necessary means to overcome extreme poverty in many areas of India. Parents send their children to work in factories to help with their family's survival (Schmitz, Traver, & Larson, 2004).

In the carpet industry in northern India, the children work twelve hours a day; they are paid low wages doing work adults refuse to do. Their wages are sent home to their parents, but the children are allowed only short breaks for meals and sleep beside their looms because they have nowhere else to stay.

The Indian government passed a law in 1989 that made it illegal to employ children under the age of fourteen, except in family-owned businesses. Unfortunately this law is rarely enforced and many times circumvented by factories stating they are hiring distant relatives (El Policy Library, 1995). In 1993 the U.S. Congress passed an act that prohibited the import of products that are made wholly or in part by children under the age of fifteen. However, abuses are still widespread and much more needs to be done to end child labor in India and around the world.

Restavecs: Slave Children of Haiti

Haiti won its independence in 1804 as a result of a slave rebellion and became the first Black nation. Ironically, today there are anywhere from 200,000 to 300,000 child slaves in Haiti. Children from impoverished homes are given away by their parents who are too poor to feed and clothe them, in hopes of a better future. In reality these children often are worked twelve to eighteen hours per day, hauling water and doing household chores for no pay, while often being abused physically and psychologically. These children are called **Restavecs**. The term, Restavec comes from a Haitian Creole word that means "stays with." The Restavec system was outlawed by the Haitian government in 2007 when it reified two United Nations' conventions banning child labor. However, Restavecs are still widespread and these laws are rarely enforced. Conditions for these children are like what fourteen-year-old Jenette describes:

> Sometimes they beat me with lengths of electrical cable and sometimes they punch me. I was grinding a coconut and I wasn't doing it very well so they took a knife and cut me with it. My mother is dead and my father doesn't care for me. I would like to run away but I have nowhere to go. . . . Sometimes I look at other children around me and I wish I was like them. (Thomson, 2009, p. 1)

The majority of these children are worked from before sunrise to late in the evening, carrying water and doing work around the house. Many of the children are beaten and endure sexual abuse regularly. Cowhide whips, specially designed to be used on children, are sold locally in stores. Many of these children are as young as six or seven when they are sold or given away.

◄ *Haitian children.*

(Photo courtesy of arindambanerjee/ Shutterstock.com)

There are organizations in Haiti that are working to end the Restavec system. However, extreme poverty, which is the root cause of the Restavec system, is widespread. Since the devastating earthquake on January 12, 2010, poverty and the number of homeless children have increased, adding to the Restavec problem. Jean Robert Cadet is the founder of the Restavec Foundation and is fighting to end the system. At the age of four he was given to another family soon after his mother died. He slept under a table for the next sixteen years and endured beatings and sexual abuse and was not allowed to speak unless spoken to. At the age of fifteen his family moved to the United States where they realized that they could not continue the Restavec system. He was turned out onto the streets of New York to fend for himself. Eventually he found success in the U.S. Army, was able to put himself through college, and is currently a high school teacher (Cadet, 1998). Unfortunately, most Restavec children's lives are not successful and they are destined to a life of poverty and abuse.

CHAPTER 12 SUMMARY

HISTORY OF FAMILY: The concept of family is always in the process of changing. It changes in response to societal norms and the need for members to survive and flourish. If you were to transport yourself back in time to 1776 to the Colonial period in the United States, you might find it hard to recognize the American family when you compare it to today's modern families.

During the Colonial period the dividing line between the average, middle-class, White family and community was more blurred than it is today. Today the domain of the family is separate from the surrounding community. What goes on in the privacy of the family is generally not the community's concern. In the Colonial family what went on in the family was the community's concern. The family and home was the center for economic survival. Everyone in the family, including children, were put to work and expected to contribute to the family's survival. Children were given tasks appropriate for their ages.

Industrialization in the United States began in the late 1700s and continued throughout the 1800s. It resulted in factories and mass production of products. More products became available at a lower cost to the average person than ever before. Industrialization helped create jobs that were located in cities and large towns. As the demand for labor expanded quickly, people began to move from the countryside to the cities to live by wage labor. What resulted was the emergence of the modern concept of childhood. Children should be protected and supported. They should go to school and be able to play and act like children. Of course this was only possible for children of middle- and upper-class families. All family members of lower-class and poor families had to work at whatever they could to bring in money to the family. During the Industrial Age, the concept of "autonomy of the family" became part of the American value system. The family was no longer as intertwined with the community as it was in the Colonial era. The nuclear family became private and "what goes on in the family stays in the family" became the norm.

During the early 1900s the whole idea of romance and love became a major component of marriage. People started to expect emotional satisfaction in their marriage. The number of children declined because families were bearing fewer children. In the late 1940s and 1950s, after World War II, there was a large jump in the number of children being born. This became known as the baby boomer generation. In the 1960s and 1970s these children were starting to grow up and many social changes took place. We had the women's movement, civil rights movement, environmental movement, anti-Vietnam War movement, and sexual revolution movement all taking place.

PLAY: Boys and girls generally have different play patterns. Boys tend to participate in more physically active activities. On the playground at school they tend to play games that are more team and rule oriented than girls. Girls tend to interact in smaller groups and have more conversations with other girl friends.

BULLYING: What exactly constitutes bullying varies, but bullying usually contains three main components: imbalance of power, intent to cause harm to another, and repetition. There are several recognized categories of bullying commonly seen today: verbal, social, physical, and cyber bullying.

CHILD ABUSE: Child abuse is a term used in Western culture to refer to bringing intentional harm to a child. What constitutes acceptable harm is culturally determined and has changed over time. When you look at the acceptable methods of discipline by parents and adults of the past, many of them would be considered abusive today. Being whipped with a belt or switch on your legs, back, or buttocks was considered an acceptable form of punishment not that long ago in our history.

Child abuse can be divided into several categories:

1. physical,
2. sexual,
3. psychological, and
4. neglect.

If a person has been abused as a child or adult, it is extremely important the person seeks help from a professional mental health expert. Abuse can cause a wide variety of severe psychological problems, or may cause the person to abuse other children when they become adults.

CHAPTER 12 VOCABULARY

Bacha Bazi
Blended Family
Child Abuse
Colonial Family
Cyber Bullying
Imbalance of Power
Industrial Revolution Family
Infanticide
Intent to Cause Harm to Another
Modern Family
Neglect
Physical Abuse
Physical Bullying
Psychological Abuse
Repetition
Restavecs
Sexual Abuse
Social Bullying
Verbal Bullying

Chapter 13

ADOLESCENTS
Physical and Cognitive Development

Adolescence is a time when kids go through many physical and emotional changes.

(Photo courtesy of Cindy Donham)

Introduction

Many young adults and teens have a difficult time transitioning into adulthood. People often mistakenly think that this is a modern phenomenon, but looking back through history, we see that adolescence has always been a difficult time. Evidence of these turbulent times in adolescence can even be seen in the 1500s in Shakespeare's *Romeo and Juliet*, where Juliet was only thirteen years old. Even though this was young for marriage when the story took place, it points out the problems of teens at that time. Part of the answer to explain why teenagers seem to have so many problems may be because of what is happening in their brains.

How Adolescents Think

In recent years neuroscientists have made great advancements of knowledge and progress in understanding how the human brain develops and works. It was believed that the brain was basically formed by the age of five or six. However, recent research by Dr. Jay Giedd at the National Institute of Mental Health in Bethesda, Maryland, and colleagues at McGill University in Montreal, shows that around the time of puberty the pre-frontal cortex starts to grow again (Giedd, 2002). This part of the brain is believed to control impulses and making judgments, and is critical in organization, working memory, modulating mood, and reasoning. Much of this growth spurt in gray matter occurs right before puberty, approximately age eleven for girls and twelve for boys.

The brain at this time overproduces neurons and synapses, the brain cells, and the connections between them. Generally the production of neurons, synapses, and brain cells is a good thing. However, the brain then starts to consolidate learning by pruning away the unused cells and synapses, and strengthens others by wrapping them with white matter or myelin. This happens in the brain of a child around age three and again in the teens and continues through the teen years into the early twenties (Giedd, 2002). This brain growth at puberty could affect teen behavior. In the past most of teenagers' mood swings, impulsiveness, judgment errors, and acting out have been attributed to hormonal changes in their bodies. Now that we know there is significant growth and change in what can be considered the CEO part of the brain, it makes sense that teen behavior may be affected (Giedd, 2002).

Dr. Giedd hypothesizes that puberty is a time in people's lives when they need to "use it or lose it" (Giedd, 2002). Activities and learning during the teen years is extremely important for development of the adult brain. For example, doing math and other forms of analytical thinking will develop the part of the

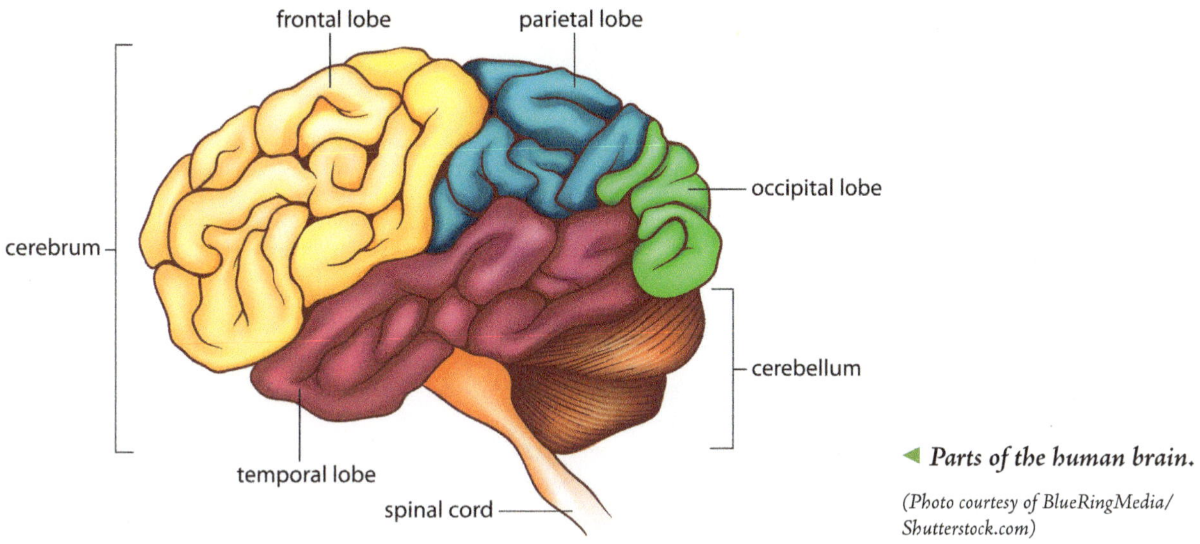

Parts of the human brain.

(Photo courtesy of BlueRingMedia/ Shutterstock.com)

brain that involves analytical thinking. Participating in sports or music then will help strengthen parts of the brain that are responsible for these activities.

The cerebellum, at the back of the brain above the neck, seems to boost processes going on in other parts of the brain. Any activities associated with a higher thought process, such as math, decision making, philosophy, and social skills, are enhanced by the cerebellum. Studies of identical twins show that many parts of the brain are closely identical in both twins; however, this is not the case with the cerebellum. Neuroscientists believe that the environment may have a stronger effect on this part of the brain.

One must be cautious when applying changes in brain structure to behavior. Behavior is a combination of biology and environment. How much each contributes is not known and probably varies a great deal from individual to individual. However, this information about brain changes does give us insight into some possible reasons for changes in teen behavior.

The Orchid Children Theory

Research shows that genetics and other biological factors put some children at higher risk than others for depression, Attention Deficit Hyperactivity Disorder (ADHD), drug addiction, and other behavioral and mental health conditions. However, Dr. David Dobbs (2009) believes that these children can also thrive and have extraordinary potential if raised in the right environment.

(orchid)

(dandelion)

◀ ***The exceptional orchid and the common dandelion.***

(Left photo courtesy of Gita Kulinitch Studio/ Shutterstock.com; Right photo courtesy of Fotofermer/ Shutterstock.com)

Dr. Dobbs (2009) believes there are basically two types of children, the "dandelions" and the "orchids." The "dandelion children" do well overall no matter what kind of environment they are raised in, like a dandelion, which can grow in most kinds of soil. This is why children that come from dysfunctional families may still do relatively well in life.

Then we have the **orchid children** that take extra care and specific greenhouse environments to survive and thrive. If orchid plants do not get specialized care they die or do not bloom. If they do get special care, they flourish and produce beautiful flowers. If the orchid children grow up in a supportive environment and family they can do extraordinarily well. If they do not have the ideal environment, these kids "act out" or externalize behavior that can result in severe problems. It is postulated that these orchid children are genetically important to our society because from these children come some of our most driven, creative, and successful people.

The orchid hypothesis states that environment and genetics can steer a person up as well as down. In the past the negative side has been emphasized and studied—"Poor Tom; he has that bad gene"—and it was assumed that some people had bad genes. In reality genes can move people in either negative or positive directions, depending on the environment. In other words, a gene that in some instances can be maladaptive can be highly adaptive in other instances depending on the environment. It is a means by which evolutionary nature hedges its bet.

Of course this is a simplified explanation for a complicated and intricate interaction of genetics and environment. However, it starts to change the traditional view about "bad genes." This theory also has implications for treatment and education of kids with depression, ADHD, anxiety, or other disorders. For example, children with ADHD may thrive and bloom in a certain kind of educational environment in ways that differ from dandelion children. This may mean that the educational system needs to change from trying to make kids fit the system to being more flexible for orchid kids to bloom.

Puberty and the Physical Transition to Adulthood

When children go through physical puberty it is a time of transition. Children go through puberty at different rates. Boys and girls go through many of the same changes as well as changes unique to their genders. Girls on the average reach puberty two years earlier than boys. The term "puberty" is derived from the Latin word *pubescere*, which means, to grow hairy. As we know, there are many other changes at puberty as well.

Body Growth

The first sign that puberty is starting is a rapid gain in height and weight, often referred to as a growth spurt. The majority of girls start this growth spurt around the age of ten. For boys it starts around the age of twelve. This two-year difference in development between girls and boys continues throughout puberty. Eventually most boys eventually surpass most girls in height and weight by age fifteen. Most girls at the peak of their growth spurt will grow about 3.5 inches in a year and boys about 4.1 inches a year (Tanner, 1971). Girls usually complete their growth in body height and size around the age of sixteen and boys complete it later at around seventeen or eighteen.

During this growth spurt children's body proportions start to change. The first body parts that start to grow rapidly are the hands, legs, and feet, and then the torso. Parents often notice this because they seem to be continually buying new shoes and pants for their children. Often at this stage adolescents appear out of proportion and awkward. As adolescent boys mature one of the most obvious changes are their shoulders broadening relative to their hips. In girls their hips and pelvis broaden relative to their shoulders.

Muscle and fat distribution also begin to change during puberty. Starting around eight or nine for girls, fat begins to increase on their bodies, arms, and legs, a trend that accelerates between eleven and sixteen. In boys, on the other hand, body fat begins to decrease on their bodies, arms, and legs during this time. At the end of puberty boys have on the average have about three times as much muscle as fat. Girls have about four-fifths as much fat as muscle (Grumbach, Roth, & Kelch, 1974).

During puberty there is also a change in motor development, particularly in boys. Girls gain in gross motor or large muscle skills. The large motor skill development in girls is gradual and tends to level off at around age fourteen. Interestingly, during puberty boys show a big increase in gross motor skills, which results in a significant increase in speed, strength, and endurance. This is one reason boys' sports ability can show a big increase between the beginning and end of high school.

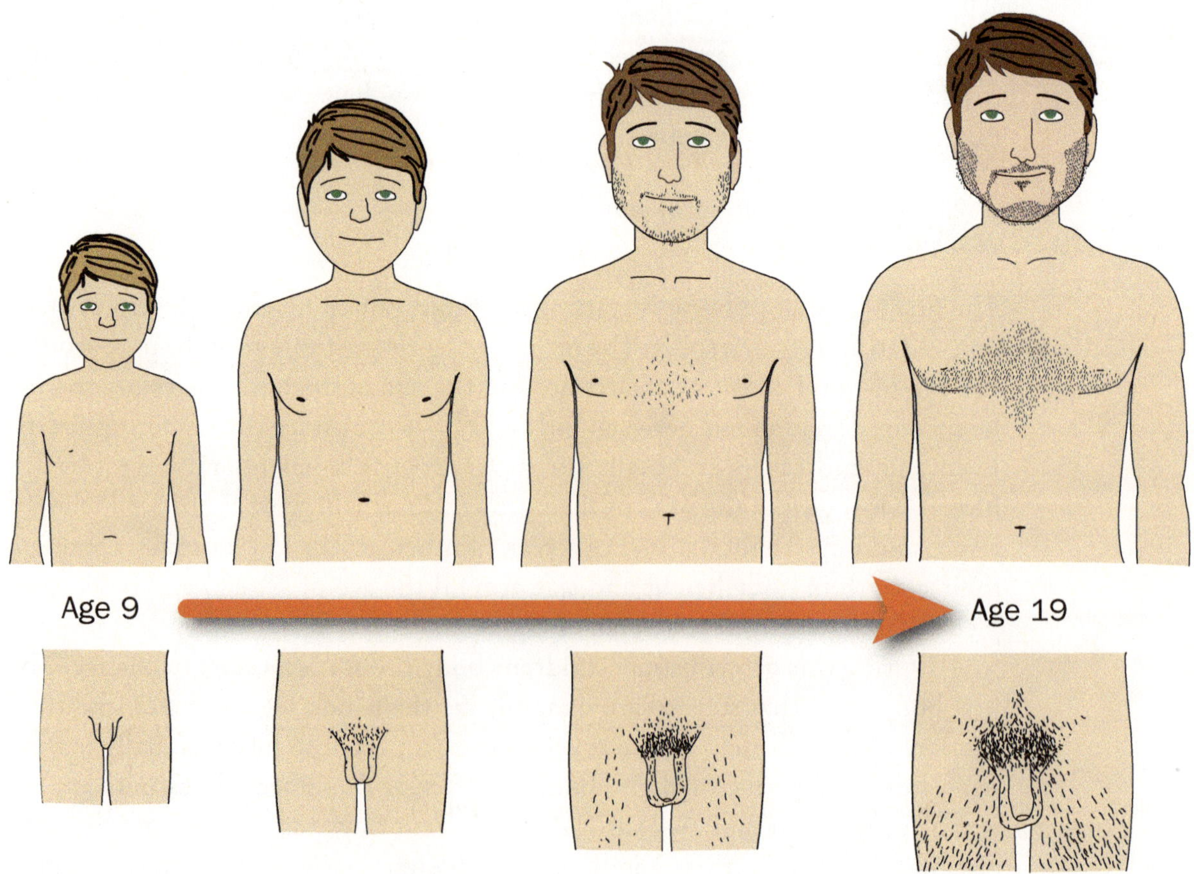

▲ *Physical changes during puberty for males.*

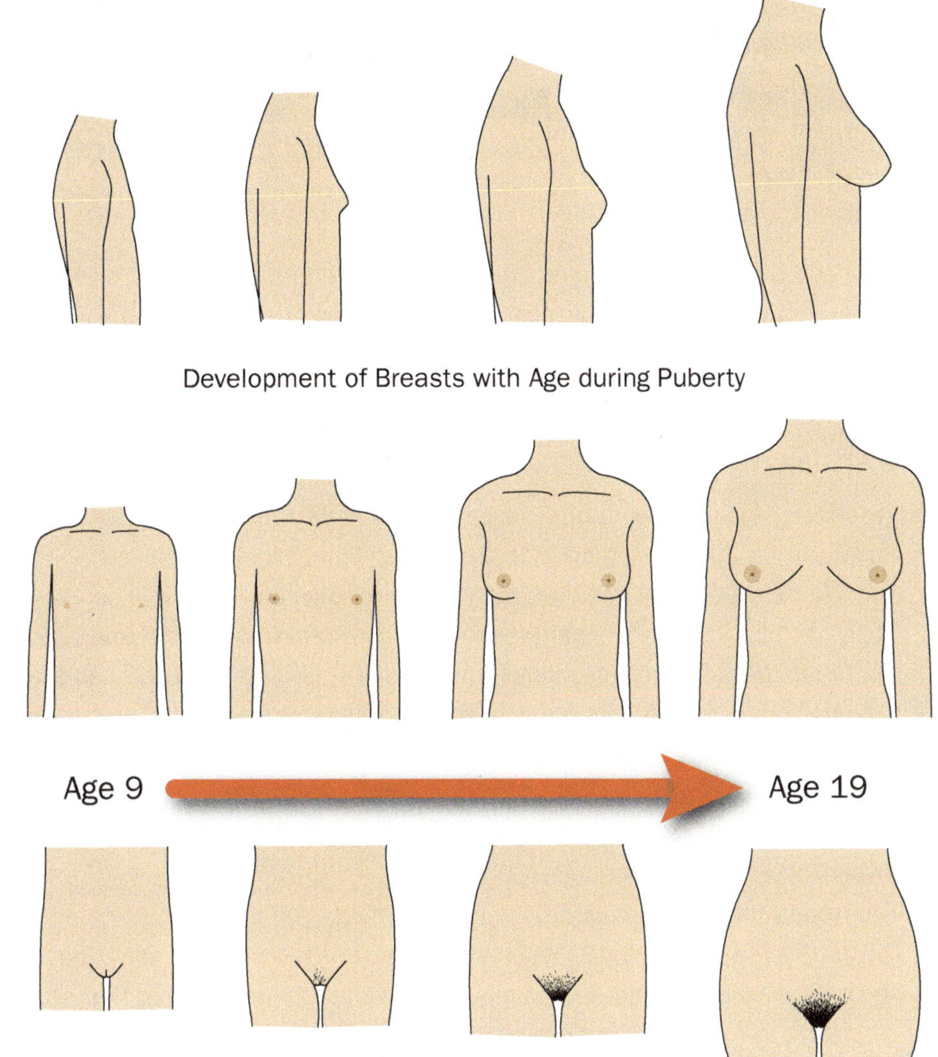

▲ *Physical changes during puberty for females.*

Sexual Changes during Puberty

There are two categories of sexual changes that occur during puberty. Primary sexual characteristics involve the production of eggs and sperm and the development of the sex organs. The secondary sexual characteristics are changes that occur on the outside of the body, such as development of breasts in girls, and the development of underarm and pubic hair in both boys and girls. Typically

American of Cambodian Heritage Gets Her First Period

By Sandy Khim

One of the most memorable experiences growing up was when I got my first period. In the Asian culture, when a female child gets her menstrual cycle, it is the sign of womanhood.

Being born in America, I did not understand the Cambodian tradition or importance about informing my mother about my first encounter with my menstrual cycle. I started receiving basic sex education in the third grade. I got my first period when I was in fourth. I was the first to start puberty amongst my friends and once I got it, I did not tell my mom. I just "stole" one of her pads and placed it on my underwear and felt gross. It was not until my mom saw me discarding them that she realized I had started my period.

My mom asked me when I started it and why I didn't tell her. I told her I wanted this to be a private thing and I was embarrassed. None of my other friends had little boobies forming or had to share pads with their mothers. My mother reassured me that it was okay and normal, and that I was transforming into a woman.

Upon switching to my next pad my mom told me to tell her. Before placing on my next pad, my mother taped cotton balls on top of the pad. She told me she wanted to see how I was bleeding and to save her the pad before I discarded it. I thought this was odd and gross, nevertheless I did as I was told.

Once it was time to discard the pad with the cotton balls, my mother told me to wrap it up in paper and give it to her. She told me she salvaged what she could, but it was a shame that the sample I gave her was not my first menstrual flow. She saved the cotton balls so she could get them covered and preserved in a sheet of gold paper. She then took cotton balls wrapped in gold paper to the temple and had a monk bless and chant protection spells on it. My mother then took it and incorporated it in with a waist chain for me to wear. It was supposed to protect my physical and spiritual self and being on our menstrual cycle was like cleaning your body.

At the time, it seemed a little crazy and unsanitary to me. But now that I am older and have become more in touch with my cultural background I look forward to continuing this tradition. I am truly grateful that my mother made the effort to "protect" my spiritual life as well as to encourage and support me through my transition from a child to an adolescent.

Summary of Physical Changes during Puberty

GIRLS ONLY	BOYS ONLY	BOTH BOYS AND GIRLS
▪ Formation of breasts ▪ Broader hips and pelvis ▪ Menstruation and ovulation ▪ Increased proportion of fat to muscle	▪ Facial, shoulder, and back hair ▪ Sperm production ▪ Increased size of penis and testes ▪ Broader shoulders and chest ▪ Increased proportion of muscle to fat	▪ Pubic and underarm hair ▪ Arm and leg hair ▪ Stronger and thicker bones ▪ Longer forehead ▪ Oilier skin ▪ Stronger body odor ▪ Lower voice ▪ Growth spurt ▪ More prominent nose, ears, lips, and chin

Source: Adapted from Arnett, 2010.

these physical changes occur over a span of about four years, but can take as few as two years and as long as six years.

The increase in body fat and weight is one component related to the occurrence of a girl's first menstrual cycle. Fat cells release a protein called **leptin.** The rise in the leptin level signals the brain that a girl's energy stores are sufficient for puberty. This is one reason menarche and other aspects of sexual maturation occur earlier in heavier girls, especially obese girls.

Sequence of Physical Changes at Puberty

BOYS		GIRLS	
Characteristic	**Age of First Appearance (in Years)**	**Characteristic**	**Age of First Appearance (in Years)**
1. Growth of testes, scrotal sac 2. Growth of pubic hair 3. Growth spurt 4. Growth of penis 5. Change in voice 6. Spermarche 7. Facial and underarm hair 8. Oil and sweat, acne	1. 9.5–13.5 2. 10–15 3. 10.5–16 4. 10.5–14.5 5. 11–15 6. 12–14 7. 12–17 8. 12–17	1. Growth of pubic hair 2. Growth of breasts 3. Growth spurt 4. Menarche 5. Underarm hair 6. Oil and sweat, acne	1. 8–14 2. 8–13 3. 9.5–14.5 4. 10–16.5 5. 10–16 6. 10–16

Source: Adapted from Goldstein, 1976.

Increasing rates of obesity and overweight children and teens contributes to earlier maturation of girls in the United States and Europe. Statistics in industrialized nations show that from 1900 to 1970, girls' menarche has occurred three to four months younger each decade. This is partly a result of the improvement in health care, nutrition, and sanitation. Girls who are very thin or who begin serious athletic training at early ages often experience later onset of their first period. Also in poverty-stricken regions of the world where malnutrition is widespread girls' onset of menarche is often delayed compared to industrialized nations.

Many American parents prepare their daughters for their first period or **menarche.** Schools often have programs in the fifth grade that educate girls about the basic facts. Parents often do better in preparing girls for puberty than they do boys.

Most boys get very little information or support from their parents about changes that happen during puberty. Most of the information boys get comes from reading materials or from peers. Often the first sign of puberty in boys is the enlargement of their testes and scrotum with pubic and underarm hair starting to grow soon after. Around this same time the penis begins to enlarge. Body growth spurts usually start near the end of or after the enlargement of the testes and penis has occurred, usually about the age of fourteen or so. At the peak of body growth, facial and body hair start to grow. The voice deepens because the larynx enlarges and the vocal cords lengthen. Girl's voices also become lower but to a much lesser degree than boys. **Spermarche,** the first ejaculation of seminal fluid, usually occurs around the age of thirteen to fourteen.

Endocrine System

The **endocrine system** consists of different glands in various parts of the body and these glands release chemicals that are called hormones. Hormones affect the development and functioning of the body.

The **hypothalamus**, a bean-sized structure located in the lower part of the brain, is responsible for regulation of hormones in other glands. The hypothalamus controls much of the psychological and physiological functions related to eating, drinking, motivation, and sexuality. The hypothalamus begins with a gradual increase in the production of **gonadotropin (GnRH)**. This increase in GnRH causes the pituitary gland to release hormones. The pituitary gland is about a half inch long and is located at the base of the brain. These gonadotropins cause the release of hormones that stimulate the development of the egg cells in the ovaries of females and the sperm in the testes of males. The ovaries and testes are also referred to as **gonads** or sex glands. The gonads produce two classes of sex hormones, **estrogens** and **androgens**. The most well-known estrogen is **estradiol** and most well-known androgen is **testosterone**.

Many people associate estrogens only with females and androgens only with males. When children are young, both boys and girls have about the same levels of these hormones; however, as they start puberty, these levels become significantly different in the two sexes (DeRose & Brooks-Gunn, 2006). Females have higher levels of estradiol and males have higher levels of testosterone. In both sexes estrogens are responsible for the increase of a growth hormone (GH), which fuels the growth spurt. This increase in GH, in combination with androgens, stimulates gains in bone density that continue into early adulthood. Boys' testes and adrenal glands release large quantities of the androgen testosterone, which leads to muscle growth, body and facial hair, and other male sex characteristics. In girls, estrogens stimulates the breasts, uterus, and vagina to mature. They also cause the increase in fat and the (beginning of the) menstrual cycle. In girls the renal androgens influence increase in height and stimulate the growth of underarm and pubic hair.

CHAPTER 13 SUMMARY

Around the time of puberty the pre-frontal cortex starts to grow again. This part of the brain is believed to control impulses and make judgments, and is critical in organization, working memory, modulating mood, and reasoning. In the past most of teenage mood swings, impulsiveness, judgment errors, and acting out were attributed to hormonal changes in their bodies. Now that we know there is significant growth and change in what can be considered the CEO part of the brain, it makes sense that teen behavior may be affected.

Research shows that genetics and other biological factors put some children at higher risk than others for depression, ADHD, drug addiction, and other behavioral and mental health conditions. However, Dr. David Dobbs believes that these children (the "orchid children") can also thrive and have extraordinary potential if raised in the right environment. The "dandelion children" do well overall no matter what kind of environment they are raised in, like a dandelion, which can grow in most kinds of soil.

Children go through puberty at different rates. Boys and girls go through many of the same changes, as well as changes unique to their genders. Girls on the average reach puberty two years earlier than boys. The first sign that puberty is starting is a rapid gain in height and weight, often referred to as a growth spurt.

CHAPTER 13 VOCABULARY

Androgens
Endocrine System
Estrogens
Estradiol
Gonads
Gonadotropin
Hypothalamus
Leptin
Menarche
Spermarche
Testosterone
Orchid Children

Chapter 14

ADOLESCENTS
Social and Cultural Development

(Photo courtesy of Syda Productions/Shutterstock.com)

Introduction

The teenage and young adult years are a time of great change. The adolescent years are full of situations when parents, by their very existence, seem to embarrass their children. As evidence, Susie, who was in the seventh grade, was being driven to school by her mother. She saw some friends of hers and asked her mother, "Could you please duck down as we drive by! "

It is a time when kids are trying to figure out who they are, what they believe, and what they want to do with their lives. For some adolescents it is a time of turbulence because of explorations and restrictions and freedoms that they experience for the first time. However, teens and young adults in different cultures do not share the same issues and difficulties. In this chapter we focus on the social and cultural aspects of adolescence and young adulthood in the United States and cross culturally.

Transitions to Adulthood

All cultures have **rites of passage.** Rites of passage mark the transitions from one phase of life to another. Generally these transitions include changes in social position, residence, and life conditions.

The term "rites of passage" was coined by Charles-Arnold Van Gennep, a Belgian anthropologist during the early twentieth century (O'Neal, 2008). What specific transitions or stages a person passes through vary from culture to culture, but all cultures include birth, onset of puberty and adulthood, marriage, and death. For purposes of this chapter we are looking at rites of passage associated with adolescence or the passage from childhood to adulthood. These can include graduations, becoming sexually active, learning to drive, voting for the first time, going through boot camp, bar mitzvahs, or confirmations. Many cultures around the world have traditional ceremonies that mark the transition of a child to sexual maturity and adulthood.

Customs from non-European cultures vary and many seem extreme from a Western point of view. For boys, many of the ceremonies involve some kind of test and circumcision. Boys of the Barabaig or Datoga from East Africa have their heads shaved and their foreheads cut with horizontal cuts that go from ear to ear. This purposely leaves scarring to show that the boys have been through "gar" or the coming of age ceremony; these scars are worn with pride (O'Neil, 2008). In the past, boys from the Maasai culture traditionally had to kill a lion and then were circumcised. For girls, rites of passage are more often associated with the onset of menstruation.

Graduating from college is a rite of passage in American society today.

(Photo courtesy of Cynthia Donham)

In the American culture, the passage from childhood into adulthood is not easily identified by a single ceremony or rite of passage. Instead it encompasses stages in the direction of adulthood. These steps include graduations, getting a driver's license, the right to vote, and the ability to drink and smoke legally. Many believe that true adulthood comes with economic independence and the establishment of a permanent residence apart from parents. There is no exact age associated with this last step, but is usually expected sometime in the early twenties.

Unlike many cultures around the world, puberty and sexual maturity in America are not considered a true rite of passage into adulthood. As a society Americans do not consider a girl of twelve to fourteen able to function as a fully independent adult. The legal age of marriage without the need of parental consent in most of America is eighteen. In general, most people prefer to be married before having children, though this is not the same as it was in the late 1900s. Laws as well as social customs in America help prevent young girls from becoming parents and trying to take on adult roles too early.

According to the American government, reaching the chronological age of eighteen determines that a person is an adult. At eighteen Americans can vote and sign up to serve in the military. But there is a question about whether most are truly independent adults at this age. Parents can keep offspring on their

The Maasai people dressed in traditional clothing.

(Photo courtesy of Amy Nichole Harris/ Shutterstock.com)

health insurance policies until they are twenty-six. This seems to imply that most are not able to settle into a job with health benefits until they are twenty-six. Teens in the foster care system are considered adults and expected to fend for themselves at eighteen. But sadly many of these former foster kids end up homeless and on the streets within six months.

Socially, Americans use various markers for emergence from adolescence into adulthood, such as graduation from college, living independently, and making enough money to support oneself. For Americans, the transition into adulthood has lengthened significantly since the beginning of the nineteenth century, moving from the late teens and early twenties to middle and late twenties. Many social changes have contributed to this trend.

The increase in expectations for more formal education is an important factor. In 1900, people were considered educated when they graduated from high school. By the end of that century, college education had become more the norm and a requirement for doing well in life. In the twenty-first century a college education is even more important and many careers require advanced degrees, which in the past were relatively rare. The trend in the job market toward requiring more intellectual and technical skills seems likely to continue. Educating women is also more important today than it was in 1900. According to the 2000 census, more women than men were enrolled in higher education. Most students also reported receiving some financial help from their parents. It seems that many also put off marriage and family until after completing formal education. The median age of marriage reported for men is 28.2 years and 26.1 years for women (U.S. Census Bureau, 2010).

Learning to Drive as a Rite of Passage in America

Most people remember when they learned to drive. I remember going down to the Department of Motor Vehicles (DMV) the first day I could, at 15½ to get my learners permit. I was so excited! I only missed two questions. My mom took me to a large, empty parking lot so I could learn to stop and start the car. In my case we had a car with a manual shift, so starting and stopping was a skill that was hard to learn without the car dying every time. I remember the car I learned to drive with, a Toyota Corolla. My older brother used it first to learn with and then came my turn. Poor clutch, after I finished popping and grinding it on a regular basis it finally died and had to be replaced.

I remember on the day of my 16th birthday, I was so excited to go down and get my driver's license. I remember getting into the car with the man from the DMV and he took me to a four-way intersection in a residential neighborhood that had no stop signs. I was mortified when I rolled through the "uncontrolled intersection." I failed right then and there! I had not even tried parallel parking, which I was really worried about. A few weeks later I tried again and passed.

▲ *A teen learning to drive from her mother.*
(Photo courtesy of Lisa F. Young/Shutterstock.com)

I headed out with two of my girlfriends for my first night out, now that I could legally drive! I was slightly older than both of my friends so this was the first time for all of us. We were so excited to be able to go places on our own and felt so grown up. We were driving in a newly developed area that had no streetlights yet and I made a U-turn. I thought it was safe because the only lights I could see in either direction were way off down the road. Of course with my luck, those lights turned out to be from a police car. The police put on the red lights and I remember thinking they wanted to pass so I pulled over to a different lane. Of course they followed me and then I realized they wanted me to pull over (I was not too savvy in those days). I finally pulled over and the officer told me that I had made an illegal U-turn. I handed them my new temporary driver's license and told them it was my first night out. I guess we all must have looked pretty scared and one of the officers was chuckling. They took pity on me and did not give me a ticket. If the officers had ticketed me, my parents would have forbidden me to drive for who knows how long. I never told my parents. I will always remember my first time driving and for a long time afterwards was always very careful about U-turns and stops (Donham, 2014).

Rites of Passage to Womanhood: The Efik People, Fat Is Beautiful

For the Efik people in Akapabuyo, Nigeria, the girls that are moving from girlhood to womanhood traditionally spend time in the "fattening room." This is a time and place where girls go to be taught by an older woman of the tribe about what it is to be a good wife and mother. They are taught how to walk, talk, and sit in front of their husband, along with proper sexual behavior. Wisdom is passed on concerning how to clean, sew, and care for children. Special dances are learned that the girls will use on their wedding day. In the past this period of seclusion was usually done right before they were married but this is not always the case today.

While in seclusion, girls strive to put on as much weight as possible. For an Efik woman, the fatter she is the more beautiful she is considered. Fat is a sign of good health, prosperity, and allure. Being thin is a sign of being sickly and not able to bear children. The girls are fed a special diet of yams, plantains, beans, and gari (ginger) while their physical activity is restricted. The time a woman spends in seclusion depends on the wealth of her family. In the past it ranged from several months up to two years. Today it usually is a few weeks to a few months. European and American influence is having its effect on this rite of passage for women. Health campaigns about the dangers of too much fat have influenced many urban dwellers to abandon this tradition (Simmons, 2006).

Relationships

Adolescent Family Relationships

For some families the transitional teen years are difficult years. However, research shows that only between 5 percent and 20 percent of teens have major clashes with their families. In spite of spending decreasing amounts of time with their families, most teens still express love and respect for their parents (Granic, Hollenstein, & Dishion, 2003; Larsen et al., 1996; Steinberg, 1993).

Most adolescent conflicts with parents are over ordinary things such as homework, curfews, or attending parties rather than more serious things like use of illegal drugs and alcohol. Some research conflicts with this view, concluding that adolescence is a time of turbulence. However, most of the time parents and children who had conflicts in earlier years continue to have conflicts as teens; those who did not have previous conflicts usually do not start when the kids are teens (Holmbeck & Hill, 1988; Montemayor, 1983; Steinberg & Silk, 2002).

Autonomy

Adolescence is a time of growing autonomy, the development and expression of independence. In America and in other cultures that value individual identity and thinking, it is a time when teens discover who they are separate from their parents and families. This includes the emotional side of feeling independent as well as making individual decisions and setting goals. This process can result in conflicts with parents.

Autonomy can be viewed through three interdependent domains: (1) emotional, (2) behavioral, and (3) attitudinal values (Beyers, Vansant, & Moors, 2003; Noon, Dekovic, & Meeus, 2001; Steinberg, 1990; Steinberg & Silk, 2002). **Emotional autonomy** focuses on the teenagers' close emotional relationships such as those with their peers and parents. This is the adolescents' and young adults' ability to separate their own emotional reactions from others, particularly their parents.

Behavioral autonomy focuses on teenagers being allowed to make their own decisions and to carry them out. It is the ability to look at all of the aspects of a decision (knowledge, advice from others) and to weigh it and then make an informed decision. **Attitudinal and value autonomy** is the development of teenagers and young adults toward having their own values and attitudes, separate from their parents and friends. This coincides with an increase in abstract thinking.

During early and middle adolescence, teens take in opinions, judgments, and expectations from their peers and others outside their families. In later adolescence they start setting their own standards and developing a coherent view of themselves as individuals. With this internalization of standards, teens and young adults will study because they want to get good grades rather than because their parents want them to study (Collins & Laursen, 2004; Harter, 2003; Ryan & Deci, 2004).

Adolescence is a time when teens start to question their parents' ideas and values. They start to see their parents as individual people with weaknesses and strengths rather than just "parents who know everything." The balance of power shifts to a more balanced state, rather than parents holding all the power, though parents do usually maintain the upper hand (Gehring, Wentzel, Feldman, & Munson, 1990; Noack & Buhl, 2005; Wentzel & Feldman, 1996). This power shift can be a time of conflict and negotiation when parents and teens must decide how much independence is reasonable and what will remain under the control of the parents.

Adolescent conflict is less prevalent in many non-Western cultures compared to Western cultures. Cultures where individual choices and identity are

Racial Identity of a Teen

By Gabrielle Zimmer, Student at CSULB, 2011

Well, I so happen to be half Black and half White. I used to think as a kid that racism was between Blacks and Whites, but then I grew to know more. I will say the first time I felt that race was an issue for me was in the 9th grade. I was on the school bus and these Black kids were throwing paper balls at me saying I wasn't Black. I went home crying like a baby . . . 'cuz I was wimpy and that was just plain old mean. Anyways I came home and called my mom; we had this talk about my being interracial, and that I would experience a different kind of racism. I was totally confused, but then and through life I figured that one out. My mom explained to me that, to a lot of Black people, especially the super ghetto young and ignorant ones at my school, I wasn't quite Black. I was or am what you would call an "oreo": White on the inside and Black on the out. I was called this all the time till I got to college. In high school it was the same way, people saying that I acted "White." I thought this was the dumbest thing ever. Is there any real way to act Black or White? Also I had White people asking me why I didn't act Black. Not ghetto enough for the Black people or the Whites. What was I to do?

Anyway my mom then said, "Have you ever wanted to be White?" Now do not judge me, this may come as a shock, but I was and can sometimes be insecure about race. It's tough when people don't like you based on such a small difference. But I said yes. When I was younger that's all I saw, was how cool the White people had it. My mom then said, "I know you always liked your White side better." This was true when I was younger because I guess you can say the world and the media displays White as better. But I was only being honest and at one point I did want to be White. But that was at one point. I think as I got older I realized there was no one way to act as a race. I still wish I had straight hair sometimes, but I think a lot of people want what they don't have.

I think the hard part is just being told that you should be a certain way to fit into a race. I don't want to have to act [like a] belligerent, loud and sassy nigga just to be Black. And are we saying that only White people act smart? Because when people [say] "You're acting White," it's like they are saying that I [am] acting White because I try hard in school and speak proper English . . . well not super proper, but you get what I mean. Anyways, it'd be nice if people didn't need to put each other in categories, but I have learned that I'm not acting any race, I'm just being me.

Source: Gabrielle Zimmer, Yonks South, Issue #1, Posted May 3, 2011, Yonkssouth.workpress.com, retrieved June, 1, 2011.

highly valued are called individualistic cultures. America and many of the industrialized Western cultures are individualistic. Societies where the separate individual is less valued are called collective cultures, as seen in Asian and African cultures. It appears that there is less openly expressed conflict between parents and teens in collective cultures because these teens may see what is beneficial to the family or community as a whole as more important than being an individual (Chao, 1994; Dason, 2000; Fuligni & Zhang, 2004).

Relationship with Peers in the United States

During the time of adolescence, teens spend increasingly less time with their families and peer relationships take center stage. Parental influence is still important, but kids begin to be influenced by a wider group of people (Byth, Hill, & Thiel, 1982; Schwartz, Bukowski, & Aoki, 2006). In fact, teens spend close to twice as much time with their peers compared to time with their parents and other adults (Csikszentmihallyi & Larson 1984; Fuligni & Stevenson, 1995). The peer friendships of these years fall into three categories: **dyadic** or close friendships; close clique of friends; and wider circle of friends often referred to as crowds (Cole et al., 1996).

In middle childhood, children form friendships mostly for the pleasure of doing things with another person. In adolescence, friendships become more complicated and seem to be defined by three fundamental attributes teenagers value: reciprocity, commitment, and equality (Hartup, 1993; Larson et al., 1996). In close individual friendships, reciprocity involves sharing feelings and comparing social knowledge with one other as well as sharing interests and

◀ ***Teenagers spend increasingly less time with their families and more time with peers.***

(Photo courtesy of SpeedKingz/ Shutterstock.com)

activities. Commitment refers to loyalty and trust, and equality refers to the equal status between people.

One of the things that marks all three kinds of teen friendships as different from earlier friendships is the increasing independence they have from parental or adult supervision. When younger, kids hang out in smaller supervised groups such as church groups, scouts, and sports groups. Though these kinds of groups continue into the teen years, adolescents often begin forming their own peer groups and hang out with larger groups of friends.

Adolescent friendships are different for girls and boys, though they are important to both genders. Girls spend more time with friends sharing their feelings, thoughts, and beliefs. These relationships are often intense. Early teen boys report having less intense friendships and spend more time alone than girls. Male validation of worth comes more from actions and activities than through disclosure of personal information, which is key in female friendships.

Opportunities for social comparison are an important part of teen friendships for both boys and girls, where they compare ideas, beliefs, abilities, and physical changes. These peers provide a reference group for deciding what is acceptable and what is not as teens try out different roles and identities. This often causes concern for the parents about who their children's friends are and whether or not the friends are "a good influence."

Cliques

Small groups of friends who have frequent social interaction with each other are called **cliques**. They are usually composed of up to twelve people, though the average size in American high schools is five people. Kids who consider themselves best friends are usually members of the same clique. Of course students can be friends with people from other cliques as well and may do some things with another clique.

One of the defining characteristics of most cliques is similarity among its members. They are often close in age and of the same gender, particularly in the younger adolescent years. Age separation in traditional schools probably contributes to this similarity in age. In settings where teens are not separated by age their cliques are more age mixed.

In many schools cliques also seem to be segregated by ethnicity and socioeconomic level. Kids with similar economic resources can afford the same interests and activities. For example, if a group of girls loves to shop and buy clothes as a regular activity, girls who cannot afford to do this would probably not be part of the group. Even in schools that are ethnically mixed, kids often seek out friends with similar backgrounds during middle and high school years. They may be seeking to confirm their own identities among those they see most like themselves. However, children who grow up in schools with a variety of ethnicities and backgrounds tend to continue to have a mixture of friends from various ethnicities even in middle and high school.

Members of cliques also have other similarities, such as an interest in drama or a particular sport. Often students choose a group of friends who have similar academic performance. Kids involved in substance abuse tend to find groups with alcohol or drug use patterns. As kids move through adolescence, cliques become less rigid and often include both boys and girls, reflecting growing interest in dating.

Crowds

Crowds are larger groups than cliques; members share characteristics but may not interact with each other socially on a regular basis. Crowds can be based on interests, abilities, social status, or, in some instances, ethnicity. In the American high school setting, for example, some common crowds might be the jocks, the nerds, the surfers, the Goths, the druggies, or the bandos. Most students can identify and agree on the various crowds at their schools. Crowds often hang out in a particular place on campus and many can be identified by dress or behavior. However, members of a particular crowd do not always spend social time with each other on a regular basis.

The status of a particular crowd in adolescent culture depends on the environment. For example, the smart crowd may have a high status at one school or a low status at another. Particularly in early adolescence, a higher-status crowd may make fun of or mock lower-status groups. As teens grow older, they more often just ignore the lower-status crowds. As with cliques, crowds tend to become more fluid in late adolescence, particularly after high school graduation.

Membership in a particular crowd puts pressure on kids to conform to group norms. People are said to **conform** when they change behaviors or attitudes to be more like the behavior and attitudes of other members of the group. It is often understood that acceptance in the group requires conformity. If kids want to be accepted in a group, they often conform. The desire to conform to peer groups often gradually decreases as individuals mature and move into adulthood.

American teenagers tend to consult or turn to people who are experts in a certain dimension; for example, on how to dress or act at school they turn to their peers. When it has to do with career choices, they may turn to their parents or another adult. Ultimately, as most adolescents get older and gain more confidence and self-esteem, they gain more autonomy and are less influenced by their peers and parents.

Most studies of adolescent peer relationships have been done with White, middle-class American students. Since adolescent roles and expectations can vary a great deal across the cultures of the world, the influence of peers, family, and other adults may vary considerably. One would not expect adolescence in the United States to be the same as in cultures where there are arranged marriages at fourteen years old and girls do not routinely continue in school past elementary school. Adolescence in these other cultures needs documentation and study.

Intimacy and Dating in Adolescence

One of the major developmental tasks for adolescents in American culture is learning to form close relationships with friends and romantic partners. Teenagers explore their values in close emotional and psychological relationships. This should not be confused with sexual or physical closeness between two people.

Theoretical Background

Dr. Harry Sullivan (1892–1949) was one of the earliest and most influential theorists to write about adolescence from a psychoanalytical perspective. Dr. Sullivan was born in a small farming community in New York to poor Irish

◄ *Teenagers taking a "selfie" with their smart phone.*

(Photo courtesy of Cindy Donham)

farmers. His father was reported to be withdrawn and his mother as bitter and complaining and showing little affection to their only surviving child while he was growing up. This was to have a profound effect on his life and work. He received his medical degree in 1917 from the University of Chicago College of Medicine (Patterson, 2011).

Dr. Sullivan focused on the progression of interpersonal tasks adolescents must resolve to attain maturity—completing these tasks leads to feelings of security, and not completing them leads to anxiety. In early adolescence, the drive for intimacy is often satisfied by close same-sex friendships. Development of successful, close, same-sex relationships is necessary to form close relationships with opposite-sex partners later. As a result of growing physical and sexual drives in older teens, many change their focus to opposite-sex relationships. One of the shortcomings of Sullivan's work is that he does not address the issue of homosexuality, which at the time was still considered an abnormality (Mullahy, 1968).

Erik Erikson described a series of stages throughout a child's life, each of which presented a crisis or conflict that needs to be resolved. However, Erikson focused on identity, whereas Sullivan saw intimacy as central. Erikson said adolescents must first establish identity before they can fully achieve intimacy in early adulthood. He saw the intimacy of adolescent relationships being a result of sexual drive, lacking deep intimacy and masking deep fear and anxiety.

Sullivan said intimacy leads to identity and Erikson that identity development leads to intimacy. Studies of the issue have not answered the question of which sequence is more correct. But the sequence is perhaps not as important as realizing that identity and intimacy are tied together during adolescence. They build on each other, are intertwined, and are both necessary for successful transition to adulthood.

History of Dating and Courtship in America

In Colonial times (1600–1840), marriages were most often within the same social class. Consideration of the economic survival of the couple was a major factor and parents usually had to approve of the match, even though marriages were not usually formally arranged as in some other cultures. Fathers had particular power because they could own property and were concerned about whom the land would go to. If the father did not approve of his children's choices then he could disinherit them. Men often married in their mid-twenties after establishing themselves economically; women were often younger. Love and affection were also considerations in most marriages at that time. Informal marriage was common in the colonies. Couples sometimes announced to their families and friends that they were married and from that point on were recognized by the community as being married. This was particularly common in the colonies and areas where clergy was not available and only visited periodically or not at all. A form of bigamy also occurred in many colonies when an unhappy spouse moved far way to a territory or state where they started over and remarried. They were unlikely to be caught or prosecuted (Hartog, 2000).

In the Victorian era (1840–1900) strict codes of courtship were common, especially in the upper classes. If a man was interested in a woman, he had to be formally introduced to her. If he was interested in courting her, he would usually visit the young lady in her home and be led into a sitting room where a chaperone would always be present. Often wedding proposals were made in writing and were accepted only with parents' approval. Love and affection were the basis of most marriages but, as in earlier times, social class, family reputation, and income were also important (Gillis, 1985).

After the turn of the twentieth century, courting began to take on a more modern form. The term "dating" is believed to have been coined in the 1920s by a short story in *Harper's* magazine (Baily, 1988; Rothman,1984). It referred to the custom in the working class for young couples to meet in public places, often with chaperones. Working-class homes often did not have appropriate places for more formal courtship. Public dating later became the custom in other social classes as well and eventually became what is thought of as modern dating.

Today peer intimacy moves to a new level when adolescents enter dating relationships. Dating involves a range of emotional and physical involvement. The rules and details of dating have changed for teens even in the past forty years and is often less formal and exclusive than it once was. Dating often occurs in a group setting.

Teens of the twenty-first century often consider the term "dating" as old fashioned and out of date. The term "hooking up," used today, is more ambiguous and can indicate a short-term, sexual, or casual relationship. If a commitment is made between the partners, they can be considered girlfriend and boyfriend. Adolescents often informally get together in small or larger mixed-sex groups and sometimes have an informal relationship with one partner, especially in late adolescence. However, it is not considered a serious relationship until they have discussed the matter and decided to be girlfriend and boyfriend.

Purpose of Dating

In Western cultures dating has several purposes. One of the purposes is social recreation, to have someone to go out and have fun with, and to fulfill the need for companionship and intimacy. In addition, it provides a way for adolescents to practice and learn strategies for future relationships. By dating they can experiment and learn what relationship characteristics they think are important for future, more permanent relationships. Dating is still a normal prelude to marriage and people rarely marry in the United States without dating first. Dating in the adolescent world also can bring prestige and can mean a teen is perceived as socially more advanced or more popular.

Dating in Other Cultures

Arranged marriages without previous dating are still a part of many cultures in the world today. Adolescents from these cultures do not view this as strange. These adolescents ideally assume that their parents have their best interests in mind and know better than they who would be a good spouse. They have no concerns about being rejected and do not have to worry about finding their "true love." The couple respects each other and will learn to love each other as time goes on. Many of these cultures view the Western marriage system as inefficient and a waste of time. Marriage in cultures where arranged marriage is practiced is seen as a union between two families and, as a result, the whole extended family is invested in making the relationship work.

Parents and Their Teenagers

Parenting Styles

The four main parenting styles include **authoritarian, permissive, authoritative,** and **uninvolved**. These parenting styles were talked about in significant detail in the section on toddlers. Authoritative parenting (or supportive parenting) is considered the most successful form used by middle-class White Americans in dealing with adolescents. However, before World War II, most parenting advice books encouraged authoritarian parenting style.

Parenting is complicated, and though these styles are useful classifications they do not tell the whole story. The personality of the teenager and parents, the circumstances, and the fact that parents do not always consistently use one parenting style, all play a role in successful parenting of adolescents.

Parenting a teenage child is a two-way process or reciprocal socialization. **Reciprocal socialization** refers to the phenomenon of parents and children socializing each other at the same time. Adolescent behavior affects parenting, just as parenting style affects teenage behavior. Which behavior causes the other, in the child–parent relationship? This question is almost impossible to answer because the two are so intertwined from birth on.

Recent research shows that this interplay has a significant role (Granic et al., 2003). For example, if a teenager tends to be dependable, conscientious, and confident, then the parents tend to be more authoritative (supportive). However, if the teenager tends to be more stubborn, angry, and "needy," the parents may be more authoritarian.

Parenting Styles Used in Other Cultures

The parenting styles discussed so far mainly apply to Western cultures. Styles in other cultures vary. For example, in China parents are expected to be loving but strict, firm, and in tight control of their adolescents' behavior. It is considered their duty to make sure that their children are successful and adhere to cultural norms. This is particularly true when it comes to educational success. Most Chinese adolescents see accepting parental controls as a sign of respect. For the most part, this more authoritarian style works well in China. In American culture many adolescents see this kind of control as oppressive. Conflicting cultural parenting styles can make it very difficult for first-generation immigrant families when traditional parents have one expectation and their children grow up in a different cultural environment.

In conclusion, no one particular parenting style is universally appropriate or the "best" for raising healthy, well-adjusted teenagers. Child rearing practices reflect the norms and values of the prevailing culture.

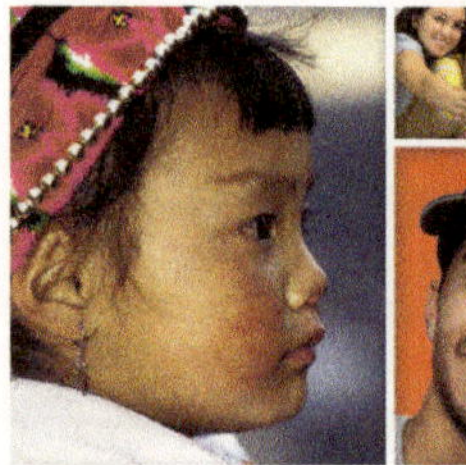

Role, Significance, and Mechanism of Intergenerational Mentoring: A Vygotskian Approach

By Nicole Jafari, EdD, California State University, Fullerton

ABSTRACT

Intergenerational mentoring and teaching are crucial aspects of a child's healthy development. Teaching and educating children is a process that continues beyond classroom and teacher-student interaction. The depth of Vygotsky's theory and its emphasis on the role of culture, adults as tutors, and collaborative teaching methods should be examined and closely looked at in order to re-evaluate the role of grandparents in children's development. In an informal and/or formal educational setting, grandparents can be instrumental in creating a colloquial classroom atmosphere; teaching new skills and gauging children's capabilities and developmental process through scaffolding and zone of proximal development. Furthermore, investigating Urie Bronfenbrenner's theory of contextual influences on shaping children's behavior can shed new light on the importance of microsystem's members, which includes grandparents and extended family. The chronological child is greatly impacted by these micro-members, who shape and influence the early childhood development (Brooks, 2011). These early microsystem imprints could further be investigated through Vygotsky's explanation on interpersonal growth through culture as a mediator (Brooks, 2011). This mediation is mostly possible through grandparent-child interaction, which could take place through intergenerational and mentoring programs as part of a more structured interaction. Grandparents make excellent teachers and mentors bearing a great deal of simple life lessons taught using differential levels of teaching. This paper will examine "Grand Mentoring," and of the role it plays on child and adolescent development.

▲ ***Mentoring can play a significant role between grandparents and grandchildren.***

(Photo courtesy of Monkey Business Images/ Shutterstock.com)

INTRODUCTION

Transfer of knowledge from one person to another can be done in many ways. Mentoring, tutoring, teaching, and guiding are all techniques used by adults to teach children. According to Vygtosky's sociocultural theory, children learn through social interaction with adults. The interaction is built on tutor and apprentice relationship where the tutor is the adult, the mentor, the more experienced, and the one teaching the novice, who is the child and the apprentice. The title of mentor is given to a person who teaches and/or advises a less experienced and often a younger person. A mentor is also a trusted counselor or guide whose teachings are based on experience, wisdom and intelligence (Pulce, 2005). Mentoring is not a new concept as it can be traced back to Greek mythology. Historical narratives indicate that Odysseus, a legendary Greek king, had trusted Telemachus, the wise counselor half-god, half-female, half-male teacher to be his son's counselor and mentor. The practice of handing down knowledge from someone with more experience to a novice has been around for centuries. That is one way cultural values and traditional practices are preserved. Today, many corporations, educational institutions, or even ordinary people use the same method of enlisting a mentor to ensure a good quality education (Pulce, 2005).

To be a mentor requires specific characteristics. An eligible mentor is generally someone who is loyal, a worthy role model, loving, knowledgeable, virtuous, accomplished, patient, supportive, enthusiastic, and overall worthy of shaping another person's mold (Pulse, 2005). These characteristics can easily be attributed to elderlies which can then be

(continues)

(continued from previous page)

role modeled by a novice. Previous research has indicated that benefits of mentoring youth include a decreased rate in risky behavior, such as declined overall drug and alcohol use. Mentees also experience higher academic achievement and better interpersonal relationship with friends and family, leading to healthier social skills. A similar study showed that grandparents' involvement in the lives of grandchildren is an important investment, and it can be mutually beneficial to both generations (Weston, 2009).

The ecological theory refers to the developmental stages in terms of contextual systems where different layers influence children's development. Concepts such as self-perception, identity formation, and self-worth can be handed down to generations through social interactions, particularly of those between grandparents and grandchildren. Conclusively, these studies suggest that bringing grandchildren and grandparents together creates an affirmative connection that has positive impact on grandparents as well as the grandchildren. Being involved in the lives of their grandchildren could be perceived as an investment, which could also be extended to great grandchildren. The practice of being active in the microsystem of the child's context is more common in the non-Anglo than the Western culture. For example, in Australian families, only 2.9% of preschoolers have face-to-face contact with their grandparents. In 1978, the United States of America established a day to be a distinct holiday as "Grandparents' Day." These policy makers understand the influences and the benefits of having elderlies involved in the lives of the younger generation. In 2002, Australia followed suit and the Governor of Victoria created an association, Grandparents Victoria, reiterating the significance they have on the children's microsystem (Lumby, 2010). Another study by Block (2002) showed that college student expectation of grandparents, even step-grandparents, is positive and mentor like.

Similar research showed the benefit of mentoring is a mutual contribution to the healthy well-being of grandparent as well as the grandchild. According to a Generations United Report (2002), older people who take on the role of a mentor develop a more productive lifestyle that is instrumental to the person's sense of purpose and community connection. In today's world, the age of retirement is increasing each decade. Despite the increase in the number of elderly persons seeking to be active, physically and psychologically, the options for active socialization opportunities decline with age, limiting the older age group opportunities for volunteerism or mentoring. This of course does not mean it is a negative phenomenon (Muir, 2006). The formula for demand and supply can be applied here; the availability of members of the older generation for mentoring and volunteerism is the supply, and the need of the youth is the demand. This makes a very productive interaction between the past and future generations.

METHODOLOGY

Eighty-nine college students comprised of mixed gender, ethnic background, and socioeconomic status volunteered to participate in this study. A structured survey questionnaire (a copy of the structured survey questionnaire is available upon request) was designed based on the adaptation from the Grounded Theory (Smith & Biley, 1997). Questions were of open and closed ended nature for the purpose of collecting data on the role grandparents played in their lives and the type of relationship they maintained with each other. The make up of the ethnicities were as follows: 24 Caucasians, 31 Latinos, 4 African American, 17 Asians, 8 Middle Eastern, and 5 others. In the pool of participants, 10 were male and 79 female, which fits the typography of student body in humanity sciences ranging in age from youngest to be 19 and the oldest to be 44 years old, averaging 20.7 years old. Seventy-one participants reported their parents to still be married to each other, while 14 claimed to have either separated or divorced parents. Nine of the students reported that grandparent(s) they described lived with them, whereas 57 reported they lived independently or with some other relative.

For the purpose of better understanding the reciprocal relationship between students and grandparents, they were asked to describe the role their grandparent(s) played in their lives. These open-ended questions were asked in different structures to give the participant the autonomy to further elaborate on this relationship. The questionnaire also considered the elements of Urie Bronfenbrenner's ecological theory (Brooks, 2011) encompassing the micro, meso, exo, and macro systems investigating the significance of the role the grandparents played in the participants' lives and the influence it marked on each child.

The analysis of data collected was based on the grounded theory methodology taking into consideration social processes (Charmaz, 2008). This qualitative research method was originally developed by Glaser and Strauss arguing that human beings are active agents that construct their own social processes (Corbin & Strauss, 1990). This methodology allows the researcher to operate in reverse fashion of research by collecting data, analyzing, and developing a theory in opposition to the traditional method of starting with a hypotheses, which would lead to data collection and ultimately a theory. There was no manipulation of data and none of the variables were controlled. The technique used in collection data was micro-genetic and cross-sectional using open and closed ended questionnaire type survey.

The method is appropriate and applicable in this particular study because of its relevancy to inductive and deductive thinking. In a traditional research methodology, the researcher constructs a hypothesis, collects data to test the assumption, and then develops a theory; however, this methodology has shortcomings such as a theoretical framework is chosen, then it is applied to the population being studied. As discussed in the introduction, the role of grandparents and grandmentors has been elaborately described; therefore, the structured questions were designed to lead to the same conclusion meaning construction of a theory using collected data. This type of methodology aims to conceptualize a theory rather than testing a hypothesis, thus avoiding a theoretical framework before a conclusion can be reached.

RESULTS

Overall, regardless of the ethnicity background, the majority of the participants expressed satisfaction in having an interdependent relationship with their grandparents. Seventy of the

(continues)

(continued from previous page)

students surveyed claimed they receive advice from grandparents and sixty seven stated that when applicable they applied such advice to their particular situations. The type of advice received from grandparents included simple life lessons such as staying in school, being respectful to others, following proper etiquette, all the way to important cultural continuity and traditional mentoring. Eighty three of the participants expressed happiness in regards to have a grandparent involved in their lives and sixty three considered them part of their support system. Due to the open ended nature of some of the surveyed questions, participants were able to elaborate on the nature of grandchild/grandparent social interactions. The nature of these social engagements and interactions ranged from conversing, having occasional meals one on one to having ritualistic cooking engagements, storytelling, discussing cultural values, and family history narratives. The study also analyzed several criteria including commonality of events, mentoring practices, cultural influences, degree of influences, and nature of influences. A previous research study conducted by Robbins, Scherman, Holeman, and Wilson (2005) showed similar findings on the type of impact of grandmentoring and frequency of these influences.

Furthermore, a previous study conducted by Lumy (2010) indicated the bond between grandchildren and grandparents staying solid even after a separation between parents. This holds true for both maternal and paternal grandparents. More than half the subjects in one study maintained that even a separation between a parent and a partner did not adversely affect the relationship between the grandchild and the grandparent. This result shows the significance and the strength of the bond between these two generations, which is an important characteristic of a mentor. As described before, a mentor is someone who is loyal, trusted, and respected, loving, and knowledgeable. These characteristics can easily be applied to grandparents, which make them one of the same as a mentor, and showed loyalty of grandchildren to mentors (Muir, 2006).

DISCUSSION

The result of this research study on the role of grandmentors showed that grandparents are seen as transmitters of culture, family value, and tradition. The study described the relationship and interaction between grandchildren and grandparents as being based on scaffolding since students described time spent with grandparents being quality time involving teaching of values and traditions. As Vygotsky considered culture as a developmental mediator, the study also showed that students are more than willing to observe, listen, and carry on advice given to them by their grandparents. Majority of participants in this study showed genuine interest in spending time with grandparents. They also had no difficulty recalling the nature of interaction with grandparents and showed willingness to learn life lessons from them. Furthermore, the practice of mentorship being an old idea dating to ancient Greek societies makes it an established system that over the years has shown success and results. Mentoring is an effective teaching method and it seems that the older generation has plenty of knowledge to transmit, and younger mentees are willing individuals ready to receive this transaction. Therefore, the study clearly showed that grandparents want to contribute and grandchildren are willing to participate in this ritual.

In conclusion, family value teaching and cultural lessons take on many shapes and forms. There are various teaching methods that human beings practice, adopt, and apply to everyday life lessons. Mentoring is one of these techniques that has been practiced to transmit information, skills, and traditional values to the younger generation. The participants in this study showed appreciation and acknowledged the significant role their grandparents play in their lives instilling these cultural inheritances. As the result of this study was discussed in detail, participants greatly appreciated the opportunity to observe, imitate, and apply these valuable intergenerational life lessons when the opportunity arose.

LIMITATIONS AND RECOMMENDATION FOR FUTURE STUDIES

This study was conducted in California, Orange, and Los Angeles Counties using volunteer student participants in the college of education and liberal arts at two major state university campuses. The socioeconomic status of the majority of the participating students was in the range of low to medium. The findings of the study were reflective of previous studies, which showed the importance of grandparents' involvement in grandchildren's lives. The researcher arrived at this conclusion using inductive and deductive reasoning based on grounded theory methodology (Strauss & Corbin, 1990). However, a more direct methodology in a comparative study deems to be useful in further accreditation of this study and previous research in the area of specific contributions grandparents make to cultural continuity and family values. In addition, a more systematic formula detailing such contribution the older generation can make would further be indicative of the specific role they can play. Secondly, future studies based on variety of demographic and intergenerational typography of ethnic groups would be useful in shedding more light on the particular area of grandmentoring. Thirdly, the study was successful in showing the positive role of grandparents in grandchildren's' cultural and heritage building; however, the study did not a make a connection between the quality of the relationship and time spent. Further detail in this area would be helpful and future studies can offer more insight into the specifics of such relationship. As the Muir (2006) study showed, grandparents can effectively mentor grandchildren improving quality of life such as academic success, self-esteem improvement, and development of a healthy self perception. If such a relationship is set up reciprocally, it can be mutually beneficial to both grandparents and grandchildren.

CHAPTER 14 SUMMARY

Teenage and young adult years are a time of great change. Rites of passage mark the transitions from one phase of life to another. Generally these transitions include changes in social position, residence, and life conditions. All cultures have some form(s) of rites of passage.

For some families the transition years of the teens are difficult years. Most adolescent conflicts with parents are over ordinary things, such as doing homework, curfew, or attending parties, rather than more serious things such as use of illegal drugs and alcohol. Adolescence is a time of growing autonomy, the development and expression of independence. In America and in other cultures that value individual identity and thinking, it is a time when teens discover who they are separate from their parents and families. Autonomy can be viewed through three interdependent domains: (1) emotional, (2) behavioral, and (3) attitudinal values.

During adolescence, teens spend increasingly less time with their families and peer relationships take center stage. In middle childhood, children form friendships mostly for the pleasure of doing things with another person. During adolescence, friendships become more complicated and seem to be defined by three fundamental attributes teenagers value: reciprocity, commitment, and equality. Small groups of friends who have frequent social interaction with each other are called cliques. Crowds are larger groups than cliques and share characteristics but may not interact with each other socially on a regular basis. Crowds can be based on interests, abilities, social status, or in some instances ethnicity.

In Western cultures, dating has several purposes—recreation, practice, and to learn what is wanted in future relationships, as well as a prelude to marriage. In many cultures dating is not practiced and arranged marriages are the norm.

CHAPTER 14 VOCABULARY

- Attitudinal and Value Autonomy
- Authoritarian
- Authoritative
- Behavioral Autonomy
- Conform
- Cliques
- Crowds
- Dyadic
- Emotional Autonomy
- Permissive
- Reciprocal Socialization
- Rites of Passage
- Uninvolved

Chapter 15

PROBLEMS IN ADOLESCENCE

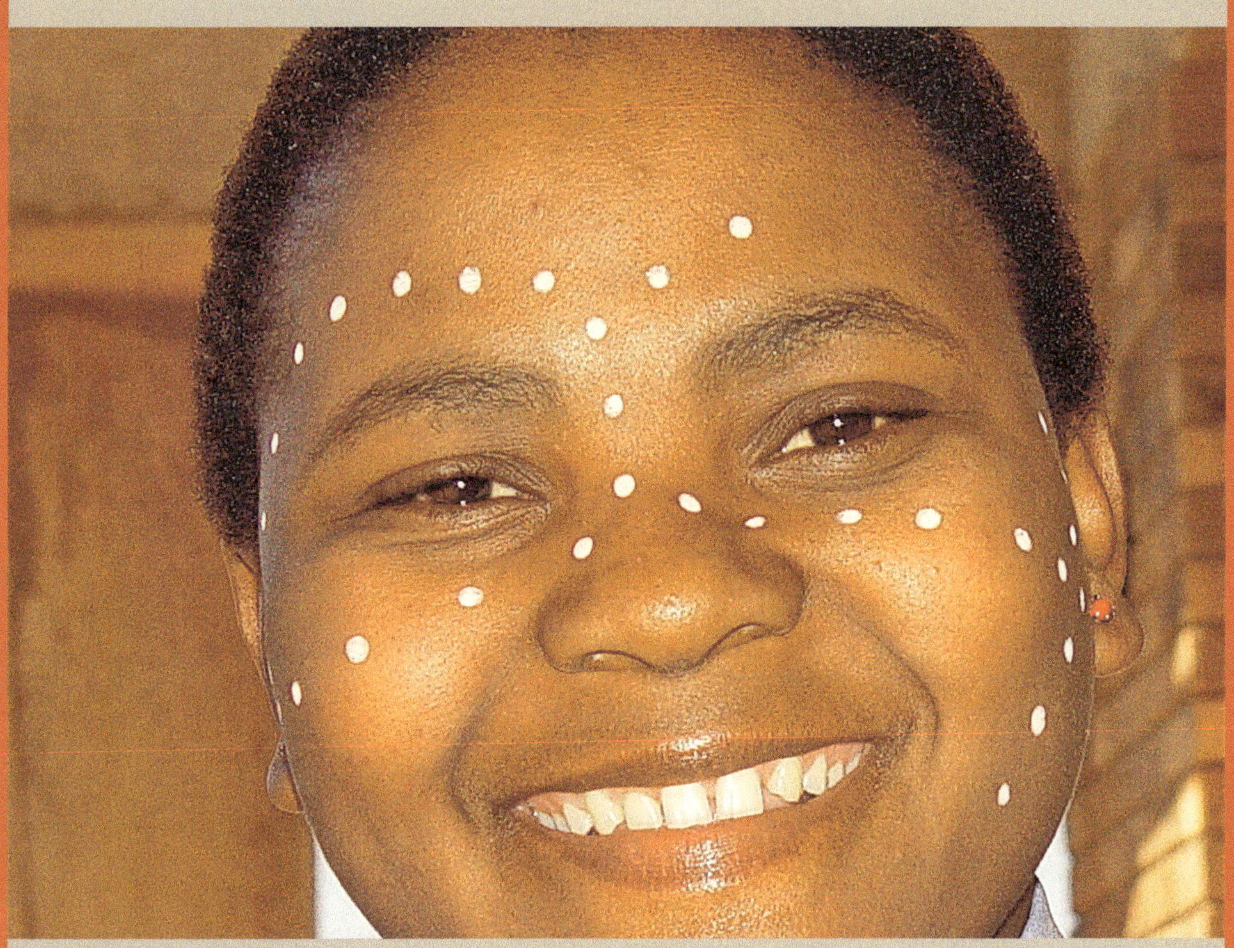

A Zulu girl.
(Photo courtesy of Margaret Goetz)

Sulu Girl Age 10

by Margaret Goetz

Afraid is something I can talk about, she said, her eyes wide in the dark of her young face.

I was afraid my mother would die because she took care of us and she was my mother. She died in spring. I was afraid my father would die and it would be only me and my little brother. He died the next winter.

Now I am afraid when I hear animals at night, there's a leopard here. I'm afraid when I hear the men's voices drunk outside, even baby girls are not safe here. I use different voices and rattle things to make them think we are not alone.

I am afraid when I have no candles left, night comes so soon. I am afraid when our measly-meal is running out, I know I will have to teach my little brother to steal. I am afraid I cannot get to school when it rains, and then there is no hope. Afraid is something I can talk about.

Sexually Transmitted Infections

In the United States youth under the age of twenty-five are at a higher risk than older individuals for contracting a sexually transmitted infection (STI). It is estimated that half of the twenty million people with an STI are between the ages of fifteen and twenty-four and four out of every ten teenage girls have had an STI (U.S. Department of Health and Human Services, 2014). People these ages are likely to have a higher number of partners than people who are older. This age group is also more likely to have higher-risk sexual encounters without the use of condoms or other protective methods. Also people in this age group are less likely to be tested for STIs. The most common STIs in American youth are **human papillomavirus (HPV)**, **trichomoniasis**, and **chlamydia**, with HPV being the most common. The incidence of chlamydia is about five times higher in fifteen- to twenty-five-year-olds than in the general population (Centers for Disease Control and Prevention [CDC], 2010). It is estimated by the CDC that 35 percent of sexually active thirteen- to nineteen-year-olds have been infected at one time.

HIV/AIDS

The disease AIDS has been known to exist only since the late 1970s or early 1980s. There are about 50,000 new cases in the United States in all age groups every year. One out of every four new cases of HIV is diagnosed in youth between the ages of thirteen and twenty-four. Most of these cases are bisexual or gay young men, particularly gay Black young men (CDC, 2014). Originally HIV/AIDS in the United States was in the homosexual and illegal drug-using populations, but now the disease is commonly found in the heterosexual population as well. Girls and minority youth are particularly at risk. Sexually active African American youth between the ages of thirteen and twenty-four have the highest rate, with 68 percent contracting HIV/AIDS (CDC, 2014).

HIV/AIDS is believed to have mutated from a similar disease found in chimpanzees in Africa (Gao et al., 1999). The infected chimps were probably killed and eaten for food. In Africa the disease seems to have started in the heterosexual population. Today there are medical treatments that help slow the disease, but there is still no known cure. Treatment involves an arsenal of drugs that must be taken on a strict schedule and some strains of the virus are more resistant to treatment than others. One of the main difficulties for many people, particularly the poor, is the cost of these medications.

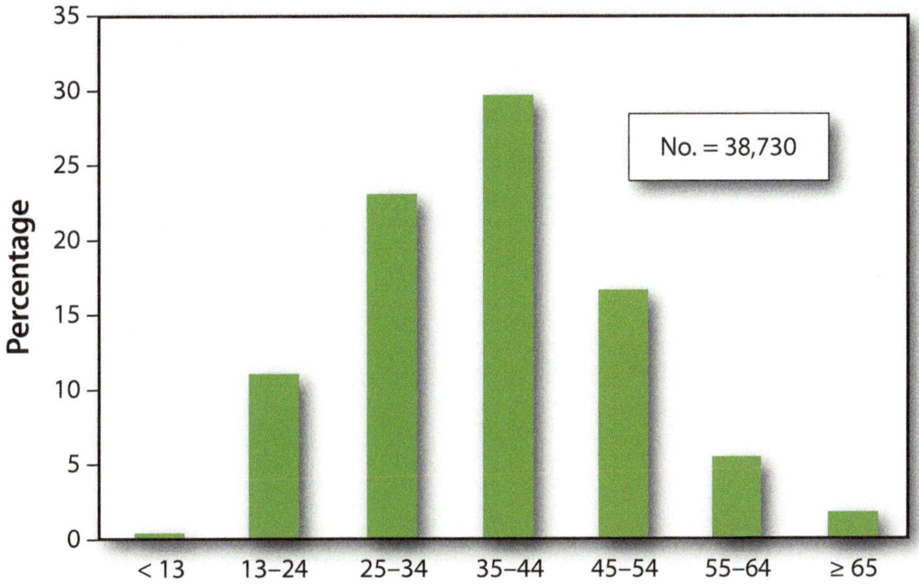

▲ ***Age of persons with HIV infection or AIDS diagnosed during 2004 in the United States.***

NOTE: Based on data from 35 areas with long-term, confidential name-based HIV reporting (Centers for Disease Control and Prevention, 2014).

How Is HIV Primarily Spread?

HIV is spread primarily by not using a condom when having sex with a person who has HIV. All unprotected sex with someone who has HIV contains some risk. However: ■ Unprotected anal sex is riskier than unprotected vaginal sex. ■ Among men who have sex with other men, unprotected receptive anal sex is riskier than unprotected insertive anal sex.
Having multiple sex partners or the presence of other STIs can increase the risk of infection during sex. Unprotected oral sex can also be a risk for HIV transmission, but it is a much lower risk than anal or vaginal sex.
Sharing needles, syringes, rinse water, or other equipment used to prepare illicit drugs for injection.
Being born to an infected mother—HIV can be passed from mother to child during pregnancy, birth, or breastfeeding.

Source: Centers for Disease Control and Prevention, 2014.

International HIV/AIDS Infection

HIV is the virus that causes AIDS. AIDS is present in every country in the world and the disease has killed more than thirty-six million people. Beyond making people sick and killing them, the disease impacts the lives of children and adolescents who lose family members. Worldwide in 2011, there were more than 3.3 million children with HIV/AIDS. In addition an estimated 1.7 to 2.4 million children died of AIDS in 2008 (CDC, 2014). In developing and transitional countries many of the people who are in immediate need of treatment do not have access to it. Only about 42 percent of the people in the world with the disease have access to the life-prolonging drugs used to treat the disease (CDC, 2014). There is a drug treatment that prevents pregnant women who are HIV positive from transferring the disease to their unborn child. Unfortunately many women in developing countries do not have access to these drugs.

Sub-Saharan Africa contains some of the poorest countries in the world and they have been severely affected by the AIDS pandemic. Two-thirds of the cases of HIV in the world occur in these countries (CDC, 2014). In Africa alone there are more than fourteen million children who have been orphaned by AIDS. In 2007, more than nine countries reported that at least 10 percent of their population between the ages of fifteen and forty-nine were infected with HIV (Avert, 2010). Botswana has one of the highest rates of infection with about 24 percent of the adult population infected. South Africa has more people

A Zulu family in South Africa devastated by AIDS. Both parents died leaving five children and only the elderly grandmother to care for them.

(Photo courtesy of Peggy Goetz)

living with HIV than any other country in Africa. In many of these places high rates of AIDS/HIV have affected the structure of families and communities. AIDS is not just a problem in Africa but is a serious issue in many other developing countries. Many countries do not have the infrastructure to keep track of the number of cases so statistics can be scarce and unreliable.

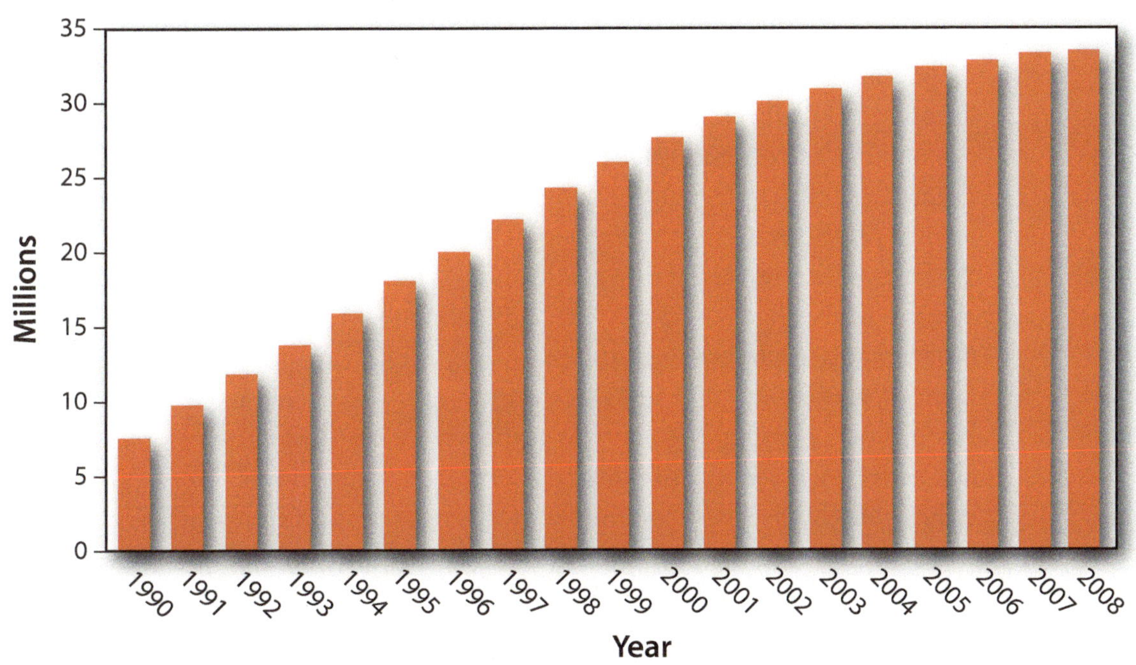

The number of people living with HIV has risen from around 8 million in 1990 to 35 million today, and is still growing. In some African countries one in five adults is living with HIV (Avert, 2014).

Teen Pregnancy

Of the world's developed countries, the United States has one of the highest rates of teen pregnancy. About 42 of every 1,000 teen girls became pregnant in 2006 (CDC, 2010). The cost to the government for teenage pregnancies is significant, about $9.1 million in 2004. This funding includes child welfare, public assistance, and health care.

One reason the rate is higher in the United States than in other developed countries is the contradicting message that American society gives to adolescents and young adults about sex. Youth are told not to have sex before marriage and at the same time are bombarded by media and other social influences that seem to promote sex. Another factor is inadequate sex education. Many people believe sex education should be left to parents. Overall the sex education offered in many high schools is inadequate and taught too late.

Lack of independent access to contraception and health care for teens in the United States is another reason for the high teen pregnancy rates. For example, in the Netherlands teens have socialized medicine. There are vending machines on the streets that sell condoms as well as advertisements on television encouraging youth to use them.

However, birth rates among teenagers are declining in the United States. In 2010 the rate was lower than any year since 1946. The birth rates among teens has fallen 44 percent from 1991 to 2010 (CDC, 2014). Despite the decline in teen birth rates, the number of unmarried teen mothers has increased. Apparently the age of the "shotgun marriage" is passing and society and families do not necessarily expect pregnant teens to marry as was once the case. In fact the number of teen marriages as a whole in the United States is declining. The average age of marriage in the United States is now twenty-five for women and twenty-seven for men.

Sex education is not universal in high schools across the United States, with about two-thirds offering some sex education (Villarosa, 2003). In addition the percentage of high school students who report having had sexual intercourse fell from 51 percent in 1991 to 43 percent in 2001. The general use of birth control has increased among high school students. In 2001, about 57 percent of sexually active high school students reported using condoms. Unfortunately, about a third of teen pregnancies end in abortion, an option that is more available to teens now than in the past. There is also some indication that oral sex is becoming more common and may substitute for sexual intercourse.

Rape

Rape is defined as a sexual act forced on one person by another. Most victims of rape are female, but males can also be raped. Rape is more common than many people would expect, and most are committed by acquaintances. In research studies, about 10 percent of girls between the ages of fourteen and eighteen report being forced to have sex by a date and about half of these instances include additional assaults like hitting, slapping, and pushing (Feldman, 2008). A national study said about 12.5 percent of college women report having been raped. Many of these rapes include **date rapes**, which are committed by acquaintances and first dates (Koss et al., 1993).

In most cases, the motivation for rape is to show power rather than sexual gratification. For the rapist, the positive reward comes from forcing the victim to be submissive, not sexual pleasure (Gowaty, 2003). Rage and anger are also motivation factors for rape. The anger can be directed at the victim in particular or at women in general. Differences in expectations about how much sex is permissible and different views of gender roles can also contribute to rape. For example, some males seem to think they should have sex whenever they want it or see sexual encounters as competitions they must win. Some men also have the mistaken idea that when women say "no," they really mean "yes" and want to be coerced. Women in general do not hold these views.

Ways for Women to Avoid Date Rape

- Set clear sexual limits and do not send mixed messages. "No" should always mean "no."
- Be assertive when being pressured to have sex. It is not a time to worry about hurting someone's feelings or to be passive.
- Be aware of situations that may be risky, like being alone with someone not well known.
- Alcohol and illegal drugs are often associated with date rape. Be especially careful in situations where they are being used.
- Trust yourself and your instincts. If something feels wrong, leave or confront the person.

Source: Adapted from Feldman, 2008.

Coercion or force is never acceptable but it is surprising how many people think that at times it is. High school students were asked in a survey if holding someone down and forcing sex was ever permissible. Forty-four percent of the girls and 24 percent of the boys said forced sex was never permissible. The rest said under some circumstances rape was permissible (Monnier et al., 2002). Teenagers need to realize that when a person says "no" they should always stop, even if they feel the person is giving mixed messages. There is no permissible rape. Rape, no matter what the situation, is a traumatic experience for the victim and can have a long-lasting impact. It can affect future relationships throughout life. Rape should never be taken lightly and victims should seek professional help.

Rape Cross Culturally

Virginity is highly valued in many cultures around the world. If a girl is raped, she is considered tarnished and shamed for life. This is one of the reasons that girls forced into prostitution do not return to their hometowns, even if they can escape. In parts of the world if a woman is raped she has dishonored her family and traditionally is expected to commit suicide.

> Mukhtar Mai grew up in a peasant family in the village of Meerwala in southern Punjab. When people ask her age, she tosses out one number or another, but the truth is that she doesn't have a clue as to when she was born . . . (and) never attended school.
>
> Then, in July 2002, her younger brother, Shakur, was kidnapped and gang-raped by members of a higher-status clan, the Mastoi. (In Pakistan, rapes of boys by heterosexual men are not uncommon and are less stigmatized than the rapes of girls.) Shakur was twelve or thirteen at the time, and after raping him the Mastoi became nervous that they might be punished. So they refused to release Shakur and covered up their crime by accusing him of having had sex with a Mastoi girl, Salma. Because the Mastoi had accused Shakur of illicit sex, the village tribal assembly, dominated by the Mastoi, held a meeting. Mukhtar attended on behalf of her family to apologize and try to soothe feelings . . . the tribal council concluded that an apology from Mukhtar would not be enough. To punish Shakur and his family the council sentenced Mukhtar to be gang-raped. Four men dragged her, screaming and pleading, into an empty stable next to the meeting area and, as the crowd waited outside, they stripped her and raped her on the dirt floor, one after the other.
>
> "They knew that a women humiliated in that way has no other recourse except suicide," Mukhtar wrote later. "They don't even need to use their weapons. Rape kills her." Mukhtar's mother and father kept watch over her and prevented that option [from killing herself]. (Kristof & WuDunn 2009, p. 71)

As you can see from this story the tribal courts in rural parts of Pakistan use rape as a form of punishment. Mukhtar was lucky because her family encouraged her not to commit suicide and she decided to help other women that had been in her situation. She ended up opening a school for women in her small village. In some places if a man's marriage proposal is refused he might kidnap and rape his intended bride. Thus her family is forced to arrange a marriage with him as he has taken her virginity and no other man will marry her.

Homosexuality

The period when adolescents start to be physically attracted to others can be a challenging time for all teens, but it is a particularly difficult time for those who are attracted to people of the same gender. Most homosexual teenagers prefer the terms "gay" or "lesbian" to "homosexual." **Gay** refers to male homosexuals but it is also used as a general term referring to both males and females. **Lesbian** refers to female homosexuals. **Bisexual** or **pansexual** refers to people who are sexually interested in others regardless of gender.

The National Health Statistics Report (Ward et al., 2014) states that 1.6 percent of the U.S. population report being gay or lesbian, 0.7 percent as bisexual, and 96.6 percent as straight. The Williams Institute, UCLA School of Law, a sexual orientation of law and public policy think tank, estimates that 3 percent to 5 percent of the American population are homosexual or bisexual (Gates, 2011). These are all estimates because of the difficulty of collecting accurate statistics. Gay and lesbian people say they have known about their sexual

The period when adolescents start to be physically attracted to others can be a challenging time for all teens, but it is particularly difficult for those who are attracted to people of the same gender.

(Photo courtesy of Pekic/Shutterstock.com)

orientation since they were very young, but only admitted it even to themselves when they were teens or even older.

Gay and lesbian teens face a higher-than-average risk for depression and suicide (Harris, 2004; Ryan & Rivers, 2003) and they still face discrimination and prejudice from many segments of the population. Some are verbally and physically threatened or assaulted by peers and adults.

Several studies in the United States indicate that teens often tell their mothers about their sexual orientation before they tell their fathers (Savin-Williams & Ream, 2003). Though teens often fear telling their parents, in most cases this fear is unfounded. Most parents are supportive or do not know how to react. For most homosexuals, telling parents about sexual orientation does not change their relationship with their parents. Adolescents report relationships with parents worsening only about 5 percent of the time (Savin-Williams & Ream, 2003).

Children with Homosexual Parents

Families today take on many forms. There are increasing numbers of teenagers who have a homosexual parent(s). A good example of how society is becoming more accepting of these families it is our former Republican Vice-President Dick Cheney's daughter, who is lesbian and has a son with her partner. It has not been very long historically that a politician with a gay child could openly support that child and stay in politics. Estimates show that between one and

There are an increasing number of gay couples deciding to have children.

(Photo courtesy of Dubova/Shutterstock.com)

five million families in the United States are headed by parents who are homosexual and over six million adolescents have a parent who is gay (Patterson & Friel, 2000). Same-sex couples often have children, some from a previous heterosexual marriage or via liaison, adoption, or sperm donor.

Studies have found that children raised by a homosexual parent when compared to a comparable heterosexual parent have no significant differences. In other words, there are no significant differences in the emotional, psychological, educational, or well-being of the children. What seems important is not the gender of one's parents but the quality of parenting. Most studies conducted have been on White middle- and upper-class parents (Carpenter, 2007). There have not been very many studies on minorities that have a same-sex parent(s), even though 45 percent of same-sex parents are African American and Latino according to the U.S. census (Carpenter, 2007).

When children with gay parents do have problems with their parents' sexual orientation, it usually has to do with other people's reactions to the situation. Teens in particular sometimes fear letting peers know their parents are gay, fearing teasing or social stigma. They may keep quiet about the situation and hesitate having friends over to their homes. Adolescents are trying to come to terms with their own identities and want to be accepted by their peers. Therefore, some may hesitate to reveal that their parents are "different," be the parents gay, recent immigrants, disabled, or anything else that might set them apart. A difference that is controversial may be particularly challenging for a teen. This fear seems to lessen as adolescents move into young adulthood.

One thing that some people believe is that children raised by gay parents will be gay. However, studies have shown that most children raised by homosexual parents are heterosexual. The percentage of gay children is about the same whether from gay or heterosexual parents (Carpenter, 2007).

Multicultural Perspectives on Homosexuality

Homosexuality occurs in all cultures. However, how gender-orientation is defined varies a great deal across cultures. U.S. society has comparatively strict and conservative views on sexuality in general and any sexual act between two people of the same gender is considered homosexual. This is not the case in all cultures where same-gender sexual contact is an interwoven part of life and development.

In Lesotho (a small country surrounded by South Africa), there exists what anthropologists have coined, **mummy-baby relationships**. It is a mentoring relationship between an older woman and a girl coming of age in her middle teens. The older woman, or "mummy," is usually married and has children of her own. The older woman's role is to teach the younger girl how to be a good wife. This includes how to cook certain dishes, how to handle their husbands, and advice about sex. This mentoring process often includes hugging and kissing and sexual relations between the two. It is taboo for a girl's mother in this culture to teach their daughter about sex. The mummy-baby relationship ends when the girl marries, however the bond of friendship still continues (Blackwood, 2001).

Among the !Kung people of southern Africa, virginity is not expected at marriage and sex outside of marriage is considered normal behavior. Growing up, adolescents normally experiment with partners of both genders and the activity is just part of growing up and learning about sex (Blackwood, 2001).

The coming of age ritual among the Sambia people of Papua New Guinea includes oral sex between boys and older men. The process is considered necessary for the normal development of male fluids, masculinity, and reproductive ability. When these rituals are completed, young men are ready for marriage (Blackwood, 2001).

The Etoro people of the same region believe boys ages ten to twenty need to be inseminated with sperm via oral sex with men on a regular basis in order to become complete men. It is a normal part of male heterosexual development (Blackwood, 2001).

Among the warrior class of the Azande of Sudan, prospective apprentice warriors aged twelve to twenty take on the role of "wives" to official warriors and live together with them in special warrior quarters. The young warriors even pay a "bride price" for the apprenticed boys. The apprentices perform all the duties of a female wife, including cooking, harvesting, and being a sexual partner. In this culture sex with women is thought to weaken men, and warriors do not marry women and have children until they retire (Blackwood, 2001).

Despite its geographical proximity, the general attitude in Mexico toward same-gender sex differs from that in the United States. Sexual classification is based more on gender power than the gender of the partners.

A Mexican male is considered heterosexual as long as he plays the dominant power position (the inserter) in the sexual act. The male who plays the passive or receiving role is defined as homosexual. Being defined as homosexual is considered socially unacceptable and carries a strong cultural stigma in the traditional Mexican culture. Even those men defined as homosexual traditionally marry women and have children, regardless of whether they continue to have sex with other men (Thing, 2010).

Homosexuality is culturally defined, and as a result varies in definition and cultural acceptance. Some cultures, as previously discussed, have culturally accepted forms, while others go to the opposite extremes. There are many cultures where a sexual act between people of the same sex is taboo and has extreme consequences. For example, in Afghanistan and Iran homosexuals are executed.

◄ ***Teenagers today have grown up with computers and have fully integrated them into their lives.***

(Photo courtesy of Monkey Business Images/Shutterstock.com)

Technology and Teens

Changing technology impacts nearly every aspect of life, so it is no surprise that things such as cell phones, texting, e-mailing, computers, video games, social networking, and the Internet have changed the world of youth in the past decades. Research in this area is still in its infancy but some information is available.

Cell Phones

Most twenty-first century teens in the United States carry cells phones and most people who do can be reached almost any time and any place. Most include access to texting and photos as well as voice communication. The availability of cell phones has been a relatively rapid change in U.S. culture. The first cell phone call was made in 1973 by Martin Cooper of Motorola, but the units were expensive ($3,995), weighed 2.5 pounds, and were ten inches long. It only had a battery life of ten minutes (Buck, 2013). It was not marketed until 1983 (Motorola DynaTAC 8000X) after the Federal Communications Commission allocated analog frequencies for use by mobile phones. In 2013 the cell phone had its fortieth birthday. By 1990, smaller and more affordable phones were available and, by 2010, they got smaller and were able to do more things each year.

In surveys, most teens and young adults prefer texting to voice communication on the phone. Exchanges are shorter and less detailed than in the past when most communication was by voice. Students find arranging social gatherings and even dates via texting faster and easier. Texting is also less threatening

◀ *Cell phones have come a long way in a relatively short time.*

(Photo courtesy of Picksell/Shutterstock.com)

when asking someone for a date or confronting someone. For example, Beth had two college roommates. There had been some tension developing among them the last part of the fall semester before she went home for the holidays. While she was home her roommates texted her to let her know that she should look for a new place to live the second term. JoeAnna broke up with her boyfriend by texting him. In some ways, today's young adult or teen is rarely alone or without possible contact with peers. Whether this constant availability has helped make personal communication skills better or worse, or just different, is still in question. Many cell phones since 2014 are also "smart phones" and allow access to the Internet, e-mail, social networking, video games, music, and taking photos. This instant availability of information and entertainment has undoubtedly had a large impact on youth and this area still needs more research.

In third-world countries cell phones have brought communication and information to formerly remote areas where landlines are not available. For example in a small village in the Tibetan mountain area of China, there is a small public phone charging shop for those who do not have electricity in their homes, and it is not uncommon to see someone in a yak-drawn cart talking on a cell phone (Goetz, 2006).

Teens and young adults today have grown up with computers and the Internet. Personal computers have been commonplace in the United States since the early 1980s. High-speed Internet access became widely available in the early 1990s. Most people in the United States under age thirty never used a typewriter and increasingly research is conducted via the Internet rather than by going to a library. To keep in contact with friends they do not need to write a letter or call them on the phone. Writing a letter and sending it by "snail mail" is fast becoming a lost art. Instant communication with friends is only a short tap of the fingers away through texting, emailing, Facebook, or Instagram. The mother of teens recently commented on the change:

> A few years ago my children's grandparents gave our children a dictionary. Little did they realize that my children never use a physical dictionary any longer, but only the computer to look up words. They looked at the traditional dictionary as an antique. (Donham, 2014)

Teenagers are now able to look up almost limitless information faster and more easily than ever before.

The Internet is a phenomenon that has spread around the world. Even in developing countries small towns often have Internet cafes filled with mostly younger people learning about and communicating with the world.

Mass Media

Mass media is any means for communicating with large numbers of people at the same time. There is more mass communication today than ever in mankind's known history, including TV, radio, newspapers, magazines, movies, books, regular mail, e-mail, blogging, social networks, telephone campaigns, and more.

People today, including teens and children, spend more time listening to mass communication than ever before and spend less time directly interacting with live information sources. This is referred to as the **displacement effect**, where people spend less time directly interacting with friends, family, and being outside doing other things.

The **numbing effect** of media goes along with these ideas. For example we hear and see so much profanity and violence in the media that it does not shock us any longer. We come to expect it. To shock us we need to see higher and higher levels of violence in a movie or television show. When we see violence or hear profanity in "real life" we are not as shocked by it because we have come to expect it from what we see in different forms of media today.

Mass media is thought to influence how people perceive the world and whether they think of the world as a friendly or dangerous place. For instance, if a child or youth sees a great deal of violence on TV or in video games, they are likely to think of the world as a violent and dangerous place. This is so even when they know that what they have seen on TV or in video games is fiction. This tendency is called the **cultivation effect**.

The cultivation theory goes hand in hand with the **social learning theory** that states that children also imitate behavior they see in the media. They learn that society rewards or punishes behavior—both negative and positive behaviors—seen via media. Though research often focuses on kids' learning negative behavior such as violence, positive behaviors such as caring and helping others can also be learned from media.

Of course, just as in interactions with other people, individuals make different choices and respond differently to media. People make individual choices about what media they consume depending on personality and opportunities. In addition there is wide variation in the way people respond to the same media, also depending on personality and social settings.

Uses of Electronic Media by Adolescents

Teens use mass media that fall into six categories: education, entertainment, stimulation, youth cultural identification, identity formation, and coping with stress. Students use electronic media as an educational source both in and out of the classroom. They use media to view documentaries, research papers, study with other students, and take online classes. Many schools now recommend that students have computers of their own and many colleges require it. The number of students that have home access to computers has steadily increased from 18 percent in 1997 to 75.6 percent in 2011. In 2011, the U.S. Census Bureau found that Hispanics at 58.3 percent, followed by Blacks at 56.9 percent, had the lowest Internet access at home compared to Whites (non-Hispanics) with 76.2 percent and Asians with the highest access at 82.7 percent (U.S. Census Bureau, 2013).

◀ *Brothers playing a video game together.*

(Photo courtesy of Phoenixns/Shutterstock.com)

Electronic media entertainment has mushroomed in the past 20 years. Computer and video games have come a long way since the first popular video game "Pong" was introduced as an arcade game in 1972. In 1974, Atari introduced it as a home video game. This paved the way for the current $65 billion video industry in the United States today (Dolasie, 2012). Texting, instant messaging, e-mail, chat rooms, social networks, blogs, and just surfing the Internet have joined the world of entertainment that once was dominated by radio, TV, and movies.

Teenagers are at a time in their lives when they are seeking an identity and attempting to discover who they are. The Internet gives them easy access to friends and outside information. These kids have had access to varying and increasing forms of media since they were born. It is not surprising that they are quick to embrace new developments and forms. It is second nature to them and is embedded in Western middle-class youth culture.

Electronics and other media also influence identity formation. The very choices of which media to use and the content reflect and reinforce identity. For instance, a young man who loves hard rock and wants to have his own band may share his practice on his electric guitar, listen to music and music videos, and talk to friends all using electronic media. Some people, including adolescents, use media experiences to **heighten sensations**. This can take the form of "thrill seeking" or seeking new or varied experiences that will heighten their feelings. Examples can include going to a horror movie to be scared, playing a stimulating video game, or watching violent films or music videos. Many teens also use electronic media as a way to cope with stress. For instance, listening to particular music or playing a video game may help them relax. Talking to friends via texting, social networking, or instant messaging may help kids cope with being upset or stressed.

For most teens, it is important to feel connected with peers and the peer culture. Having access to cell phones, computers, and the Internet is a part of this connection in modern U.S. youth culture. For instance, Myspace, Facebook, Instagram, texting, and Twitter, are examples of Internet sites and programs that kids use mainly to connect with friends.

Media and Child Pornography

Child pornography is defined as anyone under the age eighteen years photographed in the nude, in sexual poses, or engaged in sexual activity. These images include photographing real people as well as computer generated images. It is not a new phenomenon and has been around since mass media began. Child pornography is child abuse and it is illegal in the United States. However, it is often difficult to track and enforce, and, as a result child pornography has become a multi-billion dollar industry. During the past twenty years the Internet has become a new way to easily distribute all kinds of pornography, including child pornography, using computer-generated images as well as photos and films. It is estimated that of the unknown thousands of pornography sources on the Internet, about 20 percent involve children.

Some distributors of such material try to avoid legal consequences in the United States by sending the images from less regulated countries. The U.S. Federal Bureau of Investigation attempts to monitor the Internet for such sites, but most perpetrators are not caught or prosecuted.

Sexting

Sexting is when nude, partially nude, or pornographic messages and photos are sent with a cell phone by texting or e-mailing. It is a phenomenon that has developed because of the increase ease of taking, texting, and transmitting photos via cell phones. It is unknown exactly how common sexting is. One survey of thirteen- to eighteen-year-olds found one in five kids had participated in sexting (Cox Communications, 2009). Sexting in itself is bad enough but what often happens is that the pictures get broadcast onto the web. Because of the nature of the Internet, photo exchanges that start out as a private matter may reach unintended recipients and can be placed on websites. Once on the Internet, material can be difficult or almost impossible to remove. The exchange of underage photos is illegal, even if someone willingly sends photos of him- or herself to a friend.

Disastrous results can come from sexting. In 2010, eight students ranging from age thirteen to seventeen in Pennsylvania sent, via computer, nude or semi-nude photos of themselves to each other. They were all charged with breaking the child pornography laws in Pennsylvania (Miller & Hirschkorn, 2010). In 2012 Audrie Potts, a high school sophomore, went to a party where she got drunk and passed out; she was stripped and graffiti was written all over her body with a marker. This was photographed and the picture posted on the Internet. Audrie hanged herself as a result. In 2011 Savannah Dietrich, age sixteen, got drunk and passed out and then someone sexually abused her and took pictures. They then shared the pictures with friends. She went to the police with the pictures and the boys were eventually charged with a misdemeanor, which stays on their records for life (Burleigh, 2013). These kind of stories repeat themselves over and over again across the country. Teenagers and young adults need to realize the possible damage and abuse they are committing when sexting.

Sex Trafficking, Prostitution, and Teens

United States

Sex trafficking is when another person forces someone against his or her will into the sex trade across state and national borders. Prostitution is when someone sells his or her body for money. **Prostitution** can be voluntary or involuntary.

Teenaged girls and young women are coerced or forced into prostitution in all parts of the world, including the United States. The Federal Bureau of Investigation estimated more than 100,000 U.S. children were victims of this industry and ranged in age from nine to nineteen (ABC News, 2006).

Some are girls who have run away from abusive situations at home or are involved in illicit drug trade. But others are from what most would consider normal homes. One lure used to draw girls in is the promise of a job in the movies or modeling; some girls are simply kidnapped. They are often threatened, raped, beaten, and drugged into submission.

Many sex traffickers use the Internet to advertise sexual services and their bases of operation move frequently. This makes it more difficult for authorities to track them down than if they were pitching to customers on the street (ABC News, 2006).

Worldwide

In many parts of the world, the situation for girls in the sex trade is even worse than in the United States. In many places governments and police are corrupt and laws are not enforced. Girls forced into prostitution are often from poor families and are seeking work to help their families survive. They are offered a job, such as in a restaurant or as domestic help. Then, transported far from their villages, they are forced into prostitution. In some cases they are sent to neighboring countries where they do not even speak the language (Kristof & WuDunn, 2009).

The traffickers beat, rape, and drug the girls and often tell the girls they will hurt their families if they do not cooperate. Many girls cannot go home even if they could escape the brothels because once they practice prostitution, even when it is against their will, they will be considered unclean and unacceptable for marriage at home. Some become addicted to drugs and must remain in prostitution to support their habits.

The number of girls forced into the international sex trade is not known. All available statistics on the subject are estimates, and such estimates are usually on the low side. In India in 2008 it was estimated that there were two million to

Abducted from Her Own Driveway, Teen Says

Debbie's story is particularly chilling. One evening Debbie said she got a call from a casual friend, Bianca, who asked to stop by Debbie's house. Wearing a pair of Sponge Bob pajamas, Debbie went outside (in her driveway) to meet Bianca, who drove up in a Cadillac with two older men, Mark and Matthew. After a few minutes of visiting, Bianca said they were going to leave.

"So I went and I started to go give her a hug," Debbie told [us] "And that's when she pushed me in the car."

As they sped away from her house, Debbie said that one of the men told Bianca to tie her up and said he threatened to shoot Bianca if she didn't comply.

"She tied up my hands first, and then she put the tape over my mouth. And she put tape over my eyes," Debbie said. "While she was putting tape on me, Matthew told me if I screamed or acted stupid, he'd shoot me. So I just stayed quiet."

Debbie said her captors drove her around the streets of Phoenix for hours. Exhausted and confused, she was finally taken to an apartment 25 miles from her home. She said one of her captors put a gun to her head.

"He goes, 'If I was to shoot you right now, where would you want to be shot—in your head, in your back or in your chest?'" Debbie said. "And then I hear him start messing with his gun. And he counted to three and then he pulled the trigger. And then I was still alive. I opened my eyes, and I just saw him laughing."

Debbie said her captors then drugged her and other men were brought into the room, where she was gang raped.

"And then that's when I heard them say there was a middle-aged guy in the living room that wanted to take advantage of a 15-year-old girl," she said. "And then he goes, 'Bend her over. I want to see what I'm working with.' And that's when he started to rape me. And I see more guys, four other guys had come into the room. And they all had a turn. It was really scary."

After the horrifying gang rape, police say Debbie was trapped in one of Phoenix's roughest neighborhoods. In a rundown, garbage-strewn apartment, her captors were trying to break her down.

"They were asking me if I was hungry," she said. "I told them no. That's when they put a dog biscuit in my mouth, trying to get me to eat it."

After a sleepless night, Debbie was tossed back into the car and again driven around Phoenix. She said they talked to her about prostitution, and that one of the men forced her to have sex with him in the car and then later in a park.

The same man took her back to his apartment, and Debbie said, "I ended up in the dog kennel."

Greg Scheffer, an officer with the Phoenix police department, said Debbie was kept in a small dog crate for several days. Lying on her back in the tiny space, her whole body went numb.

"She was subject to various abuses while in there," Scheffer said. "This is all part of the breaking down period where [he] gains complete control of this girl."

Unbeknownst to Debbie, police say her captors had put an ad on Craig's List—a national website better known for helping people find apartments and roommates. Shortly after the ad ran, men began arriving at the apartment at all hours of the day and night demanding sex from her.

She said she had to comply. "I had no other choice," she said.

Debbie said she was earning hundreds of dollars a night—all of it, she said, going to the pimp.

Scheffer said Debbie was forced to have sex with at least 50 men—and that's not counting the men who gang-raped her on a periodic basis.

Debbie had no idea who the men were. "I didn't know them," she said. "But most of them were married, with kids. And every single one of them, I asked them why they were coming to me if they had a wife at home. . . . They didn't have an answer. So, like, I felt so nasty."

For more than 40 days, police say Debbie remained captive, often beaten and forced daily to have sex of the most degrading kind. During that time, she said she did not try to escape because her captors had done what police say so many pimps do—threatened her and terrified her.

Debbie said that the pimps told her they would go after her family, and they even threatened to throw battery acid on her 19-month-old niece.

"After they told me that, I didn't care what happened to me as long as my family stayed alive," she said. "And that's pretty much what I had in my head. Staying there to keep my family alive."

For Debbie, who police said was held by her captors at gunpoint and kept in a dog cage for more than 40 days, the chances of getting out alive seemed slim. But then police investigating the case heard tips that she was being kept in an apartment in the Phoenix area.

Police searched the apartment but didn't find Debbie.

But they were still suspicious. So on Nov. 8, police broke down the doors to the same apartment and realized with a shock why they'd been unable to find Debbie—she was there, but she was tied up and crushed into a drawer under a bed.

Debbie said she heard Officer James Perry calling her name but was too frightened to answer. "I didn't know what to say; I was just lying under the bed, stiff as a board, shaking," she said. "And then he opens the middle drawer, and he was like, 'Oh my God!'"

Source: ABC News, 2006, pp. 1–5.

three million women working as prostitutes. In a study of brothels, about half of the women from India and Nepal were forced into the trade when they were teens (Kristof & WuDunn, 2009). Estimates of the number of prostitutes in China are about ten million women, but fewer say they were forced into the business than in India.

Many of the countries with the strongest social sexual prohibitions, such as India, Pakistan, and Iran, also have high percentages of prostitutes forced into the business. Young men in the upper classes in these societies rarely have sexual relations with their girlfriends, so it is socially acceptable for them to seek out women in brothels who are from poor villages. This protects the virtues of the upper-class women while sacrificing poor, uneducated girls (Kristof & WuDunn, 2009).

How You Can Help

One of the best ways to help the millions of girls forced into the sex trades around the world is to educate the public about the problem. Many people are not even aware of the issue and the large number of girls involved.

Poverty is one of the main reasons girls from poor areas can be tricked into prostitution by the promise of jobs to help support their families. Lack of educational opportunities is also an underlying factor. Anything that can be done to alleviate poverty and encourage education of these girls can help.

Americans can also encourage adoption of foreign policy that puts pressure on foreign governments to help end sex slavery. A number of organizations work to help end sex slavery in the United States and abroad. They work with government officials and also help the girls directly.

Image and Beauty

Obesity and Eating Disorders

Obesity in Americans of all ages continues to increase. Beyond just overweight, obesity is defined as being at least 20 percent over one's ideal body weight. Particularly disturbing is the increase in obesity among children and teens. According to the CDC (2009–2010), 18.4 percent of twelve- to nineteen-year-olds, 18 percent of kids six to eleven years old, and 12.1 percent of two- to five-year-olds are obese.

Serious health problems that can be caused by obesity include high blood pressure, high cholesterol, heart disease and type 2 diabetes. All have

The American ideals of beauty have changed significantly over time. Marilyn Monroe in the 1950s was considered extremely beautiful and was a size 12. Stamps were printed all over the world with her pictures on them.

(Photo courtesy of Sergey/Shutterstock.com)

been and continue to be occurring more and more frequently in American children and youth.

Although the causes of obesity are complex, the two major causes among those under age twenty seem to be lack of physical exercise and unhealthy eating habits. Many youth spend too much time sitting, be it at home or school. Some children come home after school to an empty house while parents are working and must stay inside until their parents return. Some live in neighborhoods where it is not safe to play outdoors and there are few parks. Many schools now emphasize sit-down homework and budget cuts for education have reduced physical education programs, especially at the elementary school level.

Convenience foods with high amounts of fats and sugars are more common than ever, and kids often have easy access to them. Busy parents find less time and energy for cooking and rely more and more on an array of prepared and fast foods. Snacks and convenience foods are the fastest growing segment of the food market in the United States, and these are the foods that often contain unhealthy amounts of fats and carbohydrates.

Both being overweight and underweight are associated with depression, low self-esteem, and eating disorders. Teen girls in particular seem vulnerable to being overly concerned about weight and can have distorted views of their own bodies. Even normal or underweight girls can see themselves as needing to reduce their food intake and diet (Moses, Banilivy, & Lifshitz, 1989). In popular media girls are often given the impression that ultra-thin is the ideal, an impossibility for girls of many basic body types. This image contributes to the growing rate of eating disorders among girls and women. It was estimated that about one in five women ages twelve to twenty-five years suffered with an eating disorder. The number of men and boys diagnosed with eating disorders is also growing and makes up 10 percent to 15 percent of the twenty-four million affected Americans of all ages (Alliance for Eating Disorder Awareness, n.d.). Eating disorders can result in serious health problems including organ damage and even death.

The most commonly diagnosed eating disorders are anorexia nervosa, bulimia nervosa, and binge eating. Psychologists define **anorexia nervosa** as someone who has abnormally low body weight, an intense fear of gaining weight, and a distorted body image (Mayo Clinic, 2015). Even a small amount of weight gain can result in excessive exercise or abuse of diet pills, laxatives, or diuretics. With extreme weight loss, women's menses can cease.

I Am Good Enough for My Recovery

By Annie Vitti

The first time that I thought that I wasn't good enough was in second grade. My best friend at the time was suddenly friends with the popular girls and she believed that bullying me would mean a reserved spot with them. I'd lost my best friend. I tried to get over this, but I never really could because I could not comprehend not being wanted by someone. My cousin came to visit me in Chicago from New York City during the fall of fifth grade. He promised me that the next time that I would see him, he would take me to see his photography company in the city. I was so excited to go because I've never been. I took my time with my cousin for granted, for just a couple months later he died suddenly from a heart attack. His promise to me was broken. After his death, I become depressed. The summer before I was going into middle school, I wanted to get more friends. And I thought that I'd try to fix my appearance, improve my grades and become more athletic. I started changing my behaviors. Every day, I went on the scale. When school started, I fooled everyone at school that I was a "perfect" kid; my grades were some of the best in the class, I could keep pace with the boys in PE and girls always complimented my style. Some would think that this is what would be happiness, but I wasn't. No one wanted to hang out with me outside of school. I asked and they would always reply with a lame excuse. My weight dropped even more. The words, "Maybe if I was thinner," always pounded through my head. One day I got so scared of my appearance that I told my mom. She talked to me and we decided that I was going to get professional help. When I met the doctor, I was not diagnosed with anything, but she said that if I hadn't come in when I did, I would have been diagnosed anorexic within a month. The thing about middle school that bothered me was that everyone seemed to have a group of friends. Everybody belonged besides me. Everybody called me perfect or nice or smart or pretty. But I felt like I wasn't ever good enough for anyone. By freshman year, I was determined to find myself. I filled up my schedule with outrageous classes, put on a happy mask and tried to be a friend to everyone. Things started to get better; my weight had started to increase, I had a football player boyfriend and finally discovered who at least I thought I was and I thought I was getting better. Then the tables started to turn. I found out that my boyfriend was lying to me and was doing things behind my back. To me, my "friends," my boyfriend and what felt like the whole school, didn't tell me because I wasn't good enough. My grades dropped. My friends stopped talking to me because they didn't understand me or decided that being friends with my ex-boyfriend was a better idea. By the end of the school year, I was diagnosed with depression and anxiety. I even attempted suicide twice. During the summer after freshman year, I purposefully stopped talking to all of the "friends" that were not supportive of me when I really needed them. I was also finally diagnosed with anorexia. At one point I almost tried to force myself into different eating disordered behaviors when I was at summer camp. I personally thank my counselor for deciding to never leave me alone. I don't even know if it was intentional, but that little gesture meant so much to me. She was the first person who was able to make me believe that I was and am good enough. Because of my counselor, I've dedicated myself to recovery. But, I still relapsed. I went to my mom again and I was entered in a hospital. I spent eight weeks receiving treatment. I lost support from some of my closest friends because they thought that my eating disorder was a choice. Instead, I turned to my passion of singing and my choir. Everyone encouraged me while I was gone. Recovering is hard. But it is worth it and I can actually say that I'm happy. I've learned who my real friends are and what I want in life. I'm strong enough to be able to encourage other teens to get help. And most importantly, I finally believe that I'm good enough, because I always was! Yes, I've lots of catch up work to do for school, but I have teachers and peers that help me. I wear everyday a small ring that says "Hope" as a reminder to be positive. And instead of writing and thinking negative things I now draw the recovery symbol with pride and write the words, "I am enough." It has taken over four years of hard work to be able to say those three words, but I've never been more proud of myself. Finally, I want to enforce that many people think that there is such a thing as "perfect" but there is not. Everyone is an individual and is beautiful in his or her own way. Everybody has his or her own story to be told. Whether you know it or not you are worth it. Don't be too quick to judge people, but be supportive of everyone. Most importantly, even if you can't believe it now, you are good enough.

Source: National Eating Disorders Association, 2014.

Bulimia nervosa is characterized by repeated episodes of binge eating and purging. These patients often eat large amounts of food and then purge by inducing vomiting or using laxatives. They often maintain normal weight or have only small changes in weight. However, bulimia is often accompanied by depression, low self-worth, and shame. The cycles of binging and purging can also become addictive.

Repeated **binge eating** can also occur without the purging of bulimia. These patients continue eating excessively even when they are not hungry. They often feel they have no control over this eating followed by guilt and shame. Large weight gains are typical.

The causes of eating disorders are complex. It is thought to be a combination of psychological (depression, low self-esteem, or other mental health issues) with biological/genetic predisposition, social/environmental contributions, and family dynamics. For example, emotional, physical, or sexual child abuse can be a factor; feelings of depression, anxiety, the need for perfection, and lack of control are common in these patients. Although teens and young adults often hide their eating disorder from family and friends, treatment is critical, because eating disorders can cause death (Alliance for Eating Disorders Awareness, 2013).

Eating Disorders

How Can We Help?	1. This disorder cannot be cured or helped by a friend or family alone. Do not diagnose the problem. If you think they have a problem then encourage them to get professional treatment/help. 2. Do not oversimplify the problem or downplay the problem. 3. Call their parents or spouse and let them know. Do not promise to not tell anyone.
Treatment Options	A combination of the following: 1. Therapy (individual, group, family) 2. Medication to treat depression, anxiety, or other psychological issues 3. Enter a specialized eating disorder program
Causes	A combination of the following: 1. Biological/genetic predisposition 2. Environmental/social dynamics 3. Family dynamics

Source: Modified from Alliance for Eating Disorders Awareness, 2014.

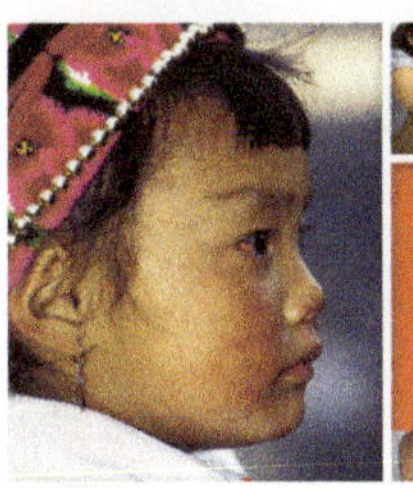

I Hate My Body

"I hate my body. Although I had absolutely no choice in its creation, I have managed to let it become what it is. Double chinned, gapped toothed, acne scarred. So many scars. I can't even see my own vagina without sucking in my fucking stomach. I hate how I look in pictures. I hate how fucking beautiful you are. I hate how you know it. How everyone of your Facebook friends knows it too. Fucking narcissists. Fucking photobooth. Fucking virtual lives. I hate your brand new clothes. Your brand new shoes. Your gym membership. All your brand new little everythings. I hate your money. I hate my $.75 in savings. My $4.68 in checking. Hate working so hard, and still feeling hungry.

I hate how I can't appreciate all that I have. That I can drink clean water that won't kill me. That I can go to school and get an education, when most people in the world can't. That I can abuse drugs and alcohol, watch movies, listen to all kinds of music, read books, make art, drive cars, ride bikes, explore parties,hang with friends, go to bars, clubs, dance and play.

I hate how, despite all that I have, I am still filled with so much anger. Sometimes it just makes me throw up. Like somehow all my painful knots, and fucked up thoughts would come undone, spilling out my mouth, sinking to the bottom of the toilet. But they don't. They cling onto my insides like leeches. Sucking the optimist's blood.

I am a happy person, I really am. But I am also a very sad, destructive person as well. You will never see this side of me. I will never let any of you see how fucked up I really am."

Source: Anonymous CSULB college student (Yonic South, 2011).

Depression

Depression in teens is common and is often unrecognized and therefore untreated. One in five children may have an emotional, behavioral, or mental illness and, in adolescents, one in eight are said to suffer from mild to severe depression. It is estimated that only about 30 percent receive any treatment and 70 percent of adolescents suffer through on their own. We are seeing higher and higher instances of depression in middle school-age children. When depression goes untreated it can contribute to an increased risk of substance abuse, inappropriate sexual activity, delinquency, low performance at school, and suicide.

Recognizing depression in teens can be difficult. Some mood swings during the adolescent years are normal and a part of maturing. Even parents who have

Depression in teens is common and is often unrecognized.

(Photo courtesy of MitarArt/Shutterstock.com)

good communication with their kids can miss symptoms of depression. Kids may not recognize depression within themselves and even deeply depressed teens may think their feelings are normal. They can lose interest in activities, friends that they once had, and school that they did well in.

Some teens whose depression goes untreated may seek self-medication with drugs or alcohol. Eating disorders are also associated with depression. One of the most common signs of depression in teenagers is frequent and intense outbursts of anger and irritability. This particular symptom often seems at odds with the more traditional symptoms of depression.

Self-mutilation, like cutting, is also a symptom of depression in teens. It is not so much an attempt at suicide as the need to experience physical pain as a distraction from psychological pain. Attention deficit hyperactivity disorder (ADHD) can also be confused with depression as the symptoms sometimes overlap. Problems with attention, sleep, behavior, school performance, and peers can occur in both. It has been shown that children with ADHD are at an increased risk of suicide because of shared genetic risk factors (Dickerson, 2014).

Clinical depression can also lead to suicide, the third leading cause of death in the United States for fifteen- to twenty-four-year-olds. About 16 percent of teenagers in high school have reported that they seriously considered suicide, 13 percent created a plan, and 8 percent tried to take their own life in the last year (CDC, 2014). Threats of suicide should always be taken seriously and professional help should be sought immediately.

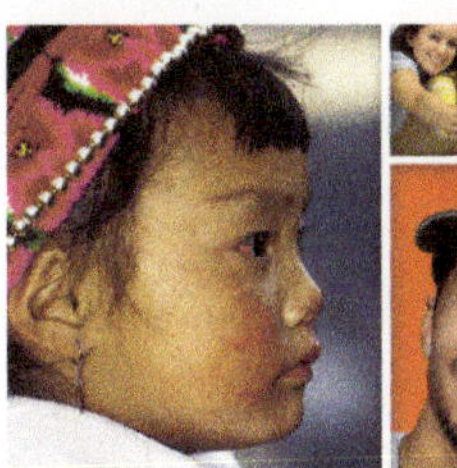

Feelings of a Depressed Teen

Chronic hopelessness, harsh self-criticism, and feeling unlovable and unwanted create a pain that cannot be described. The following was found in the diary of an older teen after her successful suicide: "It feels like the pain is feeding off of me. Like I am the host and it is the leech. It owns me and the only way that I will get rid of it is to destroy the host. The only way I will find peace is to kill myself. I wish people would just give me permission to die. They want me alive for their sake and just don't understand how intolerable the pain is."

Source: Shepps Battle, 2002

Causes of clinical depression are not completely understood and seem to have genetic as well as situational components. Teenaged girls are more likely than boys to develop depression. Reasons are complex and it may be that girls face more challenges than boys the same ages, that hormonal changes are involved, or that boys underreport symptoms of depression (Person, Sarigiani, & Kennedy, 1991).

The teen years involve a great deal of pressure on both boys and girls—at school, as well as from parents and peers. Academic performance is a priority for many families and schools. Peer acceptance involves looking and acting according to peer standards.

Clinical depression does seem to involve chemical changes in the brain, which are becoming better understood. Vulnerability to some kinds of depression seems to be inherited and a family history of depression is a red flag. Onset is often at puberty or in young adulthood. Traumatic events or long-term trauma can trigger depression. Onset can be sudden or can develop gradually.

Treatment of depression should begin with seeking out a mental health provider specializing in teens in order to get an accurate diagnosis and to develop a treatment plan. Psychiatrists can write prescriptions for medication, but ongoing therapy is also an important component. A psychologist or therapist can provide this necessary therapy. The most successful treatments usually involve both therapy and medication.

Some parents and teens are reluctant to seek out professional help because of the stigma still attached to mental illness and the need to take medication. However, treatment of mental illness, including depression, is as important as treatment for any other illness. If a teen has cancer or diabetes, parents would not hesitate to get treatment and it should be the same for depression. In most cases, mental illness will not go away by itself. Parents need to be persistent in getting their children the needed help.

In some cases, teens or children need residential treatment for depression, eating disorders, or other psychological problems. There are programs specially designed for children and teens. Some are hospital-based and others include therapeutic wilderness programs and therapeutic boarding schools.

Alcoholism and Drug Use

Experimentation with street drugs and alcohol is common among teens in many places in the United States. The substances are readily available to most high school students and it has been reported that marijuana is often easier to get than alcohol. According to a survey done by the National Institute on Drug Use (2013), 60 percent of kids in the twelfth grade do not view regular marijuana use as harmful. The findings also state that 36 percent of seniors in high school have smoked marijuana in the last month. The belief that regular marijuana use is harmful has been on a steady decline over the last twenty years. Attitudes are likely to continue in this direction with the legalization of marijuana in Colorado in 2013, and with twenty-three states as of 2014 legalizing the medical use of marijuana, with three additional states pending (ProCon.org, 2014).

Though the exact nature and causes of addiction are still not well defined, it seems clear that some people have a genetic predisposition to addictive substance abuse. In other words, some people are more vulnerable than others to becoming addicted. Although some genetic markers for addiction have been identified, additional research is still needed to understand the complex process and the interaction of genetic wiring and the environment.

Another area of addiction that has received more attention in recent years is sex addiction and promiscuity in teens. Though it seems to occur in both males and females, it comes to light as a problem in girls more often than in boys. This difference may be due partly to the remaining double standard for sexual behavior in males and females. A boy who has sex with many partners may be considered more acceptable or even admired, while a girl may be thought of as a slut.

Promiscuity is often a symptom of other psychological disorders like depression, oppositional defiance, among others. The dangers of unprotected sex include unplanned pregnancy and exposure to sexually transmitted diseases.

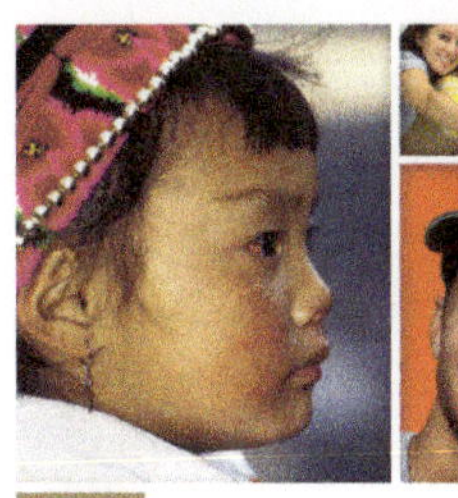

It Happened to Me

Methamphetamine became a part of my life when I was 19 years old. I was instantly hooked—there was none of that "only on the weekends," or "I'll only stay up for two days." I eventually tried to do that, but control was impossible.

I was powerless over meth. I just didn't realize it or wouldn't admit it at the time. I couldn't quit. I used almost every day for seven months and then I hit bottom. Seven months. That's all it took for me to lose everything. When I started using meth, the only thing I knew about it was that it was a drug. At the time, I had the mentality that "it" wasn't going to happen to me.

▲ ***Over just a matter of months, eyes become sunken, skin becomes paler, and blotchy marks appear.***

(Photo courtesy of Sylvie Bouchard/Shutterstock.com)

We've all seen the egg and frying pan commercials, or the junkies on the street downtown. We all know what could happen to our health years later, but we light up that cigarette anyway. We all think "It's not going to happen to me." In the end, "it" did.

Over the next seven months, meth became the most important thing in my life. Everything I did, I did to get more meth, to stay high. I didn't know what else to do. I stopped talking to my family because I didn't want them to know I was using. I went to work high and I was tired because I hadn't slept in days. I only called my mom after I'd slept and only to borrow money. I wasn't able to pay my car payment, car insurance, rent, or any other bills because I spent my money on meth. I lost sixty pounds because I didn't eat when I was high. Showering and brushing my teeth regularly didn't happen. Maintaining my hair and makeup twenty-four hours a day for a week was impossible for me, so I just quit doing it.

I used people and manipulated people for more meth. I began to consider dancing so I could have more money to buy meth. I changed my values so they matched my behavior; it was "right" if it got me high. I tried to jump out of a car moving at over seventy miles per hour, and yet I did more meth. I blacked out and hallucinated, and yet I kept getting high.

Some would say I had a choice: meth or a life—and I chose meth. Before I used that first line, I did have a choice. After that, I was in the grip of a disease more powerful than myself. I lived to use and used to live. There was no choice, I had to get high. I did anything to get more meth.

(continues)

(continued from previous page)

I even went to jail for meth. This is where I got my first dose of humility. Everyone I used with had been to jail because of meth, whether it was possession or something stupid they had done while on meth. I flat out told people I didn't have a meth problem because I'd never gone to jail. The people I used with didn't have a place to live, a car, a phone, electricity or heat, and until the end, I had those things. I compared myself to others to prove I wasn't an addict. I was wrong. And as I sat in jail, coming down—I finally admitted I was an addict.

The way I was living was hopeless; I was barely surviving. I knew that if I didn't do something, meth was going to kill me. I was living in a prison created by myself, for myself.

(Taken from Partnership for Drug Free Kids, 2012)

Severely Troubled Teens

Some teenagers become completely out of control and are at grave risk of doing physical or psychological harm to themselves or others. They completely disregard their parents' rules and as a result their parents have little or no control over them. We are not talking about your average teen that is acting out or rebelling, though it is often difficult to tell the difference between a teenager severely acting out and one that is gone beyond the cultural "norm." Normal parenting discipline techniques fail to work. Parents are often at a loss as to how to help their child and what direction they should take.

These teenagers often have a combination of different problems and issues. The problems can range from low self-esteem, eating disorders, alcohol and drug abuse, depression, anxiety, bipolar disorder, adoption issues, divorce issues, oppositional disorder, as well as many others. The causes are often from three main areas:

1. Biological/genetic predispositions and conditions
2. Cultural and environmental dynamics
3. Parenting or family dynamics

Under less severe conditions, parents seek out counseling and psychiatric help for their children and families. In many cases this is enough, but when these do not work the child often needs to be in a highly structured therapeutic setting, different from the home environment. There are programs available that will help these teens but many Americans are unaware of the programs available.

Therapeutic Wilderness Program

In **therapeutic wilderness programs**, teenagers are usually divided by gender into small groups. These groups camp, hike, cook their own food, and learn other outdoor survival skills. The staff is trained to deal with difficult teens and in basic therapeutic methods. Certified therapists also come in regularly, as well as nurses, to check on the students and any medications the teenagers are on. The idea of these programs is to get teenagers out of their normal environment, away from all other distractions, into a place where they have a structured environment and have to contribute to their own survival. This setting forces them to be accountable for their own actions and to face their emotions and the motivations behind them.

The average length of these programs are about two months and costs on average between $12 and $13 thousand per month (Donham, 2014). These programs are not "boot camp"-type programs. They are therapeutically based and personal-safety conscious. At the end of these programs the team that has been working with the child recommends if the child should return home or move to a longer-term program. If the child returns home, the team offers parents support and advice.

The long-term success rate of therapeutic wilderness programs has been questioned. These programs take "the edge off" of an "out-of-control teen" so

◂ *A fourteen-year-old at a therapeutic wilderness program in Oregon.*

(Photo courtesy of Cindy Donham)

the teen will be willing to start changing his or her behavior. When teens start facing their issues, negative behavior, and resulting consequences, follow-up therapy and therapeutic programs can continue the work that the wilderness programs started. More often than not, an adolescent needs a longer-term program, depending on that child's individual issues. It takes time and maturity to change a person's behavior. If the kids who need longer term programs return home, they often just revert back to old behaviors because they are back in the environment that helped cause the problems in the first place. Environment plays a significant role in a teenager's behavior. Many teenagers continue on to therapeutic boarding schools (Donham, 2014).

Therapeutic Boarding Schools

Therapeutic boarding schools provide a very structured environment and different levels of therapy. They often have a set program where teens progress at their own pace to earn privileges and learn responsibilities. Teens also attend classes so they can complete high school. Some schools are gender specific and others are mixed. Many programs are better than others and cater to different student population needs. The good programs also work with the parents and families of these teens. Therapeutic boarding schools do not usually have "boot camp"-formats or mentalities, even though they are usually highly structured. The average time to complete these programs is two years and the cost ranges from $6 to $10 thousand a month (Donham, 2014).

For teenagers to change their behavior, a program should address the three causes listed previously (i.e., biological causes, social–cultural dynamics, and family dynamics). A positive therapeutic and structured environment is required to facilitate the needed changes. The average length of time to turn around a teenager's behavior is about two years because it just takes time for an adolescent to address and internalize change, as well as increase in maturity (Donham, 2014).

Educational Consultants

When parents are faced with an out-of-control teenager and are trying to decide what they should do, it is often wise to hire an **educational consultant**. These are people whose job it is to keep track of the many different therapeutic programs out there. Some programs are better than others and many focus on specific population groups. When a family feels as though they are in crisis, it is difficult to weed through and find the correct program for the child. Most of these programs are very expensive and when investing this kind of money and time, parents want to make sure they are putting their child into the correct program. These consultants cost from $3 to $5 thousand. Usually once this fee is paid, these consultants will provide their services as long as the child needs them. They are well worth the expense (Donham, 2014).

Success Rate

There are a wide range of programs available to help troubled youth and only a few of the main categories have been discussed. It is very difficult to determine the success rate of these programs because it is very hard to define what success is. What equals "success" varies for each child and the child's individual needs. Some kids come through better than others, but most have learned and changed for the better. This does not mean that when they finish that they are cured and will not make mistakes. The biggest problem with these programs is the cost. Insurance generally pays little or none toward any of these programs. As a result only financially well off families can afford them. We need less costly programs and more of the programs to be covered by insurance. If very troubled teens do not get the help they need, the end results are adolescents who turn to prostitution, drugs, suicide, or violence. Our juvenile and prison systems are full of youth who have not gotten the help they needed. In the long term it is less expensive for society to treat troubled youth before they end up in the criminal system or on the streets. It also is a terrible waste of humanity to not have more affordable resources available for families (Donham, 2014).

CHAPTER 15 SUMMARY

In the United States, sexually transmitted diseases are common among fifteen- to twenty-five-year-olds who are sexually active, with human papillomavirus (HPV), trichomoniasis, and chlamydia being the most common. Minority youth, particularly African American men, have the highest risk of contracting HIV. Currently there are known medications that can slow the progression of the disease but there is no known cure or vaccination available. HIV is present in every country of the world today and is still an epidemic in many developing countries. It is estimated that only 42 percent of people who are infected have access to treatment drugs.

Rape is defined as a sexual act forced on one person by another. In most cases, the motivation for rape is to show power rather than sexual gratification. Rape is traumatic, no matter what the situation. Virginity is highly valued in many cultures around the world. If a girl is raped, she is considered tarnished and shamed for life.

The period when adolescents start to be physically attracted to others can be a challenging time for all teens, but it is a particularly difficult for those who are attracted to people of the same gender. Gay and lesbian teens face a higher-than-average risk for depression and suicide and still face discrimination and prejudice from many segments of the population. Studies have found that children raised by a homosexual parent when compared to a comparable heterosexual parent have no significant differences.

Most twenty-first-century teens in the United States carry cells phones and most people who do can be reached almost any time and any place. In surveys, most teens and young adults prefer texting to voice communication on the phone. Smart phones allow access to the Internet, e-mail, social networking, video games, music, and taking photos. Teens and young adults today have grown up with computers and the Internet. More detailed research needs to be done on what impact these technologies are having on youth toady.

The uses teens make of mass media fall into six categories: education, entertainment, stimulation, youth cultural identification, identity formation, and coping with stress. Mass media gives kids easy access to friends and outside information. Some people use media experiences to heighten sensations or to relieve stress. For most teens, it is important to feel connected with peers and peer culture.

Child pornography is defined as children under age eighteen years in sexual poses or engaged in sexual activity. It is often difficult to track or enforce, and as a result child pornography has become a multi-billion dollar industry over the past twenty years. The Internet has become a new way to easily distribute all kinds of pornography, including child pornography.

Sex trafficking is when another person forces someone against his or her will into the sex trade across state and national borders. Prostitution is when someone sells his or her body for money. Prostitution can be voluntary or involuntary. Many sex traffickers use the Internet to advertise sexual services and their bases of operation move frequently. In many parts of the world, the situation for girls in the sex trade is even worse than in the United States. In many places governments and police are corrupt and laws are not enforced.

Obesity in Americans of all ages continues to increase. Obesity is defined as being at least 20 percent over one's ideal body weight. Although the causes of obesity are complex, the two major causes among those under age twenty seem to be lack of physical exercise and unhealthy eating habits.

Teen girls in particular seem vulnerable to being overly concerned about weight and can have distorted views of their own bodies. This image contributes to the growing incidence of eating disorders among girls and women. The most commonly diagnosed eating disorders are anorexia nervosa, bulimia nervosa, and binge eating.

Depression in teens is common and often goes untreated and unrecognized. Recognizing depression in teens can be difficult. Some teens whose depression goes untreated may seek self-medication with drugs or alcohol or may commit suicide. Some parents and teens are reluctant to seek professional help because of the stigma still attached to mental illness and the need to take medication. However, treatment of mental illness, including depression, is as important as treatment for any other illness.

Out-of-control teenagers often have a combination of different problems and issues. The causes are from three main areas: biological/genetic predispositions and conditions, cultural and environmental dynamics, and parenting or family dynamics. Therapeutic wilderness programs and therapeutic boarding schools can help these youths. Treatment often takes a minimum of two years to change a youth's behavior.

CHAPTER 15 VOCABULARY

Anorexia Nervosa
Binge Eating
Bisexual
Bulimia Nervosa
Chlamydia
Cultivation Effect
Date Rape
Depression
Displacement Effect
Educational Consultant
Gay
Heighten Sensations
HIV/AIDS
Human Papillomavirus (HPV)
Lesbian
Mummy-baby Relationships
Numbing Effect
Pansexual
Prostitution
Rape
Reciprocal Socialization
Sexting
Sex Trafficking
Social Learning Theory
Therapeutic Boarding Schools
Therapeutic Wilderness Programs

References

ABC News. (2006, February 9). Teen girls' stories of sex trafficking in U.S. New York, NY: ABC News.

Adolph, K. E. (2000). Specificity of learning: Why infants fall over a veritable cliff. *Psychological Science, 11,* 290–295.

Adolph, K. E., & Kretch, K. S. (Updated: Friday, November 7, 2014). *Infants on the Edge Beyond the Visual Cliff.* New York, NY: New York University.

Alfonso, V. C., Flanagan, D. E, Badwin, S. (2005). The impact of the Cattell-Horn-Carroll theory on test development and interpretation of cognitive academic abilities. In D. P. Flanagan & P. L. Harrison (Eds.), *Contemporary intellectual assessment: Theories, test and issues.* New York, NY: Guilford Press.

Alliance for Eating Disorders Awareness. (n.d.). Eating disorder statistics. Retrieved from http://www.ndsu.edu/fileadmin/counseling/Eating_Disorder_Statistics.pdf

American Humane Association. (2014). Child abuse and neglect. Retrieved from http://www.americanhumane.org/children/stop-child-abuse/fact-sheets/child-abuse-and-neglect-statistics.html

American Humane Association. History, story of Mary Ellen. Retrieved from http://www.americanhumane.org/about-us/who-we-are/history/story-of-mary-ellen.html

Anonymous. (2011, May 3). I hate my body. *Yonic South, 1.*

Arnett, J. J. (2001). *Adolescence and emerging adulthood: A cultural approach* (2nd ed.). Upper Saddle River, NJ: Prentice-Hall.

Arnett, J. J. (2010). *Adolescence and emerging adulthood, a cultural approach* (4th ed.). Boston, MA: Pearson/Prentice-Hall.

Asher, H. B. (1974). "Some consequences of measurement error in survey data." *American Journal of Political Science* 28: 468–485.

Au, K. H. (1993). *Literacy instruction in multicultural settings.* Fort Worth, TX: Harcourt Brace Jovanovich.

AVERT: Averting HIV and AIDS. (2010). Retrieved from http://www.avert.org/around world.htm

Azar, B. (2002). It's more than fun and games. *Monitor on Psychology, 33*(3), 50–51.

Baby Center, Babycenter.com, accessed 2014 from http://www.babycenter.com/0_your-childs-talking-timeline_10356902.bc © BabyCenter, L.L.C. 1997–2015. All rights reserved.

Baily, B. L. (1988). *From front porch to back seat: Courtship in twentieth-century America.* Baltimore, MD: Johns Hopkins University Press.

Bandura, A. (1977). *Aggression: A social learning analysis.* Englewood Cliffs, NJ: Prentice-Hall.

Barnett, W. S. (Winter, 1995). Long-term effects of early childhood programs on cognitive and school outcomes. *The Future of Children, 4*(3), 25–50.

Baumrind, D. (1967). Child care practices anteceding three patterns of preschool behavior. *Genetic Psychology Monograph, 75*, 43–88.

Berger, K. (2004). *The developing person through the life span.* New York, NY: Worth Publishers.

Berk, L. E. (2008). *Infants and children: Prenatal through middle childhood.* Upper Saddle River, NJ: Pearson/Allyn & Bacon.

Beyers, W. G., L., Vansant, I., & Moors, E. (2003). Structural model of autonomy in middle and late adolescence: Connectedness, separation, detachment, and agency. *Journal of Youth and Adolescence, 32*, 351–365.

Biography.com. Charles Perrault.

Bjorklund, D., & Hernandez Balsi, C. (2012). *Child and adolescent development, an integrated approach.* Belmont, CA: Wadsworth.

Blackwood, E. (2001). Women's intimate friendships and other affairs: An ethnographic overview. In C. Brettell & C. Sargent (Eds.), *Gender in cross-cultural perspective* (3rd ed., pp. 237–247). Upper Saddle River, NJ: Prentice-Hall.

Briant, M. (2004). *Baby sign language basics: Early communication for hearing babies and toddlers.* Lyndhurst, NJ: Barnes & Noble.

Brooks, J. (2011). *The process of parenting* (9th ed.). New York, NY: McGraw-Hill.

Brooks-Gunn, J., Klebanov, P. K., & Duncan, G. J. (1996). Ethnic differences in children's intelligence test scores: Role of economic deprivation, home environment, and maternal characteristics. *Child Development, 67*(2), 396–408. doi: 10.1111/j.1467-8624.1996.tb01741.x

Browne, V.J. (2008). *Chemosensory Development in the Fetus and Newborn.* University of Colorado Denver School of Medicine and the Children's Hospital. Elsevier Inc.

Buck, S. (2013, April 3). Mashable: Cell-ebration! 40 years of cellphone history. Retrieved from http://mashable.com/2013/04/03/anniversary-of-cellphone/

Burleigh, N. (2013, September 26). Sexting, shame and suicide. Ed. RS1192 @RollingStone.com

Butterworth, G. (1990). Self-perception in infancy. In D. Ciccherri & M. Beeghly (Eds.), *The self in transition*. Chicago, IL: University of Chicago Press.

Byth, D. A., Hill, J. P., & Thiel, K. S. (1982). Early adolescents' significant others: Grade and gender differences in perceived relationships with familial and nonfamilial adults and young people. *Journal of Youth and Adolescence, 11*, 425–450.

Cadet, J. (1998). *Restavec: From Haitian slave child to middle class American*. Austin, TX: University of Texas Press.

Cameron, R. (1969). The international encyclopedia of the social sciences. New York, 1968. *The Journal of Economic History, 29*(3), 537–541.

Canagarajah, S., & Nielsen, H. S. (2001). Child labor in Africa: A comparative study. *The Annals of the American Academy of Political and Social Science, 575*(1), 71–91.

Carpenter, M. (2007, June 9). What happens to kids raised by gay parents? *Pittsburgh Post-Gazette*.

Centers for Disease Control and Prevention. (2010). Chlamydial infections–2010 STD treatment guidelines. Retrieved from www.cdc.gov/std/treatment/2010/chlamydial-infection.htm

Centers for Disease Control and Prevention. (2010). Publication and information products, NCHS health E-stat. Retrieved from http://www.cdc.gov/nchs/data/hestat/obesity_child_07_08/obesity_child_07_08.htm

Centers for Disease Control and Prevention. (2012). Overweight and obesity—basics about childhood obesity. Retrieved from http://www.cdc.gov/obesity/childhood/basics.html

Centers for Disease Control and Prevention. (April 10, 2012). NCHF data brief, 2012. Retrieved from http://www.cdc.gov/nchs/data/databriefs/db89.htm

Centers for Disease Control and Prevention. (2014). Fast stats: Obesity and overweight. Retrieved from http://www.cdc.gov/nchs/fastats/obesity-overweight.htm

Centers for Disease Control and Prevention. (2014). Injury center—violence prevention; suicide prevention (youth). Retrieved from http://www.cdc.gov/violenceprevention/pub/youth_suicide.html

Centers for Disease Control and Prevention. (2014, July 24). HIV among youth. Retrieved from http://www.cdc.gov/hiv/risk/age/youth/index.html?s_cid=tw_std0141316

Chagnon, N. A. (1968). *Yanamamo, the fierce people*. New York, NY: Holt, Rinehart and Winston.

Chao, R. K. (1994). Beyond parental control and authoritarian parenting style: Understand Chinese parenting through the cultural notion of training. *Child Development, 65,* 1111–1116.

Charlesworth, R. (2011, 2008). *Understanding child development* (8th ed.). Belmont, CA: Wadsworth.

Chen, J., & Gardner, H. (2005). Assessment based on multiple-intelligences theory. In D. P. Flanagan & P. L. Harrison (Eds.), *Contemporary intellectual assessment: Theories, test and issues.* New York, NY: Guilford Press.

Cherlin, A. J. (2008). *Public and private families, an introduction* (5th ed.). Boston, MA: McGraw-Hill.

Chess, S., & Thomas, A. (1984). *Origins and evolution of behavior disorders.* New York: Bruner/ Mazel. [Reprinted in 1987 as paperback; Cambridge, MA: Harvard University Press].

Christian Science Monitor Journal. Retrieved from http://www.csmonitor.com/1992/0721/ 21082.html

Cole, D. A., Maxwell, S. E., Martin, J. M., Peeke, L. G., Seroczynski, A. D., Tram, J. M., . . . Maschman, T. (2001). The development of multiple domains of child and adolescent self-concept: A cohort sequential longitudinal design. *Child Development, 33,* 447–460.

Cole, M., Cole, S. R., & Lightfoot, C. (2005). *The development of children* (5th ed.). New York, NY: Worth Publishers.

Collins, W. A., & Laursen, B. (2004). Parent-adolescent relationships and influences. In R. Learner & L. Steinberg (Eds.), *Handbook of adolescent psychology* (2nd ed.). New York: Wiley.

Cox Communications. (2009). Teen online and wireless safety survey; cyber bullying, sexting and parental controls. (Cox Communications teen online and wireless safety survey in partnership with National Partnership of Missing and Exploited Children and John Walsh).

Crichton, J. (Producer), & Graham, J. G., Edward (Director). (1995). American experience: The orphan trains (WGBH Boston). [Video/DVD] Edward Gray Films Inc.

Crombie, G., & Desjardins, M. J. (1993). Predictors of gender: The relative importance of children's play games, and personality characteristics. Paper presented at the Meeting of the Society for Research in Child Development, New Orleans, LA.

Csikszentmihaliyi, M., & Larson, R. (1984). *Being adolescent.* New York: Basic Books.

Dasen, P. R. (2000). Rapid social change and the turmoil of adolescence: A cross-cultural perspective. *World Psychology, 7,* 114–122.

de Vries, M. W. (1987). Cry babies, culture, and catastrophe: Infant temperament among the Masai. *Culture, Illness and Healing Journal, 11,* 165–185.

DeCasper, A. J., & Fifer, W. P. (1980). Of human bonding: Newborns prefer their mothers' voices. *Science, 208,* 174–176.

DeCasper, A. J., & Spence, M. J. (1986). Newborns prefer a familiar story over an unfamiliar one. *Infants Behavior and Development, 9,* 133–150.

Deloache, S., & Gotlieb, A. (2000). *A World of Babies.* Cambridge University Press. United Kingdom.

DeRose, L. M., & Brooks-Gunn, J. (2006). Transition into adolescence: The role of pubertal processes. In L. Balter & C. S. Tamis-LeMonda (Eds.), *Child psychology: A handbook of contemporary issues* (2nd ed., pp. 385–414). New York, NY: Psychology Press.

Dickerson, K. (2014). People with ADHD may have a higher risk of suicide. *Live Science,* Oct. 10, 2014.

Diessner, R., (2008). *Sources in human development* (3rd ed.). Guilford, CT: McGraw-Hill.

Dirix, C. E. H., Nijhuis, J. G., Jongsma, H. W., & Hornstra, G. (2009). Aspects of fetal learning and development. *Child Development, 80*(4), 1251–1258.

Dobbs, D. (2009). The orchid children. Retrieved from http;//daviddobbs.net/articles/orchid-children-web-title-the -science-of-success.html

Dolasie, M. (2012, December 5). Pong—the video game that started it all, turns 40! *DoGoNews, Fodder for Young Minds.*

Donham, C. (2014). Personal story. Unpublished manuscript.

Donham, C. (2014). Rite of passage, learning to drive. Unpublished manuscript.

Education Encyclopedia, S. U. Stages of growth child development. Retrieved from http://education.stateuniversity.com/pages/1826/Child-Development-Stages-Growth.html

Ekvall, S. W. (Ed.). (1993). *Pediatric nutrition in chronic diseases and developmental disorders: Prevention, assessment, and treatment.* New York, NY: Oxford University Press.

El Policy Library. (1995, July). Congress resolutions, resolution on child labor. Retrieved from http://pages.ei-ie.org/library/libraries/detail/137

Exton, M. The cultural conflict over toilet training. Plymouth State University. http://jupiter.plymouth.edu/~megp/webct/culturalconflict.htm. Accessed March 2015.

Fagot, B. I. (1994). Gender role learning and preschool education. In T. Husen& T. N. Postlewaite (eds.), *International Encyclopedia of Education,* pp. 2449–2452) Oxford: Pergamon.

Fagot, B. I., & Haden R. (1991). Observations to parent reactions to sex-stereotyped behaviors: Age and sex effects. *Child Development, 62,* 617–628.

Fav Meth Heads of the Day. (2014) Faces of meth. Retrieved from http://fav-meth-head-of-the-day.com/faces-of-meth/

Feldman, R. (2008). *Adolescence.* Upper Saddle River, NJ: Pearson/Prentice-Hall.

Fisher, C. B., Jackson, J. E., & Villarruel, E. A. (1998). The study of African American and Latin American children and youth. In W. Damon (editor in chief) & R. M. Lerer (vol. ed.), *Handbook of Child Psychology, Vol 1. Theoretical model of human development* (5th ed., pp. 1145–1207). New York: Wiley.

Floyd, R. G. (2005). Information processing approaches to interpretation of contemporary intellectual assessment instruments. In D. P. Flanagan & P. L. Harrison (Eds.), *Contemporary intellectual assessment: Theories, tests, and issues.* New York, NY: Guilford Press.

Foderaro, L. (2010, September 29). Private moment made public, then a fatal jump. *The New York Times.*

Fuligni, A. J., & Stevenson, H. W. (1995). Time use and mathematics achievement among American, Chinese and Japanese high school students. *Child Development, 66*(3), 830–842. doi:10.1111/1467-8624/r[9506152728

Fuligni, A. J., & Zhang, W. (2004). Attitudes toward family obligation among adolescents in contemporary urban and rural China. *Child Development, 75,* 180–192.

Gao, F., Bailes, E., Robertson, D., Chen, Y., Rodenburg, C., Michael, S., . . . Hahn, B. (1999). Origin of HIV-1 in the chimpanzee Pan troglodytes. *Nature, 397,* 436–441.

Gardner, H. (2000). *Intelligence reframed: Multiple intelligences for the 21st century.* New York, NY: Basic Books.

Gardner, H. (2003). Three distinct meanings of intelligence. In R. Sternberg & J. Lautrey (Eds.), *Models of intelligence: International perspectives.* Washington, DC: American Psychological Association.

Gates, G. (2011). The Williams Institute: How many people are gay, lesbian, bisexual or transgender? Retrieved from http://williamsinstitute.law.ucla.edu/research/census-lgbt-demographics-studies/how-many-people-are-lesbian-gay-bisexual-and-transgender/

Gehring, T. M., Wentzel, K. R., Feldman, S. S., & Munson, J. (1990). Conflict in families of adolescents: The impact on cohesion and power structures. *Journal of Family Psychology, 3,* 290–309.

Gessel, A. (1925). *The mental growth of the pre-school child.* New York, NY: Macmillan.

Gesell, A. (1943). *Infant and child in the culture of today: The guidance of development in home and nursery school.* New York, NY: Harper & Row.

Gibson, E.J., & Walk, R.D. (1960). The "visual cliff." *Scientific American, 202,* 67–71.

Giedd, J. Interview from, Frontline "Inside the Teenage Brain" website copyright 1995–2014 WGBH educational foundation. http://www.pbs.org/wgbh/pages/frontline/shows/teenbrain/interviews/giedd.html first broadcast January 2002.

Gillio, R. G. (1999). Bitter pills: Inside the hazardous world of legal drugs. *Journal of the American Medical Association, 281*, 469.

Gillis, J. R. (1985). *For better or worse: British marriages, 1600 to the present.* Oxford, UK: Oxford University Press.

Glenn, E. N. (1983). Split household, small producer and dual wage earner: An analysis of Chinese American family strategies. *Journal of Marriage and Family, 45*, 35–46.

Glionna, John M. (June 19, 2011). "South Korean pastor tends an unwanted flock" 7:55 PM PDT, *Los Angeles Times.* Reporting from Seoul latimes.com/news/nationworld/world/la-fg-south-korea-orphans-20110620,0,2908922.story

Goetz, M. (2006). Interview by Donham C. with M. Goetz about travel adventures in China. Not published.

Goldberg, L., Brinkley, G., & Kukar, J. (1998). *Pregnancy to parenthood.* Garden City Park, NY: Avery.

Golden, C. (1977). Female labor force participation. The origin of black and white differences, 1870 and 1880. *Journal of Economic History, 37*, 87–108.

Goldstein, B. (1976). *Introduction to human sexuality.* Belmont, CA: Star.

Gonzalez-Mena, J. (1997). *Multicultural issues in child care.* Mountain View, CA: Mayfield Publishing Company.

Gonzalez-Mena, J. (2009). *Child, family, and community: Family-centered early care and education.* Upper Saddle River, NJ: Pearson.

Gottlieb, A. (2000). Luring your child into this life: A Beng path for infant care. In J. DeLoache & A. Gottlieb (Eds.), *A world of babies: Imagined childcare guides for seven societies.* New York, NY: Cambridge University Press.

Gowaty, P. A. (2003). Power asymmetries between the sexes, mate preferences and components of fitness. In C. B. Travis (Ed.), *Evolution, gender, and rape.* Cambridge, MA: MIT Press.

Gracer, B., & Alexandria, V. (2003). What the rabbis heard: Deafness in the mishnah. *Disabilities Studies Quarterly, 23*(2), 192–205.

Graham, J., & Gray, E. (1995). A production of Edward Gray Films, Inc. Copyright © 1995 Janet Graham and Edward Gray. Produced for THE AMERICAN EXPERIENCE is a production of WGBH/Boston. http://www.pbs.org/wgbh/amex/orphan/orphants.html

Granic, I., Hollenstein, T., & Dishion, T. J. (2003). Longitudinal analysis of flexibility and reorganization in early adolescence: A dynamic systems study of family interactions. *Developmental Psychology, 39,* 606–617.

Grumbach, M., Roth, J. K. S., & Kelch R. (1974). Hypothalamic-pituitary regulation of puberty in man: Evidence and concepts derived from clinical research. In M. Grumbach, G. Grave, & F. Mayer (Eds.), *Control of the onset of puberty.* New York: Wiley.

Harris, C. M. (2004). Personality and sexual orientation. *College Student Journal, 38,* 207–211.

Harris, J. R. (1998). *The nurture assumption: Why children turn out the way they do.* New York, NY: Free Press.

Harter, S. (2003). The development of self-representation during childhood and adolescence. In M. R. Leary & J. P. Tangney (Eds.), *Handbook of self and identity* (pp. 610–642). New York, NY: Guilford Press.

Harter, S., & Pike, R. (1984). The pictorial scale of perceived competence and social acceptance for young children. *Child Development, 55,* 1969–1982.

Hartog, H. (2000). *Man and wife in America: A history.* Cambridge, MA: Harvard University Press.

Hartup, W. W. (1993). Adolescents and their friends. In B. Laursen (Ed.), *Close friendships in adolescence: New directions for child development* (No. 60, pp. 3–22). San Francisco, CA: Jossey-Bass.

Haugaard, J. J. (2000). The challenge of defining child sexual abuse. *American Psychologist, 55*(9), 1036–1039.

Hay, D. F., Payne, A., & Chadwick, A. (2004). Peer relations in childhood. *Journal of Child Psychology and Psychiatry, 41*(1), 84–108.

Holmbeck, G., & Hill, J. P. (1988). Storm and stress beliefs about adolescence: Prevalence, self-reported antecedents, and effect of an undergraduate course. *Journal of Youth and Adolescence, 17,* 285–306.

Hotchner, T. (1995). *Pregnancy pure and simple.* New York, NY: Avon.

Hulbert, A. (Winter, 1999). The century of the child. *The Wilson Quarterly, 23*(1), 14–29.

Iconis, R. (1995). A rash of childhood diseases hits young adults. *Current Health, 21*(7), 27–29.

Izard, C. E. (1983). *Maximally discriminative facial movement scoring system.* Newark, DE: University of Delaware Instructional Resources Center.

Izard, C. E. (1991). *The psychology of emotions.* New York, NY: Plenum.

Izard, C. E. (1992). Basic emotions, relations, among emotions and emotion-cognition relations. *Psychological Review, 99,* 561–565.

Jafari, N., & Badiesabet, N. *Street children in Iran.* Unpublished manuscript.

Jambunathan, J., & Stewart, S. (1991). *Hmong women in Wisconsin: What are their concerns in pregnancy and childbirth.* Ann Arbor, MI: University of Michigan Press.

Johnson, M. H. (1999). Developmental neuroscience. In M. H. Bornstein & M. E. Lamb (Eds.), *Developmental Psychology: An advanced text* (pp. 199–230). Mahwah, NJ: Erlbaum.

Johnson, M. H. (1999). Functional brain development in infants: Elements of an interactive specialization framework. *Child Development, 71*(1), 75–81.

Kagan, J. (1984). *The nature of the child.* New York, NY: Basic Books.

Kisilevsky, B. S., Hains, S. J., Jqxquet, A. Y., Grainer-Deferre, C., & Lecanuet, J. P. (2004, October 20). Maturation of fetal responses to music. *Developmental Science, 7*(5), 550–559. doi: 10.1111/j.1467-7687.2004.00379.x

Klinnert, M., Campos, J. J., Sorce, J. F., Emde, R. N., & Svejda, M. (1983). Emotions as behavior regulators: Social referencing in infancy. In R. Plutchick & H. Klellerman (Eds.), *Emotion in Early Development, Vol. 1. The Emotions* (pp. 57–86). New York, NY: Academic Press.

Koss, M. P., Godman, L. A., Browne, A., Fitzgerald, L. F., Keita, G. P., & Russo, N. F. (1993). *No safe haven; violence against women, at home, at work and in the community.* Washington D.C.: American Psychological Association.

Kottak, C. P. (2002). *Cultural Anthropology.* McGraw-Hill Publication, N.Y.

Kristof, N., & WuDunn, S. (2009). *Half the sky: Turning oppression into opportunity for women worldwide.* New York, NY: Alfred Knopf.

Kuczmarski, R. J. (2000). *CDC growth charts: United States, advance data from vital and health statistics* (No. 314). Hyattsville, MD: National Center on Health Statistics.

Larson, R. W., Richards, M. H., Moneta, G., Holmbeck, G., & Duckett, E. (1996). Changes in adolescents daily interaction with their families from ages 10 to 18: Disengagement and transformation. *Developmental Psychology, 32,* 744–754.

Le Roux, J., & Smith, C. S. (1998). Causes and characteristics of the street child phenomenon: A global perspective. *Adolescence Magazine, 33,* 131.

Lennenberg, E. H. (1967). *Biological foundation of language.* New York: Wiley.

Lieberman, E., Gremy, I., Lang, J. M., & Cohen, A. (1994). Low birth weight at term and the timing of fetal exposure to maternal smoking. *American Journal of Public Health, 84,* 1127–1131.

Lipsitt, L. P., Engen, T., & Kaye, H. (1963). Developmental changes in the olfactory threshold of the neonate. *Child Development, 34,* 371–176.

Lipson, J., Dibble, S., & Minark, P. (Eds.). (1997). *Culture and nursing care: A pocket guide.* San Francisco, CA: University of California San Francisco Nursing Press.

Londoño, E. (2012, April 4). Afghanistan sees rise in "dancing boys" exploitation. *Washington Post.*

Lubinski, D. (2004). Introduction to the special section on cognitive abilities: 100 years after Spearman's (1904) "general intelligence" objectively determined and measured. *Journal of Personality and Social Psychology, 86,* 96–111.

Maimbolwa, M., Yamba, V., & Diwan, A. R. (2003). Cultural childhood practices and beliefs in Zambia. *Journal of Advanced Nursing, 43*(3), 263–74.

Martin, C. L., & Ruble, D. (2004).Children's search for gender cues: Current directions in psychological science, *13*(2), 67–70.

McDevitt, T. M., & Ormord, J. E. (2002). *Child development, educating and working with children and adolescents.* Upper Saddle River, NJ: Pearson.

Mehlman, M., & Borkin, J. R. (1998). *Access to genome: The challenge of equality.* Washington, DC: Georgetown University Press.

Miller Center, University of Virginia, "life before the presidency," http://millercenter.org/ copyright 2015 Rector and Visitors of the University of Virginia.

Miller, H. P. (2011). *Theories of developmental psychology.* New York, NY: Worth.

Miller, M., & Hirschkorn, P. (2012, June 5). Sexting leads to child porn charges for teens. *CBS Evening News.*

Monnier, J., Resnick, H. S., Kilpatrick, K. G., Seals, B., & Holmes, M. (2002). Patterns of assault in a sample of recent rape victims. *Violence Against Women, 8*(5), 585.

Montemayor, R. (1983). Parents and adolescents in conflict: All families some of the time and some families most of the time. *Journal of Early Adolescence, 3,* 83–103.

Moses, N., Banilivy, M., & Lifshitz, F. (1989). Fear of obesity among adolescent girls. *Pediatrics, 83*(8), 393.

National Institute on Drug Abuse. (2014, January). 2013 monitoring the future announcements. Retrieved from http://www.drugabuse.gov/related-topics/trends-statistics/monitoring-future

National Library of Medicine (1997, August 28). Thalidomide: Potential benefits and risks. Available at http://www.nlm.nih.gov/pub/cbm/thalidomide.html

National Sleep Foundation. (n.d.). Sleep and school aged children. Retrieved from http://sleepfoundation.org

Nevitt, A. (1998). *Fetal alcohol syndrome.* New York, NY: Rosen Publishing Group.

Noack, P., & Buhl, H. M. (2004). Relations with parents and friends during adolescence and early adulthood. *Marriage & Family Review, 36,* 31–51.

Noon, M. J., Dekovic, M., & Meeus, W. (2001). Conceptual analysis and measurement of adolescent autonomy. *Journal of Youth and Adolescents, 30*, 577–595.

Nurrenbern, S. C. (2001). Piaget's theory of intellectual development revisited. *Journal of Chemical Education, 78*(8), 1107.

O'Neil, D. (2008, March 14). Rites of passage. Retrieved from http://anthro.palomar.edu/social/

Paneth, N. (1986). Etiologic factors in cerebral palsy. *Pediatric Annals, 15*(3), 191–201.

Papalia, D., Cross, D., & Feldman, R. (2003). *Child development: A topical approach.* New York, NY: McGraw-Hill.

Partnership for Drug Free Kids. (2012). It happened to me. Retrieved from http://www.drugfree.org/Portal/Stories/It_Happened_to_Me

Pasquariello, P. S. (1999). *The Children's Hospital of Philadelphia book of pregnancy and child care.* New York, NY: Wiley.

Patterson, C. (2008). *Child Development.* McGraw-Hill Higher Education.

Patterson, C., & Friel, L. V. (2000). Sexual orientation and fertility. In G. R. Bentley & N. Mascie-Taylor (Eds.), *Infertility in the modern world; biosocial perspectives* (pp. 238–260). Cambridge, U.K.: Cambridge University Press.

Patterson, M. (2011). Arlington National Cemetery website. Retrieved from http://www.arlingtoncemetery.net/hssullivan.htm

Person, A. C., Sarigiani, P. A., & Kennedy, R. E. (1991). Adolescent depression: Why more girls? *Journal of Youth and Adolescence, 20*, 247–271.

Piaget, J. (1952). *The origins of intelligence in children.* New York, NY: International Press.

Plumert, J. M., & Nichols-Whitehead, P. (1996). Parental scaffolding of young children's spatial communication. *Developmental Psychology, 32*(3), 523–532.

Prior, V., & Glaser, D. (2006). *Understanding attachment and attachment disorders: Theory, evidence and practice.* PA: Jessica Kingsley publishers.

ProCon.org. (2014, July 31). Medical marijuana pros and cons. Retrieved from http://medicalmarijuana.procon.org/view.resource.php?resourceID=000881

Qobil, R. (2010, September 8). The sexually abused dancing boys of Afghanistan. *BBC World Service, South East Asia.*

Ramsden, S., Richardson, F., Josse, G., Thomas, M., Ellis, C., Shakeshaft, C., . . . Price, C. J. (2011). Verbal and non-verbal intelligence changes in the teenage brain. Nature, 479, 113-116. doi:10.1038/nature10514

Rathus, S. A. (2006). *Childhood and adolescence, voyages in development* (2nd ed.). Belmont, CA: Thomson Wadsworth.

Rieser, J., Yonas, A., & Wikner, K. (1976). Radial localization of odors by human newborn. *Child Development, 47,* 856–859.

Rothman, E. K. (1984). *Hands and hearts: A history of courtship in America.* Cambridge, MA: Harvard University Press.

Ryan, C., & Rivers, I. (2003). Lesbian, gay, bisexual and transgender youth: Victimization and its correlates in the USA and UK. *Culture, Health and Sexuality, 5,* 103–119.

Ryan, R. M., & Deci, E. L. (2004). Autonomy is no illusion; self-determination theory and the empirical study of authenticity, awareness and will. In J. Greenberg, S. L. Koole, & T. Pyszczynski (Eds.), *The handbook of experimental existential psychology* (pp. 449–479). New York: Academic Press.

Savin-Williams, R., & Ream, G. (2003). Sex variations in disclosure to parents of same-sex attractions. *Journal of Family Psychology, 17,* 429–438.

Saylor, C. F., Finch, A. J., Jr., Spirito, A., & Bennett, B. (1984). The Children's Depression Inventory: A systematic evaluation of psychometric properties. *Journal of Consulting and Clinical Psychology, 52,* 955–967.

Schmitz, C. L., Traver, E. K., & Larson, D. (Eds.). (2004). *Child labor: A global view.* Santa Barbara, CA: Greenwood Publishing Group.

Schneider-Rosen, K., & Ciechetti, D. (1991). Early self-knowledge and emotional development: Visual self-recognition and affective reaction to mirror self-image in maltreated and non-maltreated toddlers. *Developmental Psychology, 27,* 471–478.

Schoff, F. (1916). The National Congress of Mothers and Parent-Teacher Associations. *Annals of the American Academy of Political and Social Science, 67*(1), 139–147.

Schwartz, K. D., Bukowski, W. M., & Aoki, W. T. (2006). Mentors, friends and gurus: Peer and nonparent influences on spiritual development. In E. C. Roehklepartain, P. E. King, L. Wagener, & P. L. Benson (Eds.), *The handbook of spiritual development in childhood and adolescence* (pp. 310–323). Thousand Oaks, CA: Sage Publications.

Shepps-Battle, J. (2002). About teen depression: It's hard to be a teen. Retrieved from http://www.about-teen-depression.com/teen-suicide.html

Shimoni, R., Baxter, J., & Kugelmass, J. (1992). *Every child is special.* New York, NY: Addison-Wesley Publishers Limited.

Signorello, L. B., Nordmark, A., Granath, F., Blot, W. J., McLaughlin, J. K., Anneren, G., Lundgren, S., Ekbom, A., Rane, A., Cnattingius, S. (2001). Caffeine metabolism and the risk of spontaneous abortion of normal karyotype fetuses. *Obstetrics and Gynecology, 98,* 1059–1066.

Simmons, A. (2006). Where fat is a mark of beauty. In E. Angeloni (Ed.), *Annual editions of anthropology 06/07* (28th ed., pp. 137–138). New York, NY: McGraw Hill.

Simon, F., & Butterworth, G. (Eds.). (1998). *The development of sensory, motor, and cognitive capacities in early infancy: From perception to cognition.* Philadelphia, PA: Psychology Press.

Simonson, B. M., & Glenn, S. (2001).The effects of suggestions on ratings of attention deficit hyperactivity disorder. *Psychology and Education: An Interdisciplinary Journal, 38*(2), 42–47.

Small, M. F. (2004). How many fathers are best for a child? In E. N. Junn & C. J. Boyatzis, Annual Editions: Gender 2010/2011 (pp. 186–188). Guildford, CT: McGraw-Hill.

Spearman, C. (1927). *The abilities of man.* London, UK: Macmillan.

Spinks, S. (Director). (2002). *Inside the teenage brain (work in progress-adolescent brains are a work in progress).* [Video/DVD] Frontline/Public Broadcasting Service.

Spock, B. (1946). *The common sense book of baby and child care.* New York, NY: Duell-Sloan.

Steinberg, L. (1993). *Adolescence.* New York, NY: McGraw-Hill.

Steinberg, L. D. (1990). Autonomy, conflict, and harmony in the family relationship. In S. S. Feldman & G. R. Elliot (Eds.), *At the threshold: The developing adolescent* (pp. 255–276). Cambridge, MA: Harvard University Press.

Steinberg, L. D., & Silk, J. S. (2002). Parenting adolescents. In M. M. Bornstein (Ed.), *Handbook of parenting: Vol 1: Children and parenting* (2nd ed.). Mahwah, NJ: Erlbaum.

Sternberg, R. (1990). *Metaphors of mind: Conceptions of the nature of intelligence.* Cambridge, UK: Cambridge University Press.

Sternberg, R. (2003). A broad view of intelligence: the theory of successful intelligence. *Consulting Psychology Journal: Practice and Research, 55,* 139–154.

Sternberg , R. J. (1985). *Beyond IQ: A triarchic theory of human intelligence.* New York, NY: Cambridge University Press.

Sternberg, R. J. (1991). Theory based testing of intellectual abilities: Rationale for the Sternberg triarch abilities test. In Stoller, E., & Gibson, R. (2000), *Worlds of difference* (3rd ed.). Thousand Oaks, CA: Pine Forge Press.

Tanner, J. (1971). Sequence, tempo and individual variation in growth and development of boys and girls aged twelve to sixteen. *Daedalus, 100,* 907–930.

Thing, J. (2010). Interview done by Cindy Donham with James Thing on *Personal communication on gay men in Mexico.*

Thompson, M. (2009, December 3). Haiti after the storm. *BBC News Today.*

Triandis, C. H. (1994). *Culture and social behavior.* McGraw-Hill Publication, N.Y.

Triandis, H. C. (2000). Cross-cultural psychology. In A. Kazdin (Ed.), *Encyclopedia of Psychology*. Washington, D.C.: American Psychological Association; Oxford [Oxfordshire]; New York: Oxford University Press, 2000.

Tronick, E. Z., Frank, D. A., Cabral, H., Mirochnick, M., & Zuckerman, B. (1996). Late-dose response effects of prenatal cocaine exposure on newborn neurobehavioral performance. *Pediatrics, 98*, 76–83.

U.S. Census Bureau. (July 2002). U.S. census, 2000. Retrieved from http://www.census.gov/prod/2002pubs/c2kprof00-us.pdf

U.S. Census Bureau. (2004). The foreign-born population in the United States: 2003. Retrieved from WWW.census.gov/prod/2004pubs/p20-551.pdf

U.S. Census Bureau. (Nov. 10, 2010). Newsroom archive, https://www.census.gov/newsroom/releases/archives/families_households/cb10-174.html retrieved March 10, 2015

U.S. Census Bureau. (2013). Computer and internet use in the United States, population characteristics. Thom File, issued May 2013, pp. 20–569. http://www.census.gov/prod/2013pubs/p20-569.pdf

U.S. Department of Health and Human Services Children's Bureau. (2012). Child maltreatment report 2012. http://www.census.gov/compendia/statab/cats/law_enforcement_courts_prisons/juvenile_delinquency_child_abuse.html

U.S. Department of Health and Human Services. (2014). Office of adolescent health-reproductive health. Retrieved from http://www.hhs.gov/ash/oah/adolescent-health-topics/reproductive-health/stds.html

U.S. Department of Health and Human Services. Stop bullying. Retrieved from http://www.stopbullying.gov/at-risk/factors/index.html

Van Brunschot, M., Zarbatany, L., & Strang, K. (1993, March). Ecological contribution to gender differences in intimacy among peers. Paper presented at the Meeting of the Society for Research in Child Development, New Orleans, LA.

Van Ijzendoorn, M. H., & Kroonenberg, P. M. (1988). Cross-cultural patterns of attachment: A meta-analysis of the strange situation. *Child Development*, 147–156.

Villarosa, L. (2003, December 6). More teenagers say no to sex, and experts aren't sure why. *The New York Times*.

Vitti, A. National Eating Disorders Association, stories of hope: I am good enough for my recovery. Retrieved from http://www.nationaleatingdisorders.org/node/3687

Vox, L. (n.d.). About.com, African American history, start of slavery in North America. Retrieved from http://afroamhistory.about.com/od/slavery/a/The-Start-Of-Slavery-In-North-America.htm

Vygotsky, L. (1978). *Mind in society: The development of higher psychological processes*. Cambridge, MA: Harvard University Press.

Ward, B., Dahlhamer, J., Galinsky, A., & Joestl, S. (2014, July). Sexual orientation and health among U.S. adults. *National Health Statistic Reports, National Health Interview Survey 2013, 77*, 1–12.

Watson, J. B. (1928). *Psychological care of infant and child*. New York: W.W. Norton Company, Inc.

Watson, J. B. (1930). *Behaviorism*. Chicago: University of Chicago Press.

Wentzel, K. R., & Feldman, S. S. (1996). Relations of cohesion and power in family dyads to social and emotional adjustment during early adolescents. *Journal of Research on Adolescents, 96*, 195–203.

Woyshner, C. (2004). Preparations for the duties of life: Women reformers and the functional curriculum, 1893–1918. *Educational Foundations 18*(3/4), pp. 25–43.

Index

A

B

C

D

E

F

M

N

Q

R

S

T

U

Y

Z